JOHN KNOX

Kenneth D. Farrow

John Knox

Reformation Rhetoric and the Traditions of Scots Prose 1490–1570

PETER LANG
Oxford · Bern · Berlin · Bruxelles · Frankfurt am Main · New York · Wien

Bibliographic information published by Die Deutsche Bibliothek
Die Deutsche Bibliothek lists this publication in the Deutsche Nationalbibliografie; detailed bibliographic data is available on the Internet at ‹http://dnb.ddb.de›.

British Library and Library of Congress Cataloguing-in-Publication Data:
A catalogue record for this book is available from The British Library, Great Britain, and from The Library of Congress, USA

Cover illustration: From the posthumous woodcut in Beza's *Icones* (1580).
Cover design: Thomas Jaberg, Peter Lang AG

ISBN 3-03910-138-2
US-ISBN 0-8204-6898-3

Hochfeldstrasse 32, Postfach 746, CH-3000 Bern 9, Switzerland
info@peterlang.com, www.peterlang.com, www.peterlang.net

Printed in Germany

For my Father and Brother, and in loving memory of my Mother

The author gratefully acknowledges financial assistance from The Carnegie Trust for the Universities of Scotland towards the publication of this book.

JOHN KNOX

John Knox he learn'd the Latin,
The Hebrew and the Greek:
But aften frae the poopit
His mither-tongue he'd speak.

In bane he was sma'-boukit,
But had a muckle beard
And whan he gar'd it waggle
Baith man and beast were feard.

He brocht back frae the galleys
The snellness o' the sea:
Its saut was in his sermons,
Its glitter in his e'e.

John Knox in destination
Warsl'd wi' kirk and state;
And the souchin o' his spirit
Blaws about Scotland yet.

William Soutar, 1942

Contents

Introduction: The Myths, the Writer and the Canon

Literary Reactions to Knox: 1884–2003

David Laing, the nineteenth century antiquary and the original editor of what, for the day, were accepted as the complete works of John Knox, introduces his first of six weighty volumes by observing that: 'In the long series of events recorded in the Annals of Scotland, there is unquestionably none of greater importance than those which exhibit the progress and establishment of the Reformed Religion'.[1] Like much of Laing's criticism, this now inevitably sounds a little pompous and old-fashioned, but it does entail a worthwhile point. Some may doubt the editor's sense of priority, but since the effects of the Reformation are still prevalent in the way many Scots choose to define themselves, or find themselves defined, even in an increasingly secular age, none can deny the relevance of its literature.

Accordingly, Scottish historians have expended much ink and effort on the period, and on one of its most important figures, John Knox. However, as far as the topic of Knox is concerned, the Scottish literary critic has not proved himself quite as ready to follow suit. Of course, brief literary studies of Knox are very numerous. J. M. Ross's *Scottish History and Literature to the Period of the Reformation*, (1884), Hugh Walker's *Three Centuries of Scottish Literature*, (1892), and T. F. Henderson's *Scottish Vernacular Literature: A Succinct History*, (1898), all devote some attention to him, while a study like James Moffat's *The Bible in Scottish Literature*, (1924), concentrates on one particular aspect of the Reformer's prose, albeit without going into much detail.[2] These works, however, were far from comprehensive, and this deficiency has found its way into J. H. Millar's

1 Laing I: xxv.

2 Moffat, J., *The Bible in Scottish Literature*, pp. 89–91.

epoch-making *Literary History of Scotland*, (1905). Although works such as G. Gregory Smith's *Scottish Literature: Character and Influence*, (1919), and Agnes Mure Mackenzie's *A Historical Survey of Scottish Literature to 1714*, (1933), are more recent, it is Millar's text which seems most heavily to have influenced the material on Knox now contained in modern studies such as Maurice Lindsay's *History of Scottish Literature*, (1977), Roderick Watson's *The Literature of Scotland*, (1984), Billy Kay's more language-orientated *Scots: The Mither Tongue*, (1986), and even the very recent *Scottish Literature*, (eds. D. Gifford, S. Dunnigan and A. MacGillivray, 2002). Their authors on the whole seem to have little sympathy for Knox, and it must be emphasised that he constitutes only a small part of the overall view, but in various ways, each offering might justifiably have been enhanced by deeper study. At the time of its publication, Maurice Lindsay's book was exceptionally welcome in that it broke new ground in a serious way, but its author is a literary critic who displays very many highly subjective and particular opinions.

Pr. Watson's book far surpasses Lindsay's in terms of modernity, but with regard to Knox, its author still maintains a personalised response. However, to be fair, a competent and comprehensive one volume history of Scottish literature such as Watson's is an achievement in its own right, not least because our present state of general knowledge in some areas is itself inadequate. Knox, it seems, has been the victim of an almost insurmountable cultural, geographical and disciplinary isolationism which negates the possibility of interaction between scholars. The inevitable result is that vast tracts of socially important prose are still not as well known to a cultured audience as they should be. In one area at least, these factors have apparently over-influenced Pr. Watson's work.

Billy Kay, a champion of the Scots language, comes at Knox from a very specific angle, in an attempt to convince his readers that the Reformer was heavily responsible for the decline of a healthy Scots vernacular. The present writer, however, believes that Mr. Kay's approach is too heavily influenced by prevailing stereotypes, which we will be looking at more fully later in this introduction (below pp. 14–23).

Less purposive studies of Knox are P. H. Brown's appreciation in *The Cambridge History of English Literature*, (1932), and C. S. Lewis's in *English Literature in the Sixteenth Century (Excluding Drama)*, (1954), but in both there is still a tendency to minimise Knox's literary importance. Lewis expresses this trend with characteristic sophistication. He says of Knox's works, that:

> [...] they are of absorbing interest to the historian; of less to the theologian, who may find nothing in them which is not said better elsewhere. On the literary historian their claim, though by no means negligible, is smaller. One might assess it by saying that Knox is about as important a literary figure as More would have been if he had written neither the *Utopia* nor the *Comfort against Tribulation* [...] his chief merit is his style. Except for a few alliterative passages and some apostrophes, it is very unadorned: and one's praise of it tends to be in negatives – a mere list of the faults it avoids.[3]

By his own admission Lewis's assessment is negative; in fact, it is rather *too* negative. This highly influential and admirable critic here does something of an injustice to both literary critics and theologians when he places secular historians at the top of his hierarchy. Practitioners of all three disciplines, perhaps, have an equally legitimate claim to the Reformer's writings. The literary critics, however, have allowed themselves to indulge in further dismissive comments about Knox's importance in Lewis's wake.

Even so, literary criticism of Knox has not always been of a minimising kind. In his introduction to the Saltire edition of Knox's *The Historie of the Reformatioun of Religioun within the Realme of Scotland*, (1940), (hereafter shortened titles, such as *The Historie*, are generally used after a first full citation), Ralph S. Walker provided a short and eloquent literary testimony, and R. D. S. Jack's infectiously enthusiastic commentary in *Scottish Prose 1550–1700*, (1971), his 'The Prose of John Knox: A Re-assessment', (1981), David Murison's 'Knox the Writer', (1972, 1975), Pierre Janton's 'John Knox and Literature', (1977), David Atkinson's 'The Religious Personality of John Knox', (1987), and Roderick J. Lyall's 'Vernacular Prose before the Reformation', (1988), all indicate that the tide is beginning to turn.

3 Lewis, C. S., *English Literature in the Sixteenth Century*, pp. 197–202.

But by far the greatest contribution that any writer, from any discipline, has made to Knox studies, came as long ago as 1967, when the aforementioned Janton published his monumental study *John Knox (ca. 1513–1572): L'homme et l'oeuvre*. Janton, a Professor at the French University of Clermont, united all three strands of scholarship demanded by Knox's work, and it need hardly be said that his literary criticism is particularly fine. Indeed, this book can lay fair claim to be the best work on Knox ever written. Even as a biography it is far in advance of Jasper Ridley's contemporaneous *John Knox*, (1968). Sadly, however, Janton's work is unknown to many Scottish critics, including one of the very best.[4] Janton writes in French, of course, (and very frequently even translates Knox into the language), but his erudition is prodigious and any serious student of Knox ought to consult such a scholarly work. It is ironic, but this learnéd European evidently has much to teach the Scots themselves about Scottish Reformation literature. Pr. Janton has continued to work on Knox throughout his career, and has produced an updated version of his original thesis, as well as several excellent articles during the 1990s, but since these are not exclusively literary, we shall content ourselves with merely a passing mention of them.[5] No less distinguished is the work of Edinburgh University's Pr. David Wright, an ecclesiastical historian, who has contributed an excellent study of Knox to *The Bible in Scottish Life and Literature*, (1988), and he offers another fine essay in Roger A. Mason's *John Knox and the British Reformations*, (1998). The work of Wright's colleague, Jane Dawson, also deserves mention in this context

Some critics, then, have recognised that Knox is an important and accomplished prose writer, (even if the nature of their studies has not always been literary). This is quite easy to illustrate (and we need not even refer to Knox's major work, which is of course *The Historie*). For example, in the introductory prologue to *The Reasoning Betwix*

4 See Jack, R. D. S, 'The Prose of John Knox', 293–251; n.s (3) and (4) are inaccurate.

5 The most important of these essays are: 'Prophétie et "prophesying" chez John Knox et dans la tradition puritaine'; 'La désobéissance chrétienne et le pouvoir selon John Knox' and 'John Knox et l'histoire'.

the Abbot of Crossraguel and John Knox Concerning the Mass, (1562), (Laing VI: 149–169), we find Knox mercilessly lampooning the status of the Host in the Sacrament. Bread, he says, is not literally the body of Christ, even after it has been consecrated by a priest, but rather, a meal for mice. He combines a rhetorical question with an affected naïveté, and bold, wittily conceived analogy with careful climactic balance, to produce what is perhaps the most memorable literary moment in the whole contest (although the remainder of the text is by no means dull):

> But o then, what becometh of Christes natural bodie? By myrackle, it flies to the heaven againe, if the Papistes teach treulie; for how sone soever the mouse takes hold, so sone flieth Christ away, and letteth her gnaw the bread. A bold and puissant mouse, but a feeble and miserable god [...] (Laing VI: 172–173).

This, indeed, represents devastating technique,[6] but so immensely rich are Knox's works with such rhetorical treasures that many of them have been overlooked, perhaps because they represent simply the 'norm'.

Knox was not simply a writer, however. He was a good preacher and an impressive orator. There is material to illustrate this too. The following passage was delivered orally as a response to charges levelled against him by William Kirkcaldy of Grange, and others, concerning the deposition of Mary Stewart:

> Gif sho be innocent of ony of the crymes laid to her charge be me, then may I be accused as a realer; but gif thair awin conscience bearis witnes to thame, that scho is guiltie in all the foirnamed, and in every ane of thaime, and in monie moe, lat thaim studie how thai salbe absolved befoir God, who threatenis to cast Jesabell in a bed and thame that committ fornicatioune with hir in grit afflictioune, except thai repent (Laing VI: 591).

There is a God's plenty of subtle rhetoric here, which we need not explore in any great detail at the moment (all of the techniques are recurrent and we shall identify them at more appropriate points in the study). But I have chosen this passage because it post-dates Knox's major critique of the Queen contained in *The Historie*, and later, will allow for comparison. But for now, one cannot escape the sense that

6 See also, Janton, P., *L'homme et l'oeuvre*, p. 495.

the prose is water-tight in every way and that Knox has ordered it precisely so that this is the case. The main thrust of his argument, however, depends on allusion, another recurrent feature; here it is to Revelation 2: 21–22: 'I gaue her space to repent of her fornicacion and she repented not. Beholde, I shal cast her into a bed, and them that commit fornicacione with her, into gret adversitie, excepte they turne from their dedes'. (This quotation is from Miles Coverdale's Bible, hereafter referred to simply as *Coverdale*; I have used this edition of the Bible throughout, except in cases where it has been more illuminating [or, indeed, necessary] to refer to other contemporary versions of the scriptures, such as the *Great Bible*). At any rate, here, surely, is a rhetorician who means business, and who knows how to go about it.

The Linguistic Controversy: Scots versus English

As we have seen, Knox criticism has too frequently relied upon stereotypes. The most dominant of these comes in the form of the assertion that he was an 'angliciser'. One of the earliest expressions of this belief, of course, came from Knox's admirable Roman Catholic antagonist, Ninian Winzet:

> Gif ze, throw curiositie of nouationis, hes forzet our auld plane Scottis quhilk zour mother leirit zou in tymes cuming I sall wryte to zou my mynd in Latin, for I am nocht acquyntit with zour Southeroun.[7]

Many critics apparently assume that Winzet was referring to *The Historie*, and quote a passage from that work as evidence of the kind of thing Winzet must have meant. But Winzet had no access to *The Historie*, which in fact contains a rich mixture of Scots and English forms[8] (and, for now, we need say nothing about the numerous scribes

7 See Hewison, J. K., (ed.), *Winzet's Works*, vol. I: p. 138.

8 Laing's own glossary to *The Historie* alone contains 917 Scots items, and it is very old and perhaps not fully adequate. Astonishingly, the glossary to the

who worked on it; another complicating factor). For one writer, the matter is a simple one: 'Knox', he says, 'is the first known Scot in history to attempt to conform his writing to English models'[9] (and there's an end on't). But is this indeed true?

Even waiving the textual problems of Knox's prose as it comes before modern critics (problems which, I hope to show, are quite considerable), and even if we were to admit that Knox *always* wrote English, he is still not the *first to do so*, as we shall see in chapter one. But the first issue we ought to raise in this debate is that the Laing text of Knox's works is sometimes unreliable, at least as a guide to Knox's orthography. David Murison recognises this, even while attempting to detect a pattern (which, in fact, isn't there):

> Knox himself seems to have been completely bilingual in Scots and English. The language of his work varies from pure English, as in his treatises on prayer and predestination, in *The First Blast* and in his public letters to English Protestants, to a Scots-English mixed in differing degrees in his private letters and in his *History*. His style becomes more noticeably Scottish on his return to Scotland, but he never writes pure Scots. *We do not always know how much is due to various secretaries, copyists and printers through whom most of his extant writings have been transmitted* [...] much work on this subject is still needed[10] (italics added).

The work which has in fact been done, is fairly scanty. For example, O. Sprotte's *Zum Sprachengebrauch bei John Knox*, (1906), is the earliest (and still valuable). Ronald Jack underestimated the textual difficulties in his Knox article by taking Laing's text as his basis; a mistake which M. A. Bald did not make when contributing: 'The Pioneers of Anglicised Speech in Scotland' to *The Scottish Historical Review* in 1927,[11] while Mairi Robinson probably comes the closest to appreciating them in 'Language Choice in the Reformation: *The Scots Confession* of 1560'.[12] More recently, the late Pr. A. J. Aitken has re-

modern Penguin edition of Hugh MacDiarmid's *Complete Poems* has only forty items more, and yet no one accuses MacDiarmid of having forgotten Scots!

9 Kay, B., *Scots: The Mither Tongue*, p. 69.

10 Murison, D., 'Knox the Writer', 40, n. (2).

11 See Bald, M., 'The Pioneers of Anglicised Speech in Scotland', 179–193.

12 See McClure, J. D., (ed.), *Scotland and the Lowland Tongue*, pp. 59–78.

assessed Bald's work in an important essay in *Scottish Language* entitled 'The Pioneers of Anglicised Speech in Scotland; a second look'.[13]

What, then, of Laing's text? Between 1846 and 1864 the editor brought the Knox volumes together from a number of sources. If we leave *The Historie* aside for the time being, one of Laing's primary manuscripts was the so-called M'Crie MS., now in Edinburgh University Library (MS. reference, La. III. 345). This contains all of Knox's intimate letters to his immediate family (but not all of his personal letters), and many (but again, not all) of his public admonitions to Protestants, even though many of the latter were available to Laing in their original printed form. However, the M'Crie MS. was transcribed in 1603, by an unknown scribe, for the use of Margaret Stewart (Knox's second wife),[14] and this is a full thirty years after Knox's death. The question, then, is moved back one remove. What manuscripts or printed texts did the scribe have before him? Almost certainly, he had the original handwritten letters of Knox to Mrs. Bowes and others, and perhaps even her letters to him. Both sets of originals, however, have since been lost. The problem of the public admonitions is less clear-cut. Did the scribe have Knox's holographs, or simply the common printed editions? If he had the former, it is possible, at least, that he was restoring Knox's orthography which had been corrupted by the printers (the orthography of the M'Crie MS. and the lexis, sometimes do not agree with the printed editions in the cases where both still exist). Evidence is not hard to find. For instance, samples from Laing's version of the MS., and the printed text of, say, *A Vindication of the Doctrine that the Sacrifice of the Mass is Idolatry*, (1550), look like this:

13 See Aitken, A. J., 'The Pioneers of Anglicised Speech in Scotland; a second look', 1–36.

14 The full title is: '*The Epistles of Mr. John Knox worthy to be read because of the authority of the wryter the solidity of the matter and the Comfortable Christian Experience to be found therein*'. The marginal note on f. 473 indicates the date of transcription. Below the title is written: 'This booke belong'd sometyme to Margaret Stewart widow to Mr. Knox after married to the Knight of Faudonsyde. Sister shee was to James Earle of Arran'.

Printed Edition (1550)
How difficill it is to put forth of the hartes of the people ye thing wherein opinion of holynes standeth, declareth the greate tumult and vprore moued against Paul by Demetrius and his fellows who by Idolatry gat great aduantage, as our preistes have done by the masse in times past (S.T.C. 15064, Reel 442, Aii).

Laing Text: from M'Crie MS. (1603)
How difficill it is to put furth of the hartes of the pepill the thing whairin opinion of holynes standeth, declareth the great tumult and uprore moveit aganis Paule by Demetrius and his fellowis, who, by Idolatrie, gat great vantage, as oure preistis have done be the Masse in tyme past (Laing III: 33).

Both have some Scottish features such as 'difficill' and 'gat', but the Laing text contains by far the larger number: 'furth', 'pepill', 'whairin', 'moveit', 'aganis', 'fellowis', 'Idolatrie' and 'preistis'. There are many more instances in the corpus where something similar occurs. In Laing's edition there are versions of writings by Knox printed by Laing as *Two Comfortable Epistles to his Afflicted Brethren in England,* (1554) (see Laing III: 231–236, 239–249). These epistles, admittedly, do not constitute *different versions of one text* (as in the above examples), but at certain points, particularly the introduction, they are almost identical in content. One exists only in the M'Crie MS. (and therefore it may well have been taken from Knox's codex), the other exists only in its printed form (and, of course, in Laing). They read:

Printed Edition (1554)
When I ponder with myself (beloued in the Lord) what the state was of Christes true Churche, immediately after his death and passion, and what were the changes & great mutations in the commonwealth of Iudea, before the final desolation of the same: as I cannot but feare that like Plagues for the like offences shal strike the Realme of England, and in fearing, God knoweth, I lament and morne; so can I not but reioice, knowing that Gods most merciful prouidence is no lesse careful this day ouer his weake and feeble seruants, in the Realme of Englande, than it was that day ouer his weake and sore oppressed flocke in Iurie (S.T.C. 15072, Reel 555).

M'Crie MS. (Actual Text)
When I ponder wt my self ryt deirlie belovit brethrene what was ye estait of Chrystis trew kirk immediatlie efter ye deth & passione of our savior Jesus, and what were the changeis & greit mutationis in ye common weill of Judea, befoir

ye finall desolatione of ye same, as I can not but feir lyke plageis to stryke ye realme of inglande, and in feiring god knawith I lament & murn, sa can I not but reiose, knowing yat godis maist mercifull providence is na les cairfull yis day over his weak and feabill servandis yan he was yat day over his dispersit and sair oppressit flock (La. III. 345. f. 313).

R. J. Lyall has suggested that the first text was 'probably printed by Humphrey Singleton at Wesel', but the text contains no such overt claim. However, Pr. Lyall is right to highlight: 'the consistency with which the printed version substitutes English forms for Scots ones' ('ed' for 'it, 'a' for 'ai', 'es' for 'is', 'a' for 'e', 'ea' for 'ei', 'o' for 'oi', 'i' for 'u', and so on).[15] We have already seen that the scribe working on the second version may have had Knox's original; the question which subsequently arises from this, is: did the scribe in any way alter it? A partial solution can be found from other evidence. If we compare Knox's letters contained in *The Historie* with the originals in Laing or the State Paper Office, it becomes evident that scribal fidelity *did not* extend as far as orthography. Take the letter on which Knox was arraigned for treason (see Laing II: 395–397). At his trial, he even praised the 'fidelatie' of scribes: 'that willinglie thai wald nocht adulterat my originall' (Laing II: 404). A quick glance, however, at Laing's version (what there is of it) in volume VI (Laing VI: 528) immediately shows differences. Laing of course found them insufficient 'to require notice'.[16] The M'Crie scribe could just as easily and unconsciously have introduced his own system.

Further proof of scribal alterations can be found. Pr. Jack uses the English of *The First Blast of the Trumpet Against the Monstrous Regiment of Women*, (1558), and the Scots of an epistle to Mrs. Bowes, to illustrate that Knox *deliberately switched registers* from one text to another,[17] but this conclusion actually ignores the question of scribes altogether. As far as Knox's letters to Mrs. Bowes are concerned, we *do* in fact possess one version of such a text, which pre-dates the M'Crie MS. by thirty years (but again it is not an original holograph). We find it appended to Knox's final publication *An Answer to a Letter Written by James Tyrie, a Scottish Jesuit*,

15 Lyall, R. J., 'Vernacular Prose before the Reformation', 178.

16 See Laing VI: 527–528, n. (4).

17 See Jack, R. D. S., 'The Prose of John Knox', 240–241.

(1572), and it was included, as he says, to: 'declare to the worlde what was the caus of our [Knox's and Mrs. Bowes's] great familiaritie and long acquentance' (Laing VI: 513). If we again juxtapose the two versions:

> *Version from Tyrie*
> Right dearely beloued Mother in our Saviour Jesus Christ, now is our dolour, appointed by God and forespoken by his prophetes, come upon vs, as ye dolour of a woman in ye birth of her first chylde; and so is it come, as with your eares, both openly and privately, oftentimes you have hard declared (S.T.C. 15062, Reel 473).

> *Version from M'Crie MS. (Actual Text)*
> Ryt deirlie belovit mother in or Savior Jesus Chryst now is or dolor apoyntit be god & foirspoken be his prophetis cum upon ws as the dolor of a woman in ye birth of hir first child as sa it is cum as wt your eiris baith opinlie & privatlie oftentimes ye haif hard declarit (La. III. 345. f. 250).

The first text was printed by Robert Lekprevik, but even he is known to have anglicised his material, although we cannot be absolutely sure that this has happened here. But the transcriber of the second text *has* probably adulterated the original spelling-system.

Another indication of the dangers inherent in using Laing's edition for morphological analysis can be seen from his version of Knox's *An Exposition Upon the Sixth Psalm of David, Addressed to Mrs. Bowes*, (1554), (see Laing III: 119–156). It seems that Laing, in fact, concocted this text from four different sources. One of them, a fragment, is in Knox's own hand, and now survives in the British Museum (Harleian MS. no. 416. ff. 40–45) (see Laing III: 114). As Laing says, the fragment forms part of a collection of papers which belonged to John Foxe the martyrologist. Laing's other sources were the M'Crie MS. which, in this instance, is not likely to have been taken from the Harleian MS. in its complete form, and two printed texts (1556(?) and 1580), with which he collated the manuscripts. The first printed edition bears no printer's name, but the second was printed at 'London at the three Cranes in the Vintree by Thomas Dawson' under the title *A Fort for the Afflicted* (S.T.C. 150722, Reel 555). Laing follows the Harleian MS. as soon as he can, which is at Laing III: 121, line 24, with the word 'Remitte', and this text continues until the end of the first part of the work (see Laing III: 133). The remainder of the Laing edition recreates the M'Crie MS. with only a few observations from the old printed version. A close reading of *An Exposition* shows that all the Scots forms of the M'Crie scribe, such as 'steir', 'ane', 'wreachit', 'whair', (Laing III: 119), 'yit', 'yow', 'whilk' (Laing III: 120), 'wecht' (Laing III: 121), as well as Scots suffixes in general, tend to disappear when Laing turns to the original MS. The editorial transition point can be seen in the following passage (in which King David is addressing God):

> "[...] Thow whippis me and scourgeis me bitterlie; yea, sa thow vexeis me, that, unless thow withdraw thy hand, and remit thy displeasure, thair resteth nothing unto me but utterlie to be confoundit. I beseche thee, O Lord, rage not, nether be commoveit aganis me above measure.
> [TRANSITION POINT]. Remitte and take awaie thy hevie displeasure which, by my iniquitie I have provoked against my selfe." This appeareth to have bene the meanyng of David in his first wordes, wherebie he declareth himselfe to have felt the grevous wraith of God before that he bursted forth in these wordes (Laing III: 121–122).

However, getting behind the printed versions and late manuscripts, to Knox's own English, does not mean that Knox *always* wrote English. Even allowing for the fact that Lekprevik is not wholly reliable, we can at least be reasonably sure that he did not *reverse* his process of Anglicisation (i.e. *Scotticise* his text). But his edition of Knox's answer to Tyrie the Jesuit contains some definite Scotticisms, which cannot therefore belong to anyone other than Knox himself:

> Wonder not (gentill Reidar) that sic ane argument suld proceid fra me in thir dolorois days, after that I haue taken gudenight at ye world and at all ye fasherie of the same, except to lament for my awin sinnis [...] In the progres of the said letter, he [Tyrie] planely furthshawis, what is his scope and purpois: to wit, to alienat your mynd from the treuth of God, now of Goddis greit mercy, efter long darknes, offered to this Realme (S.T.C. 15062, Reel 473, Aii).

The mix is irregular with items such as 'fra', 'sic', 'ane', 'thir', 'awin' and 'efter' existing side-by-side with English forms. But by far the most richly textured Scots words are 'fasherie' and 'furthsawis'.

What of Laing's other sources? Where he could not use the M'Crie MS., he took the printed editions of works such as *The First Blast* and *On Predestination, In Answer to the Cavillations by an Anabaptist*, (1560), as his sole basis, but the instances where he had to rely on such texts are comparatively rare. Among those who undertook to print Knox's writings were N. Dorcaster (?), J. Day, H. Singleton, T. Dawson, J. Lambrecht, E. van der Erve, E. Poullain, A. Rebul, J. Crespin, R. Lekprevik, R. Field, J. Scott, R. Hall, H. Denham, R. Waldegrave and T. Vautrollier.[18] Where they were Europeans it is less likely that they altered Knox's orthography, but where they are English, or even Scottish, it is possible. The remainder of Knox's correspondence is drawn from three other main sources: David Calderwood's *The Historie of the Kirk of Scotland* (in which Knox's letters to Mrs. Locke make their literary début, and no earlier versions are to be found), *The Calendar of State Papers Relating to Scotland and Mary, Queen of Scots*, (H. M. Stationery Office, vol. II), and *The Calendar of State Papers, Foreign Series, of the Reign of Elizabeth*, (H. M. Stationery Office). The latter two categories are the most trustworthy, and often show Knox to be using the kind of Scots / English that we find in his epistle to Tyrie.

Other sources, unknown to Laing, have come to light since he completed his great edition. A number of 'Knox-Papers' were printed for the first time in Peter Lorimer's *John Knox and the Church of England*, (1875), taken from a group of manuscripts called the 'Morrice Collection'. Two of Knox's works: *John Knox to the Congregation at Berwick*, (1552), and a *Memorial to the Privy Council*, (1552)[19] we owe to Lorimer. These fascinating manuscripts belong almost to the very earliest part of Knox's preaching career, but unfortunately they are, as Lorimer observes, 'contemporary transcripts' rather than originals.[20] The scribe may have been an Englishman, or one of Knox's Scottish circle mentioned by Northumberland (see Laing III: 83). Whatever the case, the manuscripts contain much Scots.

18 See Hazlett, I., 'A Working Bibliography of the Writings of John Knox', 185–194.

19 See Lorimer, P., *John Knox and the Church of England*, p. 251 and p. 266.

20 ibid., p. 250.

Examples are 'mycht', 'heipit', 'spreit', 'mak', 'rychteouslie', 'ferde', 'depone', 'vincuste', 'heidlings', 'trew', 'wes', 'hes', 'latt', 'yitt', and consistent use of '-ioun'.

General Conclusion

Strictly speaking, less than 10% of Knox's work comes before us in Laing's edition taken from the Reformer's handwritten scripts. However, having said that, we can get behind the Laing text and catch a glimpse of Knox *certainly* writing English, usually with a few occasional Scotticisms. We can also see a scribe reversing the process, perhaps unconsciously. It is also possible, but not always provable, that Knox's printers enhanced his anglicisation. Generally speaking, however, it is a vain task to look for, and wrong to impose, audience-related patterns on the orthographical systems, at least when dealing with texts other than *The Historie*. The evidence of *The Historie* itself, for all its intrinsic difficulties, shows clearly that Knox himself had a healthy command of Scots and that he probably used it quite extensively in his own original drafts, particularly when recording narrative speech (if he wrote, rather than dictated, this work). Ninian Winzet's charge against him, which has formed the basis of so many studies, should not be so influential, since Winzet had nothing like the literary information on Knox that we have (although, as we shall see in subsequent chapters, he *did* have unique historical material which he alone has preserved for us; below p. 150, p. 156). It would certainly not be admitted to a court of law, at any rate. The whole question of anglicisation is extremely difficult, and the answer to it cannot be expressed without multiple reservations. Knox, it seems, never forgot his 'auld plane Scottis', even if he didn't always choose to use it. When he did, particularly in *The Historie*, he used it extremely well. He was never guilty of 'anglicised pretensions'[21] as such, nor can we always be sure that he consciously adopted English models (admittedly George Buchanan said that he did, as we shall see

21 Lewis, C. S., *English Literature in the Sixteenth Century*, p. 202.

in chapter four, but Buchanan was in fact referring to Knox's vehemence, not his language).

Exhaustive research into the textual problems of Knox's work, then, inevitably terminates without real and definitive conclusions. So what is the purpose of an analysis which simply shunts the problem into a siding, and leaves it there? For one thing, the perennial English/Scots controversy has, all too often, been taken as the most important aspect of literary Knox studies. But, as we have seen, to say he wrote English, and therefore falls outside the domain of Scottish literary study, is an assertion that does not hold much water. So any effort which removes the possibility of such an approach cannot be without at least some value. And with this recognition, we can move on to better things.

Images of Knox

It is undeniable that Knox could do with a good public-relations officer, and before getting down to the business of literary criticism, it is probably best to clear up many of the misconceptions about the Reformer which at times and in places are still prevalent. There is a description of Knox written by a young contemporary, which, for all its glorious readability, has entered so pervasively into Scotland's perception of him, that one might almost wish it had never been written. When James Melvill was fifteen years old he saw Knox at St. Andrews University, and afterwards wrote it up in his diary. James's observations have placed Knox forever in the tradition of the '*Boanerges*' which, being interpreted, (as they say), means, 'The Sons of Thunder' (see Mark 3: 17):[22]

> Bot of all the benefites I haid that yeir was the coming of that maist notable profet and apostle of our nation, Mr. Jhone Knox, to St. Androis, wha, be the faction of the Quein occupeing the castell and town of Edinbruche, was compellit to remove thairfra with a number of the best [...] I hard him teatche ther the prophecie of Daniel that simmer, and the wintar following. I haid my pen and my litle book, and tuk away sic things as I could comprehend. In the

22 Perhaps it is even significant that one of the '*Boanerges*' is called 'John' (the other being 'James').

> opening upe of his text he was moderat the space of an halff houre; bot when he enterit to application, he maid me sa to grew and tremble, that I could nocht hald a pen to wryt. I hard him oftymes utter these thretenings in the hicht of their pryde, quhilk the eis of monie saw cleirlie brought to pass [...] Being in St. Androis he was verie weak. I saw him everie day of his doctrine go hulie and fear, with a furring of martriks about his neck, a staff in the an hand, and guid godlie Richart Ballanden, his servand, holding upe the other oxtar, from the Abbay to the paroche kirk; and be the said Richart and another servant, lifted upe to the pulpit, whar he behovit to lean at his first entrie; bot or he haid done with his sermont, he was sa active and vigorous that he was lyk to ding that pulpit in blads and fly out of it![23]

Despite Melvill's liveliness, these are much, and often tiresomely, quoted passages, so it is apt to point out here that he wrote much else besides (nearly a thousand pages in fact). Quoting continually choice fragments of any work such as the above can be a very misleading activity.[24] (Indeed, Knox himself, Melvill and Ninian Winzet have all been misrepresented as a result of it).

But what of Melvill's image of Knox? Is it accurate? Certainly, his physical descriptions are always interesting, since otherwise we do not really know what Knox looked like, although a later description, comparable to Melvill's, survives in a Latin letter by Peter Young.[25] From the above, we learn what Knox wore, and how he behaved in the pulpit. Moreover, as we shall see in chapter five, (below p. 218), the book of Daniel was especially significant to Knox, and had been for a long time. Melvill's mention of 'thretenings' also rings true. Indeed, there can be no doubt that he has captured one facet of Knox's character with remarkable vividness and complete accuracy. But it is not the whole story, nor does it mean that only Knox behaved like this. The rest of this study explores the other sides of Knox, as well as the one Melvill saw (and let there be no doubt, he admired Knox enormously).

23 Pitcairn, R., (ed.), *The Autobiography and Diary of Mr. James Melvill*, p. 26, p. 33.

24 If anyone objects that I am doing precisely such a thing myself, I would reply that the author of this study, more than any general critic of Scottish literature, has the right to appropriate Melvill's comments.

25 This letter is quoted in Janton, P., *L'homme et l'oeuvre*, p. 513.

We are indebted to Melvill for other glimpses of the Reformer, and although these are less important than the above, they still deserve to be quoted. It is Melvill, for instance, who tells us that Knox saw a play, made: 'at the mariage of Mr. Jhone Colvin'[26] and this does not tally very well with the idea that Knox was hostile to art or gaiety. The final observation we ought to note is Melvill's account of the Regent Morton's speech at Knox's funeral: 'He lovit Mr. Knox whill he was alyve. At his deathe and buriall he gaiff him ane honorable testimonie: "That he nather fearit nor flatterit anie fleche!"'[27] In the following chapters, we shall see why the latter part, at least, of that eulogy is a myth which must be stripped away.

What, then, of Knox's image in the Scotland of today? Certainly, no historical character has been so continually pilloried, (he lends himself easily to satirical representation!) even if there are many scholars who are prepared to probe deeper. But even dramatists, such as Liz Lochhead, are now commendably willing to turn back to his original words for their information on him, and this is surely a healthy sign.

Literary Divisions in Knox's Works and the Structure of this Study

All that remains for us to do now is to outline the categories into which Knox's work falls. His writings, however, like those of Martin Luther, are hard to classify because they are very much occasional and *ad hoc*. They are nearly always written to address a specific situation. Laing himself identifies four divisions (which Dr. Murison follows)[28] and, with one or two reservations, this study adopts these, although it excludes a number of works which Laing included, such as *The Book of Common Order or The Form of Prayers and Ministration of the Sacraments, Approved and Received by the Church of Scotland*, (1564), (Laing VI: 275–333), *The Psalmes of David in English Meter, Edinburgh, 1565*, (Laing VI: 335–343), *Prayers Subjoyned to Calvin's Catechisme, Edinburgh*, (1564), (Laing VI: 343–360), and *Additional*

26 Pitcairn, R., (ed.), *The Autobiography and Diary of Mr. James Melvill*, p. 27.

27 ibid., p. 60.

28 See Murison, D., 'Knox the Writer', 33.

Prayers Not Contained in the Edinburgh Volume of 1564–65 (Laing VI: 361–379), sometimes collectively and eponymously known as *Knox's Psalms and Liturgy*. These texts, hardcore religious writings, are of minimal interest to the literary critic.

The first division is that of 'admonitory public epistles'; works such as *An Epistle to the Congregation of the Castle of St. Andrews, With a Brief Summary of Balnaves on Justification by Faith*, (1548), *A Godly Letter of Warning, or Admonition to the Faithful in London, Newcastle and Berwick*, (1554), *A Letter to the Queen Dowager, Regent of Scotland*, (1556, 1558), *The Appellation from the Sentence Pronounced by the Bishops and Clergy, Addressed to the Nobility and Estates of Scotland*, (1558), *The First Blast of the Trumpet Against the Monstrous Regiment of Women*, (1558), and so on. Also in this category we can place *The Reasoning Betwixt the Abbot of Crossraguel and John Knox Concerning the Mass*, (1562), since the published text begins with a series of letters.

The second is Knox's 'private letters' written between the early 1550s and his death in 1572; a division which is wholly unproblematic. Laing's third category, 'devotional works' is, however, unsatisfactory. 'Controversial/theological' is better, since most of Knox's works in this division are polemical and disputatious. It includes *A Vindication of the Doctrine that the Sacrifice of the Mass is Idolatry*, (1550), *An Exposition Upon Matthew IV, Concerning the Temptation of Christ in the Wilderness*, (1556), and the important *On Predestination*, (1560). The last text is especially valuable because of its connections with *The Historie*, and we shall explore these in chapters four (below, pp. 160–168) and five, (pp. 206–210). All we need say here is that it contains a translation from John Sleidan's history of the continental Reformation: *Commentariorum de Statu Religionis et Reipublicæ, Carolo V, Cæsare*, (1556). The general connection between Knox's work and Sleidan's should be obvious (although it is worth pointing out that the *Ecclesiastica Historia*, or *Magdeburg Centuries* of Matthias Flacius Illyricus, is a better Continental equivalent to *The Historie*).

The final 'historical' chapters contain lengthy studies of Knox's *magnum opus*: written probably between 1558–1571, and which has stimulated magnificent tributes. The most singular of these comes from Dr. David Murison:

> Granted its self-confessed limitations, his [Knox's] *History* is a picture of his times which for depth of insight, brilliance of presentation and animation of style could hardly be bettered, and though critics have censured the slabs of documentation which break up the flow of the narrative, Knox's genius and single minded dedication to his one theme, the triumph of the Reformation against all odds and vicissitudes, give his story compelling dramatic force and unity. For Knox it was, *mutatis mutandis*, the drama of the Old Testament re-enacted in Scotland, with himself as Moses, Joshua, Isaiah, Jeremiah, Ezekiel and Daniel rolled into one. The *History* is the *αγων* or struggle between great forces, Catholicism versus Protestantism, State versus Church, Monarchy versus People, future versus past, revolution versus reaction, at the point of no return and when no compromise remained possible, a situation in many ways like that of our own present day.[29]

This powerful critique sets beyond doubt that *The Historie* is worthy of extensive consideration (and hits upon the fact that, for Knox, *history is theology* and *vice versa*; it is the cosmic battleground which manifests God's sovereignty and lordship. *The Historie* is Knox's testimony or witness to this experience, as he sees it, in sixteenth century Scotland). But the present study not only analyses *The Historie*; it assesses how the rhetorical skills that Knox developed in his lesser texts enabled him to write his greatest work. First, however, we must tackle 'pre-Knoxian' prose, with a similar concern to illustrate continuity.

29 ibid., 43.

Chapter One: Scottish Vernacular Prose before Knox, from the *Meroure of Wyssdome* to *Archbishop Hamilton's Catechism*

Knox's *The Historie* begins its narrative: 'in the year of God 1422' (Laing I: 5), almost one hundred and fifty years before the setting up of a Reformed Scottish Church in 1560. Obviously, reform was no easy process and only came about after a long struggle, which was by no means consistent. A recognisable pattern first appears some ten years after Knox's inception point, when the beliefs of Wycliffe and Hus found their way into Scotland, but complete political impotence was a concomitant of such views and they generally passed away without much notice. Only comparatively isolated individuals such as Paul Craw (Pavel Kravar) held them, and there was no known corresponding attempt to propagate any through manuscripts other than the *New Testament*. The first significant religious controversy which Knox describes took place in 1494, when the so-called 'Lolardis of Kyle' (Laing I: 8) were called before James IV by the Archbishop of Glasgow, but that whole affair collapsed into farce (see Laing I: 12).[1]

Quite coincidentally, it was probably in the same decade of the fifteenth century that original Scottish religious prose really began, and it emanated from a thoroughly orthodox source. John Ireland's *Meroure of Wyssdome*, a predominantly theological treatise in seven books, composed for personal use by the same King James, dates from around 1490, and its author was a man who had little sympathy for

1 J. M. Ross considers this episode in his *Scottish History and Literature to the Period of the Reformation*, but he is rather too enthusiastic about Knox, and some of his conclusions may be unreliable. For instance, he could 'hardly resist' the suspicion that the religious articles of the Wycliffites found in *The Historie* had been given a Reformation 'tint' by Knox. However, Knox was very careful to differentiate between his own comments and the articles (see Laing I: 8, 9, 10 and I: 8, n. (7)). He even translates, as he says, 'according to the barbarousnes of thair Latine and dictament' (Laing I: 8).

'heresy'. For example, in Book VI, which deals at length with the 'haly sacramentis', he discusses the implications of their administration by sinful clergymen (a topic raised in Wycliffe's *De Civilii Dominio*). Ireland neatly employs *reductio ad hæresim*:

> [...] in this mater Errit and fell in herresie iohnne wicleif of ingland about a hundreth yer syn in the tym of the truble of the kyrk and scisme / that trowit that quhen the paip bischop or preist is nocht in the stat of grace / that thai minister nocht the sacramentis na has nocht power / this was ane auld and paralus heresie / lang tyme befoir him / condampnit / and eftir his deid the haly kyrk condampnit him as herretyk / and the kyrk of ingland condampnit him in his lif / and eftir his deid war condampnit *iohannes huse* and *ieronimus de praga* and brynt in the counsall of constaunce / that followit his Errouris. Veritie is [...][2]

Ultimately the Scottish Reformation owed little to Wycliffe, except perhaps that which it inherited *via* Luther,[3] but what is significant about the above passage is the fact that it is fundamentally concerned with identifying religious errors and offering reliable alternatives. When the Reformation gained strength, the prose which gathered round it (with the two exceptions of Murdoch Nisbet's *The New Testament in Scots* and James Harryson's *James Harryson, a Scottishman's Exhortacion to the Scottes to Conform to the Will of Englande*) was very often intent upon those basic aims, no matter what doctrinal standpoint authors held. Admittedly, Ireland dealt mainly with the heresies of antiquity, those of Pelagius, say, or Nestorius, and as he says himself, by the time he wrote the *Meroure of Wyssdome*, Wycliffe had been dead for over a hundred years. In any case, he had never posed much of a threat to Rome in his life-time. It is clear, however, that there are at least some points of contact between Ireland and the Reformation era. The very fact that he chose to write theology in the vernacular is significant, although he seldom quotes scripture in Scots since that would bring him perilously close to one aspect of the very heresy which he was in the process of condemning. There are never-

2 See McDonald, C., (ed.), *Meroure of Wyssdome*, vol. 3: p. 84.

3 According to Alister McGrath, the Roman Church regarded Luther as 'a Wycliffite in his doctrine of confession, a Hussite in his theory of contrition'; see *The Intellectual Origins of the European Reformation*, p. 29.

theless a few stimulating instances, however; for example: 'as jhesus sais in þe euangel, the realme of heuin is likynnit to a tressoure, hid in a *croft* [...]', 'the angell said, 'Lady, this *barne* sal be of gret powere''[4] (italics added), and so on. The above passage is also valuable in other ways. 'Heresy' is a particularly theological topic. Ireland was a trained theologian, who thinks (and in fact writes) mainly in Latin. His thought-patterns impinge upon his vernacular style (look at how the verb 'condampnit' is in end-position in the phrase: 'lang tyme befoir him / condampnit'. Compare, for example, Virgil's: '[...] tot adire labores / impulerit'). This is not as likely to happen when Ireland's material is less, or non-, theological.

Broadly speaking, Ireland's literary relevance to the later prose of the Scottish Reformation falls into about three main areas (we must bear in mind, however, that the *Meroure of Wyssdome* had no popular circulation and belongs, in Scotland at least, to an age before printing). First of all, it is the work of a schoolman; a thoroughbred scholastic who studied at the Sorbonne and took there a doctorate in theology around 1475. There are indeed many sections of the text which illustrate just how deeply Ireland was immersed in this academic world-view. The following is perhaps the most elaborate example of this author's 'gymnastique intellectuele':[5]

> The vii verite is at the prescience of god is / at the iugement sal be and yit that presciens is nocht necessar bot contingent tharof. This I prove / for it followis in consequens logical necessar / god wait at the iugement sal be / *ergo* the iugement sal be / and the conclusioun and consequent of this logicale consequens is contingent and nocht necessar / for yit be the power of god it is possible that the iugement be nocht na neuir cum / tharfor the antecedens of the logicale conesquens is nocht necessar bot contingent for / and the antecedens war necessar and the conse-quens contingent / of a trew antecedens in a gud consequens folowis a fals consequens / and that is impossible.[6]

This kind of thing may strike readers as typical of medieval scholasticism; plodding, convoluted and pedantic, and indeed it is, but one must admit that it is also solidly, if excessively, rational. As an intel-

4 Macpherson, C., (ed.), *Meroure of Wyssdome*, vol. 1: p. 40, p. 134.

5 Janton, P., *L'homme et l'oeuvre*, p. 411.

6 Quinn, F., (ed.), *Meroure of Wyssdome*, vol. 2: p. 139.

lectual world-movement, scholasticism like Ireland's was probably on the decline, but it was obviously still a force to be reckoned with by any potential Reformer who sought to operate through the Universities. Thus, at Wittenberg in the subsequent century, Luther had to meet it head on, while Zwingli and the Swiss Reformers, who were steeped in the learning of Erasmus and in a more distinctive Swiss humanism, were comparatively free of it (although it is well known that Luther himself, at least initially, was much influenced by Erasmus, and without the latter's Greek *New Testament*, the German Reformer could not have made his own version). The Reformation in Scotland, in this respect, is undoubtedly closer to the Lutheran movement. Ireland's younger contemporary, John Major, who probably taught the young Knox at St. Andrews, was, of course, the last great Scottish scholastic, and when Knox began his reforming career he couched his message in the terminology of the medieval universities, and then gradually blended into it the very best of a later Renaissance eloquence as his knowledge and experience deepened, presumably as a result of private study.

The correlation between the intellect and religious belief influences other aspects of Ireland's work and interlinks again with broad aspects of Reformation prose. For instance, Book III contains a lengthy exposition of the *Apostolicum*, the Apostle's Creed, and has parallels in John Gau's fascinating little treatise entitled, appropriately enough, *The Richt Vay to the Kingdom of Heuine*, (hereafter *The Richt Vay*), a Lutheran text printed in 1533 at Malmö by John Hochstraten, and in *Archbishop Hamilton's Catechism* of 1551, which was written in order to codify orthodox belief and as a reaction to Protestant infringement. (Gau's text, in fact, is a translation of a Danish theological work by Christiern Pedersen;[7] hence the printer and place of

7 Christiern Pedersen (1480–1554) was a Danish humanist and Reformer who attended Greifswald before taking priest's orders in 1505. Three years later he produced a translation of Saxo Grammaticus's *Gesta Danorum* under the title *Historia Danica*. In 1514 he was translating the Psalms and in 1515 completed a *Book of Homilies* (Jærtegnspostil). After attaching himself to the Lutheran Reformation he followed Christian II into Holland in 1525. His translation of the *New Testament* appeared in 1529 and was adapted from the Vulgate and Luther's edition of 1522.

publication. Gau himself was a Scot who had fled to Denmark, where his Lutheran beliefs would not result in persecution or martyrdom).[8]

It is one of the fundamental assertions of this study that language and vocabulary are deeply influenced by religious belief and that, logically, where religious beliefs are either Protestant or Catholic, one can trace distinctive prose features to each corresponding system of thought (and each system of thought, of course, entails a differing system of religious practice and worship). For example, in the ninth or tenth articles of the Creed, there are differences due to religious factors. Ireland represents his belief in the Church: 'I trow it that the halikirk catholic and universal determinis the communioun of haly thingis',[9] and this more-or-less agrees with *Archbishop Hamilton's Catechism*. Gau has: '*I trou that thar is ane halie chrissine kirk*' and: '*I trow forgiffine of sinnis*'. For Ireland and the author of the later catechism, the forgiveness of sins is dependent upon the Catholic Church. The two necessarily go together. For Gau there is a Christian Church which is not Catholic. If there are differences in the Creeds, the differences in their expositions are greater still, as we might expect. For instance, Ireland says under the tenth article ('he sal cum one the day of iugement / to iuge baith thame that salbe deid and lyffand [...]'):[10]

> The sext ressoune / quharfor god has ordand this final iugement is / we se that euill persouns in this waurld / of-tymes has gret digniteis in the kyrk & temporalite / and gud and haly persouns has gret pouerte and oppressioun / and mony merwalis tharof / Tharfor god that is of infinit wisdome and liberalitie / that for ony gud deid in the waurld gevis reward / and for euill has ordand punicioun in this warld / for gud deidis of wertu morale and done in grace / wtout perseuerance thar-in / gevis heir temporale reward lordschip plesance and dignite at ar lest / *In genere bonorum* And eftir punysis richt sar [...][11]

Interestingly, Ireland sees the final judgement as a solution to the social injustice which occurs in ecclesiastical circles, while both Gau and *Archbishop Hamilton's Catechism* emphasise its relevance to the

8 Mitchell, A. F., (ed.), *The Richt Vay*, p. 34.

9 Quinn, F., (ed.), *Meroure of Wyssdome*, vol. 2: p. 62.

10 ibid., vol. 2: p. 52.

11 ibid., vol. 2: p. 54.

personal life of the individual. In fact, Ireland comes quite close to a major strand in early Reformation thought concerning the clergy, although decades would pass before it found more forceful expression. Indeed, there are parallels elsewhere in Gau's work. For example, in his concluding epistle to the noble lords and barons of Scotland, he attacks, in his view, the most corrupt clergyman of them all, the Pope.

> Our halie fader ye paip and his bischopis giffis ane part of ye spulze quhilk thay reiff fra ye pwir to thir forsaid sekkis and thinkkis yat they supple thair office the quhilk is notht in veritie for sanct Paul sais in the iii c. of his first epistil to timothe ane bischoip man be ane prechour heir Paul sais notht yat it is sufficient to ane bischoip to haiff ane preacher to supple his office but hime self suld be ane techour and prechour [...][12]

Ireland, of course, would be appalled at this kind of talk, but in it we can see a sharpening and a more specific application of his own comments, worked into the prose through Gau's Protestant world-view. Furthermore, while Ireland's tone is level and restrained, Gau uses irony and sarcasm, and this is certainly symptomatic of the keener, more crucial and indeed violent religious controversy which the Reformation provoked. Protestant vehemence, like Gau's, was to permeate Knox's later prose and there is nothing as forceful in Ireland's work. And it seems to be basically true that prose which took shape in an atmosphere of real and not just academic controversy, such as Gau's, Knox's and say, Ninian Winzet's, more effectively brings out the author's personality.

However, if there is any parallel between Ireland and Knox himself, it is in their skill as preachers. Charles MacPherson, Ireland's first editor, rather inadvisedly says: 'that Ireland ever preached much [...] may be doubted',[13] but as J. H. Burns rightly counters: 'Ireland's own references to his preaching cannot be so lightly dismissed',[14] and much of the text of the *Meroure of Wyssdome* confirms that the author was a man of the pulpit. Indeed one of his favourite phrases: 'we may weill knaw and understand [...]' closely echoes Robert Henryson's

12 Mitchell, A. F., (ed.), *The Richt Vay*, pp. 104–105.

13 MacPherson, C., (ed.), *Meroure of Wyssdome*, vol. 1: p. xxvi.

14 See Burns, J. H., 'The Meroure of Wyssdome', 94.

preaching swallow,[15] and Ireland constantly teaches by similitude, which is, of course, a favourite recourse of preachers. But passages like this must catch the drift of Ireland's sermonising:

> O man repleit and fillit of all foly and wikitnes / quhow may thou cheris the wikkit thef dedly syn / in thi hert mynd and curage / that is sa cruell and agan the / and lauboris to bring the to eternall dampnacioun / sene thou knawis weill that for the distruc/cioun of it / and for thi saluacioun help and suple be werray necessite and cherite / god of maieste tuk humanite / and deit on the croce / thou will nocht haue ane euill govn / ane euill hois ane euill scho thou will nocht haue an euill wif / na ane euill possessioun eftir thi will thi plesaunce and desyr *And thou will haue ane euill saulle conseruand syn mortall in it* [...][16] (italics added).

This is pretty close to the type of preaching identified by G. R. Owst as 'satire and complaint',[17] with just an inflexion of the 'snares of costume' theme, and these are worked out through the stock address to foolish man. Interestingly, it is man and not woman who is: 'singled out to suffer at [the preacher's] hands',[18] but the most appealing feature is Ireland's use of mimesis, and there is real control of language here ('thou wil nocht haue ane euill govn [...] hois [...] scho [...] wif [...] possessioun', effectively switches to what one '*will haue*' in consequence; namely: 'ane euill saulle conseruand syn mortall in it'). Of course, Ireland's language is from the standard religious register ('syn', 'eternall dampnacioun', 'saluacion', 'cherite', 'deit on croce') but on the whole, we do get the impression that he was a fairly competent preacher. Knox was undoubtedly in touch with the type of preaching tradition which Ireland epitomises here, and the Reformer himself was perhaps the last of the great old Scottish preachers. Anyhow, no other prose writer between 1490 and 1550 is so close to Knox in this respect as Ireland.

There is another striking similarity between the two writers, although it would be foolish to make too much of it. Ireland, upon occasion, indulges in what one might legitimately label the 'merry

15 See Fox, D., (ed.), *The Poems of Robert Henryson*, p. 68, l. 1737.

16 See McDonald, C., (ed.), *Meroure of Wyssdome*, vol. 3: p. 71.

17 Owst, G. R., *Literature and Pulpit in Medieval England*, pp. 375–471.

18 ibid., p. 405.

tale', although this is by no means all that typical of his writing as a whole. Even so, it is there, it ties in with preaching, and it ties in with Knox. In Book V of the *Meroure of Wyssdome*, Ireland attacks the notion of inescapable destiny, and presents the following little narrative which is a fine example of *reductio ad absurdum* in action:

> As the woman in parys quhen sche knew that hir cousing was drownit in the rywer of sayn cryit and said / that it was his destany & he mycht be na maner euade it / for it was ordand for him sche said or euir cot or govne was schapin for him Than come a clerk *as my self* / and hard hir criand sayand and affermand this / and *be gret wisdome* he thocht he wauld schaw hir foly / and gaf hir twa gret blawis and strakis on baith hir chekis / that sche was gretlie abasit of / And sone sche turnit her purpos and cryit agane the clerk / quhy he had sa felony strikin hir wtout caus or reassoun / and that he suld be had to presoune and punyst for it *The wys clerk an/suerit sobirly* and said / lady this god wist lang befor that I suld fall in sic a rage / and foly to strik you and that ye suld thole and suffer this for your daft and wykit langage / that ye haue spokin agane *his honour and wisdome* / and sene this was destany and ordand for you / that ye suld nocht wyt me And thus the lady gat twa gret blawis tholit gret scorne and passit schamefully hir gait[19] (italics added).

This has parallels in the humorous narratives of Knox (which we shall consider later in the book; below pp. 255–278), and its generic affiliations are those which the Reformer also draws upon. Similarly, the none-too-modest self-references may personally bring Knox to mind (below p. 195, Laing II: 297), but the broadest similarity must be expressed in terms of the sermon exemplar. Owst identified it as: 'the humorous sermon-anecdote' which: 'we recognize as one more natural, typical product of that early pulpit realism and feeling for raw humanity'[20] and if Ireland was pretty good at this kind of thing, Knox was a master.

Ireland's passage, however, deserves fairly lengthy consideration since it is far from artless. It smacks of realism, first of all, because it is localised in Paris, where Ireland was very much at home; secondly because the woman's dialogue, although it recalls Chaucer (whom

19 Quinn, F., (ed.), *Meroure of Wyssdome*, vol. 2: pp. 140–141.
20 Owst, G. R., *Literature and Pulpit in Medieval England*, pp. 167–168.

Ireland had read),[21] may independently catch at an idiom which both Ireland and Chaucer knew. There is also a transition from indirect to direct speech, the honours going of course to the clerk, (and *that* specifically anticipates Knox, as we shall see), which allows a steady focusing to take place, while Ireland moves from slapstick (the 'twa gret blawis [...]') through naturally realised emotions such as the woman's anger and outrage, to shame, as the clerk finally exposes her undoubted stupidity. In the context of this study, a more detailed analysis of Ireland's work is not possible, and I have attempted to discuss the *Meroure of Wyssdome* only insofar as it has any relevance to later Reformation prose and to Knox's works. But as we have seen, connections can, and should, be made. In *The Historie*, Knox passes from the 1490s to the late 1520s, 'the year of God 1527' (Laing I: 13), to the story of 'Maister Patrick Hammyltoun'. Even so, Knox was not in possession of all the literary facts, and the modern literary historian can find significant material some seven years before this date.

Around 1520, a certain Murdoch Nisbet, who was an Ayrshireman and who may have had some connection with the Lollards mentioned earlier, (above p. 29), transcribed John Purvey's revision of Wycliffe's Bible into Scots, and Knox certainly had no knowledge of this. Like the *Meroure of Wyssdome*, the text was never printed, and the translation seems to have been made for secret study. Nisbet's Bible, however, is prefaced by a translated version of Martin Luther's introduction to his German *Das Neue Testament*, comparing *Old* and *New Testaments*. It discourses on the etymology of the term 'evangelion', introduces Christ as a new David and His gospel as a remedy for sin. Finally, it differentiates between the Law and the Gospel, and ends with a three-fold address to noblemen, clerics and commons. Each book is accompanied by pre-Vulgate argumentations, found in most of the Wycliffe manuscripts and in the Vulgate itself,[22] and towards the end of his text, Nisbet includes sundry lessons from the *Old Testament*. He concludes with a translated version of Luther's

21 See MacPherson, C., (ed.), *Meroure of Wyssdome*, vol. 1: p. 74, l.15, which shows that he had definitely been reading 'the persounis taill, and vtheris'.

22 See Biblia Sacra*: Vulgate Editionis Sixti V Pontifica Maximi jussu Recognita et Clementis VIII*, pp. ii–xxviii.

preface to Romans (and in this there is a parallel with Gau's work).[23] Luther's first preface dates from 1522, although Nisbet's work on the Purvey Bible was probably begun before this, since a scribe capable of translating the German, might just as well have translated the whole Lutheran Bible instead of Purvey's old-fashioned text. William Tyndale's edition of the same preface, of which the Scots translation is independent, was published along with his own English Bible in 1526, and his version of Luther's prologue to Romans was not printed until 1535, when Tyndale revised the text of the 1526 Bible. This Tyndale preface *is* included in Nisbet, although some modifications have been made, and due to the later date of the 1535 English edition, Nisbet could not include it in its proper place, so he finally put it at the end of his manuscript. Such, then, are the contents and complexities of Murdoch Nisbet's *The New Testament in Scots*. It is a valuable text only insofar as it allows us to examine the earliest Lutheran influences in Scotland and in no sense does it lay claim to originality. Its progressiveness is inextricably linked with its Lutheranism, but in terms of its language and style, it is certainly backward-looking. After all, the earliest Wycliffe Bibles go back to the 1380s and the Purvey version is only about fifteen years later. Here is Nisbet's version of 'The Parable of the Unforgiving Servant' from Matthew 18, juxtaposed with John Gau's rendering of the same passage (which is the longest scriptural extract in *The Richt Vay*):

> *Nisbet (1520)*
> [...] the kingdom of heuinis is liknit to a king, that wald rekkin with his seruandis. And quhen he began to rekkin, aan that aucht ten thousand talentis was broucht to him. And quhen [he] had nocht quharof to yelde, his lord comandit him to be sald, and his wif and his childer, and al thingis that he had, and to be payit. Bot the ilk seruand fel doun, and prayit him, and said, Haue pacience in me, and I sal yelde al thingis to thee. And the lord had mercy on that seruand, and leet him ga, and forgafe to him al the dette. Bot that ilk seruand yede out, and fand aan of his euen seruandis, that awcht ane hundreth pennyis; and he held him, and stranglit him, and said Yeeld that that thou aw. And his euen seruand fel doun, and prayit him, and said, Haue pacience in me, and I sal quite al thingis to thee. Bot he wald nocht; bot went out and put him into presoun, till he payit all the dette. And his euen seruandis, seand the thingis

23 See Mitchell, A. F., (ed.), *The Richt Vay*, p. xxxvi.

that war done, sorowit gretly, and thai com and tald to thar lorde al thingis that war done. Than his lord callit him, and said to him Wickit seruand, I forgafe to the al the dette, for thou prayit me. Tharfor quhethir it behuvit nocht alsa thee to haue mercy on thin euen seruand, as I had mercy on thee? And his lord was wraathe, and betuke him to tormentouris, till he payit al the dette. Sa my fader of heuen sal do to you, gif ye forgef nocht euiry man to his bruther of your hartis.[24]

Gau (1533)
[...] ane similitud of ane king quhilk haid mony seruandis and ane of thaime vesz awand ane thowsand pennis to hime / and quhen he had na thing to pay with thane he commandit to sel hime and his wiff and his barnis to pay his dettis / this seruand fel apone his kneis befor hime / and said lord be marciful to me and I sal pay the al thy det thane this king vesz marciful to hime and forgaiff hime al his det / thane this seruand passit fourtht and fand ane oder seruand ane of his awne marousz / quhilk vesz awand ane hundreth pennis to hime / Thane he twik hime be the halsz and said pay quhat thou aw to me / thane he fel apone his kneis and said be marcifull to me and I sal pay ye al ye det / he vald noth bot he keist hime into presone vnto he suld pay it / quhen his marousz saw this thay var displesit and schew to thair maister quhow it haid hapnit / this king callit hime / befor hime and said to hime / thow vikkit seruand I forgaff ye al thy det quhen thou desirit of me / suld thow noth siclik be merciful to thy marrow and forgiff hime his dettis as I forgayff ye thyne? yane he vesz crabit and deliuerit hime / to ye tormentouris vnto he suld pay al his dettis sua sal my heuinlie fader dw to zow and ye forgiff him noth euerie ane oder with zour hartis quhat thay sine aganis zou [...][25]

As we noted earlier, Gau's text, like Nisbet's, is a translation (although he has had to work slightly harder than Nisbet). His source is Pedersen's *Den Rette Vey till Heimmerigis Rige*, (Malmö, 1531), itself mainly a translation of Urbanus Rhegius's *Die Zwölff Artickel unsers Christliche glaubens mit anzaigung d'hailigen geschrifft Darin sie gegründt seind*, (Augsburg, 1523).[26] (Gau also seems to have known

24 Law, T. S., (ed.), *The New Testament in Scots*, vol. 1: pp. 80–81.
25 Mitchell, A. F., (ed.), *The Richt Vay*, p. 60.
26 Urbanus Rhegius (German name Urban Reiger) (1489–1544) is also known as Phoenix von Roschach, Mattheas Gnidius or Simon Hessus. Formerly a secular priest, he adopted Lutheranism in the 1520s and left his monastery to propagate the Reformer's doctrines. He had been educated at Freiburg and lectured on poetry at Ingolstad where he enjoyed the tutorship of Johann Eck, who later became Luther's principal Catholic opponent. His background as a humanist

the original, and, indeed, seven copies still exist).[27] An English version entitled *A Declaration of the Twelve Articles of the Christen fayth with annotations of the holy Scriptures where they be grounded in*, (London, 1548), translated by Walter Lynne, indicates that the parable belongs not to the original but was added by Pedersen to clarify a point.[28] The study of Nisbet's source is less fruitful. First of all, the Lollard *New Testaments* were copied by numerous scribes at a time when there was no standardisation of spelling or literary dialect. Thus, there is a great diversity among the remaining manuscripts which have come down to us, especially among the early versions. For a medieval text, the Purvey Bible is remarkably uniform,[29] but it would be facile to compare Nisbet's text with, say, Forshall and Madden's printed version of the best extant manuscript. Disparities such as 'leet him ga / suffride hym to goo' and 'callit/clepide' might be traced solely to the fact that Nisbet was using another manuscript. Again it falls outside the scope of this study to determine which English MS. is closest to Nisbet's. Rather, our task at present is to explore the texts and their disparities, keeping in mind how they might have been studied by nascent Scottish Protestants. Gau's work, like John Johnsone's contemporaneous *An Confortable Exhortation of Our Mooste Holy Christen Faith and her Frutes*, (hereafter *An Confortable Exhortation*), may have been a still-born project, seized by port authorities,

made him a shrewd rhetorician and augmented his theological skills. One of his correspondents was Erasmus, who called him: 'Virum quod indicant literæ, comditum prudentem, facundum, eruditum, in summa omnibus omnium gratiarum ac musarum dotibus vndique præditum'; see *Erasmi Epistulæ*, tom. II: 1514–1517, p. 204; see also Nichols, F. M., (ed.), *Epistles of Erasmus*, vol. II: p. 244.

27 Mitchell, A. F., (ed.), *The Richt Vay*, p. xxxii.

28 See S.T.C. 20843, Case 24, Reel 142 (U.M.N. 2846) and also Brandt, C. J. and Fenger, B. T., (eds.), *Danske Skrifter; Den Rette Vey till Hiemmerigis Rige* is in vol. IV: III; in particular, see p. 277, l.23 – p. 278, l.11.

29 For instance, only the Bodley MS. no. 227 and the Corpus Christi MS. no. 147 of the 'Purvey text' contain significant signs of further revision, and these lack the methodical technique of the mainstream translations. For a workable, but old-fashioned commentary on the slighter disparities, see Skeat's Introduction to Forshall, J. and Madden, F., (eds.), *The New Testament in English by John Wycliffe and John Purvey*, pp. xi–xii.

but as A. F. Mitchell suggests, copies were more probably 'recovered by the magistrates after they had been for a time in circulation'.[30]

Certainly the two parables read very differently. Gau, following Pedersen, includes his version of course to substantiate the tenth article of his creed, which is appropriate enough. Neither the *Meroure of Wyssdome* nor *Archbishop Hamilton's Catechism* have any use for the same parable, although in the same part of his Creed, Ireland includes a similitude which has a similar ring:

> And geve a temporale king / of his wertu and liberalite / quhilis forgevis men thar fautis / and takis thame to grace / and nane makis of his will ordinance or liberalite disqui/sicioun / but humely thankis him / tharfor gret is the foly of men that makis inquisicioun of godis deidis [...][31]

Ireland, however, has a different intention. He aims to encourage 'our pennaunce and turnyinge to god',[32] not the forgiveness of others. *Archbishop Hamilton's Catechism* has comparatively little time for figures and only says: 'nane can get fra God remissioun of thair synnis, except thei forgeue to thair nychtbour all offencis done to thame'.[33]

Nisbet's version of the narrative performs no specific justificatory function of course but there is no reason to suppose that the parable was not discussed during secret meetings, along with other scriptural texts. On the contrary, evidence from many fourteenth century heresy trials in England confirms this kind of activity among the Wycliffites. Perhaps the most curious of all the differences between the two versions are brought about by the kind of minor errors we find in Gau. For instance, in Nisbet, the first servant owes 'ten thousand talentis'. Gau on the other hand gets both the number and the currency wrong. He has '*ane thousand pennis*'. We know that, when the wrote, he had before him not only Pedersen's *Den Rette Vey till Hiemmerigis Rige* and Urbanus Rhegius's work, but also Pedersen's Danish translation of the Latin *Vulgate*: *Det Ny Testamente*, Luther's

30 Mitchell, A. F., (ed.), *The Richt Vay*, p. xxvii.

31 Quinn, F., (ed.), *Meroure of Wyssdome*, vol. 2: p. 72.

32 ibid., vol. 2: p. 73.

33 Mitchell, A. F., (ed.), *Archbishop Hamilton's Catechism*, f. cxx.

Das Neue Testament and Tyndale's 1526 version of the *New Testament*. It seems that he has produced a conflation of the two Danish texts (although elsewhere, he sometimes quotes Tyndale *verbatim*, or translates Luther). Obviously, all this is not very important, since Gau evidently did not consider the figure to have any theological significance, (although in fact, *it does*), but as a rule it was not advisable to tamper with scripture. Moreover, Gau has not been as attentive to detail as he was elsewhere. The age, after all, was one in which comparatively precise linguistic scholarship, pioneered by Lorenzo Valla, Cardinal Francisco Ximenes de Cisneros and Desiderius Erasmus,[34] ultimately led to the rejection, by Protestants, of at least some of the Catholic sacraments (such as Penance), and stimulated the whole of the Eucharistic controversy.[35] Even the old Augustinian interpretation of Biblical parables, (particularly, 'The Parable of the Good Samaritan'; see Luke 10: 30–35), with its ingenious allegories, paid specific attention to the most minor details. It is against this combined backdrop that we should view Gau's error, although no really important point of doctrine rests upon his presentation. Another, more significant dissimilarity between Gau and Nisbet comes towards the end of the parable. Where Nisbet's manuscript suggests that the fellow servants acted out of great sorrow, Gau attributes their motive to revenge. This differs again from the earliest Tyndale and *Det Ny Testamente* which has 'da sorgede de der faar'.[36] Gau's source seems to have been *Den Rette Vey till Hiemmerigis Rige*'s 'bedroffuede', which, to Gau, may have denoted a mixture of sorrow and anger. He may well have associated this with the Scots 'feid'.

34 See Greenslade, S. L., (ed.), *The Cambridge History of the Bible*, pp. 79–80, 50–62. Cardinal Ximenes published his *Complutensian Polyglot* in 1522, but Erasmus was the first textual critic to make the Greek New Testament widely available. In 1516, Froben's press issued his *Novum Testamentum Omne*. The text itself was far from perfect, (indeed the Polyglot was superior), but it was Erasmus's edition that caused the controversy.

35 See, for example, McGrath, A., *Reformation Thought*, pp. 110–116.

36 See Pedersen, C., *Det Ny Testamente*; also Offor, G., (ed.), *New Testament*, for Tyndale's version of 1525. The latter has 'they were very sory'. Similarly, Luther has 'Worden sie seer betrubt'; (*Dr. Martin Luther's Werke: Die Deutsche Bibel*, (*W.A.D.E.*, 6. 84. 10).

Despite the title of Nisbet's transcription, it is much more anglicised than Gau's work. Where Nisbet has 'childer', Gau has 'barnis' (from Pedersen's 'børn'); where Nisbet has 'seruandis' Gau has the splendid Scots 'marousz',[37] (which is not cognate with the Danish 'stalbrødre'), Nisbet has 'stranglit', Gau has 'took him be the halsz' (from the Danish 'halsen'), Nisbet has 'Lord', Gau 'maister' (not cognate with 'Herre') and finally, where Nisbet has '(he) was wraathe', Gau has 'he vesz crabbit' (again not cognate).[38]

Just as Knox apparently had no knowledge of Nisbet, he was likewise ignorant of Gau's project and of John Johnsone's *An Confortable Exhortation*, or at least, he never mentions them. Like *The Richt Vay,* Johnsone's text was probably printed by Hochstraten in Malmö and shipped to Scotland in the mid-1530s, and it probably shared a similar fate. There are two imperfect copies of the text, from which a whole copy can be assembled.[39] It is written throughout in a fairly uniform English, although Johnsone was undoubtedly a Scot. He addresses his readers as: 'the Christian brethernein in Scotlande' and calls them 'my brethren (which are my kinsmen pertayning to the flesche)'.[40] If we add to this the indisputable evidence that he was an eye-witness at Patrick Hamilton's martyrdom in St. Andrews in 1528,[41] his book begins to occupy its proper place in our perception. Like Gau's and Nisbet's works, it is minor literature (but not a translation). Tyndale's early Bible has influenced Johnsone more than Gau, and the text is mainly made up of quotations. There are sections dealing with subjects such as faith, unfaithfulness, hope, despair, peace, love, patience and the flesh, and the author seems to have thoroughly imbibed Luther's 'theologia crucis'. There is only one

37 Knox, too, evidently knew this word; see Laing I: 189: 'Thare did everie man reaconter his *marrow*' (italics added).

38 See Brandt, C. J. and Fenger, B. T., (eds.), *Danske Skrifter*, vol. IV: III, for 'bedroffuede', p. 278, 1.2, 'børn', p. 277, 1.26, 'stalbrødre', p. 277, 1.30 'halsen', p. 277, 1.32, 'Herre' p. 278, 1.3.

39 See Cameron, J. K., 'John Johnsone's *An Confortable Exhortation of Oure Mooste Holy Christen Faith and her Frutes*: An Early Example of Scots Lutheran Piety', 135.

40 See Johnsone, J., *An Confortable Exhortation*; also S.T.C. 2. 14668, (Al).

41 ibid., (E1) – (E2).

Patristic reference, and it is presumably to Augustine's *Quæstiones Septemdecim in Matthæum*,[42] and this is considerably fewer than the number of such references in Gau. Johnsone however does display some literary flashes, even if he was not theologically erudite:

> O erth / erth / erth / heere the woorde of thy lorde / which sayth. I come not to call the rightewes / but the synners to repentaunce. Ye whole nead not ye phisician / but they that are seke / art thou righteous and saue: then thou hath no nead of Christ / thou neadeth no other saueare but thy silfe [...] But o vayne man / thou art deceawet / for nether arte thou righteous nor whole / but because thou ymagine folischlie after thy fleshlie wisdom [...][43]

Although *An Confortable Exhortation* is remarkably irenical in tone, this passage, like our first quotation from *The Richt Vay*, uses a very penetrating sarcasm; not, however, to attack ecclesiastical institutions, but to encourage the individual to be more honest in religious self-assessment. (Knox of course combined both techniques in his prose). Johnsone uses the words of Christ to make up the core of his argument here (see Matthew 9: 13, Mark 2: 17, Luke 5: 32) but the forceful address to the earth recalls Jeremiah 22: 24, while the incisiveness of his wit and the way he punctures fondly fostered illusion are not at all unimpressive. The 'All is vanity' theme of Ecclesiastes, moreover, is not far below the surface

In another place he writes with positively palpable sincerity (and we should compare the following with Romans 4: 1–25):

> Therefore let us with Abraham beleue in hope / aboue hope / in Gods righteuesnes aboue oure vnrighteuesnes. In gods treuth aboue oure lyes. In Gods mercy aboue oure synfulnes. In Gods power / aboue oure weaknes. Let us haue faith with Abraham in gods promyses. And we shall reioy with Abraham in receawinge of the same thynges promised [...][44]

42 ibid., (C2).
43 ibid., (B7).
44 ibid., (B1).

James K. Cameron finds in these lines an 'arresting quality',[45] which probably derives from Johnsone's use of sharp contrasts which consistently emphasise the frailty of man and the power of God. And there is a kind of serenity in the language that seems to encourage faith.

Around the time that Johnsone and Gau were writing or translating their Lutheran treatises, John Bellenden translated Hector Boece's *Scotorum Historiæ a prima gentis origine, cum aliarum rerum et gentium illustratione non vulgari*, (1527), (hereafter *Scotorum Historiæ*), to produce Scotland's first popular vernacular prose history, twenty-five years before Knox began writing *The Historie* (and the relationship between these two works is something which we will consider more fully at a more important juncture). Another contemporaneous translation of Boece exists as the 'Mar Lodge' translation, although it has never been fully printed.[46] (The original manuscript is now in America and a transcript lies with the editor of the *Dictionary of the Older Scottish Tongue*; hereafter *D.O.S.T.*).[47] (Since this study is concerned only with Scottish *prose*, I shall not be considering William Stewart's verse translation of Boece). Also of particular interest and contemporary relevance is a work entitled *The Roit or Quheill of Tyme*, (1533–1538), by one Adam Bell or Abel, who was a canon regular of the Augustinian order, and who spent part of his life at Inchaffray Abbey. He later joined the Francisan brotherhood at Jedburgh. He originally composed a Latin chronicle from the creation to his own day, called *Rota Temporum* or *The Wheel of Time*, which was apparently published with the assistance of Bishop John Leslie at Rome, between 1575–8, when the bishop himself was resident there. No copies are known to have survived. Bell undertook his history at the request of George, fourth Earl of Seton. However, the author also produced a vernacular abridgement of his work which

45 See Cameron, J. K., 'John Johnsone's *An Confortable Exhortation of Oure Mooste Holy Christen Faith and her Frutes*: An Early Example of Scots Lutheran Piety', 143.

46 The first seven books only are contained in Watson, G., (ed.), *The Mar Lodge Translation of the History of Scotland*. This text is still incomplete.

47 ibid., p. vii.

is now in the National Library of Scotland (Nat. Lib. MS. 1746).[48] A transcript is held by the editors of the *D.O. S. T.* The vernacular text is heavily reliant on the work of Boece although it does not appear to be a direct translation, like the versions by Bellenden and the 'Mar Lodge' writer. We shall be looking briefly at Bell's work in due course.

It goes without saying that both of the direct prose translations of Boece constitute literary works of fairly major importance, and they ought to be considered as literature in their own right, but in the context of this study, I wish to make a very specific point which is relevant to Knox. Bellenden's *The Chronicles of Scotland* was published in the early 1530s and Knox could have had easy access to it. Certainly it contained information useful to him. Bellenden's work, it should be noted, embraces the whole range of Scottish history from the earliest times, while Knox was, of course, much more selective in his choice of period. The periods *do* overlap, however, and I have chosen one incident which the respective narratives all share: the martyrdom of Paul Craw. Boece's original text is quoted for two reasons. First of all it allows us to assess the nature of Bellenden's and the 'Mar Lodge's' translation. It is to be hoped that the second reason will become apparent when Knox's version of the events is considered.

> *Boece 1527*
> Post paucos dies ex quo solutum consilium fuerat, deprehensus est ab Henrico episcopo quidam in gymnasio sancti Andreæ, natione Bohemus, nomine Paulus Crau, nouas sectas docere, nouamque dogmata de sacramento Eucharistiæ, ac contra diuorum venerationem & confessionem sacerdotibus in aurem faciendam, quem, vt ad se accitum pertinacem cognouit, professoribus eum Theologiæ commisit, vt omnibus virtutis viribus hominem ab illis opinionibus deducerent: nec quicquam ab illis quoque effectum. Quamobrem iudici eum seculari transmiserunt, qui quæstione habita compererunt e Bohemia velut apostolum missum ad prædicandam Scotis Vvitcleff & Ioannis Hus hæresim deliram. Itaque profecto medio foro extructo rogo crematus est. Iacobus rem auditam plurima laude euexit, authoresque vnice hac re commendatos habuit. Principem in resistendo Paul Bohemo ac de fide eius inquirendo Ioannem

48 See Watson, G., 'The Franciscan Friary of Jedburgh with Some Account of Adam Bell, its Historian', 82–88.

Fogum monachum ordinis Cistertiensis sacrarum literam professorem Abbatia Melrossensi donauit.[49]

In terms of style and vocabulary, the two Scots versions are certainly different from each other, although they share the same parent text.

Bellenden

Schort tyme eftir this counsale was takin be Bischop Hary in the Vniversitie of Sanctandrois, ane man of Boheme, namitt Paule Craw, inducing new and wane superstitiounis on the pepill, specialie aganis the Sacrament of the Altare, veneracion of sanctis and confessioun to be maid to preisitis. Nochttheless, fra he was fondin obstinatte in his opinionis he was brocht afoir the theologis, and all his opinionis condampnitt. And becaus he perseveritt to the end of his pleye, but ony reuocacioun of his vane opinionis, he was deliueritt in temporall menis handis. At last thai fand be scharpe examinacioun that he was send oute of Boheme to preche the heresijs of Viccleif and Huss to the Scottis, and thairfoir he was brynt cruellye to the deth. The King commendit mekle this punycion and the autouris thairoff, and gaif the Abbacy of Melross to Iohnne Fogo, monk of Cisteris, becaus he was principale hammyr of heresye aganis the said Paule.[50]

Mar Lodge

Nocht lang eftir was tane in Sanct Androis ane man of beum namit Paull Craw preachand new and vain superstitionis to ye pepill, specially againis ye sacrament of ye altar, veneration of Sancts and confession to be made to preistis. At last he was brocht afore the Theologis and all his opinionis condampnit. And because he perseverit obstinatly to ye end of his play, he was condampnit and brint. He confest afore his deith yat he was sent out of Beum to preich to Scotland ye heryses of Hus and Wikleif. The King comendit meikyll this punition and gaif ye Abbacy of Melross to John Foggo for he was principall convickar of yis Paull.[51]

Apparently, C. S. Lewis was unaware of the 'Mar Lodge' translation, but his comments on Bellenden are of interest: 'He is not one of the great translators and does not quite succeed in getting rid of the idiom of the original. Tell-tale absolute constructions, historic presents, and

49 Boece, H., *Scotorum Historiae*, Liber XVII, f. 352.

50 See Batho, C. and Husbands, H., (eds.), *The Chronicles of Scotland*, vol. II: pp. 393–394.

51 From Liber XVII, f. 365 (as yet unpublished). I am indebted to Mr. H. Watson of the *D.O.S.T.* who supplied a copy of the MS.

excessive linking of sentences abound'.[52] R. J. Lyall reaches many of the same conclusions about Bellenden, but carries them over to a perceptive comparison with the other version, which is: 'in some respects closer to Boece's Latin', without the 'narrative vigour achieved by Bellenden'.[53] Certainly, with the above passages, we can see that, although still a fairly close translation, the 'Mar Lodge' is more concise, uses shorter sentences and is actually a slightly edited presentation of the original material. However, in what follows it will be clear that these are not general rules. Here, the 'Mar Lodge' author makes fewer attempts at linkage, while Bellenden succeeds in bringing a narratorial raciness and logic to the prose by using a 'Nochttheles' or a 'thairfoir' in the right place at the right time. We detect considerable overlapping of phrases between the two, but also one or two significant disparities. Bellenden says that Craw was 'inducing' heresies, the other, 'preachand'. The source of both is Boece's 'docere' which refers to teaching. 'Inducing', however, suggests something rather more subtle and culpable. Both translators render Boece's 'effectum' as 'pleye' or 'play', and no Scot could fail to understand the meaning here. The final difference which we shall note comes in the closing stages of the narrative. Boece has 'Principem in resistendo', which the anonymous author renders as 'principall convickar'. Bellenden, on the other hand, waxes alliterative and metaphorical with 'principale *hammyr* of heresye' (italics added). Boece says nothing about a 'malleus'. Pr. Lyall is right: 'when Bellenden expands it tends to be for rhetorical effect'.[54]

When we turn to Knox, however, we encounter a radically different interpretation of things, and the differences (for the most part) are evident down to the deepest levels:

> But our Cronikilles mack mentioune, that in the dayis of King James the First, about the year of God 1431, was deprehended in the Universitie of Sanctandrose, one named Paul Craw, a Bohame, who was accused of heresye befoir such as then war called Doctouris of Theologie. His accusatioun consisted principallye, that he followed Johnne Husse and Wyckleif, in the

52 Lewis, C. S., *English Literature in the Sixteenth Century*, p. 116.

53 Lyall, R. J., 'Vernacular Prose before the Reformation', 174.

54 ibid., 174.

opinioun of the sacrament, who denyed that the substance of braid and wyn war changed be vertew of any wourdis; or that confessioun should be maid to preastis; or yitt prayeris to sanctes departed. Whill that God geve unto him grace to resist thame, and not to consent to thair impietie, he was committed to the secular judge, (for our bischoppis follow Pilat, who boith did condempne, and also wesche his handis,) who condempned him to the fyre; in the quhilk he was consumed in the said citie of Sanctandrose, about the time afoir written. And to declair thame selvis to be the generatioun of Sathan, who, from the begynnyng, hath bein ennemy to the treuth, and he that desyrith the same to be hyd frome the knowledge of men, thei putt a ball of brass in his mouth, to the end that he should nott geve confessioun of his fayth to the people, neyther yit that thei should understand the defence which he had against thair injust accusatioun and condemnatioun (Laing I: 6).

Before we explore this passage as literature, one or two things deserve to be said about Knox's sources. In an appendix, Laing brings together all of the earlier accounts of Craw's death, such as Walter Bower's, although he refers somewhat casually to Boece).[55] However, had Laing looked more closely at *Scotorum Historiæ*, he would have found pretty solid evidence that this was Knox's source. If we return to Boece, we can see that he uses the Latin term 'deprehensus' early on in his narrative. The Scots translations both say simply that Craw 'was takin' or 'tane'. Knox has 'was *deprehended*', (italics added), which almost certainly implies corruption, in the same way that Bellenden's 'inducing' does. In his modern edition of Knox's *The Historie*, W. C. Dickinson glosses 'deprehended' as 'apprehended' but, so doing, he somewhat obscures the subtle differences in meaning which original readers would be attuned to, and he also misses the influence of Boece.[56] Knox uses the term elsewhere and the drift is clear. For instance, he says of Mary of Lorraine's Chaplain, Friar Black, that he was: 'deprehendit with his harlott' (Laing II: 68). Knox, then, has stayed too close to his source, and produced one of his occasional inconsistencies. (Other more circumstantial evidence can be found to substantiate the above. For example, Knox's use of 'principallye' occupies a position which corresponds too closely to

55 See Laing I: Appendix II: 497–499.

56 Dickinson I: p. 7, n. (4).

Boece's 'nouamque' to be coincidental, and the others have 'specialie/ specially').

However, there is nothing inconsistent about the remainder of Knox's interpretation. He elaborates on the fact that Craw was transferred from ecclesiastical to secular authorities (a detail which the 'Mar Lodge' edits out) by making a comparison between the Bishops and Pontius Pilate, from Matthew 27: 24. Knox's version is considerably more detailed than the others and he replaces the material on John Fogo (which is, in any case, inaccurate)[57] with more information about the manner of Craw's execution. Instead of being hammers of heresy, Craw's accusers are presented as the 'generatioun of Sathan' and this simultaneously evokes the mood of *Old* and *New Testament* genealogies, and condemns the temporal authority in no uncertain terms.

There are other areas in the prose of Knox, Boece and Bellenden which allow for fruitful comparison, although they are less obvious at first sight. In her doctoral thesis, *Studies in the Language of Bellenden's Boece*, E. A. Sheppard observes that: 'Boece and his translator castigate severely the vices of the pre-Reformation Clergy and the many faults of the Church organisation [...] Thus although Bellenden seems to have spent the latter part of his life contending with the secessionists, there is little in his writings of which a fair-minded Protestant would disapprove'.[58] This certainly implies a point of contact, and a close reading of Bellenden brings out passages similar to those of Knox. The following passage is from Liber X of Boece:

> *Boece*
> Christi sacerdotes sacrorum curam haberent diligentem, prophanis abstinerent, sacerdotiis viuerunt suo quisque contentus, [augendæ religionis studio populum instituerent sacro dogmate; itaque; viuerunt vt docerent:] militiæ deinceps donati immunitate, assisterent Christi templis. Non alerent equos nec canes voluptatis causa: arma non ferrent, causas non agerent profanis. Si quispiam Christo initiatorum sua munia minis diligenter obierit, quo minis Christiano

57 See Laing I: Appendix II: pp. 497–499.

58 See Batho, C. and Husbands, H., (eds.), *The Chronicles of Scotland*, vol. II, Appendix, p. 461.

populo foret consultum, primum pecunia mulctaretur, inde non resipiscens abdicaretur sacerdotio.[59]

This time it is the 'Mar Lodge' that is the longer and more involved rendering (and now we see the danger of generalisations):

Bellenden
[...] kirkmen to haif deligent cure of deuyne seruice, abstenand fra all prophane materis, and to leif content of the doviteis pertenand to thair kirkis, exoneritt of all weirfair, that thai may alanerlye assist to devyne seruice. Als, thai sall nocht nureiss horss nor houndis for thair pleseir. Thai sall bere na wappynnis, and decyde na prophane accionis. Gif preistis failye in the forsaid poyntis, thai sall pay for the first falt ane sovme of moneye, the secund tyme, gif thaij amendit nocht thair lyfe, to be deprivit of thair preisthede.[60]

Mar Lodge
[...] kirkmen, and preisitis, of devyne servuice suld have diligent cure, fra prophane curis yai suld abstene; apoun benefice yai suld life, every man of his aune suld be content: for augmentacion of godlynes and gud maneris. Yai suld interpret ye haly writt to ye pepill; to yare doctrine yare life suld be conforme; fra weirs in tyme cuming yai suld be priuilegit, and apoun ye kirk and goddis seruice awate. Thay suld nowder nuriss hors nor houndis for voluptuosite, nor plesure. Thay suld bare nane armis invasive, nor suld accep na prophane causs. Gif ony kirkman in his cure war notit with necligence, yat ye pepill be his exempill war hurt, he suld first in pecuniare sowmes be punyst, syne gif he mendit nocht, fra his benefice he suld be deprivit.[61]

Church discipline, especially as it affected the personal conduct of clergymen and ecclesiastics, was a bone of contention throughout the early stages of the whole European Reformation, and Boece's remarks probably reflect actual practices of which he strongly disapproved. Lax behaviour among orthodox Churchmen provided Scottish Protestants with a veritable gold-mine of material which they could, and did, turn to the purposes of satirical attack, but one should not make the mistake of thinking that the Reformation, anywhere, was simply about ecclesiastical misconduct. As I have suggested, Reformers (and con-

59 Boece, H., *Scotorum Historiæ*, Liber X, ff. 205–206.

60 Batho, C. and Husbands, H., (eds.), *The Chronicles of Scotland*, vol. I: pp. 60–61.

61 'Mar Lodge' translation, unpublished MS., Liber X, f. 212.

scientious Catholics like Boece) were by no means averse to condemning it, but the core of Reform was undoubtedly deeply doctrinal, not behavioural. (Dr. John Durkan on at least one occasion, may have made too little of this).[62] Prose like the above has its most coherent Protestant counterpart in the Reformation *The Buke of Discipline*, (1560), and we shall compare passages after analysing the stylistic features and variants of the above translations.

Boece and the anonymous author emphasise the priest's duty to: 'interpret ye holy writ to ye pepill' but Bellenden has nothing much to say about this aspect of religious life. However, even the Boece text implies quite clearly that the authority to interpret scripture lies exclusively with the priests. Naturally, any Protestant opponents would reply that such an arrangement perpetuated an impenetrable power-structure. This very power-structure was of course circumvented by Tyndale, and by Coverdale's first translation of the whole Bible in 1535: hence the fierce opposition to vernacular scriptures.

Interestingly, Boece deprecates Church involvement in military actions, although he rather cleverly suggests immunity instead of duty. Bellenden says the Church should be 'exoneritt', the 'Mar Lodge' 'priuilegit'. The latter reading is the more positive, but both are arguably justifiable in their own way. Bellenden, however, writes simply that priests should 'bere na wappynis'. Both Boece and the 'Mar Lodge' are much more precise about this; indeed the 'Mar Lodge' author says: 'suld bare nane armis *inuasive*' which has apparently been stimulated by: 'causa arma non ferrent [...]'. The Scots half-line implies that defensive action is legitimate; a reading which Bellenden's version does not permit. Knox was much concerned with these issues and in favour of the sword of just defence. 'Armis invasive', however, implies international war; Knox only dealt with the legitimacy of civil revolution in his writings.

On the whole what impresses us about the passages is their sincerity, although Boece only addresses the most anodyne (and perhaps the most decadent) of the priests' sensual attractions (nourishing horses and hounds) and his proposed disciplinary programme sounds too simple. Even so, Boece and the 'Mar Lodge' version are

62 See Durkan, J., 'Book Review: Dickinson's *Knox*', 158–161.

more concerned with the well-being of the Christian congregation than Bellenden, and both fasten onto the notion that the 'pepill' may be 'hurt' by bad 'exempill'. Again, Bellenden comes off the worse for this kind of comparison. At such crucial points, when a lot depends on keeping the sense of the original, the anonymous version is almost definitely to be preferred over Bellenden's.

A later Protestant parallel, *The Buke of Discipline*, is contained at the end of Book III in Knox's *The Historie*: 'to the end that the Posteriteis to come may juge alsweill quhat the wardlingis refused, as quhat Policie the godlie Ministeris requyred' (Laing II: 181–182). (Knox, of course, is only a co-author of this work).[63] Prose which most resembles Boece's, but which reflects a much more sophisticated and carefully planned system of ecclesiastical government, is the following (cf. Proverbs 6: 14, 19, Exodus 20: 16):

> Yea, the Seniouris aught to take heyde to the life, manneris, deligence, and studye of thair Ministeris. Yf he be worthie of admonitioun, thei must admonische him; of correctioun, thei must correct him: And yf he be worthy of depositioun, thay with consent of the Churche and Superintendent may depose him, so that his cryme so deserve [...]
>
> Some crymes deserve depositioun for ane tyme, and whill the persoun gyf declaratioun of gretar gravitie and honestie: as yf a minister be deprehendit dronk, in brawling or fechting, ane oppin sklanderar, ane infamer of his nychtbour, factious and sawar of discord, he may be commandit to cease from his ministrie, till he declair the signis of repentance [...] (Laing II: 235).

There is a deceptive simplicity and a directness about this, which owes much to the structural formula *parallelismus membrorum*: 'yf he be worthie of X [noun] [...] thei must Y [related verb] [...] him'. The form becomes more complex as justificatory material is necessitated: 'yf he be worthie of X [...] thei with [authorisation], [...] may Y [related verb], [justification], [...] until [...] [conclusion]'. The passage is very particular about the nature of 'crymes', although there is a balance be-

63 See Laing II: 128, 'Commissioun and charge was gevin to Mr. Johne Winram, Suppriour of Sanctandrois, Maister John Spottiswoode, Johne Willok, Mr. John Douglas, Rectour of Sanctandrois, Maister Johne Row and John Knox, to draw in a volume the Polecey and Disciplyn, as weill as thei had done the Doctrin; whiche thei did and presented to the Nobilitie, who did peruse it many dayis'.

tween generalisation and specificity which is carefully achieved. And the 'crymes' are far more basic than those outlined in Boece. One might say that the Reformation encouraged a new realism. There is no mention of pecuniary punishment and this is a case in point. A wealthy minister who could afford to pay fines ought to be a contradiction in terms. (Noteworthy stylistic features are 'yea', which is an encouraging and a positive reaction signal, and also there is a more accurate use of the verb 'deprehendit').

Now we may return to Bell's *The Roit or Quheill of Tyme*, which, for all its intrinsic interest, is undeniably a work of less importance than Bellenden's or the 'Mar Lodge' version of Boece. We cannot at the moment make any specific connection with the work of Knox, as we did with the other authors, but like John Ireland, Bell was evidently very much aware of, and opposed to, heresy. He knows about Protestantism and has definite ideas concerning it. For example, in folios 57 b and 116 b, he writes:

> Quha that is nocht blindit with error will sa at thir sanctis prayer is bundin in the hewin at had sa gret effek in this miserabill life [...] Abowt this tyme ye apostat & heresyarche martyn lutheir left his haly relegyon & beguth his herise sa yat he & his wikkit discipulis hes infekkit a gret part of euroyp viz: anno X 1520.[64]

Generally speaking, however, Bell is obviously an inferior writer to Bellenden and the other chroniclers. As Pr. Aitken has pointed out, the style is less lively than theirs, the spellings are crude and unliterary, and none of the stories which it has in common with them, are as fully or as well told (compare, for example, the story of King Kenneth's murder by Fenella in f. 71 with Bellenden).[65] One further quotation will give the reader an idea of its literary quality. In his prologue, Bell tells his audience why he chose the common medieval image of the wheel for his title, and he explains the purpose of the book:

64 See *The Roit or Quheill of Tyme*, by Adam Bell, Nat. Lib. MS. 1746, ff. 57b and 116b. I am indebted to Mr. H. Watson of the *D.O.S.T.* for access to a transcript.

65 ibid., 71a. I am also referring to Pr. Aitken's handwritten assessment, which is dated 1970; see also Batho, C. and Husbands, H., (eds.), *The Chronicles of Scotland*, vol. II: p. 117.

> In yis roit nocht allanerlie secular men or wemen may haif plesant and propetable commonyng bot alswa religious men may fynd mater of prechin and be mair reddy to gife of diuers thingis inquirit solutioune. Quharfore ane halie fadir callit mychaell de Lyra wmquhill commissar of yis prouince now kithis myrakulis. He said yat he wald all our brethir of obseruance had knawlegis of croniculis of yare land, and quhy yat, bot because monye thingis ar sperit at yame quhilk ar nocht sperit at othiris. Not with standing yis roit or quheill quhilk first with greit labour I compilit in latyne now agan to ye honour of god ye wirgin mary and our halie fader sanct francis. my merit and alswa plesour to my lord seton I haif translatit it in yngilis nocht puttand all in yngilis yat latyng reportis bot it yat is maist ganene for secular stait principalie to lordis and men or wemen of honour I haif put certane documentis schortlie to instruk ye redaris and kendill yame in lufe of god & yare nychtbour quhar throw yai mot get grace heir & hyne glore euirmair amen.[66]

We learn from this statement that Bell sees his material not only as having aesthetic appeal, but also homiletic worth, furnishing preachers with useful subject matter. Some of his observations are not especially naive for the age, but the reference to miracles reveals a superstition which was becoming unacceptable to writers such as Gau. But the creditable notion that the readers should not be ignorant of their country's history reveals a respect for knowledge and freedom of information. (This is not to say that Bell was not specific about his target audience; note the reference to men and women 'of honour'). His main purpose, is however, as he says in conclusion, to encourage the love of God and man, which has salvific import for the readers. We can safely conclude that Bell's work had no influence on Scottish prose of the period, and indeed, it remains largely unknown even to this day.[67] We may now return to more important texts.

If the two prose versions of Boece's *Scotorum Historiæ* stand independently within an incipient Scots vernacular historiographical tradition, consummated by Knox's *The Historie*, three subsequent works of prose *Ane Resonyng of ane Scottis and Inglis Merchand betuix Rowand and Lionis*, *The Complaynt of Scotland* and *James Harryson, a Scottishman's Exhortacion to the Scottes to Conform to*

66 ibid., f.1b.

67 My attention was first drawn to this rare text by Anneli Meurman-Solin's *Variation and Change in Early Scottish Prose*, p. 107, p. 223.

the Will of Englande (which display a more intimate authorial connection and an urgently shared, very topical political standpoint) in some ways represent yet another, more complex historiographical tradition, which also has certain parallels in Knox.

Ane Resonyng can be attributed safely to William Lamb, *The Complaynt* with some probability to Robert Wedderburn, and they can both be dated very specifically to the late 1540s (although *The Complaynt* as we now have it, may have been modified after the immediate issues it addressed ceased to be urgent).[68] This, then, is a full fifteen years after Bellenden and on the very periphery of the period to which Knox's writings belong (1548–1571). Unlike Knox, both authors were pro-Catholic and anti-English, but the latter emotion more than the former was, of course, exacerbated by Henry VIII's 'rough wooing' of Scotland in the mid-1540s. Both authors, however, were effective propagandists (and this they share with Knox); Lamb's work is a response to, as well as a reiteration of, the English Government's tract *A Declaration, conteyning the just causes and consyderations of this present warre with the Scottis wherin also appereth the trewe & right title, that the kings most royall maiesty hath to the soueraynte of Scotlande*, (1542), while *James Harryson, a Scottisheman's Exhortacion* is, apparently, a Scotsman's pro-English contribution to the same argument. Linguistically, this work is closest to John Johnsone's, and provides us with our second example of an apparently anglicised Scot before Knox. Furthermore it contains one highly controversial pro-Protestant and anti-French passage which anticipates exactly the sentiments of the Reformer:

> And what madness or deuill (O moste dere countremen) hath so moued, or rather distracte our myndes, eftsones to take weapon in hand, and thesame [sic] against oure promises, fidelities, honoures, and othes, hauyng on oure side, no good ground, honestie, reason, ne any iuste respecte, but onely of the prouocation of the deuil, the pope, and his rable of religious men (as thei would seme to be) & specially those, whom we cal our auncient frendes, where thei are in deede our auncient enemies, ye Frenchemen.[69]

68 See Lyall, R. J., (ed.), *Ane Resonyng*, pp. x–xviii, and Stewart, A., (ed.), *The Complaynt of Scotland*, pp. vii–x and pp. x–xi.

69 See Murray, J. A. H., (ed.), *The Complaynt of Scotland*, Appendix, p. 227.

The thoroughness, directness and logical tones of these lines place the work closer to *Ane Resonyng* than to *The Complaynt*, although the insistence does recall the latter. But if nothing else, *James Harryson, a Scottishman's Exhortacion* testifies to a less nationalistic world-view which was beginning seriously to question traditional assumptions in the light of rather more basic human values.

The Complaynt itself is a more important exercise, however. It is, for the most part a lively translation of Alan Chartier's *Le Quadrilogue Invectif*, although its author gives the impression, at least, of being a monster of erudition. C. S. Lewis's appreciation appears full of a wonderful enthusiasm which may nevertheless have eclipsed his usually very sound judgement: 'Here, unforetold, unsucceeded, unexplained, tricked out in all its heterogeneous ornaments as in jewels "that were the spoils of provinces", what we call the "Renaissance" has come dancing, shouting, posturing, nay, as it were, sweating, into Scots prose'.[70] As I have suggested, Lewis is overrating *The Complaynt* as a precursor of the Renaissance. In the same vein, he implies that the author's evident social concerns are, for the most part, independent of Chartier. Again this point might be regarded as arguable. Katharine Firth, on the other hand, identifies the text's importance as: 'one of the earliest pieces of literature to combine a plea for the reform of Scotland with a warning from prophecy'.[71] The following passage for instance could easily have been written by Knox (and has no parallel in *Le Quadrilogue Invectif*):

> It is vrityne in the xxviii. of deutronome thir vordis: Gyf thou obeyis nocht the voce of the lorde thy gode, ande kepis nocht his ordinance, thir maledictions shal cum on the: thou sal be cursit on the feildis, thou sal be cursit in the cite; the lord sal send maledictione ande tribulatione on al thy byssynes; the lord sal sende pestilens on the, the heyt feueir, droutht, the sourde, tempest and all euil seiknes, ande he sal persecut the, quhil he hef gart the perise: thou sal thole iniuris & spulye, ande ther sal be na man that can saue the: thou sal spouse ane vyfe, bot ane vthir sal tak hyr fra the be forse: thou sal big ane house, bot thou sal neuyr duel in it: thy ox sal be slane befor thy eene, & thou sal get nane of hym tyl yet: thy flokkis of scheip sal be gyffin to thy enemies; the oncoutht ande straynge pepil sal eyt the frute of the eyrd that thou hes lauborit [...] We

70 Lewis, C. S., *English Literature in the Sixteenth Century*, pp. 114–116.

71 Firth, K. R., *The Apocalyptic Tradition*, p. 110.

may persaue for certan, that ve haue bene scurgit vitht al the plagis that are befor rehersit [...][72]

This seems to be the author's direct translation (from *The Vulgate*) of Deuteronomy 28: 15–16, 21–22, 30–31), and he quite blatantly applies scriptural prophecies to contemporary events. Admittedly this is a couple of years after the Protestant Reformer George Wishart's comparable address to the town of Haddington, which we shall consider in a later chapter, (below pp. 230-233), but the author is still breaking comparatively new ground (and, in any case, Wishart's impact was almost purely oral and ephemeral). Ironically, this ground was already being absorbed into the Protestant tradition by the more enduring efforts of Knox and Sir David Lindsay of the Mount. Thus *The Complaynt* now stands out in stark relief. However, one paradox which it successfully avoids, is, as we have seen, the use of Protestant translations of scripture. *Archbishop Hamilton's Catechism*, on the other hand, which is thoroughly Catholic, is manifestly the debtor of such translations. Furthermore, even allowing for the close connection between *The Complaynt* and *Ane Resonying*, Lamb's work owes almost nothing to scripture, in any form.

It would be misleading to give the impression that *The Complaynt* was made up only of fiery jeremiads from the *Old Testament*, but as we can see, it is also a little misleading to present assessments like Pr. Lewis's. Without doubt, the work represents the high watermark of Middle Scots art prose, but one has to exercise caution and judgement. In addition to its serious prophecy, it also contains some serious satire and again, a link with David Lindsay, specifically his *Ane Satyre of the Thrie Estaitis* is pronounced. For instance, in chapter VII, Dame Scotia, who is derived from Chartier's Lady France, observes her three sons, the three estates, walking across barren fields. Here, the two passages are juxtaposed:

Le Quadrilogue Invectif

Et a celle heure apperceut trios de ses enfans, l'un estant droit en armes appuyé sur sa hasche, effrayé et songeux, l'autre en vestement long sur ung siege de costé, escoutant et taisant, le tiers, en vil habit, reversé sur la terre, plaintif et

72 Murray, J. A. H., (ed.), *The Complaynt of Scotland*, p. 24, p. 28.

langoureux. Comme doncques elle les eust choisiz á l'ueil indignee en son hault couraige, vers eulx les prist a reprendre de leur oiseuse lacheté par parolles entrerompues souvent de doloreux soupirs qui de cuer adollé lui mouoient, leur disant en cest maniere [...][73]

The Complaynt
[...] sche persauit cummand touart hyr thre of hyr auen natiue natural sonnes. the eldest of them vas in harnes, traland ane halbert behind hym, beand al affrayit ande fleyit for dreddour of his lyue. The sycond of hyr sonnis vas sittand in ane chair, beand clethd in ane sydegoune, kepand grite grauite, heffand ane beuk in his hand, the glaspis var fast lokkyt vitht rouste. hyr yongest sone vas lyand plat on his syde on the cald eird, and al his clathis var reuyn ande raggit, makkand ane dolorous lamentatione and ane piteouse complaynt. he tuke grite pane to ryise vp on his feit, bot he vas sa greuouslye ouer set be violens, that it vas nocht possibl til hym to stand rycht up.[74]

In *The French Background to Middle Scots Literature*, Janet M. Smith focuses on this passage, and observes that: 'the Scottish author has made an odd confusion by first saying that the three sons were coming towards the lady, and then that one was sitting in a chair and one was lying on the ground. He could have no clear mental picture'. Chartier's image on the other hand, Smith argues, is 'perfectly clear'.[75] Smith is right about the oddness of the image, but perhaps too ready to assign such differences to incompetence on the part of the Scots author. Detailed studies of the relationship between the two works show that the translator was consistently idiosyncratic in his use of Chartier,[76] and this could only be the product of deliberate design. His 'confused' picture is artistically stimulating, in the same way that a Cubist painting is stimulating. Arguably, Dunbar uses a similar technique in *The Golden Targe*. A less puzzling difference is the author's addition of detail such as a book (the Bible, of course) which the second son, the spiritual estate, has allowed to fall into desuetude. The implication is perfectly obvious. Another is *The Complaynt*'s use of 'the eldest [...] The sycond [...] hyr yongest' which has been adapted from 'l'un [...]

73 Droz, E., (ed.), *Le Quadrilogue Invectif*, p. 10.
74 Murray, J. A. H., (ed.), *The Complaynt of Scotland*, p. 70.
75 Smith, J. M., *The French Background to Middle Scots Literature*, p. 146.
76 Blayney, M. S. and G. H., 'Alain Chartier and *The Complaynt of Scotland*', 8–17.

l'autre [...] le tiers' (the one [...] the other [...] the third). The use of two adjectives in the superlative degree ('eldest', 'yongest'), instead of cardinal and ordinal numbers, carries with it connotations which the author may have intended. Since Dame Scotia remonstrates with the sons for their abject failure in all things, being the eldest involves a greater degree of responsibility for any faults (if we take the family structure seriously). In the context of the above passage, being the 'yongest' as well as the most ill-treated of the sons, involves a heightening of pathos. Moreover, this son is not only the youngest and lying 'sur la terre', he is: 'on the *cald* eird' (italics added). The scene is becoming more and more tailor-made to arouse our sympathy.

On the reverse side of the coin, there are stylistic omissions in *The Complaynt*. For instance, Chartier uses three doublets at strategic points; 'effrayé et songeux,' 'escoutant et taissant' and 'plaintif et langoureux'. Only the first and third of these have aesthetic equivalents in 'al affrayit ande fleyit for dreddour' and 'revyn and raggit', although the former is an exaggeration and the latter not a translation. The phrase 'en vil habit' would seem to have stimulated it. Moreover, the rhythms of *The Complaynt* are marred by a marked participial excess: 'cummand', 'traland', 'sittand', 'beand', 'kepand', 'heffand' and 'makand', which begins to displease the ear after a while, but the ultimate impression is that the author retains his individuality by offering a quirky, perhaps even mischievous translation, which cocks a snook at Chartier as well as augmenting relevant details.

Compared to *The Complaynt*, Lamb's *Ane Resonyng* is much less eccentric, and much more disappointing as literature. As the self-explanatory title suggests, the work takes the form of a dialogue, although it is a manifestly stage-handled affair for propaganda purposes. Similar, generally rather wooden dialogues were becoming commonplace in England, but like *The Complaynt*, *Ane Resonyng* also has continental parallels, although they are more tenuous than those of a direct translation. It has been suggested that the form, as we find it in Lamb, probably originated within Lutheran traditions of polemical composition in Europe, particularly those associated with the German poet and so-called *meistersinger*, Hans Sachs, who wrote seven such dialogues.[77] However, the genre is not altogether unknown in Scottish polemical prose. For instance, *The Richt Vay to the Kingdom of Heuine* contains 'Ane schort disputacione apone the pater noster betuix god and ye saul', but this, of course, also originated in other Lutheran circles.[78] By comparison, Lamb's debate, staid as it generally is, appears much more lively, since it is permeated by the perennial antipathy between the Scots and English. One point where the 'Inglis' merchant seems to get the upper hand is with the following riposte (although, as we might expect, such instances are rare):

> *Inglis*: Giff I will say the craw is blak, than yow will say that scho is quytt! Quhat man, dois it nocht appeir be historie how ye Scottis practizate to steill out of oure thesaurie diuerss of choiss instrumentis, quhilk neuer-the-les wes eftir recouerit agane?[79]

The 'Inglis' man's exasperated criticism is compellingly realised through broad humour, a familiar address ('Quhat man'), and through the more penetrating accusation which follows. A more typical clash comes with the following, where the Scottish merchant puts forward the evidence of the Italian humanist and historian of England, Polydore Virgil, (or P.V. Castellensis), who was the author of the *Historia Anglica*, and he finishes off with an allusion to Boece.

> Your buik of weir referris the probatioun of thir depositionis and restitutionis of kyngis to the nobill men that wes present at that tyme in the Cokfeild besyd Westminster; bot, nebour, oure Boece, historiane, / writis that this first Macolme wes nocht crownit kyng of Scotland quhill the jmlxj. yeir of Christ, and swa his sone Macolme maid homage to Sanct Edward fyve yeiris or his fader wes kyng of Scotland![80]

Earlier in *Ane Resonyng*, Lamb made at least one of the 'Scottis' man's intentions abundantly clear: 'I intend to impugn euerie ane of thir pretendit homagis be Polidor, your awin literate, autentik histor-

77 See Lyall, R. J. (ed.), *Ane Resonyng*, p. xxv.

78 See Mitchell, A. F., (ed.), *The Richt Vay*, pp. 97–101 and Brandt, C. J. and Fenger, B. T., (eds.), *Danske Skrifter*, vol. IV: III: pp. 321–325.

79 Lyall, R. J., (ed.), *Ane Resonyng*, p. 133.

80 ibid., p. 87.

iciane', and if need be, he says, he will quote: 'ane cuning, grave and diligent ancient air callit Hectour Boece, our trew historiciane'.[81] Lamb's use of Polydore, of course, affords him a double-edged sword. Virgil was an acknowledged English historian whose work had been undertaken upon the insistence of Henry VII, and thus, he could hardly have been accused of bias, but his account of things disagreed with *A Declaration*. Lamb was therefore able to undercut the English argument quite consistently. His estimation of Boece as: 'our trew historiciane' sounds naïve and wildly optimistic, but a close examination of *Ane Resonyng* shows that Lamb was carefully circumspect in his use of this source. Lamb's style appears fired with enthusiasm but is otherwise unremarkable, apart from its legal terminology ('probatioun', 'depositionis', 'restitutionis'). At any rate, we have seen enough to recognise that, while it is an intelligent and well-informed propaganda exercise, in terms of style and content, one cannot claim major importance for *Ane Resonyng*. Like Knox, Lamb uses sources and a method of attack which his opponents could not but acknowledge as authentic and authoritative (for Lamb there was Polydore Virgil, for Knox, a whole range of material from the Bible to the Church Fathers and his own experience of Catholic practice). Unlike Knox's work and *The Complaynt*, there is no appeal to prophecy or call for reform, and here *Ane Resonyng* certainly falls short, even if there are appealing literary ideas behind it (ideas which, it must be suggested, never quite come to fruition).[82] Like the *Meroure of Wyssdome* and *The New Testament in Scots*, *Ane Resonyng* unfortunately lies within a manuscript tradition, so its influence was necessarily minimal or non-existent, but it should be remembered that Knox's *The Historie* also lies within such a tradition, at least in Scotland.

In this chapter, we have been dealing with prose works of which Knox himself seems to have been ignorant (although *Scotorum Historiæ* is an evident exception). However, he was certainly not ignorant of the political, historical and religious environment which formed many of the works (this time with the probable exception of the

81 ibid., p. 57.
82 ibid., p. xxxiii.

Meroure of Wyssdome). Thus, while it is possible that he was ignorant of the final work which this chapter examines, *Archbishop Hamilton's Catechism*, he certainly knew of John Hamilton himself, as *The Historie* attests. In Book I, Knox says that Hamilton: 'the Abbot of Paslay [...] was called "chaster then any madyn,"' (Laing I: 124) but, to be sure, he didn't think very highly of him, as the subsequent narrative, which relates to the year 1543, suggests:

> [...] In the meantyme, arryves from France to Scotland the Abbot of Paislay, called bastard brother to the Governour, (whome yitt many esteamed sone to the old Bischope of Dunkelden, called Crychtoun,) and with him Maister David Panteyr, (who after was maid Bischope of Ross). The brut of the learnyng of these two, and thare honest lyiff, and of thare fervencye and uprychtnes in religioun, was such, that great esperance thare was, that thare presence should haif bene confortable to the Kirk of God. For it was constantlye affirmed of some, that without delay, the one and the other wald occupy the pulpete, and trewly preach Jesus Christ. But few dayis disclosed thair hypochrisye; for what terrouris, what promisses, or what enchanting boxis thei brought fra France, the commoun people knew not [...] (Laing I: 105).

David Laing was less critical of Hamilton and says that: '"the Catechisme" which usually passes under his name, from having been printed at his expense, at St. Andrews, in 1552, exhibits a solitary instance on the part of the Roman Catholic clergy to convey spiritual instruction, and is most creditable to his memory'.[83] *Archbishop Hamilton's Catechism* itself is a weighty volume expounding the Ten Commandments, the Creed and the seven sacraments (not two, as the Protestants would have it). A. F. Mitchell has demonstrated that it is largely modelled on an earlier continental catechism prepared under Herman von Wied entitled *Enchiridion Christianæ Institutionis* (the Cologne *Enchiridion* of 1536),[84] and Dr. John Durkan has argued against the traditional attribution of authorship to John Winram, in favour of Friar

83 See Laing I: 142, n. (2).

84 See Von Wied, H., *Enchiridion Doctrinae Christianiae Canones Concilii Provincialis, Coloniensis, Anno Celebrati, MDXXXVI*, published in Paris, by D. Jacobum.

Richard Marshall, who was a master at St. Andrews.[85] Interestingly, Mitchell also points out that the work exhibits some traces of Lutheran arrangement-patterns in the Commandments section and elsewhere.[86]

In its immediate context, *Archbishop Hamilton's Catechism* is the Catholic counterpart of Gau's *The Richt Vay*[87] and it is this text with which it has most in common. Its source is John Gropper in Cologne, an ecumenical Catholic, and it is not uncompromising to Protestants. Even so, some passages display a firmness of tone derived from religious orientation:

> A man yat is geuin to heresie, eftir the first and secund monitioun fle & forbeir his company, and knaw yat he yat is siclike is subuertit and synnis, euin damnit be his awin jugement, for alsmeikle as he resaiuit the fayth as trew & catholike & efterhend in sum part he gangis fra it, & impugnis it. Or we may say yat he is damnit be his awin judgement, yat is to say, he is damnit afore God, throu his awin, or for his awin electioun, wilfulnes and stifnes of his hart & will nocht leiue his herisie and return to the catholike faith.[88]

The catechism's system of belief is even more evident in this:

> The discipillis of our salviour, & the haly Apostillis haiffand knawlege of ye misteryis of Christ, hes decretit and ordanit in the feirfull & leiffand misteryis, remembrance suld be maid for yame quhilk hes sleppit faithfully, as he mycht say plainely, that the halye Apostillis of Jesus Christ, ordanit that the saulis quhilk departis of yis warld in the leiffand faith of Jesus Christ, yat yai suld be helpit be remembrance had for yame in the Mes.[89]

While on the one hand, Protestants did not deny the 'Church' a right to extirpate heresy,[90] they would contend over both a definition of the Church and the nature of heresy itself. However, when *Archbishop Hamilton's Catechism* mentions 'heresie', what we call 'Protestant-

85 See Durkan, J., 'The Cultural Background in Sixteenth Century Scotland', 326–329.

86 See Mitchell, A. F., (ed.), *Archbishop Hamilton's Catechism*, p. xi.

87 See ibid. p. xi and Mitchell, A. F., (ed.), *The Richt Vay*, pp. xlvi–xlvii.

88 See Mitchell, A. F., (ed.), *Archbishop Hamilton's Catechism*, f. xx.

89 ibid., f. cci.

90 See for instance Wishart's Zwinglian *Confession of Fayth* in Laing, D., (ed.), *The Miscellany of the Wodrow Society*, pp. 11–23. Article XXIV, p. 21, deals with 'heretykes and sysmattyckes'.

ism' undoubtedly falls into the domain which it sets up for the word. On the other hand, the second passage needs no such explanation. *Archbishop Hamilton's Catechism* recommends 'praying for the saulis departit' and no Protestant would countenance the practice in any form (you need the book of Maccabees for that, and they had excluded it from the canon). Furthermore, the first passage relies on the authority of an ecclesiastical mandate, while the second is hypothetical and the writers may well be on shaky ground, at least insofar as they attempt to justify their belief from scripture. Of course, the literary critic need not deny the legitimacy of Catholic tradition as sixteenth century Protestants did, and in this tradition there is surely justification of *Archbishop Hamilton's Catechism*, but if we are concerned with the authors' ability to argue a case given certain strict parameters, one cannot help but sense weakness in the argument here. At any rate, we have established the doctrinal orientation of the catechism. What is the overall literary impression that it gives? Mitchell says that: 'the style [...] is good, its illustrations and similes are generally well chosen',[91] and he is right. The most impressive use of figurative language comes with the examples of the torch (f. lxxviii), the mirror (f. lxxix) and the compass (f. lxxxi), but the example of the urinal (f. lxxx) may strike modern readers as somewhat vulgar, or at least, out of place. Here is the first of the four, which forms part of the exposition of the Commandments:

> First christin pepill, ye suld vse the law of God as ye wald use an Torche quhen ye gang hayme to your house in a myrke nycht, for as the Torche or Bowat schawis you lycht to descerne the rycht waie hayme to your house, fra the wrang way, and also to descerne the clein way, fra the foule way. Evin sa aucht ye to use ye law or command of God, as a Torche, Bowat or Lantern. For doutles, the law of God giffis ye lycht of knawledge to descerne your hie way hayme to your dwelling places in hevin, fra the wrang way yat leidis to hel.[92]

This is a fine example of homiletic skill, and even if, as Knox suggests, Hamilton did not preach publicly, *Archbishop Hamilton's Catechism* certainly supplies the deficit. There are clear markers which

91 Mitchell, A. F., (ed.), *Archbishop Hamilton's Catechism*, f. xix.
92 ibid., ff. lxxvii–lxxix.

facilitate the gradually shifting emphasis, from introduction, to application, to comparison, to substantiation ('First [...]', 'for as [...]', 'Evin sa [...]', 'For doutles […]'). And there is a use of antithesis ('(Torch) lycht / myrkness', 'rycht waie / wrang way', 'clein way / foule way') and parallelism (note the triple use of 'descerne'). But the most distinctive feature about the passage is its use of an everyday (or more accurately, an every night!) situation, in language which is recognisably Scottish. Moreover this language seems to work on two levels. The item 'Bowat', for instance, has the obvious meaning of 'torch'. It is frequently used as part of curfew stipulations such as this one, from the *Edinburgh Records*: 'At na persouns be fund on the hie gait fra ix houris at euin furth, without ane lanterne or bowat in his hand'.[93] When used metaphorically, however, it often takes on more profound philosophical connotations. Here is such an example from the *Meroure of Wyssdome*: 'His owne ressoune that is [...] his bowatt to lead him fra myrkness [...]'.[94] The same kind of dual application comes into play with the phrase 'hie way'. On the surface it simply means a public path, but even so, it also has a place in the language of popular piety. *The Gude and Godlie Ballatis*, a collection of Lutheran songs from the 1540s, for instance, uses the phrase in metaphors relating to Christian misconduct: 'Quhen fra the *hie way* I ga wrang […]',[95] (italics added), so obviously, the authors choose their language carefully.

Such then is the literary, political and religious environment in which Knox's own prose took shape. As we have seen, prose writings before Knox were by no means insignificant, and those works which actually passed into circulation must have heightened the religious and political awareness of their readers. To be sure, different works were designed by their authors to arouse different sympathies, and this must have produced cross and under-currents, but the literary atmosphere was lively, there is no doubt. In one or two instances, we can be very specific about the influence of earlier prose on Knox's work, but we must conclude that he was probably ignorant of the less well-known

93 *D.O.S.T.*, I: 132.
94 *D.O.S.T.*, I: 332.
95 *D.O.S.T.*, III: 131.

works which this chapter considers. (This does not mean, however, that Knox was unaware of existing Scottish literature or unconscious of literary trends). Connections can be made between Knox and the earliest original Scots prose, and when Lutheran works began to infiltrate Scotland, the connections widened to become both literary and ideological. In the 1530s, the historiographical genre became popular in the vernacular and Knox fully inherited the tradition. In the 1540s and early 1550s Catholic prose came into its own with three fine works which enhanced the polemical, hortatory and homiletic milieu that existed in Scotland, and in a sense, anticipated or pre-empted the call for Reform. It is with all of these works in mind that one can fully appreciate how Knox's *The Historie* took shape.

Chapter Two: Knox's Admonitory Public Epistles

As far as we can tell, Knox's own literary career began in 1545, shortly before he was called to preach in the Castle of St. Andrews (an episode which we shall explore more fully somewhat later; below pp. 210–213). In *The Historie*, Knox tells us how he had entered the castle in the same year, as tutor: 'of some gentilmenes childrene, whome certane yearis he had nurished in godlynes' (Laing I: 185), but before long, he saw fit to exercise his talents in other areas. It seems that a certain Dean John Annand (whom Knox later castigated with a much quoted phrase), had 'long trubled' the Protestant preacher John Rough, (Laing I: 188), and: 'the said Johne Knox had fortifeid the doctrine of the Preachear *by his pen*' (italics added). According to Knox (a man sometimes *less* modest than Ireland's wise clerk; cf. above pp. 35–37), he:

> [...] had beattin the said Dean Johne from all defences, that he was compelled to fly to his last refuge, that is, the authoritie of the Church, "Which authoritie, (said he,) damned all Lutheraines and heretikes; and tharefoir he nedith no farther disputatioun." (Laing I: 188).

To be sure, *The Historie* contains most, if not all of this first literary gesture (see Laing I: 188–189) and most of the text of Knox's subsequent sermon, which he was called to preach, but Knox's writing does not enter into print until the following year, when, as a prisoner in the French galleys, he composed his first admonitory public epistle, addressed to those who had been with him in the Castle. The text is contained in Laing III: 5–11, which we shall use for reasons of convenience.

Although very short by the standards of Knox's later published texts (it runs only to some two thousand two hundred words in length), *An Epistle to the Congregation of the Castle of St. Andrews*, (1548), (so, Laing), is particularly important for two reasons. It is the first in a series of such works, and it is clearly written according to certain recognisable rhetorical principles which are maintained right throughout the Knox canon. The letter contains two distinct sections (see Laing III: 5–8, paragraph 2 inclusive, then paragraph 3 to the end of the work). In the first section, Knox discourses on a general Biblical theme: that the afflicted are in fact instruments of God's glory (an old theme to modern readers perhaps, but to Knox's congregation, who were redefining their Christian heritage, surely an absorbing one). He tells his audience that one or two scriptural examples will suffice in order to prove such a theme, and already we can see that he takes little for granted, unless it has a scriptural sanction. Of course, we have already met this use of a constant referential base in Gau's *The Richt Vay*, but Knox is not writing a Protestant catechism, like the earlier reformer. That would come later. He is communicating, as a known individual, to an intimate group of his own acquaintance, and his model is surely the 'grand épîtres pauliniennes'.[1] (Unlike Dean Annand, however, he makes no reference to proscriptive ecclesiastical authority, and a definite shift in popular religious orientation is epitomised here). In fact, he offers three Biblical parallels to his readers: the narrative of Joseph's affliction in Genesis 37: 5–30, Satan's introduction of idolatry into Israel (which has many possible sources), and the example of the Apostles' confusion after the crucifixion of Christ in Acts 11: 19: 'They that were scatred abrode thorow ye trouble yat rose' (*Coverdale*).

The second part of the letter suggests a similarity between these and current events with special implications both for Knox and his congregation. He goes on to speak highly of Henry Balnaves's treatise *On Justification by Faith*, (which we shall consider below, pp. 157–160); its presence being a manifest sign of God's work amongst them, before he concludes by reassuring the readers that the Lord will visit the wicked with retribution.

This, then is the overall structure of the epistle. Its real literary value, however, emerges when we analyse specific passages in order to establish something of the flavour of the prose. One of the things which is immediately evident is Knox's use of long, heavy periodic sentences, and the most weighty, elaborate and profound of these, is

1 Janton, P., *L'homme et l'oeuvre*, p. 418.

the first. As Janton writes: 'un court préambule comprend l'adresse et une formule de bénédiction':[2]

> Blessed bee God, the Father of our Lord Jesus Christ, whose infinite goodness and incomprehensible wisdome, in every age, so frustrats the purpose, and maketh of none effect the slight of Sathan, that the same things, which appeare to be extreme destruction to the just, and damnage to the small flocke of Jesus Christ, by all men's expectation (yea, and Sathan himselfe) by the mercy of our good God, are turned to the laude, praise and glorie of his own name, utilitie and singuler profite of his Congregation, and to the pleasure, confort, and advancement of them that suffer (Laing III: 5).

When confronted with such an introduction, modern readers may find it necessary to read the sentence over two or three times before they can comprehend its overall sense, but once they have done so, initial difficulties disappear, and its eloquence will come to impress. Perhaps the best word to describe it is 'pregnant'. In terms of sixteenth century rhetoric, this passage probably comes closest to a *propositio*, or a brief introductory section, which outlines what is to follow in the pamphlet.[3] Knox manages to express complex theological notions with much greater control than, say, Ireland, at his most theological (even if Ireland was never compelled to treat such a personal theme), and he is combining the strains of a doxology with those of exhortation, producing material which is simultaneously devotional and potentially very practical. Although his overall model is the epistles of Paul, here it seems that he began by meditating on 1 Peter 1: 3: 'Blessed be God, and the Father of oure Lorde Jesus Christ, which accordynge to his greate mercy hath begotten us [...]' (*Coverdale*), before incorporating probable references to Psalms 33: 10 and Romans 15: 11: 'The Lorde bryngeth the councell of the Heithen to *none effect*' (*Great Bible*), '*Praise* the Lorde all ye Gentiles, and *laude* him all ye nacions' (*Coverdale*) (italics added). The first reference, to 1 Peter, concerns us here, because as we shall see at a later point, Knox had adopted the role of St. Peter in the 'Wishart Narrative', now contained in *The Historie*

2 ibid., p. 418.
3 Sonnino, L. A., *A Handbook*, p. 150.

(see Laing I: 125–171, especially p. 139), immediately prior to his own entrance into the Castle; (below, p. 285).

The sentence itself is dominated by a great number of highly abstract nouns (such as: 'goodness', 'wisdome', 'age', 'purpose', 'effect', 'destruction', 'expectation', 'mercy', 'laude', 'praise', 'glorie', 'utilitie', 'profite', 'pleasure', 'confort' and 'advancement'), which Knox often couples with equally abstract adjectives ('infinite' and 'incomprehensible'). Thus, his language moves one's attention away from present suffering (his own as a galley-slave and that of his readers as persecuted Protestants in an, as yet, Catholic country). He redirects it towards an ethereal, even celestial, plane. The majority of his lofty phrases occur towards the end of the passage, which is its most important phase, given the overall periodic structure which Knox favours. His reason for using such a structure is to stimulate simultaneously a state of mental fixity, an expectation of fulfilment on the reader's part, and to tease these out as long as possible without overdoing things. To achieve such effects, of course, is difficult, but to sustain them properly without exasperating the reader, is harder. Suspending one's sense for too long is an obvious danger for any prose writer, and a fine degree of judgement is necessary.

Not that Knox's epistles were made up solely of this kind of rhetoric. If this were the case, he could no more hold his audience than a Shakespeare who was constantly soliloquising. In what follows, we can see him progressively shortening his sentences and tightening his syntax as he comes to the important point where he can turn to his scriptural exemplars. Here we have sentences two and three of the treatise:

> *[Sentence 2]* How the name of the onely living God hath beene magnified in all ages by them which were sore troubled, by persecution of tyrants, exiled from their owne countrey, *long were to rehearse*.
>
> *[Sentence 3]* Yet one or two principall will wee touche, for probation of our words foresaid (Laing III: 5; italics added).

It is at this stage that we realise Knox has constructed his opening paragraph very carefully. Sentence Two, which is also periodic, but less complex than the first, culminates with *dubitatio*. The orator gives the impression that his matter is so multifarious that he does not know where to begin; long it 'were to rehearse [...]'. The directness of Sentence Three is, in the light of this, particularly striking. Knox then acts as editor, choosing from a vast range, such subject matter as will edify his readers, without them having to go to any great trouble.

The second part of the epistle is less impersonal, but more overtly hortatory than the type of prose we encounter above. Here are two further examples from it:

> Therefore, most deare Brethren (so call I all professing Christes Evangell), continue in that purpose which yee have begun godly; though the battell appeare strong, your Captaine is unexpugnable: To him is given all power in heaven and earth. Abide, stand and call for his support; and so the ennemies which now affraye you, shortly shal be confounded, and never againe shall appeare to molest you (Laing III: 10).

The mood of *familiaritas* or *syntomia* is clearly Knox's goal, as he increases the personal intensity of the letter, and he also echoes Matthew 28: 18 and Galatians 3: 3. (The following passage has, in the context of Knox studies, at least, become rather famous):

> Consider, Brethren, it is no speculative Theolog which desireth to give you courage, but even your Brother in affliction, which partly hath experience what Sathan's wrath may doe against the chosen of God. Rejoyse (yet I say) spiritually, and bee glad; the time of the battell is short, but the reward is eternall (Laing III: 10).

The optimism and warm confidence of these passages leaves a deep impression, not least because Knox is intent on removing all troublesome barriers between himself and his audience. In the first, he even includes a definition of 'Brethren', to assure others that they fall into such a category; in the second, he tells them that he is no academic theologian, happily dispensing advice on matters of which he has no real experience. Rather, he is on equal footing in every way (in fact, he probably had *more* experience of affliction than they, but he tactfully omits to mention this). The mood of the prose recalls Johnsone's work *An Confortable Exhortation* (which we considered above, pp. 43–45), but to be sure, there is something different; Knox's language is full of military terminology ('battell', 'Captaine', ‘ennemies’). This is not altogether new; in fact, it is of great antiquity in Christian thought. Indeed, it still survives in many well-known Christian hymns. The Reformation, however, *did rediscover* the idea (it was, after all, the age which enthroned the *Old Testament* and St. Paul). Erasmus’s *Enchiridion Militis Christianæ* (*Handbook of the Christian Soldier*), a cult work in the sixteenth century, was not idly named. This work went through two editions in 1503 and 1509, to a rather luke-warm reception, but suddenly found a vast audience on the eve of the Continental Reformation. Knox must have encountered this sort of language as a student of the *Vulgate Bible* in his youth, but he probably first heard it in action, in the vernacular, on the lips of his mentor, George Wishart, in the 1540s (below, p. 284). A later chapter deals with Wishart’s enduring influence on Knox, but even after his own very first sermon, which of course, predates the above letter, Knox was calling himself: ‘God’s weak *soldeour*’ (Laing I: 201; italics added). The attractions of this kind of thing are obvious; militancy has a wide appeal, it transforms religious belief into high drama and allows the intermingling of two different, indeed, sometimes opposite, facets of human experience.

In addition to this, like St. Paul in Acts 27: 22 (‘[…] and now I exhorte you to be of good cheare, for there shal none of our lyues perishe […]’ (*Coverdale*)), Knox is using *boni ominis captatio*, or predictions of troubles soon to be over-powered by good, and by rewards for endurance. This fits in nicely with his perceived role as a prophet who has secret access to future events. The syntax too is made to work to good effect in these passages. Verbs come in a memorable pattern of three in the first (‘Abide, stand and call’) evoking different yet parallel responses to danger, while in the second, Knox parenthetically splits verb and adverb in a phrase which draws upon the Sermon on the Mount: ‘Rejoyse (yet I say) spiritually, and be glad […]’ (cf. e.g. Matthew 5: 12). Knox was apparently afraid that his readers would rejoice in an all-too-worldly fashion, which, of course, wouldn’t do. At any rate we have seen that *An Epistle to the Congregation of the Castle at St. Andrews* contains a rich abundance of deliberative rhetorical techniques, certainly enough to captivate and motivate the author’s first readers.

Knox was released from the galleys in 1549 and, as he says in *The Historie:* 'was first appointed preachar to Berwik, then to Newcastell; last, he was called to London' (Laing I: 231). His second epistolary production, an unpublished letter to his new congregation at Berwick, (as we have seen, one of the texts which was unknown to Laing; above pp. 21–22), has never received any literary attention because it is so little known, but this text is a very valuable one, not only in its own right, but also because it allows us access to Knox's hitherto unknown thoughts at a significant phase in his development as a preacher, and because it contains one passage, at least, of profound literary importance (more of this later, however). It is entitled *John Knox to the Congregation at Berwick*, (1552).

This text seems to comprise four or five sections (one dealing with the pervasive powers of Satan, another with the disparity between real and merely nominal piety, others with the failure of the prophets to move the people, with a Paulinian definition of the gospel and some personal details about Knox; his physical and mental condition). As we might expect, given his changed life-situation, he is much less concerned with suffering than he was in his previous epistle, and in his second section of the letter, he develops a more judgmental theme:

> The wheit and dornall growing in one ground, and nurissed with lik moistour and rayne, albeit they be permitted to grow togydder, yitt before the tyme of harvest do bothe shew to the faythfull and vigilant servands of their lorde some tokins and signs how the one is known distinctlie from the other. Even so it is in Christis church; for albeit the wicked shall remane in the Lord's fielde and husbandrie, even to the end, yit be synes of some that sumtymes appeared godlie so manefest and plane, that we shall cease to wunder when we shall see tham gaddered, bound in faggots, and so cast in the fyyr to burn for evir.[4]

This shows that, as early the 1550s, Knox was constructing his homiletic material around Christ's parables; this time it is the 'Parable of the Tares' in Matthew 13: 24–30, 37–43, and we can be certain that many of its symbols, such as 'the tyme of harvest', had a lasting influence on his thought (according to Matthew 13: 39, harvest is: 'the

4 Lorimer, P., *John Knox and the Church of England*, p. 255.

ende of the worlde' (*Coverdale*)). (Indeed, in chapter three we shall encounter the same image in Knox's personal correspondence with Mrs. Elizabeth Bowes; see below pp. 129–130). Knox's method here is especially important because it unites two strands of rhetorical practice which we have already examined. He combines a *parable*, such as we find in Gau, with a *similitude*, such as we find in *Archbishop Hamilton's Catechism*. As we shall see later, Knox had his own sources and models, but here literary facets have surely come together to produce an appeal on two levels: narrative and figurative.

In his third section of the letter, we can also find formative material; notably it reveals Knox's early preoccupation with two major and related subjects: history and prophecy:

> These things are to be seen in the histories and prophecies from the beginning. Ffor in the first aige God cryed, "My spreit shall not strive with men for evir. I will appoint unto him a hundreth and twentye yeres;" as God would say, "I cry by my prophets, I threaten and strive, even as man wer able to resist me; so will I do no more; my worde shall not thus be mokked; I will revenge the dishonour done against my veritie, I shall destroy all fleshe by watter." Butt, O bretherne, who feared these threatnynges and eschaipped the plagues? Noe and his familie – aucht persons of the holle world.[5]

He is contrasting Genesis 6: 3 with 7: 23 ('I will yet geue him respyte an hundreth and twenty yeares' with '[...] all these were destroyed from the earth, saue Noe onely remained, and they that were with him in the Arke' (*Coverdale*), but the most striking feature is the distinctive Knoxian paraphrase of God's words, presumably included to clarify things for the benefit of his readers. (This is a feature of his preaching which recurs in similar forms and we shall consider these in his published sermons, below pp. 182–183). Knox's: 'Butt, O brethrene [...]' in contrast to the affected naïvete of the passage that we considered in the introduction (above, p. 13), is straight-forward in its function and demands an inner response to Knox's personal appeal.

The most compelling passages in *John Knox to the Congregation at Berwick*, however, are those which deal with Knox's personal thoughts and his self-conception. For instance, he says:

5 ibid., p. 256.

> These words I writte with dolor of hart. Amongst my uthers grevous offences daylie committed against Godd's majestie, no ane do I more lament than yat I for man's pleasure so long resisted the godlie and just request of such as sought my companye, neither for pleasure of flesche nor worldlie dignitie, but onlie for increase of hope and desyre of Godd's everlasting kyngdom [...] Wythe life and deathe, deir brethrene, I am at poynt, they before me in equalle ballances. Transitorie life is not so sweate to me that, for defence thairof, I will jeopard to lose the life everlasting. Nor yit is corporall deathe to me so fearful that, albeit most certainlie I understand the same shortlie to follow my godlie purpose, that yet, thairfore, I wold depone myself to dee in Godd's wrayth and anger for ever and ever, which, no doubt, I did yf for manis pleasur I refused Godd's perfitt ordinance [...] This day I am more vile and of low reputation in my awin ees than I was either that day that my feitt was cheyned in the presen of dolor (the galeis I meane), or yit that day that I was delivered by his only providence from the same.[6]

For the most part this passage is a *confessio*; in a purely rhetorical context also known as *paramologia* or *paralogia*, but there is much else at work. With this example we can break through to behind the written word and perhaps catch just a glimpse of Knox as he was before he entered the pages of literature. As we shall see, Knox began his life in all probability as a devout Catholic (this of course he shares with such figures as Luther, Calvin, Zwingli, Bucer, Bullinger, Melanchthon, Beza, Oecolampadius, Musculus, Pellikan and many more 'fathers' of Protestantism). Orthodox sacramental confession would thus have formed part of his early routine. We do not know how long it took for him to reject Catholicism; perhaps he spent a number of years subconsciously kicking against the pricks of a new religion. According to Calderwood's *The Historie of the Kirk of Scotland*, it was in 1543 that Knox first: 'receaved anie taste of the truthe', from: 'Thomas Gwilliam [...] a Blacke frier, borne beside Elstone-furde, in East Lothiane, and provinciall of the Blacke friers of Scotland'[7] and by 1545 he had become Wishart's disciple, to make his own rather splendid entrance into the pages of *The Historie* carrying the double-handed sword (see Laing I: 137, 139) with which he was entrusted, presumably as a mark of his special zeal. At any rate, it is

6 ibid., p. 260.

7 Calderwood, D., *The Historie of the Kirk of Scotland*, vol. I: pp. 155–156.

unlikely that Knox underwent a Lutheran *Turmerlebnis* experience, since he would probably have told us about it if he had. And this is about all we can say of his conversion. Whatever happened, when his incipient Protestantism deprived him of confession, he probably found himself with a newly awakened belief in salvation 'through faith alone' ('durch Glauben allein' or 'sola fide'). For all his confidence in this redemptive power, however, he seems to have retained vestiges of his old practices. The psychological need to confess, to reach out for a spiritual panacea, has perhaps found its way into prose like the above, and its fullest expression in Knox's letters to Elizabeth Bowes, with whom his relationship was especially intimate. Penance too, which is a logical corollary of confession, may find an 'outgate' in phrases like: 'dolor of hart' and 'I […] lament'. From these lines we can also tell how deeply Knox had meditated upon his own apparent unwillingness to become a preacher, and when we come to look at *The Historie*, these emotions should become more understandable (below, p. 211).

Knox moves into another rhetorically appealing phase, by combining methaphoric language with a *partitio*: 'Wythe life and deathe, deir brethrene, I am at poynt, they before me in equalle ballances'. The structure and something of the sentiment reminds us very much of Brutus's famous comment to Cassius: 'Set honour in one eye, and death i' th' other, / And I will look on both indifferently' (*Julius Caesar*, Act.1., Sc. 2., ll. 86–87), but Knox's vocabulary comes from a different register. 'At poynt', for instance, refers to a position on a scale measuring weight, and this comes to represent any crucial juncture in one's life: for example, 'when it cometh to the poynt ther as strokes shall be gyuen'.[8] We have already met something similar in *Archbishop Hamilton's Catechism* (see above, p. 66), with the metaphorical use of the phrase 'hie way'.

Our next two sentences are made up of interlocking but contrasting statements which we might paraphrase (excluding sub-ordinate clauses) thus: 'Transitory life is not so sweet to me that I will lose everlasting life because of its sweetness / Corporal death is not so fearful that I will die under God's wrath because of my fear of it'. Here we have *commutatio*, a device which was defined in, say,

8 *O.E.D.*, VII: 1048, 22 (b).

Publius Rutilius Lupus's *De Figuris Sententiarum et Elocutionis* and later in Angel Day's *The English Secretarie*. Knox finishes, as he had begun, in self-deprecation, by providing information about his suffering in the galleys, which is probably more interesting to modern readers than to his contemporaries, and this information probably constitutes some of the evidence which Peter Lorimer regarded as irrefutable proof of Knoxian authorship here.

The Morrice collection (as it is known) also contains Knox's *Memorial to the Privy Council*, (1552), a text which is less impressive than the above, but in it we can detect almost for the first time, Knox's sarcasm. It comes out very clearly in these lines, in which he ponders on the issue of sitting at the Lord's Supper (echoing Colossians 2: 3):

> The contempte of Christ's institution and daungers that may ensue if men shuld syt in the Lord's Table, Jesus Christ, our Lord and Master, in whome all treasures of wysdome and knowledge be hidd, did never see nor suspect; for no mencion is mayd in his holie Scriptures that syttyng at the table shuld bryng contempt of his institution. *Wonder it is that men are become more circumspect and wyse than God himself*[9] (italics added).

Using *attributio*, (ironically) attributing the prerogatives of God to man, Knox completes his argument with a dry touch, which, although we have met it briefly in our introduction, we will come to recognise as his most distinctive motif. Of course, his real concerns were theological, but words are his weapons; the more deadly that these are, the more chance his theology has of establishing itself and surviving in the hostile world of sixteenth century religious controversy.

It was not until mid-1554, however, that Knox's first major admonitory epistles were published. They were *An Admonition or Warning that the faithful Christians in London, Newcastel, Berwycke & others, may avoide Gods vengeaunce, both in thys life and in the life to come*, (S.T.C. 15059), which includes a colophon: 'from Wittomburge by Nicholas Dorcaster; Anno M.D.liiii, the viii of May' and *A Godly letter sent too the fayethfull in London / Newcastell / Barwycke / and to all other within the realme off Englande / that love the cominge of oure Lorde Jesus, by John Knox*, (S.T.C. 15073). We

9 Lorimer, P., *John Knox and the Church of England*, p. 270.

shall consider the latter first. This text carries the further information: 'Imprinted in Rome, before the Castel of S. Aungel, at the signe of sainct Peter. In the moneth of July / in the year of our Lord 1554'. Of course, only the date is reliable: the work was in fact printed in London by Hugh Singleton, and perhaps we should be wary of attributing the 'sardonic imprint' to Knox himself.[10] The second of these texts is in fact a revision of the first, and it was therefore the second which found its way into the M'Crie MS. and subsequently into Laing's text, with the overall title *A Godly Letter of Warning or Admonition to the Faithful in London, Newcastle and Berwick*, (1554). The editor refrained from detailed collation of the various versions and, given the nature of this study, literary criticism of a reasonably reliable single version (Laing's) is better than detailed textual comparisons.

As Knox says in *The Historie*: 'Edwarde the Saxt, that most godly and most verteous King [...] departed the miserie of this lyef the vj of Julij, Anno, & .c., 1553', (Laing I: 242–243), and thereafter:

> [...] Sathan intended nothing less than the light of Jesus Christ utterly to have bein extinguissed, within the hole Ile of Britannye; for after him was rased up, in Goddis hote displeasur, that idolatress Jesabel, mischevous Marie, of the Spaynyardis bloode; a cruell persecutrix of Goddis people, as the actes of hir unhappy regne can sufficiently witnesse. And in to Scotland, that same tyme, (as we have hard,) rang that crafty practisar, Marie of Lorane, than named Regent of Scotland; who, bound to the devotioun of hir two brethrein, the Duck of Gueise, and Cardinall of Lorane, did onlie abyd the opportunitie to cutt the throttis of all those in whome she suspected any knowledge of God to be, within the realme of Scotland (Laing I: 244).

It was in such a climate and with little option that many Protestants in England, Knox among them, had left the country for the comparative safety of the continent, and ultimately, of Geneva. *A Godly Letter* itself was addressed from Dieppe where, as Laing says, Knox: 'remained till the end of February' [1554] (Laing I: xvi). It is hardly surprising that one of his main themes in this work was that the persistence of idolatry under the reign of Edward, 'of whome the

10 Murison, D., 'Knox the Writer', 36.

godless people of England, (for the most parte,) was nott worthy' (Laing I: 244), had brought punishment in the shape of Mary Tudor.

A Godly Letter is both a more carefully constructed and stylistically accomplished text than *An Epistle to the Congregation of the Castle of St. Andrews* and other letters which we have considered, but between 1548 and 1554, Knox had had ample opportunity to enhance his literary techniques. To this period one can assign *A Vindication of the Doctrine the Sacrifice of the Mass is Idolatry* and *An Exposition Upon the Sixth Psalm of David, Addressed to Mrs. Bowes*, which we shall be looking at in chapter four (below, pp. 177–180). Again, the best way to approach the text is to examine its basic structure before isolating passages of prose. Knox uses a more complex Biblical conceit than hitherto, in this instance linking the events in England under Edward, with those in Judæa, under Josiah (2 Chronicles 33: 25–35). Inherent in such a parallel is the association between reformers and the prophet Jeremiah, who, as Elizabeth Whitley observes with some enthusiasm, 'also was a prophet in troubled times; whose book, so full of battle-cries and trumpets had come alive to Knox'[11].

The first phase of the work apparently came about as a refutation of arguments propounded by John Dudley, Earl of Warwick and Duke of Northumberland,[12] while the second outlines the dangers inherent in idolatry. As we might expect, 'the Masse' is the subject which triggers this section. We began our analysis of *An Epistle to the Congregation of the Castle of St. Andrews*, by examining Knox's highly contrived (but impressive) opening sentence. Since the kernel of his public letters is often contained in the opening lines, it is logical to begin our analysis of *A Godly Letter* the same way. It opens:

> When I remember the feirfull threatnyngis of God, pronunced aganis realmes and nationis, to whome the lycht of Godis Word hath bene offerit, and contemptouslie be thame refusit; as my heart unfeanedlie mourneth for your present estait, Deirlie Belovit in oure Saviour Jesus Chryst, so doith the haill poweris of bodie and saull, trembill and schaik for the plagues that ar to cum (Laing III: 165).

11 Laing I: xvi, and Whitley, E., *Plain Mr. Knox*, p. 76.
12 See Laing III: 169, n. (3).

According to the marginal note to the text, added perhaps by the printer, these lines refer to Matthew 10 and Leviticus 26: (presumably 'yf no man wil receue you, nor heare youre preachinge, departe out of that house or that cite [...] it shall be easyr for ye lande of Sodom and Gomorra in ye day of judgement' and 'I wyl vyset you shortly with swellynges and feuers [...]', which are verses 14 and 16 respectively, (*Coverdale*). Knox is sounding a new note. This is not like the highly conceptual introduction we found in his first letter; he is writing now about what he sees as an imminent crisis of dire proportions and the prose reflects his urgency. Adjectives like 'feirfull' and verbs 'trembill and schaik' are less overstated than we might at first expect. For Knox, like causes produce like effects, and he had scripture as substantiation of that. This is a *prædictio*, though one might argue that it is not specific enough to constitute full-blown prophecy, and this is the position we shall adopt (more of this later, however).

Knox becomes more convincing when the parallelism *implicit* in his choice of Biblical conceit becomes antithetical parallelism *explicit* in his language. Here is one example, although there is a whole host of such passages from which to choose:

> (1.) Thair King was led by pestilent preistis. Who guydis your Quene; it is not unknawin. (2.) Under Zedekias and his counsaill, the ydolatrie whilk be Josias was suppressit came to the light agane. But more abominabill idolatrie was never in the earth than is that whilk of lait is now set up againe by your pestilent Papistis amangis yow. (3.) In Jerusalem, was Jeremie [...] (Laing III: 187).

In the first example, Knox uses opposites in terms of possessive adjectives: 'Thair / your' and main nouns: 'King/Quene'. Towards the end, he brings in a double negative '*not un*knawn', which, incidentally, he also uses in the opening to *The Historie*: 'It is *not un*knowen, Christeane Reader [...]' (Laing I: 3; italics added; see below, p. 196). By this device, he achieves, first of all, *litotes*, and then *brachiepeia*, a figure which exploits omission and brevity. In the second example, he makes a simple, definitive statement concerning Zedekiah's discovery of idolatry. Then, for added emphasis, he points out that the idolatry of the 'Papistis', although it is much worse, is (implicitly) encouraged.

In terms of imagery, *A Godly Letter* is one of Knox's most sophisticated pamphlets. This of course is a sweeping statement and demands justification. The following two extracts should supply the deficit. In his *John Knox to the Congregation at Berwick*, we saw Knox adapting Biblical similitudes; in *A Godly Letter*, however, he *fashions his own*. These can be deeply attractive (and illustrative at the same time):

> The sunne keipeth his ordinare course, and starteth not back frome the West to the South; but when it goeth doune, we lack lycht of the same till it ryse the nixt day towards the Eist agane. And sa it is with the lycht of the Gospell [...] (Laing III: 206).

Knox goes on to warn, with a sinister fatalism, that if the gospel: 'be contempnit, darknes suddenlie followeth' (Laing III: 206), and E. G. Rupp has drawn some significant parallels between this kind of observation and those of Martin Luther, who likewise believed that nations did not have 'infinite last chances'.[13] Knox, however, excels the above passage shortly afterwards. He suggests to his audience that only those devoid of practically *every* worthwhile human quality ('naturall love', 'fatherlie affection', 'reverence of God', to name but a few) will worship at the Mass. Nevertheless, if such appallingly wretched creatures *do* exist, and the Mass is maintained:

> [...] allace! the sunne is gone doun, and the lycht is quyte lost; the trompet is ceissit, and ydolatrie is placeit in quyetness and rest. But gif God sall strenthen yow [...] then is thair but ane darke mistye cloude overspred the sunne for ane moment, whilk schortlie sall vanische, so that the beames efter sal be sevinfold mair brycht and amiabill nor thai were befoir. Your patience and constancie sal be a louder trompet to your posteritie, than wer all the voyces of the prophetis [...] (Laing III: 207–208).

Our first passage fulfils all the demands of *tempus* or *chronographia*, outlined in Desiderius Erasmus's *De Duplici Copia Verborum Rerum Commentari Duo* as: 'the description of time [season], sometimes [...] employed simply for the sake of giving pleasure'.[14] The vividness of

13 Rupp, E. G., 'The Europe of John Knox', 8.
14 Sonnino, L. A., *A Handbook*, p. 176.

Knox's description, which recalls Isaiah 30: 26, does of course manage to meet this criterion, but that is not the point, as we know. If Knox had thought his works would have been read for pleasure, he might have indulged in one of his occasional Pauline ejaculations: 'God forbid!' (see Romans 3: 4, 6: 31, 1 Corinthians 6: 15, etc.) but the periodically resurfacing strands of imagery *do* stimulate. In the first extract from *A Godly Letter* we met 'lycht' as a metaphor, then Knox combined it with the 'sunne', then with the 'trompet' (our first encounter with one of Knox's central metaphors and one we shall meet again, to be sure) and finally, with 'cloude[s]' and 'voyces'. In addition to all this rich and complex figurative language, Knox sets up a balance between *lamentatio* on the one hand ('allace! the sunne is gone [...]') and *consolatio* on the other ('gif God sall strenthen yow [...]'). Ultimately, it was up to Knox's original readers, which mood would prevail.

Having considered such an impressive literary project as *A Godly Letter*, it is something of a disappointment to turn to two shorter letters which took shape around the same time. The first, *An Epistle to his Afflicted Brethren in England*, existed only in manuscript till Laing printed it, and is dated the tenth of May 1554; the second, *A Comfortable Epistell sente to the afflicted Church of Chryst exhortying them to beare hys crosse wyth pacience, lookyng every houre for hys commynge agayne to the great comfort and consolacion of hys chosen, with a prophecy of the destruction of the wicked*, was published some three weeks later. There is nothing about it to indicate place of publication or identity of the printer. Laing entitles these productions *Two Comfortable Epistles to his Afflicted Brethren in England*, (1554).

As we saw in the introduction (above, pp. 17–18), where we have already met them, these texts begin in very similar fashion, although as they progress, significant disparities in their argument and method begin to emerge. The former for example sounds at times almost like a diary of travelogue. It is especially useful to biographers since it provides information about a period of Knox's life not very satisfactorily covered in *The Historie* (see Laing I: 244) (cf. 3 John 13, Judges 5: 18, and 2 Samuel 23: 7).

> My awne estait is this: since the 28th of Januar, I have travellit through all the congregationis of Helvetia, and hes reasonit with all the Pastouris and many other excellentlie learnit men upon sic matters as now I can not commit to wrytting: gladlie I wold be toung or be pen utter the same to Godis glorie: Gif I thocht that I myght have your presence, and the presence of sum other assured men, I wald jeopard my awn lyfe to let men see what may be done with a saif conscience in theis dolorous and dangerous dayis; but seing that it can not be done instantlie without danger to utheris than to me, I will abyd the tyme that God sall appoint (Laing III: 235).

This is a subtle passage which draws upon *præscriptio:* description of facts and circumstances apparently not always necessary. Similarly, Knox employs *negatio* in the latter part, where he tells much by implication, and in fact, by declining to speak. We met a related device in our analysis of the opening passage to *An Epistle to the Congregation of the Castle of St. Andrews*, but here Knox's method is different. There is a veiled compliment in the phrase: '*other* assured men' (italics added), and he keeps his readers under the illusion that they are on tenter-hooks. The topics discussed during Knox's many devout and learned conversations with the *crème de la crème* of Reformation Europe (one of whom was probably Bullinger)[15] must indeed be worth waiting for.

From *A Comfortable Epistle*, the later text, I have selected a passage which is surely more declamatory than anything we have encountered so far, because it brings out something of the contrast between the two texts and because it prepares us for the better known *A Faithful Admonition to the Professors of God's Truth in England*, (1554), which we shall be looking at shortly. Knox tells us: 'why God shoulde sodenly strike the papists in England' (see Laing III: 244, marginal note; and cf. Ezekiel 22: 26):

> [...] For sufficiently they have declared the malice of their myndes. They have violated the law and holy ordinaunces of the Lord our God. They have opened their mouthes agaynst his eternal veritie. They have exyled his trueth, and establyshed their own lyes. They dayly persecute the innocentes, and stoutly maintaine open murtherers. Their heartes are obdurate, and their faces are become shameles like harlots [...] (Laing III: 244).

15 See Burns, J. H., 'Knox and Bullinger', 90–91.

This is the first time we have observed Knox consistently using short, terse sentences and here he achieves a staccato effect. Previously, we have focused on his concision as it functions in order to achieve contrast with longer, more prolix sentences. Moreover, placed together like this, the sentences constitute *disjunctio* or *diazeugma.* The use of related verbs, particularly, contributes to this effect ('declared', 'violated', 'opened', 'exyled', 'establyshed', 'persecute', 'maintaine'); each occurs at the same place in its respective clause, and helps illustrate: 'one gross crime or other' (*King Lear*, Act 1., Sc. 3., 1.5). There is plenty more of this in *A Faithful Admonition*, (1554).

A Faithful Admonition is one of the few Knox texts apart from *The Historie* and *The First Blast* ever to have received any critical attention from casual students of Knox. This is so, because, historically speaking, it is regarded as one of his most controversial exercises, ultimately exacerbating the persecution of Protestants who had chosen to remain in England under Mary Tudor. This, however, is a matter more proper for historians who are less intent on sensationalism than practitioners of other disciplines. For now, we are concerned not with history, but with literature.

In terms of its literary structure, *A Faithful Admonition* is, in fact, Knox's first short masterpiece. Undoubtedly, it contains his most concentrated, sustained and remarkable use of the Biblical conceit so far (and more besides, as we shall see). It is built around the account of Christ feeding the five thousand in the Gospels (see Matthew 14: 15–21, Mark 6: 35, Luke 9: 12–17, John 6: 5–13), with Knox himself portrayed as a disciple entrusted with distributing the bread. (And this is presumably not just a rhetorical figure but also revealing of Knox's own fundamental convictions about God's active role in history). Complementing this are the narratives of the tempest on the sea of Galilee, of Christ walking on the water and St. Peter's partially successful attempt to do the same (see Matthew 14: 24–32). As if this in itself were not enough of a challenging literary task, Knox identifies several 'trigger points' in the narrative at which he finds a way to bring in highly relevant material from the *Old Testament* to reinforce his overall argument. Consider how he identifies Peter's inability to walk on water as symptomatic of man's lack of faith in general, and then further observes:

> And this is a synne common to al the electe and chosen children of God, that when so ever they see a vehement trouble appearing to let them and dryve them backe from the obedience of God, then begynne they to feare and to doute of Goddes power and good wyll [...]
>
> With this feare was Abraham stricken [...] This storme saw Moses when [...] And Ezechias sore complaint declareth [...] (Laing III: 313–314).

This piling up of examples represents a technique which we shall examine when we come to the prose contained in *The Historie* relating to Knox's interview with Mary, Queen of Scots, at Lochleven, in the 1560s (below, p. 249). For the time being, however, we shall content ourselves with the observation that Knox's transitions from *New* to *Old Testament* never seem too contrived, but come across as natural and spontaneous diversions.

Also working within the rhetorical framework of the pamphlet is a vehemence which is extremely compelling, especially when it finds expression like this:

> But, O, thou beast! I speake to you Wynchester, more cruel than any tygre, Shal neither shame, neyther feare, neither benefytes receyved brydel thy tyrannous crueltie? Aschamest thou not, bloudi beast, to betraye thy natyve countray, and the liberties of the same? (Laing III: 298).

Janton has identified some of the forms at work here[16] but he does not mention the most obvious: *communicatio* or *anachinosis*. This is a sudden address to a member of the audience (in fact to 'wyly Winchester' himself; see also Laing III: 284–5). The effect is to engage forcefully the renewed attention of not just one, but all, the readers.

However, Knox is at his best in *A Faithful Admonition* when he combines a genuinely self-interpreting and honest autobiography, with the governing metaphors which run through the text, like quartz through a rock. As C. S. Lewis says, he apparently: 'thought himself a timid, temporizing, culpably gentle preacher'.[17] This comes out in the following passage:

16 Janton, P., *L'homme et l'oeuvre*, p. 467, n. (87).

17 Lewis, C. S., *English Literature in the Sixteenth Century*, p. 198.

> The blynd love that I did beare to this my wicked carcase, was the chefe cause that I was not fervent and faithful enoughe in that behalf: for I had no wil to provoke the hatred of all men against me; and therefore so touched I the vices of men in the presence of the greatest, that they might se themselves to be offenders; (I dare not saye that I was the greatest flatterer); but yet, nevertheless, I wold not be sene to proclaime manifest warre against the manifest wicked [...]
>
> As I was not so fervent in rebuking manifest iniquitie, as it became me to have been, so was I not so indifferent a feeder as is required of Christes stewarde (Laing III: 270).

Lewis, however, too hastily concludes that: 'no equal instance of self-ignorance is recorded until the moment at which [Samuel] Johnson pronounced himself "a very polite man"'.[18] When we come to examine Knox's autobiography contained in *The Historie* we shall see that there was a *real* basis for the above comments, and, as Donaldson says: 'Knox may have been less of a lion than is often believed'.[19] Even David Laing concurs: on 'more than one occasion Knox displayed a timidity, or shrinking from danger, scarcely to have been expected from one who boasted his willingness to endure the utmost torture or suffer death in his Master's cause' (Laing VI: lxxxi).[20] Of course Donaldson and Laing are discussing Knox's personality, not his preaching, but we cannot absolutely separate the two; they interface. Perhaps Knox's vehemence as a preacher comes from an attempt to counterbalance his acknowledged personal weakness. A study of psychology often indicates that judgement goes awry when we feel inadequate. Surely something like this has happened in Knox's case. He ultimately over-compensated for his own timidity.

Lewis's observations, however, have distracted us from the real rhetorical and stylistic issues (and Lewis, I think, has paid too little attention to these). In the above passage, we can see Knox becoming more rhetorical as he becomes more personal. The most obvious flourish comes with the phrases 'manifest warre / manifest wicked / manifest iniquitie' and when Knox levels the most damning charge against himself he has returned to his literary conceit.

18 ibid., p. 198.
19 Donaldson G., 'Knox the Man', 19.
20 See also Shaw, D., *Reformation and Revolution*, p. 44, n. (5).

As much as *A Faithful Admonition* tells us about Knox, we should not overlook the fact that it is addressed to others in order to encourage them. Elizabeth Whitley has, rightly, called it 'a rather beautiful sermon', in which Knox writes: 'very movingly of those whose faith wavers through fear'.[21] In the following passage we can see how he does this (cf. Psalms 107: 30):

> Consider and marke, beloved in the Lord, what we reade here to have chaunsed, to Christes disciples, and to their poore bote; and you shall wel perceave, that the same thynge hath chaunsed, dothe, and shal chaunse, to the true churche and congregation of Christe (whiche is nothing els in this miserable lyfe but a poore bote) travelying in the seas of this unstable and troublesome world, towarde the heavenly porte and haven of eternal felicitie, which Christ Jesus to his electe hath appointed (Laing II: 274).

What is admirable about this is the way the image of the boat builds into rich metaphors which follow the implications of the story through to a natural and imaginative conclusion, designed specifically to encourage rather than to warn or explain.

Knox reveals his ability to evoke pathos: 'poore' recurs, and complements 'miserable' and 'troublesome', but more than this, he is using a device which I call the synoptic vision: '*hath* chaunsed, *dothe* and *shal* chaunse' (italics added). It allows him to embrace past, present and future. Knox's phrase is of course memorable, and allows us to posit much about his thoroughness. Modern, highly media-conscious politicians can often be heard using the same technique, whether it occurs during a spontaneous discussion or functions as part of a set speech. They know its value, and so did Knox. Also, we should notice earlier lines such as 'you shall *well* perceave' (italics added). Knox is really offering his readers a pat on the back if they happen to formulate a reading of the gospel similar or identical to his own.

A Faithful Admonition also bears witness to Knox's range of metaphoric choice. Much later on in the text he observes:

> "O God! the Heathen [...] have defiled thy holye Temple and have prophaned thy blessed ordinaunce. In place of thy joyfull synges, they have erected their

21 Whitley, E., *Plain Mr. Knox*, p. 79.

abhominable ydoles. The deadly cuppe of al blasphemy is restored agayne to their harlottes hand. Thy prophetes are persecuted and none are permitted to speake thy worde frelye. The poore sheepe of thy poore pasture are commaunded to dryncke the venemouse waters of mennes traditions [...]" (Laing III: 327).

Knox is still intent on at least a degree of pathos, but the passage is dominated by mixed metaphors. His primary source is probably *Revelation* 17: 4 which describes the Whore of Babylon as: 'having a golden cup in her hand ful of abominations and filthiness of her fornication' (*Great Bible*), but the metaphors run through to 'harlottes hand', 'The poore sheepe of thy poore pasture' and the drinking of 'venemouse waters of men's traditions' (cf. Matthew 15: 3, 15: 6). Psalms 74 and 79 seem to lie behind much of the text here but even so, Knox thoroughly intergrates the imagery into a coherent, indestructible whole.

Two years separate *A Faithful Admonition* and Knox's next admonitory public letter *The Copie of a letter / sent to the ladye Mary dowagire*, a work which was 'newe augmented and explaned by the Author, in the year of our Lord 1558', and published at Geneva by Poullain and Rebul (see S.T.C. 15067). These two texts are included in Laing's fourth volume as *A Letter to the Queen Dowager, Regent of Scotland*, (1556), and *A Letter to the Queen Dowager, Regent of Scotland, Augmented and Explained by the Author*, (1558). Much had happened to Knox between *A Faithful Admonition* and his first letter to the Regent, most notably that he had been called to, and later expelled from, Frankfurt. He had presumably resumed pastoral duties in Geneva before returning to England and Scotland for a flying visit in 1555–56. Much impressed by the new religious zeal he found in Scotland (evidenced in his private correspondence, as we shall see below; p. 143), he undertook to write the above document(s) with the encouragement of: 'the Earls Marischal and Glencairne'.[22] David Murison comments on Knox's apparent naïveté when he notes that the Reformer: 'imagined he could really talk the Queen Regent, who was a Guise, into support of the Reformation'.[23] Less naïve is Knox's

22 See Laing IV: 72.
23 Murison, D., 'Knox the Writer', 40.

review of the Queen's response, as it is recorded in *The Historie* (cf. 2 Chronicles 36: 16). He says of his letter, that it:

> [...] was delivered into hir awin handis by the said Alexander Erle of Glencarne. Which letter, when sche had redd, within a day or two, she delivered it to that proud Prelate, Betoun, Bischope of Glasgw, and said in mockage, "Please yow, my Lord, to reid a pasqwill." Which woordis cuming to the earis of the said Johne, war the occasioun that his Letter he maid his additionis, as yitt may be sein (Laing I: 252).

In the augmented letter Knox further refers to these events and, echoing Ezekiel 30: 9 and Isaiah 18: 2, rejoins:

> [...] if no more ye esteme the admonition of God nor the Cardinalles do the scoffing of Pasquilles, that then he shall schortlie send you messagers with whom ye shall not be able on that maner to jest (Laing IV: 458).

It is too often overlooked that these lines merely reiterate: 'the woordis of Maister George Wisharte in Dondye' in 1545, (see Laing I: 126, marginal note), although Knox's Wishart speaks more generally:

> "[...] I am assured that to refuse Goddis Word, and to chase from yow his messinger, shall not preserve yow frome truble; but it shall bring yow into it. For God shall send unto yow messingeris, who will not be effrayed of hornyng, nor yitt for banishment [...]" (Laing I: 126).

It is possible to argue that Knox saw in Wishart's words a reference to himself, but the (perhaps apocalyptic) identification of other godly 'messagers' seems to preclude this. Alternatively one may say that Knox's prophecy, as derivative as it is, was right, and contains an unconscious reference to John Willock: 'ane of the principall ministeris within the realme' (Laing II: 71) who attended the Regent at her death-bed. Knox, however, ends the controversy over the letters by pointing out, that:

> As concernyng the threatnyngis pronunced against hir awin persone, and the most principale of hir freindis, lett thare verray flatteraris see what hath failled of all that he hes writtin. And tharefor it war expedient that hir Dochtter [...] should look to that which hath passed befoir, least that in following the counsallis of the wicked, she end more miserablie then her crafty Mother did (Laing I: 252).

We can well credit Dr. Murison's further point that the Regent's 'jibe' was one: 'for which Knox never forgave her'.[24]

The augmented letter additionally contains a full explanatory introduction and eight new sections of various lengths appended to the original. Dr. Murison admires how the texts use paradox to stimulate thought, but this is a feature which we have already explored in some detail. Notably they are devoid of the lengthy conceits which the other admonitory works exhibit. Admittedly this lack partially deprives them of the sustained argumentative thrust at all times augmented by useful Biblical imagery, which we noted in his earlier works, but Knox compensates in other ways. For instance, he persistently presents the Queen with a straight-forward choice (straight-forward to him, at any rate). *Either* she can choose to maintain the Catholic religion to the peril of her soul, *or* she can choose the Protestant faith, and be saved. Moreover, there are multifarious appeals to an impressive range of authors: Josephus, Tertullian, Democritus and Themistius among them. (This anticipates the considerable erudition which Knox displays in *The First Blast*, a work published in the same year as the augmented letter).

Thomas M'Crie says of the first letter: 'though Knox's pen was not the most smooth nor delicate [...] the letter is far from uncourtly' and contrasts this with the second, in which Knox used: 'a more pointed and severe style'.[25] In what follows we shall see that M'Crie's judgements are broadly justifiable. Knox, at his most conciliatory sounds like this:

> I am not ignorant how dangerous a thing it appeareth to the natural man, to innovate any thing in matters of religion. And, partlie, I consider that your Grace's power is not so fre as a publik reformation perchance woulde requyre [...] But if your Grace shal consider the daunger, and damnation perpetuall, which inevytably hangeth upon all mainteynars of a fals religion, then shall the greatest danger easely devoure and swallow up the smaller (Laing IV: 82; Original Letter).

24 ibid., 40.
25 M'Crie, T., *Life of John Knox*, vol. I: p. 51.

When one considers this passage, it becomes apparent that Knox is actually asking the Regent to accept the lesser of two evils; on the one hand the 'dangerous' necessity of introducing a change of religion (ordinarily a bad thing, says Knox, but not so in this instance); on the other, of maintaining a corrupt system (and it should be noted that, in the sixteenth century, Knox was by no means alone in believing that the wrong faith would entail hell-fire; witness John Annand and Richard Marshall). He begins with a concession (*concessio* or *epitrope*), which simultaneously evokes a mood of caution. Indeed, he at first gives the impression that he is as much addressing himself as the recipient of his letter. Thus he assures the reader that he is fully conscious of the magnitude of his words and has thought deeply on the matter in question (presumably to the complete satisfaction of his conscience). His final methaphors, 'devoure' and 'swallow', are integrally related but not at all tautological (unlike some of the stylistic features in prose such as Ireland's). Abraham Fraunce's *The Arcadian Rhetorike* provides a definition of the function of metaphor (*translatio*) with which Knox's use seems to be in line: 'a metaphor is nothing but a similitude contracted into one word. There is no trope more flourishing than a metaphor, especially if it be *applied to the senses* [...]'[26] (italics added).

When Knox strikes back at the Regent in the second letter he more blatantly justifies his own (genuine) attempt to get through to her:

> For what hath my life and conversation bene, since it hath pleased God to call me frome the puddle of Papistrie, let my verie ennemies speak; and what learning I have, they may prove when they please. The report of your Grace's moderation, aswell at that time as after, when sute was made for my apprehension, moved me to write this my other Lettre [...] with simplicitie I have advertised you of a mortall danger; as this portion subsequent shall prove [...] (Laing IV: 439, Augmented Letter).

Percontatio, or an appeal to the audience to present the speaker's own opinion, charges these lines, with Knox employing a neat, additional twist in that he is talking, for a moment, to his 'verie ennemies'. If

26 Sonnino, L. A., *A Handbook*, p. 182.

one's enemies will not deny the truth of a certain proposition, that seems almost to be a complete guarantee of honesty. The more subtle the appeal is, the more effective the impression of truthfulness. Noticeably, Knox seems to have moved on from the diffidence evident in *A Faithful Admonition* to a much more confident and mature position. The prose is, however, still carefully explanatory even if the 'simplicitie' with which Knox claims to write, is deceptive.

In his 1556 epistle *A Letter of Wholesome counsell how to behave ourselves in the myddes of thys wycked generacion*, published by Laing as *A Letter of Wholesome Counsel, Addressed to his Brethren in Scotland*, (1556), we find Knox dealing with very different issues. (Knox was still in Scotland when he received communication from Geneva, and decided to return to the continental city). As Pr. Jack writes, it was composed: 'to encourage those who [felt] themselves thwarted in the pursuit of truth'.[27] However, this letter is at times rather varied; now lively, challenging, even humorous, now serious, hopeful, thorough and full of spiritual wisdom born of, and justified by, experience. Particularly striking is the evidence which it provides of Knox the humanist (although he never loses sight of his own responsibilities as a preacher):

> Multiplication of wordes, prolixet interpretationes, and wilfulnesse in reasonyng, is to be avoyded at *all tymes*, and in *all places*, but *chiefly in the congregacion* [...] (Laing IV: 138, italics added).

The above presuppositions lie behind all of Knox's prose, and give us an insight into the 'mechanics' of his compositional process *in nuce*.

M'Crie observes that the letter is: 'an important document regarding the state of the Protestant Church in Scotland prior to the Reformation'[28] and although this is somewhat unimaginative, it is solid. One of the issues which Knox addressed was an apparent lack of enthusiasm for the Scriptures.

> But if such men as havynge lybertye to reade and exercise them selfs in God's holy Scriptures and yet begin to weary, because from tyme to tyme they reade

27 Jack, R. D. S., 'The Prose of John Knox', 244.

28 Quoted in Laing IV: 131; M'Crie, T., *Life of John Knox*, vol. I: p. 51.

> but one thing, I aske, Why weary they not also every daye to eate breade? Every daye to drincke wine? (Laing IV: 136)

It is difficult for modern readers to appreciate just how crucial an issue this was for Knox, but historical information can clarify things. In the early 1540s an Act of Parliament was passed allowing the Bible to be translated: 'in the vulgar tongue, in the English or Scotish'[29] but this had been a long time coming. Of course, Tyndale's *New Testament* had been circulating in Scotland as early as 1526 and we have already seen that John Gau and John Johnsone were deeply influenced by it, but possession of such literature often resulted in its owner being hereticated. In *The Historie*, for instance, Knox writes of how:

> [...] thare was one Furress of Lynlythqw tacken, who, after long empreasonment in the Sea toure of Sanctandross,[30] was adjudgeit to the fyre by the said Bischop James Betoun, and his doctouris, for non other cryme but becaus he had ane *New Testament in Engliss* (Laing I: 52–53, italics added).

Thus, when the vernacular Bible was legally sanctioned, he recorded the response with much enthusiasm in a passage which friend and foe alike have characterised as 'wonderful'. Whereas before, many:

> [...] war holdin in such bondage, that thei durst not have red the Lordis Prayer, the Ten Commandmentis, nor Articules of thare fayth, in the Engliss toung, but thei should have bene accused of heresye. Then mycht have bene sein the Byble lying almaist upoun everie gentilmanis table. The New Testament was borne about in many manis handes. We grant, that some (alace!) prophaned that blessed wourd; for some that, perchance, had never red ten sentenses in it, had it maist common in thare hand; thei wold chope thare familiares on the cheak with it, and say, "This hes lyne hyd under my bed-feit these ten yearis:" Otheris wold glorie, "O! how oft have I bein in danger for this booke: How secreatlie have I stollen fra my wyff at mydnycht to reid upoun it." (Laing I: 100–101).

One cannot overestimate the influence of the Bible on the Reformation, but Knox, like Luther, was apparently ambivalent. For Luther, subjective interpretation would lead to a 'new Babel' and much later

29 See Laing I: 100, n. (8).

30 This cosmic irony becomes relevant in Knox's account of Cardinal David Beaton's death; see Laing I: 179.

John Dryden lamented: 'The Book thus put in every vulgar hand / [...] at the mercy of the rabble lay'.[31] On the whole, however, Knox genuinely rejoiced that: 'yitt thairby did the knowledge of God wonderouslie increase, and God gave his Holy Spreit to sempill men in great aboundance' (Laing I: 101). In light of this information, we can see why reading the Bible was so important to Knox, and why it takes up part of his *A Letter of Wholesome Counsell*. Perhaps the most readily comprehensible modern parallel to those who did *not* read, is evident at a political level in today's society. Those who rather cynically refuse to vote in a free environment under tolerant laws, when in other less stable countries, many are daily facing torture and death for demanding the right to have a say in their own future, seem to fit the bill. Just as responsible members of a democracy have little sympathy for such individuals, Knox had none for the complaining Scottish Protestants. That is why his challenge to them is extremely pithy. His aim is to discredit their 'argument' (if indeed it deserves such a definition) as quickly and efficiently as possible, and having buried it, to get on with more important concerns. He succeeds by ridicule (often a great motivating force) and one cannot help but place a seal of approval on his method.

When he does address serious matters, such as the relationship between the Law and the Gospel, the tone is altogether different:

> Now, if the Law, which by reason of oure weakeness can worke nothing but wrath and anger, was so effectual that remembred and rehearsed of purpose to do it, it brought to the people a corporall benediction, what shall we say that the glorious Gospell of Christ Jesus doethe worke, so that with reverence it be entreated? (Laing IV: 134).

There is no ridicule here, but Knox is implicitly using argument *a fortiori*. I say 'implicitly using', because Knox avoids the standard formula: 'if [...] which [...] *[how] much more*' (see e.g. Matthew 6: 30), in favour of: 'if [...] *what shall we say*' (cf. Romans 3: 5, 4: 1, 6: 1, 7: 7, Hebrews 11: 32, italics added), which is rarer, but not unique. Less prominent is the presence of a temporal pronoun, 'Now', at the beginning of the argument, which implies that an earlier premise has

31 See Grant, D., (ed.), *Dryden: Poems and Prose*, p. 76.

already been granted. Knox carries his readers towards his point of view on a wave of logic, and we shall see just how useful logic was to Knox in later texts such as *The Appellation from the Sentence Pronounced by the Bishops and Clergy: Addressed to the Nobility and Estates in Scotland*, (1558). Also, there is an implicit contrast between corporal benediction (of the Law) with the (spiritual) benediction of the 'glorious Gospell' (cf. 2 Corinthians 4: 4, 1 Timothy 1: 11). Knox is indulging in a rather splendid vision (although it is much inferior to that of *A Faithful Admonition*).

A Letter of Wholesome Counsel to the Scots is the first in the series of four such productions, even if it is much more moderate in tone than the subsequent three. Laing groups them under the heading *Letters to his Brethren And the Lords Professing the Truth in Scotland*, (1557) (see Laing IV: 255–286). Knox himself includes one of them in *The Historie* (see Laing I: 269–272 and IV: 261), with some explanatory comments, to give his readers an idea of the tenor of his epistolary writings at that time. Of the year 1557, Knox writes:

> At this same tyme, some of the Nobilitie direct thare letteris to call JOHNE KNOX from Geneva, for thare conforte, and for the conforte of thare brethrein the preachearis, and otheris that then couragiouslye faught against the ennemyes of Goddis trewth (Laing I: 267).

Knox further notes how, after a thorough and solemn consultation between himself, Calvin and 'other godlie ministeris', they: 'all with ane consent, said, "That he could nott refuise that Vocatioun, onless he wald declair him self rebellious unto his God, and unmercyfull to his contrie."' (Laing I: 268). However, to his dismay, he found that after setting off and reaching Dieppe: 'thare mett him contrare letteris' (Laing I: 269). This was an unexpected setback, and granted the deep seriousness with which Knox regarded his vocation, one which inevitably convinced him of vacillating tendencies among those who had approached him. In response, he was at his most sardonic:

> To some it may appear ane small and lycht mater, that I have cast of, and as it war abandoned, asweall my particulare care, as my publict office and charge, leaving my house and poore familie destitut of all head, save God only, and committing that small (but to Christ deirlie belovit) flock, ower the which I was

> appointed one of the ministeris, to the charge of ane other. This, I say, to worldly men may appear a small mater, but to me it was [...] such, that more worldly sustance then I will expresse, could not have caused me willinglie behold the eies of so many grave men weape at ones for my cause, as that I did, in tackin of my last good nycht frome thame. To whome, yf it please God that I returne, and questioun be demanded, What was the impediment of my purposed jorney? judge yow what I shall answer (Laing I: 270).

Edwin Muir, an eminently critical biographer of Knox, uses this passage to attribute to him a tendency to exaggerate: 'the brethren in Geneva, it appeared, had been led to expect that he was going to the glorious dangers of a possible martyrdom in Scotland, and after all he had only gone to Dieppe!'[32] Muir, in fact, evinces a belief that Knox had pinioned himself between former exaggerations and his present embarrassing situation. This reading, however, is somewhat unfair. Admittedly, Knox *does* emphasise his own sacrifices, but certainly there was a core of real feeling behind this, and he works it out in the rhetorical context of the letter. It is there, not to prompt pity, or even as a reflection of Knox's putative aura of piety at the sombre Geneva conference, but to prick the conscience of the letter's recipients. One can scarcely come away with the impression that it did not do so.

There are many other rhetorical devices at work (some of which we shall pass over for later consideration in a different context). The three central features, however, are the use of *demonstratio*, *anaphora* and the Scots concept of the 'lang guid nycht'. The first involves the creation of a clear mental image and the placing of it before the eyes of the reader. Knox offers a vivid picture of his own family thrown to the winds of chance, but he has not only abandoned his family, (as if that were not enough), he has left behind his office and his congregation. The *anaphora* comes in when he catches the whole content of his first sentence with 'this' (a device which he was to use in one of his most famous post-Reformation sermons and one we shall be exploring in much greater detail later (below, pp. 227–228). For now, we shall note its use as early (-ish) evidence of the recurrence of funda-

32 Muir, E., *John Knox: Portrait of a Calvinist*, p. 124. Janton's comment: 'Si l'absence de sympathie fausse le portrait, de bonnes remarques psychologiques éclairant çà et là le comportement de Knox': see *L'homme et l'oeuvre*, p. 521, takes a positive view of Muir's work.

mental techniques in Knox's writing/preaching). The 'lang guid nycht' concept is integrally related to Knox's *demonstratio*.[33] He introduces it first of all by differentiating between 'me' and 'worldly men' (a real opposition!) and then paints the picture of weeping reformers, with whom he must part company for ever. The concept has all the compelling qualities of a valediction; it draws its dynamic from the fact that it is absolutely final (although this effect for Knox, was apparently spoiled by those reeds blown in the wind in Scotland); it exhibits dignity in its resignation to fate and creates a mood of high seriousness. With all this working within the text, Knox trenchant final questions cut to the heart of the matter like a knife.

The remaining two letters in this series are much less autobiographical than the above, although Knox does say that his purpose was to: 'renew sumwhat of my former rude wrytting' (Laing IV: 262), in a form: 'mair ampill than was that whilk I sent first' (Laing IV: 275). He is much more conciliatory, however, and he even touches on the theme which must have angered him when he read the letters he had received on reaching Dieppe (cf. 2 Corinthians 1: 7, Romans 11: 22, Colossians 1: 27).

> But my hoip is gud of yow, deirlie belovit in the Lord Jesus, that evin to the end ye sall continew in that doctrine whilk anis ye haif professit, notwithstanding that the windis of unstabill and disavibill opinions be blowin in your earis; and also, that ye shall proceid and marche forward in the batell begun, (Remember, I beseik yow, with what conditionis we did first break bread togidder in the name of the Lord Jesus,) whatsoever impedimentis be preparit in yow contrair [...] (Laing IV: 274–275).

There is perhaps just a trace of criticism aimed at the nobles' inconstancy, but he balances this with tokens of intimacy, particularly a former celebration of the Supper (a similar allusion is also found in *The Historie*: 'a great nomber of the toune [St. Andrews], openlie professed, by *participatioun of the Lordis Table*, in the same puritie that now it is ministrat in the churches of Scotland, wyth that same doctrin, that he had taught unto thame' (Laing I: 201–202, italics added). The parenthesis, '(Remember [...] Jesus)', which contains quite a tender

33 See also Laing III: 153–154, 396, 397.

recollection, is, moreover, strategically placed, at the point where Knox is outlining the most difficult phase of the Christian experience. (Since the two letters are tonally similar, and spring from the same life-situation which Knox found himself in, we need only consider one of them, the above.)

These texts, indeed, were not the only product of Knox's unplanned stay in Dieppe. We can assign the composition of two texts to this period, *An Apology for the Protestants Holden in Prison at Paris: Translated from the French; with Additions*, (1557), and a much better known work: *The First Blast*, (1558). Our understanding of both requires that we set them in their historical context.

In France, in 1557, Parisian priests connected with the Sorbonne had repeatedly observed large gatherings of Huguenots at a private residence in the *Rue St. Jacques*, presumably for Reformed religious worship. A mob-attack on the participants led to the Civil Authorities interrupting the tumult, and ultimately over a hundred Protestants were imprisoned. (One can read Christopher Marlowe's *Massacre in Paris* for a later interpretation of events; a work in which the Duke of Guise and the Cardinal of Lorraine figure prominently. As we shall see later, it would be an understatement to say that Knox had no sympathy for any such individuals; below, p. 201, p. 307). Three of these Protestants were eventually martyred while the rest remained in prison. The remainder prepared the text known as the *Apologie des Chrestiens* for purposes of self-vindication (something which Knox found himself participating in more and more), and it was subsequently published. A copy seems to have come Knox's way at Dieppe, and he conceived of a translation which could be sent to his countrymen. Janton has examined the nature of the final product in much detail,[34] even if, as Laing points out, most of the text was probably translated by an anonymous companion of Knox at that time.[35] Knox did, however, definitely contribute to the overall package. I have chosen the following passage, which is from Knox's own additions, because its significance will become obvious, when, later, we consider Knox's descriptions of George Wishart's mission to Scot-

34 Janton, P., *L'homme et l'oeuvre*, p. 433.
35 See Laing IV: 295; 'by a faithful Brother'.

land (below, pp. 280–286). He writes of the French mob (cf. Matthew 7: 15):

> But theis, as ravisching wolves rageing for blud, murderit sum, oppressit all, and schamfullie intretit both men and wemen of great blude and knawin honestie. They finallie careit Chryst, whome they had apprehendit, first to the presence of thair preistis, and eftir did present him befoir a judge, whair libertie was permittit to declair his innocencie [...] (Laing IV: 300).

We have already met traces of the passion narrative in Knox's version of the Paul Craw martyrdom, (above, pp. 48–50), and, as I say, the most highly developed use of this form occurs in the stories about Wishart contained in *The Historie*. The above example, however, is more sophisticated than the Craw story. Knox's phrase 'ravisching wolves rageing for blud' reminds us, perhaps, of Henryson's: 'cruell wolf, richt ravenous and fell' who comes 'rampand [...] / With girnand teith and angrie austre luke'[36] in his poem *The Wolf and the Lamb*, and although Knox is not using the figure of a lamb in this instance, Christ Himself of course is the lamb *A per se*. Knox employs the oldest and simplest opposition of world-history, good against evil.

The First Blast, has proved itself a more objectionable pamphlet. It has now become a cliché of Knox criticism to point out that it was the most ill-received of his works. C. S. Lewis (typically) spent some time getting to the bottom of why he thought this was so:

> It was embarassing because in a certain sense nearly everyone (except regnant queens) agreed with Knox. Everyone knew that it was contrary to natural and divine law that women should rule men. But then a great many political arrangements as the world now is are equally contrary to Natural Law. We are fallen. It is no use trying to make a sudden return to the Golden Age: [...] Of course, if you press it, women should be subject to men. But if positive laws have in fact placed the crown on a woman's head, pious persons had better mind their own business and say nothing about it.[37]

Lewis, however, gives the impression that the Reformer was almost completely alone in *voicing* such opinions, but this is not the case. The

36 See Fox, D., (ed.), *The Poems of Robert Henryson*, p. 97, ll. 2616 / 2629–30.
37 Lewis, C. S., *English Literature in the Sixteenth Century*, p. 199.

same critic is enthusiastic about David Lindsay, but Lindsay writes in his *Ane Dialogue betwix Experience and ane Courteour* (a text which we shall meet again later): 'Ladyis no way I can commend / Presumptuouslye quhilk doith pretend / Tyll vse the office of ane kyng, / or Realmes tak in gouernying'.[38] Similarly, Bishop Ponet's *A Short Treatise of Politique Power and of true obedience which subjects owe to Kings and other Civill Governers*, Christopher Goodman's *How Superior Powers Oght to be obeyd of their subjects and wherein they may lawfully by Godes Worde be disobeyed and resisted*, and Jean Bodin's (admittedly later) *Les Six Livres De La Republique* (*De Republica Libri Sex*), all contain parallels.[39]

In *Theology and Revolution in the Scottish Reformation*, Richard L. Greaves concentrates more on Knox's personal motivation (and Greaves actually comes close to writing literary criticism here):

> *The First Blast* is, in a special sense, a personal tract, revealing [Knox's] passionate but usually controlled temperament. The explosive passion which gave birth to the tract seethes just below the surface. The passion is a confused mixture of righteous indignation, personal bitterness, animosity, and frustration. All of this is focused not only on Mary Tudor, but also on Mary of Lorraine and Mary the Virgin, who together formed a trinity of evil in Knox's mind.[40]

Knox of course was troubled by 'Marys' throughout his life, and he was later to add a fourth to his list: Mary, Queen of Scots. For example, when telling his 'familiaris' what he thought of her, he tries to give the impression that he is a fellow: 'of exceeding honesty' who 'knows all qualities, with a learned spirit, / Of human dealings' (*Othello* Act 3., Sc. 3., ll. 262–264).'"Yf thair be not in hir (said he) a proud mynd, a crafty witt, and ane indurate hearte against God and his treuth, my judgement faileth me."'(Laing II: 286). This, Knox tells us,

38 Hamer, D., (ed.), *The Works of Sir David Lindsay*, p. 295, ll. 3247–50

39 See also Reid, W. S., *Trumpeter of God*, pp. 145–147.

40 Greaves, R. L., *Theology and Revolution in the Scottish Reformation*, p. 161. As J. Kirk observes, this is 'a somewhat misleading title, for only the sub-title [*Studies in the Thought of John Knox*] [...] does justice to the content'; see 'The Scottish Reformation and Reign of James VI: A Select Critical Bibiliography', 137.

with characteristic finality, was his judgement at first 'and ever since' (Laing II: 286, marginal note).

The First Blast causes so much controversy that most critics lose sight of the fact that, whatever its orientation, it is still a work of literature (or propaganda, if you like). Even sympathetic writers (like David Murison), who *do* consider the tract from the literary point of view, belittle its value in this field.[41] One wonders how we can make such judgements. The fact is that, in terms of rhetoric, the work contains just about every kind of deliberative device one can imagine.

One cannot accuse Knox of being slow to come to the point, because he does so straight away. He states his fundamental thesis with brevity and thoroughness:

> To promote a Woman to beare rule, superioritie, dominion, or empire above any Realme, Nation or Citie, is repugnant to Nature; contumelie to God, a thing most contrarious to his revealed will and approved ordinance; and finallie, it is the subversion of good Order, of all equitie and justice (Laing IV: 373).

With partial modifications (see for example Laing IV: 389, 410), Knox returns to this thesis time and time again (perhaps, one feels, too often). His topic of course is *rebellion(!)*: man's three-fold revolt against natural law, human law and divine law (in the final example, he further introduces the key ideas of profanation and pollution). All the oppositions are mirrored in the actual structure of the language; there is emphasis on 'to' which signals the contrasts, for instance. In fact, this first sentence is a *definitio,* which works on a multiplicity of levels.

The First Blast, along with *The Appellation from the Sentence Pronounced by the Bishops and Clergy: Addressed to the Nobility and Estates in Scotland*, (1558), is among the most 'logical' or 'scholastic' of Knox's works. Of course, one should not confuse 'reason' and 'objectivity' (very little that Knox wrote is objective or 'disinterested' in the way that we understand the words). Even so, Knox's appeal is to *the intellect*. Knox would not have agreed with Hamlet's famous Renaissance theory about the nobility of man, but he would concur in saying: 'he that made us with such large discourse, / Looking before

41 See Murison, D., 'Knox the Writer', 41.

and after, gave us not / That capability and godlike reason / To fust in us unus'd' (*Hamlet* Act. 4., Sc. 4., ll. 36–39). Dr. Murison's comments are particularly relevant in this overall context:

> Knox was in any case obsessed by the logic of God in history, and I use the word 'logic' advisedly, because Knox's mental training was mediæval and Aristotelian […] and according to Beza, he rivalled his master [Major] in metaphysics. One might indeed say that he had been brought up on the syllogism.[42]

Here is one of his syllogisms, contained in *The First Blast*:

> First, I say, if justice be a constant and perpetuall will to geve to everie person their own right, (as the moste learned in all ages have defined it to be,) then to geve, or to will to geve, to any person that whiche is not their right, must repugne to justice. But to reigne above man can never be the right to woman, because it is a thing denied unto her by God, as is before declared. Therefore to promote her to that estat or dignitie can be no thing els but repugnancie to Justice (Laing IV: 400).

This is the type of reasoning to be found in Aristotle's the *Organon / De Interpretatione*): a four-step hypothetical syllogism, the conditional premise being the first, consequential the second, adversative third and with *conclusio* in end-position. Knox, moreover, touches two bases in the context of the second premise ('to give' and even 'to *will* to give' authority to women, are both unjust). He also uses *exclusio* in conjunction with his conclusion; it is: 'no thing els but [...]'. As Roland Bainton says: 'Aristotelian physics was regarded as an exercise in thinking God's thoughts after him'.[43]

In *The Appellation*, Knox responds to being accused of sedition by addressing the magistrates in the following manner:

> […] if you be powers ordeined by God (and that I hope all men will graunte,) then, by the plaine wordes of the Apostle, is the sworde geven unto you by God for maintenance of the innocent, and for punyshement of malefactors. But I and my brethren with me accused do offre not onely to prove ourselves innocents in all thinges laid to our charge, but also we offre most evidently to prove your

42 ibid., 34.
43 Bainton, R., *Here I Stand: A Biography of Martin Luther*, p. 27.

Byshoppes to be the verie pestilence who have infected all Christianitie. And therefore, by the plaine doctrine of the Apostle, you ar bounde to maintaine us, and to punysh the other, being evidently convict and proved criminall (Laing IV: 482–483).

The same four-step structure ('if' / 'then' / 'but' / 'therefore') permeates this syllogism as it did the last, but it works alongside a different rhetorical trope. Knox is aiming for *epiplexis* or *increpatio*, vehemently turning an argument upside down and back on the accusers. Within this scheme, there is the use of: 'not onely [...] but also', which suggests to readers that for Knox to be so frank and accommodating, he must be right and have nothing to hide (and Knox did not believe he was bluffing either). His most virulent touch comes with the items 'pestilence' and 'infected'.

Knox's *A Vindication of the Doctrine that the Sacrifice of the Mass is Idolatrie*, (1550), however, contains what is probably his most powerful series of syllogisms, and we shall deal with the feature here, rather than bring it up in each chapter (although inevitably we shall run into it again, albeit briefly, in our analysis of *The Historie*; below, pp. 242–243). Knox's *A Vindication* is built around the following propositions:

THE MASSE IS IDOLATRIE. All wirschipping, honoring, or service inventit be the braine of man in the religioun of God, without his own express commandment, is Idolatrie: The Masse is inventit be the braine of man, without any commandment of God: Thairfoir it is Idolatrie (Laing III: 34, 47).

The second syllogisme.

All honoring or service of God, whairunto is addit a wickit opinioun is abominatioun. Unto the Masse is addit a wickit opinioun. Thairfoir it is abominatioun (Laing III: 52).

Unlike the type of syllogism we find in *The First Blast* and *The Appellation*, these are three-step, although in the first at least, Knox really places the conclusion in front, as well as at the end, of the manoeuvre. Moreover, they are both categorical; they constitute syllogism in *darii*, the third mood in the first figure of the Aristotelian system. In *A Vindication*, however, the logical device has a different function from those in the other texts. Here, Knox constructs great arguments on their basis, and having proved the point to his own satisfaction, he restates his fundamental thesis again, and subsequently each premise takes on a much greater import. In fact, Knox combines the repetitive techniques of *The First Blast*, with logistic techniques. He does not always achieve the same fusion in other works.

Nor is the syllogism confined to public displays. In chapter three we shall be looking at Knox's private letters and it is not out of order to give here a taste of these. In Letter III, he ponders:

> […] the office of the faithfull is to keip promeis; but God is faithfull, ergo, He man keip promeis [...] let this collectioun of the promissis be maid; God promisses remissioun of synis to all that confessis the same, but I confes my synnis, for I sie the filthines thairof, and how justlie God may condemp me for my iniquities. I sob and I lament for that I can not be quyt and red of syn; I desyre to leif a mair perfyt lyfe. Thir are infallible signis, seillis and takinis, that God hes remittit the syn (Laing III: 341–342, Letter I).

There are actually two syllogisms here. Knox knew of the distinction between a preceding *pro*syllogism ('the office […] be maid') which, like the examples from *A Vindication* is in *darii*, and a subsequent *epi*syllogism, which stands in relation to it ('God promisses […] the syn'). Notably, however, the members of the episyllogism are more loosely connected than any of the others, but this is because Knox works in a good deal of revealing autobiographical detail about his own experience of repentance. These, then, are his most spectacular uses of the device (but see also Laing III: 342, IV: 400, V: 91, 110, 218, 224, VI: 218).

Obviously, the logical rhetoric of texts such as *A Vindication*, *The Appellation* and 'Letter I' grew out of different circumstances from *The First Blast*, to which we now ought to return and say something further. Initially, it seems, Knox did not envisage the tract becoming the notorious political *faux pas* that it turned out to be. He even considered a second and third blast, concealing his name until the publication of the final work. As elaborate as the scheme was, it never came off, and Knox left only a summary of the proposed *Second Blast* (see Laing IV: 539–540). This text is very short, but in it Knox can be seen adopting an even more radical politico-religious stance. He was preparing to speak out not only against female rulers, but non-

Protestant sovereigns in general. He may have found some consolation in the fact that less than a year after prophesying that woman's reign was a 'rotten proppe' and 'a wall without foundation' (Laing IV: 420) Mary Tudor was dead. Some years later, Ninian Winzet busied himself in preparing the comically entitled *The Last Blast of the Trompet*, but when he tried to have the work printed, the government intervened.[44]

At any rate, having composed *The First Blast*, Knox made his way back to Geneva, perhaps to face the questions he had envisaged to his Scots brethren, perhaps not. We have no way of knowing if he was embarrassed because he has nothing whatsoever to say about these events in *The Historie* (see Laing I: 274). It was probably on his return to the city that he received news of events concerning himself in Scotland, dating back to his 1555 visit. About all this, however, *The Historie* is brimful of information. During his preaching tour in 1555–56, Knox had received a summons from 'the Black Freiris' (the '*Fratres Predicatores*'; Laing I: 251), challenging him personally to appear before them in Edinburgh, presumably with a view to discrediting him as a heretic. Knox relates how he both kept the summons and got the better of the Friars:

> Butt that dyet held nott; for whitther that the Bischoppis preceaved informalitie in their awin procedyngis, or yf thei feared danger to ensew upoun thare extremetie, it was unknown unto us. Butt the Setterday befoir the day appointed, thei cast thare awin summondis; and the said Johne, the same day of the summondis, tawght in Edinburgh in a greattar audience than ever befoir he had done in that toune: The place was the Bishope of Dunkellis his great loodgeing, whare he continewed in doctrin ten dayis, boyth befoir and after nune (Laing I: 251).

The charge however was renewed when Knox had left the country and when he was in no position to answer. Like the Mare in Henryson's *The Trial of the Fox*, he was: 'callit [...] *contumax*'[45] and *in absentia* the Provincial council sentenced him to death and burned him in effigy, for, as he says, 'none compeirance':

44 See Hewison, J. K., (ed.), *Winzet's Works*, vol. I: lxxxi, xcii, pp. 35–45.

45 See Fox, D., (ed.), *The Poems of Robert Henryson*, p. 42, l. 1004.

> Fra the which injust sentence the said Johnne maid his APPELATIOUN, and caused to print the same, and direct it to the Nobilitie and Commounes of Scotland, as yitt may be redd (Laing I: 254).

The dry humour which characterises the original narrative is nowhere evident in *The Appellation*. It is a long, serious, angry, political and theological treatise dealing at length with the right of the people to rebel against unjust figures of authority, be they King, Queen, Magistrate or commoner. Again Richard Greaves very perceptively assesses Knox's emotional state: 'Consumed with prophetic indignation, he poured his feelings into his summer tracts of 1558. God must be avenged. Knox his prophet must be avenged'.[46]

Knox is at his most scornful when he writes of Mary Tudor's English subjects, who, according to him, must stand servile before her:

> He whome, in his membres, for the pleasure of a wicked woman, they have exiled, persecuted and blasphemed, doth now laugh them to skorn; suffereth them to by pyned in bondage of most wicked men, and finally, shall adjuge them to the feir everlasting, except that spedely and openly they repent [...] (Laing IV: 516–517).

Knox obviously takes much comfort from the fact that the Englishmen, who were ultimately responsible for his own leave-taking, must now endure that which he warned them against, the 'regiment' or government of a woman. Of course, Knox is not playing games but we must remember that by this time the daggers were out he is striking a blow in retaliation. And for all his anger, the above passage still works within the rhetorical framework whereby he turns everything on its head.

Furthermore, we saw earlier that Knox uses figures of omission. In *The Appellation*, he can be seen combining such a figure with some others which we have not yet encountered. Take this single sentence which comes towards the conclusion of the work:

> The pride, ambition, envie, excess, fraude, spoile, oppression, murther, filthie life, and incest, that is used and meintained amongest that rabble of preestes,

46 Greaves, R., *Theology and Revolution in the Scottish Reformation*, p. 138.

freers, monkes, channons, byshopps and cardinalls, can not be expressed (Laing IV: 513).

Anyone familiar with Knox's biography knows that before he was forced to become an active preacher, he was initially a priest and papal notary. In the latter capacity he drew up legal documents (all now collected by Thomas Thomson)[47] and something of their structure can be seen in this passage. It follows the pattern, perhaps, of a bill of sale complete with rights of ownership. The specificatory list of nouns (and this time they are far from abstract) is especially prominent. In rhetoric this would come closest to *congeries* or 'piling up' towards a climax. The printed text of *The Appellation* must still have been doing the rounds in 1566 when Knox referred to it in his *The Historie*, but C. H. Kuippers states that even before its publication it: 'had been circu-lating in manuscript'.[48] Certainly it must have shaken its recipients, and as Janton observes, the text: 'meant a great deal more for them than for us'.[49]

The much shorter *Letter Addressed to the Commonalty of Scotland*, (1558), represents the last of Knox's pre-Reformation admonitory works written to Scotland. Of the four remaining letters, two are written to England, *An Epistle to the Inhabitants of Newcastle and Berwick*, (1558), and *A Brief Exhortation to England for the Speedy Embracing of the Gospel*, (1559), and two, *The Reasoning Betwixt John Knox and the Abbot of Crossraguel*, (1562), and *An Answer to a Letter Written by James Tyrie*, (1572), are post-Reformation. The text of the *Letter Addressed to the Commonalty* was published along with the *Appellation* to which it refers the reader, and we can date its composition to mid-July 1558. Knox of course was not conscious of discontinuing a series in any sense.

47 See Reid, W. S., *Trumpeter of God*, p. 19, Laing VI: xix and Thomson, T., (ed.), *Proceedings of the Society of Antiquaries in Scotland*, vol. III: p. 67.

48 See Kuippers, C. H., (ed.), *Quintin Kennedy (1520–1564): Two Eucharistic Tracts*, p. 61.

49 Janton, P., 'John Knox and Literature', 423.

This letter is a particularly compelling one. Its real strength lies in the way it addresses the whole of the commonalty but gives the impression, at the same time, of speaking directly to each individual. It has the evocative power of a finger-pointing recruitment poster, and in a sense, this is exactly what it is; a call to rally around the Protestant cause as it comes to a head. In chapter one we saw how John Ireland used mimesis to penetrate the minds of his congregation (above, p. 35). In the passage to come, Knox shows that he has fully inherited this preaching trend (and expanded on it considerably). He characterises what he sees as the evasiveness of the commoners, like this:

> […] We were but simple subjects, we could not redresse the faultes and crimes of our rulers, bishoppes, and clergie: we called for Reformation, and wished for the same; but Lords brethren were Byshoppes, theyr sonnes were Abbottes, and the frendes of greate men had the possession of the Churche, and so we were compelled to give obedience to all that they demaunded (Laing IV: 535).

In his subsequent *Epistle to the Inhabitants of Newcastle and Berwick*, Knox says: 'ye judge me rather to mock you then to exhort you to repentance by this means' (Laing V: 493), and mockery is what he is about here. This prose would perhaps be at its best if read in a simpering, insipid voice. An imaginative way of assessing these lines is to think of them functioning as a kind of mirror into which contemporary readers were invited to look. If they saw their 'reflection', or thought they did, Knox had all but succeeded in moving them. Only those without self-respect could remain idle.

Pr. Jack has admired the *Epistle to the Inhabitants of Newcastle and Berwick*, (S.T.C. 15065): 'as the finest short literary piece [Knox] composed'[50] and certainly the Reformer draws on *all* his previous literary experience, which by this time was quite considerable, but perhaps *A Godly Letter* more properly deserves Pr. Jack's description. However, the *Epistle* is unique in that it shows Knox dealing for the first time with the problem of 'back-sliding'; apparently the erstwhile Protestants he once knew were returning to Catholicism. Knox's feelings of betrayal and alarm are so strong in this letter that the text seizes our attention immediately (and won't let go). In his earlier *A*

50 Jack, R. D. S., 'The Prose of John Knox', 427.

Letter of Wholesome Counsell, we observed how Knox used the item 'now' as part of the reasoning process, as a signifier of consent in accepting previous propositions (above, pp. 96–97). In this pamphlet, he uses it in an entirely different way (cf. Proverbs 7: 12):

> *Now* he offerethe himself unto you; *now* he is neare; *now* he is to be founde, whyle he callethe you to repentance by his Messingers and Worde (Laing V: 490, italics added).

Each use has the effect of crystallising a fleeting moment in time which quickly gives way to another. Readers may be reminded of a child's visual toy with synthetic surface, which alternatively shows one image, then another.

Knox, however, is at his most deadly when he makes use of his own personal authority:

> My conscience dothe neither accuse me, that amongst you was I a false prophete, mercenary nor idle person, and yet I quake, feare and tremble, remembring your horrible fall; and ought yow to rest, be quyet and rejoyse, against whome God's vengeance is so plainly pronounced? (Laing V: 482).

In that second 'I', Knox has invested his own personality (it is rather like Julius Caesar's: '*I* could well be mov'd, if *I* were as you' (*Julius Caesar*, Act 3., Sc., 1. 58) or Brutus's: 'Must *I* give way and room to your rash choler?' (Act 4., Sc. 3., 1. 39). If Knox himself, a true preacher and no deceiver, is afraid (and he is not *just* afraid; he is quaking, fearing and trembling), the sinful, complacent turncoats ought to awaken to the danger immediately (and they are not *just* complacent, they are resting and rejoicing). Knox is telling them that they are fiddling while Rome burns (not that he would be altogether hostile to the latter part of such a prospect). *A Brief Exhortation* is a companion piece to *An Epistle to the Inhabitants of Newcastle and Berwick*, and it is remarkably similar (indeed they were printed together in Geneva); so much so that we can pass it by with this, the briefest of mentions.

Only two texts now remain: *The Reasoning* and *An Answer to a Letter Written by James Tyrie*. The former has left its traces in the narrative of *The Historie* in the same way as *The Appellation*, the letter[s] to the Regent and *The First Blast*. In 1562:

> The Abbot of Crosraguell requyred disputatioun of Johne Knox for mantenance of the Messe, which was granted unto him, and whiche held in Mayboll thre dayis. The Abbot had the advantage that he requyred, to wit, He took upoun him to prove that Melchisideck offered bread and wyne unto God, which was the ground that the Messe was builded upoun to be a Sacrifice, & C. But in the travaill of thre dayis thair could no prooff be produced for Melchisedeckis oblatioun, as in the same disputatioun (which is to be had in print) clearlie may appear. The Papistis constantlie looked for a wolter, and thairfoir thei wold maid some bragg of reassonying. The Abbote farther presented him self to the pulpit, but the voice of Maister George Hay so effrayed him, that efter anes he wearyed of that exercise (Laing II: 351–352).

The copy of *The Reasoning* to which Knox alludes was printed by Robert Leprevik in Edinburgh in 1563, (S.T.C. 15074), apparently the first of Knox's works to be published by a Scottish printer. Knox himself made the work public apparently to dispel the rumour, currently circulating, that Kennedy had soundly vanquished him in debate. Indeed, he stimulates in *The Historie* the counter-rumour that Kennedy was much 'effrayed' of George Hay. The reality of the matter, is, however, as Kuippers observes. The debate: 'ended in complete dead-lock'.[51] One can still assess the merits of Kennedy's arguments in the copy made available by Knox, and additionally in the Abbot's *Two Eucharistic Tracts: Ane Litil breif Tracteit maid be master Quintine Kennedy, abbot of Crosraguel, provand cleirly the real body of Iesu Crist to be present in the sacrament of the altare, contrar the vickit opinion and heresy of Ecolampadius and otheris diuerss in thir miserabill dais falslye deniand the Sammyne* and *Ane Compendious Ressonyng, be the quhilk is maid manifest, truelie, and propirlie, conforme to the scripturis of almychtie God (bayth new Testament and auld,) the messe to be institute be Iesu Christ oure saveour* [...].These are both fine works which have unfortunately been neglected by literary critics, but which fall outside the range of this

51 Kuippers, C. H., (ed.), *Quintin Kennedy (1520–1564): Two Eucharistic Tracts*, p. 39.

study. However, in chapter four we shall have the good fortune to meet one of them again (see below, p. 171).

Knox's version of the copy is made up initially of letters between the two potential participants, arranging for the debate to take place. This is from Knox's response to 'the Abbote's first letter':

> That ye offer unto me familiar, formall and gentill reasoning, with my whole hart I accept the condition, for assuredlie [...] chiding and brawling I utterlie abhor, but that ye require it to be secrete I nether se just caus why that ye should require it, nether yet good reason why that I should grant it [...] (Laing VI: 177).

As we can see, the correspondence is mainly taken up with practical matters, but nonetheless it does contain some valuable information. Knox for instance asserts his own gentility in a way which recalls William Dunbar's address to another Kennedy: 'Flyting to vse gritly I eschame: / For it is nowthir wynnyng nor rewaird [...]'.[52] Knox even sounds amiable. As we might expect by now, he is deeply distrustful of clandestine theological reasoning. He wants things 'out in the open' (so to speak) and 'above-board'. This, perhaps, is more in keeping with the openness which the Reformation stimulated and demanded.

In the actual debate, Knox is just as mannered as in the above passage (but this contrasts markedly with the sarcasm of his introduction, as we have seen). Our treatment of this encounter anticipates assessment of the debate between Knox and Friar Arbuckle contained in *The Historie*, which comes in for extensive treatment a little later, (below, pp. 240–246), so we shall content ourselves with a swift look at Knox's contribution to the debate with Kennedy, and reserve the more detailed work in a similar area for later on. Knox was very good at debating. Here he is in action:

> Your Lordschip is not ignorant that in everie definition there oght to be *genus*, which I take your Lordschip here maketh this term *Sacrificium*, but because the term is generall, and in the Scriptures of God is diversely taken, therefore it must be brought to a certane kinde (Laing VI: 198).

52 See Bawcutt, P., (ed.), *The Poems of William Dunbar*, p. 200, ll. 18–19.

This represents Knox's most explicit use of logical forms which we have yet encountered. In *The First Blast* and *The Appellation* the scholarship really belonged to the sub-text. It functioned subtly and our attention was diverted by the progression of the arguments which were rolling by us, like a circus coming to town. Here, the schoolmanship is of supreme importance (and perhaps at this point it is apt to quote some phrases from the remainder of the Knox canon to assess the contribution which this kind of language brought to his work). Just a smattering of them will suffice: 'paralogism' (Laing V: 109) 'equivocation' (Laing V: 132), 'sorite' (Laing V: 195), 'preterit, future' (Laing V: 153), 'conditional' (Laing V: 190) '*causa propinqua*' (Laing V: 99), '*causa causæ et causa causata*' (Laing V: 113), '*agens et patients*' (Laing V: 129), '*scopæ dissolutæ*', (Laing V: 132), '*necessaria concludentia*' (Laing VI: 205) and so on. Janton has gathered many of these together in his analysis of 'la langue et le style' of Knox[53] and he expands: 'Le vocabulaire reflète le vaste champ d'activité du réformateur'.[54] In *The Reasoning*, Knox, for once, is objective and disinterested and this too has its useful function (more of this, however, when we see Knox in conflict with Arbuckle in *The Historie*).

Ten years separate *The Reasoning* and the publication of Knox's final pamphlet *An Answer to a Letter Written by James Tyrie*, (S.T.C. 15062). Apparently, Knox had composed his answer in 1566, but refrained from publishing the material until July 1572, because at that time Tyrie had become particularly active as a pamphleteer in France.[55] This letter, like the earlier *On Predestination*, is especially valuable because it indicates much about Knox's own literary knowledge of Continental historiography, and about his erudition in general. Katharine Firth has pointed out that Tyrie, in his original letter, refers to a certain writer of the twelfth century, and Knox picks up the reference.[56] The author was Abbas Joachim of Corazzo (ca. 1135–

53 See Janton, P., *L'homme et l'oeuvre*, p. 478.

54 ibid., p. 477.

55 Ridley, J., *John Knox*, p. 509.

56 Firth, K. R., *The Apocalyptic Tradition*, p. 129.

1202),[57] 'a man', according to Knox, 'sometymes of great authoritie and reputation amonges the Papistes' (Laing VI: 505) and the work was (I think) his *Expositio magni prophete Abbatis Joachimi in Apocalypsim* etc., first published 1527. Knox additionally refers to 'Joannes Aventinus' or, more accurately, Johann Turmair, the so-called 'Bavarian Herodotus' and author of *Annalium Baiorum Libri Septem*, (known in the vernacular as *Bayersche Chronik*). A special story lies behind Knox's knowledge of this book.

In the late 1950s, Dr. John Durkan discovered a copy in Edinburgh University Library, which was certainly owned by Knox, and had been annotated, on his instructions, by his nephew, Paul. C. P. Finlayson subsequently published a short study of the material in *The Scottish Historical Review* of 1959 entitled: 'A Volume Associated with John Knox'.[58] The book, it seems, once belonged to the same George Hay that we have just met (in connection with the Maybole reasoning). The above information becomes significant again when we examine the manuscript of *The Historie*[59] (below, p. 199).

Anyhow, here is Knox combining the double authority of these two authors, to confute Tyrie:

> Let the wrytings, we say, of these two, beare witness what has bene the judgement of divers men in divers ages, of Rome, of the pryde of the prelacie, of their corruption in lyfe and doctrine, and finally, of their defectioun from the trueth.
>
> Abbas Joachim, wrytting upon the wordes of the Revelation of Sanct Johne, "the sext angel powred furth his phyole upon the great flood Euphrates," hes this sentence, *Si autem aquæ huius fluminis quod vocatur Euphrates, populi sunt, et gentes, et linguæ, quæ parent Romano imperio; si quidem civitas Romano ipsa, est nova Babilon* [...] This place, and that which ensewes of the drying up of the watters, evidently shawes what was the judgement of the wryter in his dayes of Rome [...] (Laing VI: 505–506).

To find anything like such an effective use of sources, we have to think back to the Scots merchant in Lamb's *Ane Resonying,* but in this instance, the debate is for real, and Knox's response more-or-less

57 See Laing VI: 505, n. (2).

58 See Finlayson, C. P., 'A Volume Associated with John Knox', 170–172.

59 ibid., 170.

spontaneous. He probably considered it part of his duty to keep in touch with the opinions of 'divers men in divers ages' in case an opponent like Tyrie cited evidence from antiquity, and as we have seen, his learning paid off (more than once).

We have now considered the majority of Knox's admonitory prose in texts which are not as similar as many critics have usually suggested. In Knox's work, we can see continuity between his own and pre-Knoxian prose, and an enormous range of rhetorical devices which we have not begun to do justice to, and we have built up a mental picture of the techniques which find their finest expression in *The Historie*. Chapter three, however, deals with Knox's personal correspondence, and as far as literary history is concerned, takes us into largely unexplored terrain.

Chapter Three: Knox's Personal Correspondence

In his essay 'Knox the Man', the historian Gordon Donaldson points out that: 'with Knox, we have, almost for the first time in Scotland, a quantity of intimate personal letters'[1] and this point is surely of profound importance. Laing divided Knox's private correspondence into four divisions: epistles to Mrs. Bowes and her daughter Marjory; 'familiar epistles' to other close friends; letters concerning the progress of the Reformation in Scotland, and finally, those relating to the later period of Knox's life. However, the literary critic can dispense with two categories, grouping the epistles to Mrs. and Miss Bowes together with the 'familiar epistles' and merging the final two categories also. Thus we have letters of spiritual counsel and letters relating to historical matters.

As a religious adviser and pastor, Knox undoubtedly excelled, and we shall see how and why in this chapter. First of all, however, his relationship with the two most important recipients of his letters (the Boweses) needs a little explanation. When Knox was appointed preacher in Berwick he had become attached to three members of the Bowes family, primarily Elizabeth (who became his mother-in-law), Marjory (subsequently Knox's first wife) and George (son to Mrs. Bowes).[2] As we would naturally expect, Knox was much concerned with the two devout ladies, although it is to *Mrs*. Bowes that the bulk of his letters are addressed. They were often separated, although he records only one such instance in *The Historie*. On leaving Scotland in 1556: 'he send befoir him to Deape, his mother in law Elizabeth Bowes, and his wyef Marjory, with no small dolour to thare hartes, and unto many of us' (Laing I: 253). In an impressive article in an edition of *Manuscripta* (1987, 31, no.1),[3] A. Daniel Frankforter has

1 Donaldson, G., 'Knox the Man', 18.

2 See Reid, W. S., *Trumpeter of God*, p.79.

3 See Frankforter, A. D., 'The Chronology of the Knox-Bowes Letters', 28–41.

broken new ground in dating these texts, although matters of chronology are only of peripheral interest to the literary critic.

Among his other correspondents, Knox can number Jean Calvin (in Latin), John Foxe, Thomas Upcher, William Cecil, Thomas Randolph, Harry Wycliffe, John Wishart, Christopher Goodman, the Earl of Moray, William Douglas, Gregory Railton, Queen Elizabeth of England (to name one of the more important recipients), and so on. Knox knew, and had dealings with, a great many people. But what differentiates Knox's personal correspondence from the public letters that we have just considered is the *size* of his audience, and audience, after all, is the major concern of a rhetorician like Knox. In the personal texts, the audience is of one, or at most, four or five. At the risk of presenting a truism, one can say that such a situation shows Knox in a more intimate light. But this intimacy has a crucial effect on many features of his writings. Moreover, it allows us to perceive Knox's innermost fears as the dramatic events of his life are reflected in the texts. We can illustrate this quite easily. Here are samples from letters written in circumstances of comparative ease, and some danger, respectively. The first comes from Geneva just before Knox and his friend Christopher Goodman were re-elected as ministers to the English congregation (cf. Acts 9: 19, and 1 Thessalonians 2: 18).[4]

> The chosin weschell of Chryst Jesus, St Paule, apoyntit to his ministrie and preaching, not be man, but be the imperiall voce of the Sone of God speiking unto him from heavin, aschamit not to confesse (deirlie Belovit), that albeit he had ane ernist zeall and desyre to have visitit the congregatioun of Thessalonica in thair greatest necessitie, that yit he was impeidit be Sathan of his jurney and purpois (Laing IV: 248–249).

When writing to Anne Locke, one of his most trusted confidants and, for her time, a distinguished woman (who later translated *Sermons of John Calvin upon the Songe that Ezechias made after he had bene sicke and afflicted by the hand of God, conteyned in the 38 chapiter of Esay* and Jean Taffin's *Of the markes of the children of God, and of*

4 See Laing I: xviii.

their comfort in Afflictions),[5] Knox is altogether less mannered in his approach:

> Our deere brethrein and sisters of Edinburgh and Lothiane, who ly neerest these blood thristie tyrannes, are so trubled and vexed, that it is pitie to remember their estate. Our God comfort them. We stand universallie in great feare, and yit we hope deliverance (Laing VI: 100–101).

The first, which is: 'to his sisteris in Edinburgh', makes use of the same elaborate introduction that we met in the public letters, but Knox also relies occasionally on Romance words ('imperiall voce') and so, creates the air of sophistication. But for all his artifice, indeed *because* of his artifice, the passage is nothing like as compelling as the second.

A binary phrase like 'jurney and purpose', from the first, may not be repetitive, but 'trubled and vexed' from the second, arouses much greater emotive effect ('vexed' in particular is a striking word, used in the early translations of the Bible to stress tribulation; see for example Psalms 6: 2 or 2 Peter 2: 8, *Great Bible*). Moreover, the hurried section beginning: 'it is pitie to remember their estate', conveys a deep wealth of compassion. And the short, one-clause sentence ('Our God comfort them') is, to say the least, not a very recurrent feature in the epistolary writings we have so far examined. Fatalistic realism is mitigated by a glimmer of hope in: 'We stand universallie in greate feare, and yit we hope deliverance'. This gives a vivid impression of Knox's mood. And yet clearly Knox is not aiming for an aesthetic response.

Here we have surely hit on an intrinsic paradox in Knox's private correspondence. Sometimes, when he has no intention of applying consciously artistic devices, he reaches a stage at which he reveals psychological honesty and deep emotions, without any kind of artifice. The paradox lies in the fact that the crystallisation of these

5 See Collinson, P., 'The Role of Women in the English Reformation illustrated in the Life and Friendships of Anne Locke', 258-277; also Hannay, M. P., *Silent but for the Word: Tudor Women as Patrons, Translators and Writers of Religious Works*, p. 9, p. 59, and Stevenson, R. L., 'John Knox and his Relations to Women', 202-204.

mental patterns is, in itself, thoroughly compelling (not only in artistic terms). This perhaps suggests that, for Knox, real feeling and rhetoric do not *always* go together. This may seem like an obvious point, but we must remember that we are dealing with Knox; a man *immersed* in oratory, who used it nearly always as his natural medium. This brings us to a related point. C. S. Lewis says that Knox's rhetoric is: 'the rhetoric of passion, not affectation'.[6] This is a somewhat curious thing for Lewis to say. If by 'affectation' he means 'decoration' then he is partly right. But the logical implications of his remark, as it stands, are that there are two types of rhetoric. The latter requires skill, the former only emotion. Any such conclusion cannot be entirely sustained. After all, one can be passionate about a great many things and not be at all eloquent. Still less do we need a knowledge of rhetorical practice to be passionate. We can clarify the matter like this. W. B. Yeats once said: 'Irish poets, learn your trade'.[7] As a sixteenth century preacher, Knox also learned his trade, and it was a difficult but worthwhile 'trade'. In fact, he learned it so well that it almost became part of him. It is, then, surely misleading to talk of *passion* as if it were the source of one's *eloquence*. If they come together, so much the better. But one is not a guarantee of the other. Our passage from the letter to Mrs. Locke makes this clear. Knox, for a moment drops his rhetoric, and we see a subconsciously self-expressive side of his character. Even so, it must frankly be admitted that such insights are comparatively rare. In the very same letter we can trace overt rhetorical control:

> Least that the rumours of our trubles truble you above measure, deare Sister, I thought good in these few words to signifie unto you, that our esperance is yit good in our God [...] (Laing VI: 100, Letter XLV).

Knox apparently knew that: 'Rumour is a pipe / Blown by surmises, jealousies, conjectures [...]' (2 *Henry* Act 4, Induction, ll. 15–16) and he was out to scupper it. The most obvious devices here are the switch from 'trubles' to 'truble' (which effectively expresses the infectious

6 Lewis, C. S., *English Literature in the Sixteenth Century*, p. 198.

7 See Jeffares, A. N., (ed.), *Poems of W. B. Yeats: A New Selection*, p. 286. The line is from 'Under Ben Bulben', V.

nature of rumour) and the counter-balancing word 'esperance' (which again seems to come from the catalogue of Romance).

At any rate, this introduction ought to give us some idea of the riches to be found in the epistles. It is without further ado that we can turn to this body of texts. The letters often begin with the standardised expression, 'une phrase de type', as Janton calls it.[8] For instance, Knox's letters to Mrs. Bowes, and others, open in the following ways (variants are italicised): 'Rycht deirly belovit Mother', (Laing III: 357, Letter I), 'Rycht *dearly* belovit Mother' (III: 343, II), 'Belovit *Sister*, efter maist hartlie commendatioun' (III: 348, III; repeated exactly, without orthographical variants, III: 352,V), 'Belovit Sister, efter *my* hartlie commendatioun' (III: 397, XXVI), 'Belovit Mother, – *With my* maist hartlie commendatioun' (IV: 218, XXVIII), 'Deirly belovit Sister in *Jesus oure Lord*' (III: 350, IV; 365, XIII), 'Deirlie belovit Sister in *our Saviour*' (III: 353, VI), 'Deirlie belovit Sister in *Jesus our Soverane*' (III: 356, VIII), 'Deirlie belovit Sister in *Jesus oure Saviour*' (III: 360, IX.2), 'Deirlie belovit Sister in *our Lord Jesus*' (III: 361, X), 'Deirlie belovit Sister in *our Saviour*' (III: 364, XII), 'Deirlie belovit Sister in *Jesus oure Lord*' (III: 365, XIII), 'Rycht deirlie belovit Sister in *oure Soverane Jesus Chryst*' (III: 369, XIV), 'Deirlie belovit Sister in *our Saviour and onlie Mediatour Jesus*' (III: 355, VII), 'Deirlie belovit Sister, in *the commoun faith of Jesus our Saviour*' (III: 394, XXIV), 'Maist deir Sister, *whome I reverence as it becumis in all godliness*' (III: 358, IX), 'Deir Mother *and Spous, unfeanidlie belovit in the bowells of oure Saviour Chryst Jesus*' (III: 369, XV) and 'Deirlie belovit Sister, *whome I no less tendir than it becumis a weak member to do another*' (III: 387, XXII). He is in all cases concerned with one of the following: heartfelt greeting, the metaphorical expression of the location of the believer in Jesus Christ, (who is simultaneously Saviour, Lord, Sovereign or sole Mediator), and with the propriety and sincerity of his conduct in writing the letter. Above, we have noted twenty variants. In some of the letters, for example XXIII (Laing III: 392–394), XXV (Laing III: 396–397) and XXVII (Laing IV: 217–218), Knox is apparently so eager to

8 Janton P., *L'homme et l'oeuvre*, p. 416.

communicate that he omits the introduction altogether, and begins *in medias res.*[9]

His conclusions too are worth exploring (variants again italicised); 'Your Sone' (Laing III: 372, Letter XV), 'Your Sone *unfeanid*' (III: 343, I), 'Your Sone, *with trubillit hart*' (III: 348, II), 'Your *Brother*' (III: 350, III), 'Your Brother *in Chryst*' (III: 352, IV), '*In greit haist*, [...] Your Brother' (III: 353, V), 'Your Brother *in Jesus Chryst*' (III: 356, VII), 'Your *Brother unfeanid*' (III: 361, IX.2), 'Your Brother *in Chryst Jesus*' (III: 365, XII), 'Your*is* to *his* power' (III: 374, XVI), 'Yours to his power' (III: 382, XIX), 'Youris *at* his power' (III: 387, XXI), '*Be youris unfeanid in Chryst*' (III: 379, XVIII) and 'Your *Brother to power*' (IV: 244, XXXIV). Again, Knox is often concerned with the spiritual location of the believer, although there is noticeably no attendant metaphorical expression. Here, although expressions of sincerity abound, they take second place to phrases emphasising the recipient's authority to command him within proscribed limits (to the glorification of Christ). We have noted fourteen variants in this instance. Sometimes he even used a pre-arranged pseudonym to sign off: 'Johne Sinclair'; 'This was his mother's surname, whilk he wrait in tyme of trubill'[10] (see Laing IV: 245).

The real value of these letters, however, is in their contents. Perhaps at this point it is necessary to say something about Mrs. Bowes's very distinctive character, since this information will help us understand why Knox had to write to her so frequently. Without any exaggeration, she might fairly be called a spiritual hypochondriac. As we saw in the introduction, (above, p. 19), Knox mentions her in an Appendix to his *An Answer to a Letter Written by James Tyrie* and there he says that she had:

> [...] a troubled conscience upon hir part, which never suffered her to rest but when she was in the company of the faithful, of whome (fra the first hearing of the word at my mouth) she judged me to be one (Laing VI: 513; see also Laing III: 333).

9 ibid., p. 416.
10 This is clearly a scribal interjection.

Thus Knox was forever being called upon by her to provide comfort and solace. A few examples from his frequent replies should give us an idea of what she was like, and of the lengths to which he would go to calm her spirit. Here, Knox is exasperated with her, since she has evidently been informing him, in solemn terms, about temptations that he believes she does not feel. It is hardly surprising that, for once, he deals with her rather testily:

> I am sure that your hart nether thristis nor desyris to invocat or mak prayer unto breid, nor unto any uthir creature [...] Allace, Sister! your imbecilitie trubillis me, that I suld knaw you sa weak that ye suld be moveit for sa small a matter (Laing III: 361, Letter X).

Or here he is assuring her that her union with Christ is inviolable (cf. Romans 11: 29 and 1 Corinthians 12: 27):

> To embrace Chryst, to refus idolatrie, to confes the truth, to love the memberis of Chrystis bodie, ar the giftis of God: thairfoir he can not repent that he hath maid you pertaker thairof (Laing III: 349–350, Letter III).

Knox is using a four-fold series of infinitive constructions ('to embrace', 'to refus', 'to confes', 'to love'), which is incantatory as well as inculcatory, in order to placate her. Or again, she has apparently suggested to him in one of her own letters that he has been lying to her all along. So troubled is she that she now doubts the trustworthiness of her most intimate companion. In response, Knox posits Satanic subterfuge, (of course), (see Revelation 12: 9, 1 Corinthians 1: 23) and says:

> That fals and leying spreit dois according to his wickit and dissavabill craft, when he wald caus you beleif that I knaw your rejectioun. Na, fals Devill! he leis: I am evin equallie certified of your electioun in Chryst as that I am that I myself preacheth Chryst to be the onlie Saviour (Laing III: 369, Letter XIV).

Knox realises the presence of Satan in terms of pneumatology ('fals and leying spreit', cf. 1 Kings 22: 22), but he is also using forceful exclamation ('fals Devill!'), and a kind of formula with which he expresses absolute truth. For Knox, the fact that he preached Christ truly, was the core, the very heart, of his existence. If that wasn't true, then nothing was. He didn't use the expression lightly, and anyone who knew *him* would know *this*. Additionally, he equates his most solemn pronunciation with his assurance of Mrs. Bowes's worthiness in the phrase: '*evin equallie* certified' (italics added; cf. Galatians 1: 11). The two adverbs lend a special weight to his remark.

However, I am not suggesting that Knox always indulged her (and this was probably the right thing to do in the circumstances. Individuals like Mrs. Bowes often want attention, which they would not otherwise get, rather than advice). Once or twice, it seems, he got rather fed up with her persistent demands on his time:

> [...] my daylie labouris must now incres, and thairfoir spair me sa mekkill as ye may. My ald maladie trubillis me sair, and na thing is mair contrarious to my helth then wrytting (Laing III: 364, Letter XI).

> Yit, Mother, depend not upon me too muche, for what am I but a wreachit synner? (Laing III: 376, Letter XVII).

In the first of these, Knox points out that he is a busy man, which, of course, is laudable, but he is still trying to duck her. In the second, he combines self-deprecation with a point of doctrine (he is a sinner), but his idea is the same in both.

This brings us to a recognition of the fact that the correspondence tells us as much about Knox as it does Mrs. Bowes. He is a counterpart to her, and *vice versa*. This finds its most engaging expression in lines like these, which deal with the prospect of Knox and she, meeting:

> Your messinger faund me in bed, efter a sair trubill and maist dolorous nyght, and sa dolour may compleane to dolour when we twa meit (Laing III: 352, Letter V).

Knox would certainly endorse the saying 'misery loves company', but he is writing here with just a touch of wry humour, and is building on the fact that, for all their complaining, he and she, both, actually *enjoy* it. Along the same lines, Thomas Hardy's wife could comment that the poet was never happier than when writing melancholy poems like 'The Darkling Thrush'.

Nor was Mrs. Bowes the only one to make mountains out of mole-hills. Knox's introduction to Letter XIII, a very accomplished work, shows him moving ever so much closer to a bombastic style (cf. Philippians 2: 1):

> Albeit I do thrist, deirlie belovit Mother, no less to sie yow than sumtymes I have thristit to sie that whilk of erthlie creaturis is maist deir unto me, yit do the daylie trubill discorage me in a part, that oure temporall meitting sall not be sa suddane as we baith require; and yit my esperance and hoip is in God, that we sall meit, evin in this lyfe, to baith oure comfortis; and thairfoir I hartlie requyre yow, in the bowells of Chryst Jesus, to be of gud comfort, and pacientlie to beir this distance of oure bodies (Laing III: 392, Letter XIII).

All this is to say that Knox longs to see his loved ones, but certain difficulties hinder him. The Bowes ladies must resign themselves to the fact that he will not be able to visit them for some time, if at all. The phrase: 'that whilk of erthlie creaturis is maist deir unto me' is as decoratively formal as, say, Macbeth's use of: 'dearest partner of greatness' (*Macbeth*, Act 1., Sc. 5., ll. 13–14). Knox might even have been capable of an *epistula amatoria*. His most striking metaphor is 'thrist' which he applies to his desire to see both women. However, he writes at a moment when his thoughts are towards Elizabeth, and when those for Marjory are in the past ('I *have* thristit [...]'). Elsewhere, he reveals that he could not remember having written to the younger woman: 'I *think* that this be the first Letter that ever I wrait to you' (Laing III: 395, Letter XXIV; italics added). This is certainly odd, but disarming, for all that.

This, then, ought to suffice as a general introduction to Knox's correspondence with his close friends. In chapter two, our analysis of *A Faithful Admonition* touched on the fact that Knox's prose was, at least in places, tentatively confessional. In these 'familiar epistles' we find, broadly speaking, three types of prose: Knox comforting Mrs. Bowes, Knox 'confessing' to Mrs. Bowes (among others) and Knox apparently *responding* to her epistolary confessions. Two of these divisions, the first and third, deserve sub-division, or at least, further clarifying comment. Knox 'comforts' Mrs. Bowes in two ways: by offering sober, even-toned religious advice on the one hand, and more authoritative exhortations on the other. When Knox responds to Mrs. Bowes's confessions, he combines self-revelatory comments with the more straight-forward advice which constitutes our second division.

When he does this, he is at his most compelling, since the rhetoric of a truly great preacher perfectly complements material which is double-edged: both confessional and consolatory. However, in what follows I hope to show that whatever Knox is about in his letters, analysis of the prose itself can often tell us more about him than he means to reveal.

We can work through the divisions exploring the kind of language which is at work to build up this picture. Take letter IV, for instance: Knox tells Mrs. Bowes that he was sitting at his book and 'contemplating Mathowis Gospell' in the 'instant moment' (Laing III: 350) that her messenger delivered her letter to him. This letter (presumably) posed spiritual dilemmas to which the very passage that he had been meditating upon (Matthew 13: 1–8, 19) offers the solutions. Knox is so impressed by the incident that he evidently considers it something of a minor miracle,[11] and, judging by his subsequent comments, he turned to a text which he apparently identifies as St. John Chrysostom's commentaries on the gospel, for further clarification and enlightenment. One might expect the text in question to be *In Evangelium Sancti Matthæi brevis enarratio, nunc primum in lucem edita* (*Homilies on Matthew*), but Pr. Wright has recently shown clearly that Knox's ultimate source was the 'Pseudo-Chrystostomian' *Opus Imperfectum in Mattheum*, perhaps in conjunction with a gospel commentary composed of catena from the Fathers.[12] But whatever his source, Knox continues:

> In reiding of this his halie judgement, your battell and dolour was befoir my eis; and as I prayit God that ye myght be assistit to the end, sa wissit I that ye had bene present with me; and even at the sam instant callit your servand, whairof I praisit my God, and addressit me to wryt efter the reiding of your letter as I might (Laing III: 351, Letter IV).

11 St. Augustine reveals a very contrary response to this type of occurrence in general, but is more favourable when referring to his Christian reading experiences; see Pine-Coffin, R. S., (tr.), *Confessions*, p. 74; Bk. 4: 3, and cf. p. 177, Bk. 8: 12.

12 I am indebted to Pr. David Wright for pointing this out to me; details can be found in his essay, 'John Knox and the Early Church Fathers'; 110–111.

Although there is no actual advice in this passage, the above lines belong to a train of thought which culminates in orthodox spiritual counsel, so we ought not to cavil. Clearly this belongs to our first division (and falls short of 'authoritative exhortation'). But it still tells us much. For example, there is emphasis on 'instant'. We remember that the 'miracle' which Knox is celebrating depended on his reading the gospel at the 'instant' Mrs. Bowes's letter arrived. Knox, then, carries over the language which makes the miracle *what it is*. Moreover, the phrase 'sa wissit I' with its first person pronoun situated after the verb, stands out in contrast with the more common constructions ('I prayit', I praisit' and 'I myght'). Even in the sixteenth century, this was an elevated way of talking. We might think it pompous, but for Knox it was probably a (subconscious) means of expressing his own dignity. Today, telephone conversations have an uncanny knack of stimulating changes in register. There are subtle codes at work in these letters, there is no doubt.

If we step back from the actual words on the page, it is also possible to assess the general effect of this passage on its reader (and we may have to think ourselves, as far as we may, into a frame of mind which is consistent with sixteenth century religious thought). Mrs. Bowes, we know, was by all accounts a very foolish woman, but even she must have got the impression from Knox's observations that, if she is diligent in Bible-study, she too will reach that plane of spiritual knowledge which posits the hand of God in all things, no matter how trivial, and subsequently find consolation. It is because Knox thinks along these lines that he can respond to her letter as he does.

We can trace some of the above features recurring in other letters, and one of these in particular has great potential for Knoxian apologists:

> The verie instant hour that youre letteris was presentit unto me, was I talking of yow, be reassone that thrie honest pure wemen wer cum to me, and was compleanying thair greit infirmitie, and wes schawing unto me the greit assaultis of the enemy, and I was opinnying the cause and commodities thereof, whereby all our ëis wypit at anis [...] (Laing III: 379–380, Letter XVIII.2).

In *The Literature of Scotland*, Pr. Watson comments on: 'Knox's cantankerous views about the female sex',[13] but, as I suggested in my general introduction, we should be wary of assuming that Knox *always* viewed the fairer sex in such a way (even if *The First Blast* provides some evidence to confirm this interpretation). Although this epistle probably pre-dates *The First Blast* by four or five years,[14] the way in which godly 'wemen' gravitate towards Knox is remarkable (and would they do so if he were consistently a boorish bear?) Pr. Gordon Donaldson's observation is, I think, closer to the truth: 'It would certainly not be an overstatement to say that Knox was not indifferent to women or to say that in his own way he was also attractive to women'.[15]

Cynics among us might view the passage with suspicion, but as Knox says to Mrs. Bowes: 'I wryt na lie unto yow, but the verie treuth of oure communicatioun what tyme I ressavit youre letteris' (Laing III: 380, Letter XVIII.2). Nor is there any trace of hyperbole in statements like: 'all our eis wypit [wept] at anis'. I would not go so far as to say that Knox was emotionally weak (that would be *lèse-majesté*) but he *is* known to have wept, publicly, on more than one occasion; (more of this, however, when we look at *The Historie*; see below, p. 211, or Laing I: 198).

The stylistic features which impress us now are past-progressive tenses: 'was compleanying', 'wes schawing' and 'was opinnying', and in one case, the past-progressive links up with the kind of inversion we met in Letter IV: 'was I talking'. Knox in fact seems to be suggesting that religious experience is sometimes a matter of gradual illumination. As with the experience recorded in Letter IV, (Laing III: 350–352), Knox finds a miracle in this encounter, but when he mentions the 'verie *instant hour*', (italics added), divine intervention, at least initially, seems rather less credible (but see again Laing III: 380; Letter XVIII.2).

Knox's advice is not just quirky and codified. It is often full of memorable, even charming, insights. Letters VII and XX can provide

13 Watson, R., *The Literature of Scotland*, pp. 95–96.

14 See Ridley, J., *John Knox*, p. 452.

15 Donaldson, G., 'Knox the Man', 29.

the evidence of this. The former ponders the theological problem of why the Elect are allowed to suffer:

> [...] sumtyme He dois turne away his face apeirandlie evin from His elect, and than ar thai in anguische and cair; but mercifulliere turnis He unto thame, and gevis gladnes and consolatioun whilk, albeit it remane but the twinkling of an eie, yit is it the arlis-penny of his eternall presence. Rejois, Sister, and continew (Laing III: 356, Letter VII).

Here we can imagine Knox at first speaking *sotto voce* and then warming up to his task of encouraging Mrs. Bowes to believe in the certainty of her salvation. And there is also a deep tenderness about the lines. The image of a 'twinkling [...] eie' is from 1 Corinthians 15: 52 where it precedes the Last Trumpet on Judgement Day, but the 'arlis-penny' which is from a financial register (not frequent in Knox), most probably derives from another source. As Laing says it is: 'a piece of money given in earnest of a bargain or mutual agreement'.[16] The use of such a figure is surely pleasing (just as it is in, say, Burns's poem 'My Tocher's the Jewel').[17] Knox's final sentence seems to be 'invested' (to borrow and adapt his metaphor) with a new significance. It is full of reassurance and encouragement. This section from Letter VII is also noteworthy in other ways. For example, Knox uses an adverb *in the comparative degree*, (which, therefore, shares some of the properties of an adjective, and which is almost totally unexpected): 'but *mercifulliere* turnis He unto thame'. (George Buchanan does something similar in that memorable piece of contorted prose *The Chamæleon*: 'for yis monstre being vnder coverture [of a] manis figure, may *easeliar* endommage [...]')[18] (italics added, all instances). Knox is not known for his use of neologisms, but this (perhaps together with 'monstriferous' in *The First Blast*; see Laing IV: 401), is one of them.

Letter XX contains one passage at least which is even richer than the above. Towards the conclusion of the letter he tells Mrs. Bowes:

16 See Laing III: 356, n. (1).

17 See Kinsley, J., (ed.), *Poems and Songs of Robert Burns*, vol. II: p. 605, no. 345.

18 See Brown, P. H., (ed.), *Vernacular Writings of George Buchanan*, p. 43.

> Abyd, Mother, the tyme of harvest, befoir whilk must neidis goe the cald of winter, the temperat and unstabill spring, and the fervent heit of summer: to be plane, ye must neidis saw with teiris or ye reap with gladnes; syn must in yow ga befoir justice, deth befoir lyfe, weaknes befoir strength, unstabillnes befoir stabilitie, and bitterness befoir comfort (Laing III: 385, Letter XX).

This is perhaps one of the gentlest expressions of the Christian message that any reader will ever encounter. It is even more attractive than our samples from John Johnsone's work (above, pp. 43–45). Again we meet the image of 'harvest' time (first encountered in *John Knox to the Congregation at Berwick* and drawn from Matthew's gospel). We may indeed, then, have another (veiled) apocalyptic reference. But the antithetical structure of this section seems to suggest Genesis 8: 22 ('Nether shall sowynge tyme and harvest, calde and heate, summer and wynter, daye and night ceasse, so longe as the earthe endureth'), Proverbs 25: 13 ('Like as the wynter coole in the harvest, so is a faithfull messenger to him that sent him'), Psalms 126: 5 ('they that sowe in teeres, shal reepe in ioye') and perhaps 1 Corinthians 15: 43 ('It is sowne in corrupcion and shal ryse in uncorrupcion, it is sowne in dishonoure and shal ryse in glory, it is sowne in weakness and shal ryse in power') (*Coverdale*) (cf. also Joshua 3: 15, 2 Samuel 23: 3, Jeremiah 8: 20, 50: 16, 51: 30, Isaiah 33: 6, Zechariah 14: 8, Psalms 74: 7, Solomon's Song 2: 1, 2 Peter 3: 10, 12). It may have been passages like this, more than any in *The Historie*, that Carlyle had in mind when he said of Knox: 'it must be a little mind that cannot see that he was a poet – one of the wild Saxon kind, full of deep religious melody that sounds like Cathedral music'.[19]

More than this, the above lines contain language at its most functional. Knox uses disjunction ('Abyd, Mother, the tyme of […]'), and antonyms ('cald/heit', 'saw/reap', 'syn/justice', 'weaknes/strength', 'unstabillnes/stabilitie' and 'bitterness/comfort'), all of which revolve around the same preposition ('befoir'). Additionally, there is some (pardonable) deception, since the phrase 'to be plane' really leads into a passage which is, in terms of imagery and structure, no simpler. But

19 Carlyle, T., *Lectures on the History of Literature*, p. 157.

even St. Paul approved of deceiving people into the truth (see 1 Corinthians 9: 20).

Competent and subtle homiletics continue in Letters XXVI and XIII. Knox expounds the story of Jacob wrestling with an angel in Genesis 33: 24–32:

> The Angell touchit the marie or principall synow of Jacobis thigh, whairby he become crukit, and did halt, to witness unto him, that it was not be his awn power that sa lang he had resistit. The thigh, ye knaw, is the principall part that susteanis man to stand; and thairfoir being maymit or crukit in that part, he is unabill to wersell: And yit (a matter greatlie to be wonderit,) Jacob wald not suffer the Angell to depart whill he gave unto him the benedictioun, (a response befoir written,) and this was done at the spring of the morning. Heirby is signifeit [...] (Laing III: 399, Letter XXVI).

As well as explaining all the symbolic meanings of the narrative, Knox poses his reader (presumably Mrs. Bowes) a problem, which he pretends to wonder at, while all along he knows the solution. And Mrs. Bowes gets from Dr. Knox an anatomy lesson into the bargain. Furthermore, Knox is using a conversational tone ('ye knaw' marks this clearly) which very effectively narrows the gap between teacher and pupil. Pr. Jack is obviously right when he notes: 'Knox appears to have known that the orator who talked down to his audience or bored them with extended grave analysis would soon have no audience to bore or condescend to [...]'.[20] Pr. Janton makes the same point (perhaps just a little more memorably) when he draws attention to a reference in Leonard Cox's *Arte or Crafte of Rhetoryke*:

> [...] for lack of invencion and order with due elocucion, great tediousnes is engendred [...] by occasion whereof the speker is many times ere he have ended his tale, either left almost aloon to his no little confusion, or else (which is a lyke rebuke to him) the audience falleth for werynes [...] *fast on slepe*[21] (italics added).

One of the most impressive pieces of advice to Mrs. Bowes (in our first category) comes in Letter XIII. Knox has to address two

20 Jack, R. D. S., 'The Prose of John Knox', 248–249.

21 Janton, P., 'John Knox and Literature', 426.

issues in this text. Mrs. Bowes has written to tell him that she finds herself doubting the existence of a Saviour and she has apparently heard about the disturbing case of Francis Spira (although it is still too early for Nathaniel Bacon's account of Spira's life, published in the early seventeenth century). As Laing notes, Spira was: 'a lawyer of Padua, whose case is well known: He died under great remorse of conscience, in consequence of having, by terror of the Inquisition, abjured the Protestant faith'.[22] The way Knox destroys these (silly) notions reveals him as a true master of dialectic art. As we saw in Letter XIV, the devil gets the blame for all things, but Knox does more than knock *him* on the head. He tells Mrs. Bowes:

> Do ye not espy ye are not within his girne; for gif ye wer, to what purpois suld he trubill you? He is a roaring lyon, seiking whome he may devour; whome he hes devourit alredie, he seikis na mair. Befoir he trubillit yow, that thair is not a Saviour, and now he affirmis that ye salbe lyke to Francis Spera, wha denyit Chrystis doctrine; doith not the ane of theis tentations mak the uthir a lie, sa that ye may espy thame baith to be leis? (Laing III: 368, Letter XIII).

W. Stanford Reid admires Knox's: 'mixture of scriptural principles [the reference which forms the core of the argument here is, of course, to 1 Peter 5: 8] and [the] hard lowland common sense that he manifested',[23] but like most of the Reformer's biographers, Reid passes over literary merit. Knox takes both of Mrs. Bowes's complaints, has a good look at them, decides (rightly) that they are mutually contradictory, and subsequently sets them against each other. In this 'pincer' movement he creates *reductio ad impossibile*. (One cannot help but think of John Bunyan, who often did something similar with apparently contradictory scriptural passages. Bunyan was forever matching them off in great imaginary controversies, until one emerged the victor. In Knox's passage, however, *both* propositions are vanquished, each by the other).

But Knox did not always need elaborate methods to make his points in spiritual matters. He was also capable of lightning strokes. Take Letter XXII; this provides us with fine examples of what Pr.

22 See Laing III: 367, n. (2).
23 Reid, W. S., *Trumpeter of God*, p. 80.

Jack would call 'sudden incongruity'.[24] Knox talks of those desirous of salvation, who cry out:

> "Brethren, what shall we do?" Whilk wordis declair thame to be lambis weak, yea deid, and yit desyrous to be fed. And lyke unto theis ar all this day, that [...] unfeanidlie thristis to knaw the treuth and obey the same (Laing III: 388, Letter XXII).

The image of a dead lamb, which is, nevertheless, still desirous to be fed, is a striking one, and yet, given Knox's theological standpoint and religious vocabulary, one can understand how he arrived at it: by *imaginative creative extension*. But it also trips up any reader who may be mentally snoozing (Mrs. Bowes would not be doing so; she, no doubt, was too absorbed in assimilating the information which, after all, meant a lot to her), and returns him or her to the complex issues under discussion. Knox then goes on to clarify things by indulging in a more conventional similitude (which, incidentally, also guarantees his own job):

> For lyke as scheip hes na judgement to descerne betwix the hailsum and noysum gers, (but be the regement of thai pastour,) sa hath not the flock of Chryst wisdome to avoid sectis and heresies, (yea, abominatioun and idolatrie,) but by Godis Word, whilk aucht purelie and sinceirlie to sound fra the pastouris mouth (Laing III: 389, Letter XXII).

Although the imagery is consonant with that which went previously, no-one could have any difficulty seeing Knox's point in this instance.

Or in Letter XXXI (which is not to Mrs. Bowes) he reveals a mastery of alliteration when he is requested to arbitrate on the topic of proper 'Apparell of Wemen' (Laing IV: 225), by some latter-day Daughters of Jerusalem (Luke 23: 28) in Edinburgh. It:

> [...] is verie difficill and dangerous to apoynt any certantie, leist in sa doing we either restrane Christiane libertie, or else loose the brydill too far to the folische fantassie of facill flesche. For gif we sall condempne [...] And gif we say [...] (Laing IV: 225–226, Letter XXXI).

24 Jack, R. D. S., (ed.), *Scottish Prose 1550–1770*, p. 21.

David Murison calls this manoeuvre: 'a masterpiece of tact and diplomacy, or, if you like, wilines, a quality which was to stand him in good stead later in many a weightier matter'.[25] And, in the same letter, for the first time in this chapter, we run across moods which anticipate *The Historie*:

> Thair be sum whilk will not be sene altogether ignorant of Godis Word, and yit, nevertheless, armit as it wer with the exampill of the multitude in apparell, ar mair lyke to courtesinis than to grave matronis (Laing IV: 226, Letter XXXI).

(cf. Laing II: 368, or p. 205, below). It is in this chapter more than any other that we can see formative strands of Knox's major work emerging ever so gradually, and we shall meet similar signs later on; below, pp. 145–149).

When Knox is addressing his close friends (apart from the Bowes women), he is just as compelling. Sometimes the prose even takes on the persuasiveness of the devil (although this is part of Knox's plan). In Letter XXX, to a 'Sister', we can see this:

> I knaw that not onlie the Divill in his awn face, wirking into the sonis of unbelief, sall stryve and contend, as aganist that whilk is the subversioun of his haill kingdome; but also sall he cleith him self in ane Angel of lycht, and cum to yow under the colour of freindschip (as in ane uthir letter I have tuichit), and sall allure and solist yow be persuasionis of the naturall man, that ye neid not to be sa strait and sa seveir, for God is mercifull; and thairfoir that ye may beir with the tyme, for avoyding danger and displeasure baith to your self and to uthiris. Yea, perchance he salbe so bold, that he [...] (Laing IV: 223, Letter XXX).

For all concerned, Satan is obviously a very insidious character, tireless and super-subtle in his machinations. Knox, in fact, pictures him persuading this particular lady that (like Lady Macbeth), to beguile the time by looking like the time (*Macbeth*, Act 1., Sc. 5., ll. 61–62) is perfectly acceptable. According to Knox, Satan also clothes himself, allures, solicits and generally tempts the 'naturall man'. Knox also thinks in terms of kingdoms and he introduces earthly and heavenly

25 Murison, D., 'Knox the Writer', 38.

figures ('sonis of unbelief' and 'Angel of lycht'). Alliteration, however, like that of Letter XXXI, is the most impressive feature, and here it has a more definite purpose. Prevalent 's' sounds come in when Knox is outlining the devil's most fiendish designs, and these have a relaxing effect. But Knox immediately alters the effect by bringing in plosive 'd's ('danger and displeasure') to create dissonance and to warn his reader that temptations are only superficially attractive. It is with full appreciation of his own skills that Knox later observes: 'Be yow assured, deir Sister, that all theis persuasionis ar nothing ellis but sweit songis [...] to bring your saule asleip' (Laing IV: 224). 'Sleeping', obviously, is not just a metaphor.

I said earlier that Knox's conventional spiritual guidance fell into two divisions; advice and exhortation. We have now fully explored the first of these. The second involves a more familiar picture of Knox. No one can deny that passages like the following sound a different note to that which we have just heard. In Letter II, for example, Knox tells Mrs. Bowes:

> But, O, Mother! thocht na erthlie creature suld be offendit with yow, yit feir ye the presence and offence of Him, who, present in all places, searcheth the very hart and reynis; whais indignatioun, anis kendillit agains the inobedient, (and na syn mair inflameth his wraith than idolatrie doith,) na creatur in heavin nor in earth, that onlie is creatur, is abill to appeas the same (Laing III: 346, Letter II).

I have taken this out of its context, and indeed, Knox goes on immediately to comfort his reader, after warning her to flee idolatry as from eternal death. Even so, it is clear that Knox is 'thundering'. He draws primarily on Psalms 7: 9 ('manteyne the iuste, thou rightous God, that triest the very hertes & the reynes') and Hebrews 4: 13 ('ye worde of God is a iudger of the thoughtes & intentes of the hert, neither is there any creature invisible in ye sight of him', *Coverdale*). Moreover, the idea of 'kindling' or 'inflaming' God's wrath is a common Biblical notion. Just as the Deity is present in all places, He is represented in nearly every clause of Knox's warning ('Him', 'who', 'whais', 'his', 'the same' are appositives of God). For Mrs. Bowes, Knox makes His presence compellingly real.

Similarly in Letter VIII we can see Knox adopting vehement language. This time, he is in a very apocalyptic vein:

> O miserable, unthankfull, and maist mischevous warld! what salbe thy condempnatioun, when He, that hes sa oft gentillie provokit ye to obey his treuth, sall cum in his glorie, to punish thy contempt? Wha sall hyd thee frome the presence of that lyoun whome thou did persecut in everie age? What sall excuse thee, that sa tiranfullie hath sched the bluid of sic as faithfullie labourit to bring thee from blind ignorance and idolatrie, when that stubburne contempneris sall cry, "Mountanis fall on us, and hyd us fra the presence of the Lord!" (Laing III: 357, Letter VIII).

As before, Knox goes on to reassure Mrs. Bowes that, in contrast: 'Deir Sister, *we* salbe placeit in maist securitie with the Lamb, in whais blud we are purgeit' (Laing III: 357, italics added; cf. Hebrews 9: 22, 1 John 1: 7, Revelation 5: 9, 7: 14, 12: 11).

For anyone interested in apocalyptic typologies this is a splendid passage. The framework constitutes *interrogatio* and the central image is that of Christ's Second Coming as a 'lyoun' (the enthusiasm and zeal may even remind us of Dunbar's 'Surrexit Dominus de Sepulchro'). We saw previously that Knox borrowed the 'roaring lion' from 1 Peter and there it referred to Satan (above, p. 132). Here, then, we have a complete contrast. Of course, Knox may be thinking of Revelation 5: 5: 'the lyon which is off the trybe of Iuda, ye rote of David' (*Coverdale*), the only one who is worthy to open the Book of Seven Seals, and indeed, Knox actually quotes Revelation 6: 16 directly.

For all this, it would be wrong to give the impression that the stern tones in the above selections are really typical of Knox's letters. We ought to move on to more prominent features; to the confessional aspects of the prose. If we are still astonished at the idea of Knox being partial to 'confession', what is to come should dispel disbelief entirely, but it should perhaps be noted that, in this respect, Reformation theology transferred emphasis away from an obsession with particular individual sins, and involved a more radical concern for inescapable original sin, which only Christ could cure and which is harder to confess.

First of all, we might consider a passage where Knox actually uses the term 'confess' himself. Here he is telling Mrs. Locke about his experiences in Geneva:

> In other places, I *confess* Chryst to be trewlie preachit; but maneris and religioun so sinceirlie reformat, I have not yit sene [...] besydes; Sathan I *confess* rageth aganis the ane and the other [...] (Laing IV: 240, Letter XXXIII; italics added).

We cannot and should not make much of this, but surely his use must signify something about his frame of mind and natural associations between language and subject matter.

On other occasions, we can observe him revealing intimate truths in the presence of God. Two instances come to mind. He tells Mrs. Bowes and Mrs. Locke respectively:

> *God I tak to recorde in my conscience, that* nane is this day within the Realme of Ingland, with whome I wald mair gladlie speik (onlie sche whome God hath offirit unto me, and commandit me to lufe as my awn flesche exceptit,) than with you (Laing III: 370, Letter XV; italics added).

> *God I tak to record in my conscience, that* or I suld knaw yow so far convictit as to bow to idolatrie and daylie confirme the same be your presence, I rather wold chuse unto your company to beg my breid [...] (Laing IV: 219, Letter XXIX; italics added).

(cf. 2 Corinthians 1: 23, Philippians 1: 8). We meet the same sort of type-phrase as those in Knox's introductions,[26] but he combines with them the 'truth-guarantee' of comparisons such as: 'evin [...] as that I am that I myself preacheth Chryst to be the onlie Saviour' (see Letter XIV; above, pp. 123-124). Despite the surface similarities between the two sections, they in fact reflect different sides of related situations. In XV Knox is expressing what holds he and his correspondent together, in XXIX he describes what would keep them apart. And for good measure he adds: 'I rather wold chuse [...]' (cf. 'I had rather be a dog [...] / Than such a Roman', *Julius Caesar*, Act. 4., Sc. 3, ll. 27–28, 'I had rather be a toad / And live upon the vapour of a dungeon', *Othello*, Act 3, Sc. 3, ll. 274–275, Psalms 109: 10).

26 For further uses of these type phrases, see Laing III: 133.

Real and deep confession, however, only comes into play when Knox says things like this. He finds himself stung by his own preaching (!), and concludes:

> But now, albeit that I never lack the presence and plane image of my awn wreachit infirmitie, yit seing syn sa manifestlie abound in al estaitis, I am compellit to thounder out the threattyngis of God aganis obstinat rebellaris; in doing whairof (albeit as God knaweth I am no malicious nor obtstinat synner) I sumtymes am woundit, knawing my self criminall and giltie in many, yea in all (malicious obstinacie laid asyd,) thingis that in utheris I reprehend. Judge not, Mother, that I wrait theis thingis debassing myself uther wayis than I am; na, I am wors than my pen can express […] And thus in conclusioun, thair is na vyce repugnying to Godis halie will, expressit in his law, whairwith my hart is not infectit (Laing III: 338–339, Letter I).

Modern Scots, who are on occasion accustomed to thinking of Knox as a 'whited wall' (Acts 23: 3), must here accept the fact that he fully recognised canting, self-righteous hypocrisy as the most insidious sign of complete corruption that there is. Of course, loud professions of humility (after the fashion of Uriah Heep) may themselves fit into the arsenal of pompous clap-trap that quasi-pious individuals exhibit, but this is certainly not so in Knox's case. David Murison is quite right when he selects this passage as evidence that Knox was a 'sincere and thoughtful preacher'.[27]

What makes these lines so interesting is the fact that they reveal Knox caught between his (necessarily high) religious and moral standards, and the realities of his own being. He may well be a Reformed preacher, professionally schooled in theology, but when it comes right down to it, he is no different from anybody else, he says, except for the fact that his vocation compels him to reprehend others. For what it's worth, Knox would never have considered himself a burning and shining light, to anyone, or to any place. He is surely writing with a deep concern to be properly understood (after all he is making quite a difficult point) but also, in a state of some agitation. He *means* what he says; he is not 'debassing' himself 'uther wayis' than he is, and he is constantly reminded of his frailty.

27 Murison, D., 'Knox the Writer', 37.

Most of these things are evidenced in the structure and syntax of the text. For example, the frequency of parentheses at times makes the letter rather hard to follow (and that is why Dr. Murison in his quotation leaves some of it out). The phrase: 'malicious obstinacie laid asyd', coming as it does between 'all' and 'thingis', may be tentatively labelled as awkward, but there is no doubt that it is introduced spontaneously, at the most crucial point of the argument. The other non-essential: 'albeit as God knaweth, I am no malicious nor obstinat synner', together with 'obstinat rebellaris', allows us to conclude that Knox was rather concerned with 'malice' and 'obstinacy'. He wants, in fact, to suggest that he is guilty of neither. (Mary Stewart, one feels, would not have agreed with him, to be sure. Perhaps she would have found in these remarks one of the richest unconscious ironies that he ever achieved. Indeed, intransigence is a charge which modern minds must level at Knox, justifiably I think, but let us not forget that what we regard as tolerant and accommodating would often be seen as weak and puny in the sixteenth century).

At any rate, we seem to have linguistic evidence of definite psychological patterns here. Just as Shakespeare's Edmund in *King Lear* is obsessed with 'baseness' and 'bastardy' (see *King Lear*, Act 1, Sc. 2., ll. 1–22), so too is Knox with the subjects outlined above. A good parallel in religious literature is perhaps Paul's Galatians, one of his most hurried and mentally revealing texts. Other engaging features are Knox's use of the 'thounder' metaphor, and we meet with judicial, legal terminology ('criminall', 'giltie', 'judge') as opposed to contractual, which we discussed earlier. However, it is obvious that the whole piece is charged with vitality and is highly attractive to any unbiased literary critic.

We have seen how Knox the preacher impinges upon, and affects the character of, Knox the revealing letter-writer. But he was also, as he thought, a prophet. When prophecy begins to mingle with confession we get what is, in anyone's terms, a quite extraordinary mixture. Letter XXIX to Mrs. Locke and Mrs. Hickman, contains something of this mixture. After detailing his relationship with certain women, Knox asks them if they recall how, once he had established a bond of trust with them, he felt it necessary to reveal certain secret prophetic truths:

> But when I considder and call to mynd how God, I dout not, brocht us in sic familiar acquaintance [...] and how my hart was opinit and compellit in your presence to be mair plane in suche matteris as efter hath cum to pass, then ever I was to any. For ye remember, as I suppois, how efter great angusche and sorrow of hart, whilk many dayis I susteanit, at last I was compellit, with weiping tearis, to oppin unto you that whilk almaist no man culd haif beleiffit. Ye remember my judgement, and what communicatioun we had upon the same (Laing IV: 220, Letter XXIX).

In the colophon, Knox further defines himself as: 'Your Brother, that schewit this visioun unto yow *when no such thing was suspectit*' (Laing IV: 222; italics added). We saw the author of *The Complaynt of Scotland* using prophecy, (above, pp. 57–58), but not like this. In fact *The Complaynt* stands more in line with the type of prediction found in the public letters and Knox's *The Historie*. Here, however, we get a much clearer insight into Knox's mind. If we are to be rigorously and ruthlessly objective, we must allow for the possibility that Knox the prophet was the product only of his own mythopoeic self-image (although we should also bear in mind that a belief in genuinely predictive prophecy is not at all naïve; St. Paul calls it one of the gifts of the Spirit [1 Corinthians 13: 2 and elsewhere] and it is a major strand of thought in the gospels as well as the *Old Testament*). But in this instance, we do not need to address the issue of prophecy in itself; rather, we should explore how Knox uses the concept as a factor working within his personal relationships. Obviously he did not want to reveal his terrible visions to the ladies for fear that it would upset them, but he felt himself 'compellit' (by God, presumably) to do so. He ended up weeping, yet again, but the women probably came away with a sense of his magnetic and charismatic qualities. When he wrote this letter, sometime later, he may have been worried that the dazzling impression which he had made was fading away, so he took the opportunity to remind them of it. And he now has the 'proof' of what had: 'efter hath cum to pass' (Laing IV: 220) to boot. 'Almaist no man culd haif beleiffit', but Knox believed, and true enough, he was no ordinary man.

This brings us on to his most explicitly situation-conditioned, confessional prose. Take for example the letter in which Knox tells Mrs. Bowes how he approached the brother of her husband, Robert

Bowes, to ask for his permission, which he didn't get, to marry Marjory Bowes:

> Amangis utheris his maist unpleasing words, whill that I was about to have declarit my hart in the haill matter, he said, "Away with youre rethoricall reassonis! for I will not be persuadit with thame." God knawis, I did use no rethorick nor collourit speach; but wald haif spokin the treuth, and that in maist simpill maner [...] I am not a gud oratour in my awn caus; but what he wald not be content to heir of me, God sall declair to him a day till his displeasure, unles he repent (Laing III: 378, Letter XVIII).

In his biographical analysis of this encounter, Edwin Muir selected the words: 'I am not a gud oratour in my awn caus' as evidence that Knox was being less than wholly truthful, and went on to contrast them with the brilliant rhetoric of Knox's *A Vindication of the Doctrine that the Sacrifice of the Mass is Idolatry* (published a few years before) in which he does speak in his own cause.[28] But Muir is perhaps overlooking the fact that, in at least one sense, there *is* no contradiction. To denounce the use of rhetoric is the supreme sign of the rhetorican. For example, we cannot take Mark Anthony at face value when he says: 'I am no orator as Brutus is / But, as you know me all, a plain, blunt man' (*Julius Caesar*, Act 3., Sc. 2, ll. 217–218). Robert Bowes, in fact, is a lot closer to that cynical, worldly-wise old politician Caius Cassius, who says of Anthony's words: 'they rob the Hybla bees / And leave them honeyless' (Act 5, Sc. 1, ll. 33–34). Similarly, Bowes will not be persuaded by Knox's 'rethoricall reassonis'. Moreover, this is almost the first time that we see Knox using reported speech and he was to go on to develop this technique a great deal more, as *The Historie* shows. He winds up his presentation of Mr. Bowes by accusing him of wickedness, but certainly Knox himself was much stung by the encounter, and he lashes out.

We see Knox, as it were 'on the edge', again, in texts such as Letter XXXVI, in which he ponders the reasons why he fled the country at the succession of Mary Tudor. He exploits *ante occupatio*

28 Muir, E., *John Knox: Portrait of a Calvinist*, p. 49; see also Laing III: 47, 52, 57.

to anticipate putative counter-arguments and to answer them well in advance. Thus *preoccupatio* gives way to *prosopopoeia*:[29]

> Gif any object, I follow not the counsell whilk I gif to uthiris, for my fleing the contrey declaireth my feir; I answer, I bind na man to my exampill; and yit I trust to God that I do not expressedlie against the Word, whilk God uttereth be me. Gif the lufe of this lyfe, or the feir of corporall deith, causit me to deny the knawin veritie, [...] then wo unto me for ever, for I wer nathing but a tratour to Chryst and his religioun (Laing IV: 247, Letter XXXVI).

David Murison selects a similar letter as evidence that Knox could display: 'the frankness of a man in an agonising re-appraisal of himself'[30] and indeed Knox does not hesitate to pronounce his own condemnation if he were to abandon Christ. He has not backed himself into a corner, but he has come perilously close to it. The whole thing rests, however, on a series of hypotheses ('Gif any [...]' 'Gif the [...]') and self-deprecation comes in ('for I wer nathing but [...]') only if we grant the conditions. The mathematicians, of course, will tell us that the more variables we introduce into a hypothesis, the less chance the conclusion has of coming into play.

Elsewhere, Knox went further, by facing up to the possibility of martyrdom (and, in fact, flinching from it):

> As for my self, albeit the extremitie suld now aprehend me, it is not cumin unlukit for. But allace! I feir that yit I be not rype, nor abill to glorifie Chryst be my death, but what lacketh now, God sall performe in his awn tyme (Laing III: 357–358, Letter VIII).

We should not lose sight of the fact that, as a devout sixteenth century Protestant, in pre-Reformation times, Knox himself was in some senses a 'victim'. In *The Historie*, he tells us that he entered St. Andrews Castle because he was: 'weareid of removing from place to place', and 'be reassone of the *persecutioun* that came upoun him [...]' (Laing I: 185; italics added). Indeed, Knox wrote the above letter in dangerous times and his fear is not ill-founded. Evidently, he was becoming quite used to having fear as a constant companion (martyrdom 'is not cumin

29 See Sonnino, L. A., *A Handbook*, p. 30 and p. 54.
30 Murison, D., 'Knox the Writer', 38.

unlukit for'). Knox does end on a positive note of trust in the Deity which is truly impressive under the circumstances.

Knox, we know, was never called upon to make the supreme sacrifice, mainly because of his own shrewd or commonsense manoeuvres. On one occasion, though, he did take a risk against the better judgement which had probably saved his life in the past. The occasion, of course, was the journey to Scotland in 1555. The impression that this has made on his private letters is far different from that on the open epistles. After all his fears and misgivings, he got, on arrival, what seems to have been the surprise of his life! Letters XXVII and XXVIII reflect his enthusiasm when he found many Scots sympathetically disposed towards Protestantism:

> Albeit my jurney toward Scotland, belovit Mother, was maist contrarious to my awn judgement, befoir I did interpryse the same, yit this day I prais God for thame wha was the cause externall of my resort to theis quarteris; [...] Gif I had not sene it with my eyis, in my awn contrey, I culd not have beleivit it (Laing IV: 217, Letter XXVII).

In fact, it seems that Mrs. Bowes herself was one of the 'cause[s] externall' that persuaded him to make the trip, and now he marvels that God should have chosen to work through her. Certainly the prose captures signs of a disbelief which has been overcome, but it is not long before remorse works its way in. Knox subsequently speaks of his exile as the 'den' of his 'awin ease' (Laing IV: 217). On the whole, however, the sense of triumph is over-powering. Knox even indulges in an almost romantic death-wish:

> The trumpet blew the ald sound thrie dayis together, till privat houssis of indifferent largenes culd not conteane the voice of it [...] O! sueit war the death that suld follow sic fourtie dayis in Edinbrugh, as heir I have had thrie [...] (Laing IV: 218, Letter XXVIII).

As we saw in chapter two, Knox's joy was to be short-lived, but these two letters surely testify to his enormous capacity for emotional self-expression.

Only one division within the 'familiar epistles' now remains: that of combined counsel and confession. The combination of the two features gives the writing both an intimacy and an added edge to the counsel. One might say that Knox places the coping stone on his former efforts. He emphasises the special relationship with Mrs. Bowes in Letter XXII, describes himself, and explains his motivation to her:

> […] knawing youre sair anguischis, and the rare noumber of thame that can rychtlie lay the medicine to the wound, my conscience prickit with verie pitie, compellit me to remane, contrarie to my determinat purpois (Laing III: 391, Letter XXII).

Like the Psalmist (Psalms 73: 21) Knox is 'pricked to ye reins' (*Great Bible*) by his compassion, and he presents himself as a doctor (metaphorically speaking, but our earlier analogy was not far off; above, p. 131). In Letter XXI, the link between the facets is more evident, with Knox setting himself up as an exemplar, or if you like, travelling ahead of Mrs. Bowes down the spiritual paths, that he might return and warn her of the dangers which lie in any particular direction (cf. Job 6: 4, Psalms 39: 1, Lamentations 3: 15).

> I drank, schortlie efter this flattrie of myself, a cupe of contra poysone, the bitterness whairof doith yit sa remane in my breist […] The lyke, Mother, mycht have cumin to yow, gif the secreit brydill of afflictioun did not refrane […] (Laing III: 387, Letter XXI).

Drinking from the bitter cup, of course has its precedents in Isaiah and Christ's passion narrative, but the main thing to note here is how Knox deflects Mrs. Bowes from making the same mistakes as he.

However, perhaps the most remarkable of all the combinations is the one which we find in Letter III. He asks Mrs. Bowes:

> Call to your mynd what I did standing at the copburd at Anwik: in verie deid I thought that na creature had bene temptit as I wes. And when that I heard proceid fra your mouth the verie same wordis that he trubillis me with, I did wonder, and fra my hart lament your sair trubill, knawing in my selfe the dolour thairof. And na uthir thing, deir Sister, meant I […] (Laing III: 350, Letter III).

Gordon Donaldson laments that this is 'all too cryptic'[31] and W. Stanford Reid points out at length why it is wrong to build innuendos from

31 Donaldson, G., 'Knox the Man', 18.

the material; 'from the fact that Mrs. Bowes was considerably older than Knox and had already borne many children, we must conclude that by this time she had lost most of her physical attractiveness'.[32] There are certainly no sexual connotations, then. Indeed, together with Reid, one is inclined to think that Knox is alluding to something altogether mundane, although it obviously signified much to reader and writer. We are reading someone else's mail, after all; we should anticipate that it will contain topics meaningful only to the correspondents.

However, in its context as part of the letter, this undoubtedly banal event, whatever it may have been (and we will never know), has become part of a *reasoning* process. With the same skill that we saw in Letter XIII, (above, p. 125), Knox tracks down and fuses together two strands of individual experience (his and hers), and with this fusion, forges his argument. Repeated items like 'trubill/trubillis' tell us something too. For Knox, without trouble there will be no triumph. This is perhaps the Christian tenet which he most took to heart (cf. for instance 2 Timothy 2: 9).

When we turn from the 'familiar epistles' to the letters relating to the Reformation and to Knox's later life, we must look for another, underlying but unifying principle, since the confessional and pastoral concerns are much less pronounced, if they are there at all. Three striking strands of material emerge from these texts; material which constitutes the *first draft* of passages in *The Historie*; which *supplements The Historie*, and finally which *exceeds the bounds* of *The Historie*. Take the first of these strands. Letter IV to Mrs. Locke is perhaps the best of all the examples which could be cited:

> In the meane time, came the Bishop of Sanct Andrewes to the towne, accompanied with a great band of warriours, and gave a strait commandement, that no preaching sould be made by me, who was both brunt in figure and horned, assuring the Lords, that if they suffered me to preache, that twelve hacquebuttis sould light upoun my nose at once. (O burning charitie of a bloodie bishop!) (Laing VI: 25, Letter IV).

32 Reid, W. S., *Trumpeter of God*, p. 81.

When composing Book II of *The Historie*, probably completed by the end of the same year (1559, that is), Knox used the same approach and humour, but we get a much more involved, vigorous and interesting version:

> The Bishope, hearing of Reformatioun to be maid in his Cathedrall Churche, thoght tyme to sturr, or ellis never; and thairfoir assembled his collegis and confederat fellowis, besydis his uther freindis, and came to the town upoun the Setterday at night, accumpanyed with a hundreth spearis, of mynd to have stopped Johne Knox to have preached. The two Lordis and gentilmen foirsaid war onlie accumpanyed with thair quyet housholdis, and thairfoir was the suddane cuming of the Bischope the more fearfull; for than was the Quene and hir Frenchmen departed from Sanct Johnestoun, and war lying in Falkland, within tuelf myles of Sanctandrois; and the town at that tyme had not gevin professioun of Christ, and thairfoir could nocht the Lordis be assured of thair freindschip. Consultatioun being had, many war of mynd that the preaching should be delayed for that day, and especiallie that Johne Knox should nocht preache; for that did the Bischope affirme that he wald nocht suffer, considdering that by his commandiment the picture of the said Johne was befoir brunt. He willed, thairfoir, ane honest gentillman, Robert Colville of Cleishe, to say to the Lordis, "That in case Johne Knox presented him selff to the preaching place, in his town and principall Churche, he should gar him be saluted with a dosane of culveringis, quherof the most parte should lyght upoun his nose". After long deliberatioun, the said Johne was called [...] (Laing I: 347–348).

In his marginal note, Knox cannot resist the summarising observation that this was: 'the Bishope his good mynde toward Johne Knox' which is a gentler, but still ironic re-statement of: 'O burning charitie of a bloodie bishop!' and one of Knox's best jokes. In fact Knox *did* go on to preach and: 'the Bishope advertisshed heirof' told the Regent and 'did so kendill hir choler', even if 'the luif was verrie cold betuix thame' (Laing I: 350). Readers of *The Historie* will recognise a connection between this narrative and the reconciliation of Cardinal Beaton and Archbishop Dunbar in Book I (Laing I: 145; see also p. 286, below). Knox, however, emerged from the maelstrom of activity which ensued with his nose very much still intact and decidedly un-punctured.

It is undeniable that the letter contains the seeds of a very fine story (which would fall somewhere between 'dramatic narrative' and ‘merry tale’ according to categories which I shall adopt later; below, pp. 255–309). Of course, there are minor differences in detail between the two versions. In *The Historie* version, Knox replaces ‘in the meane time’ with a non-restrictive and active line ‘hearing of Reformation to be maid, thoght tyme to sturr’, and he adds a statement of sardonic finality ‘or ellis never’. The ‘great band of warriours’ are further classified as ‘collegis and confederat fellowis’, which makes some of them, at least, sound like criminals. Knoxian revision between texts continues. For example, in *The Historie* he also tells readers that it was by the Bishop’s commandment that he had been outlawed and publicly disgraced. Neither is the participation of ‘ane honest gentill-man’, Robert Colville of Cleish, mentioned in the letter, and the ‘twelve hacquebuttis’ which are to light upon Knox’s nose ‘at once’, become ‘a dosane of culveringis’ which, for the ‘most parte’ will pierce his most prominent facial feature. The image of the spears flying through the air and descending in unison is indeed a delightfully comical spectacle, in both texts.

Then there is the strand which *adds* to our knowledge of events in *The Historie*. Consider Letter XCVI, written as late as July 1571. Knox writes to the now Reformed Church in Edinburgh, and advises:

> Be not ye sclandered at the multitude of them that have joyned handes with impietie: “For if they had bene of us (as Sanct Johne sayeth) they had remaned with us.” But now this their defection doeth planelie declare, that when they were with us, they were but as corrupted humoures within the body, which behoved to be expelled furthe, before the body coulde convalesce and come to perfection againe. Lament their fall, but follow not their trade [...] (Laing VI: 603, Letter XCVI).

In Book I of *The Historie*, Knox includes a narrative about one of his fellow-prisoners in the galleys, James Balfour, who at the time of writing, had become a ‘principall mysgyder’ of Scotland (Laing I: 206), and who had apparently abandoned Knox’s version of Reformed, Evangelical Christianity. The way in which Knox deals with Balfour is fundamentally the same as the way he deals with apostates in the above letter:

> This we wryte, because we have heard that the said Maister James alledgeis, that he was never of this our religioun; but that he was brought up in Martine's opinioun of the Sacrament, and tharefoir he can nott communicat with us. But his awin conscience, and two hundreth witness besydes, know that he lyes; and that he was ane of the cheaff, (yf he had not bein after Coppis,) that wold have gevin his lyef, yf men mycht credite his wordis, for defence of the doctrin that the said Johnne Knox tawght. But albeit, that those that never war of us, (as none of Monquhanye's sones have schawin thame selfis to be,) departe from us, it is no great wonder; for it is propir and naturall that the children follow the father; and lett the godly levar of that rase and progeny be schawen; for yf in thame be eather fear of God, or luf of vertew, farther then the present commoditie persuades thame, men of judgement ar deceaved (Laing I: 202).

In this case, *The Historie* text precedes the letter, but Knox (like David Lindsay) was never a man to let a good idea go to waste. Moreover, in one sense at least, revision has taken place in the letter. Knox quotes and acknowledges as his source the scriptural passage (1 John 2: 18–19) which only forms part of an allusion in his earlier writing. The verses read: 'Litle children, it is nowe the laste houre, and (as ye haue herde that Antechrist shal come) euen now are ther many become Antechrists. They went out from us, but they were not of us, for yf they had bene of us, they wolde no doubte haue contynued with us' (*Coverdale*). (John's epistles provide many passages which are useful for dealing with secessionists; ironically however, European Catholic polemicists used these verses to stigmatise the Protestant defectors themselves).

Of course, there is much more at work in *The Historie* section: the intimate reference to 'Martine' (Bucer, not Luther), the appeal to witnesses and to godly readers, but the letter brings in a developed metaphor ('humoures within the body') and is more positive in that it envisages the 'body' (of Christ: the Church) returning to health.

Sometimes the correspondence noticeably and definitely exceeds *The Historie* in dramatic sweep. The finest example of this is in Letter XXXIV to Mrs. Locke, which relates to a period immediately prior to September, 1559:

> We doe nothing but goe about Jericho, blowing with trumpets, as God giveth strenth, hoping victorie by his power alone. Christ Jesus is preached even in Edinburgh, and his blessed sacraments rightlie ministred in all congregatiouns

> where the ministrie is established; and they be these: – Edinburgh, Sanct Andrewes, Dundie, Sanct Johnstoun, Brechin, Montrose, Stirline, Aire. And now, Christ Jesus is begunne to be preached upon the south borders, nixt unto you, in Jedburgh and Kelso, so that the trumpet soundeth over all, blessed be our God. We laike labourers, alas! (Laing VI: 78, Letter XXXIV).

E. G. Rupp finds 'top secret gossip' in these lines[33], but, really, there is hardly anything muted about Knox's tones. He is not whispering, but shouting from the roof-tops. Had this passage worked its way into *The Historie*, however, it would have had great potential, perhaps with the story of Joshua and the Siege of Jericho (see Joshua 6) combining with a use of Matthew 9: 37: 'ye *hervest* is greate but ye *labourers are few*; therefore praye the LORDE of the *hervest* to send for labourers into his *harvest*' (italics added). (We need not point out the significance of the image here). The most important thing about the lines is, however, their use of place-names (and if this does not seem especially significant here, it will in a later chapter; below, pp. 227–228).

Then, there are passages which draw upon comparatively recent traditions, which *The Historie*, for all its continuity with previous Scottish cultural trends, does not. In a letter to Thomas Randolph, written in mid-1564 (in his own hand) when Knox was much occupied with the composition of his major work, he says:

> Rollettis tydingis ar as yit buried in the breastis of two within this realme, butt Maddye telleht [sic] ws many newes: "The mess shall up, the Bischope of Glaskier and Abbot of Dunfermling come as ambassadouris from the Generall Counsall, my Lord Bothwell shall follow, with power to putt in execution whatsoever is demanded, and our Soveraine will have done; and then shall Knox and his preaching be pulled by the eares, etc." Thus with ws ravis Maddye every day; but heirupon I greatlie pans not (Laing VI: 541, Letter LXXVIII).

The short satirical poems known as 'Maddie's Lamentatioun', 'Maddie's Proclamatioun' and 'The Bird in The Cage' written by Robert Sempill and published by Lekprevik in 1570, also make use of the popular fun-figure: 'Maddie prioress of the Kaill-market', and Richard Bannatyne's

33 Rupp, E. G., 'The Europe of John Knox', 12.

Memorials mention a close relative: Maddie 'of our fisch merkatt'.[34] As in the narrative dealing with the Archbishop of St. Andrews and his spearmen, Knox pictures features of his physiognomy as the object of violence. Again, he is quick to assure his reader that he is nothing moved by the prospect (although he probably was).

The later epistles also provide us with much information about the relationship between Knox, and William Maitland of Lethington, who was, according to Knox himself: 'a man of good learnyng, and of scharpe witt and reassonying' (Laing I: 247), whatever else. Lethington, of course, has gone down in history as the chamæleon of Buchanan's short prose piece, and Knox seems to have combined what amounts to a deep respect for his shrewdness with just as deep a mistrust of his person. In the penultimate chapter, we shall be looking at their major confrontation, as outlined in Knox's *The Historie*, (below, pp. 251–254), but as I said, the epistles provide interesting information about yet another, and later, conflict between the two. In 1572, it seems, Lethington wrote to the Session of Edinburgh, complaining:

> It is cum to our eires be credible report, that your minister, Johne Knoxe, asweill publict in his sermondis as utherwayis, hes slanderit me as ane atheist, and enemie to all religione, in direct speiches, that I have plainlie spocken in the Castell, that "thair is nather heavin nor hell," and that "thai ar thingis devysed to fray bairnes," with uther sic language tending to the lyke effect, unworthie of Christiane earis to be rehersit in the hearing of men. Which wordis, befoir God, never at ony tyme proceidit from my mouth [...] (Laing VI: 635, Letter CIX).

Like Ninian Winzet, Lethington must have had contacts with Knox's congregation[35] for him to be able to report such material (if it is

34 See Laing VI: 541, n. (1).

35 Winzet often refers to comments made by Knox during his sermons. One of the most curious observations Winzet makes is that: 'A sair batell aganis Longinus struk John Knox in his preching of St. Johnes Euangel and againis thir examples and siclyke'; see Hewison, J. K., (ed.), *Winzet's Works*, vols. I: p. 78 and II: pp. 34–35.

accurate) and Lethington goes on to desire the Session not to receive Knox's every word: 'as oracles; and knaw that he is bot a man subject to vanitie; and that many tymes dois utter his owin passiones' (Laing VI: 635). By the time Knox received news of this challenge, he was too ill to respond by letter, and we owe to Richard Bannatyne's *Memorials* the detailed account of how he reacted. Knox apparently cited Lethington's 'workis' in troubling the commonwealth and the Kirk as evidence, for the whole world, of the Secretary's atheism (rather too general a response, perhaps), and:

> Whair the bill said that "Johne Knox was a man subject to vanitie, and all is not oracles that comes out of his mouth.": Whairto the said Mr. Knox ansueris, That he confessit he was but a most vile creature and a wretched man; nochttheles the thingis that he hes spoken sould be fund als trew as these oracles that have bene spocken be ony of the servandis of God befoir [...] (Laing VI: 639).

As always, Knox seized the opportunity to express his own unworthiness, and on the strength of this, lends weight to the re-affirmation of his prophetic capacity. Obviously, he retained his oracular hat right to the very end.

Such, then, are Knox's private letters. They are, to be sure, deeply attractive and fascinating works; indeed, many of them are minor literary masterpieces in their own right, and abiding testimony to Knox's skill, patience, shrewdness, compassion and candour. Furthermore, a three-fold structure emerges from the 'familiar epistles' which shows Knox at his most compelling when he unites two strands of thought, but also remarkably varied throughout. The later letters are less self-expressive, but their chief value lies in their intertextuality with *The Historie*, whether they contain first-drafts or supplementary material. In nearly every case, however, they help clarify our understanding of Knox and his literary methods. But the one really extraordinary thing which emerges from this chapter is the fact that so *many* literary critics have forgone the opportunity to examine the riches of Knox's writing in this field.

Chapter Four: Knox's Theological Works

Nearly all of Knox's critics conclude that, as a theologian, he was not an original thinker. In the epilogue to his *Theology and Revolution in the Scottish Reformation*, Richard Greaves put the matter succinctly, but he is careful enough to present a fair and balanced judgement:

> [...] Knox displayed virtually no ability to develop dramatically fresh interpretations, nor will he ever be accorded a place among the theologians of the first rank in Western Civilization. Yet he was a man of no mean ability, and as the principal formulator of the theology, liturgy and polity of the Reformed Kirk in Scotland, he drew upon a wide variety of sources, ranging from native Scottish elements, to Lutheran, Reformed and English traditions.[1]

For what they are worth to the literary critic, these statements are true and one should probably make them before going any further. But it need hardly be said that theology is not our business. Like C. S. Lewis, in his *English Literature in the Sixteenth Century*, we must concern ourselves with it only insofar as it affects our understanding of literature, and Knox's literary personality.

This chapter, then, analyses how Knox's literary and rhetorical machinery enables him to make his theological points, but we shall also keep an eye open to detect material which falls under our concepts of Knoxian 'intertextuality' and psychological revelation. On examining the theological division, straight away the first of these concepts becomes relevant. In his most lengthy theological treatise, *On Predestination*, (1560), Knox combines the thought of John Bale's *The Image of bothe Churches*[2] with that of Augustine's *De Civitate Dei* and copious Biblical references (Daniel 4: 35, Isaiah 31: 2, 32: 6, Hosea 6: 8, Psalms 141: 4, Acts 8: 32, 1 Peter 2: 8, Revelation 2: 9, 14: 9, 1 John 3: 10, Matthew 7: 23, 23: 33), so that two cities become two armies:

1 Greaves, R., *Theology and Revolution in the Scottish Reformation*, p. 217.
2 See Firth, K. R., *The Apocalyptic Tradition*, pp. 40–47.

> The one of these armies; is called the Church of God; the elect spouse of Christ Jesus; the shepe appointed to slaughter, the kingly priesthode; the sonnes of God, and the people redeemed: by ancient writers it is termed the Citie of God. The other is called the Synagogue of Satan, the church malignant; cruell, deceatfull and blood-thirstie wolves; progenie of vipers; sonnes of the Devill; workers of iniquitie; and such as worship the beast and his image (Laing V: 413).

However, if we believe Book I of *The Historie*, Knox did not arrive at these conclusions after a long period of thought, but had held them even before the beginning of his preaching career. In chapter two, (above, p. 69), we touched on the fact that his clash with Dean John Annand constituted what was probably his first literary exercise (at that time Knox was still too timid to indulge in an open, oral debate). It is in this challenge to Annand, as early as 1547, that we find him formulating the above concepts and using exactly the same kind of imagery and structure:

> We must discerne the Immaculat spouse of Jesus Christ, frome the Mother of confusioun, spirituall Babylon, least that imprudentlie we embrase a harlote instead of the cheast spous; yea, to speake it in plaine wordes, least that we submitt ourselves to Sathan, thinking that we submitt our selves to Jesus Christ. For, as your Romane Kirk, as it is now corrupted, and the authoritie thairof, wherein standis the hope of your victorie, I no more dowbt but that it is the synagog of Sathan, and the head thairof, called the Pape, to be that man of syne, of whome the Apostle speakis, then that I doubt that Jesus Christ sufferred by the procurement of the visible Kirk of Hierusalem (Laing I: 188–189).

(cf. 2 Thessalonians 2: 3). And this is not the only other instance. In the presence of Mary Stewart in 1561 (see Laing II: 283–284) and in *The Confession of Faith*, (1560), (Laing II: 109–112), we find Knox forwarding much the same argument. When confronted with the above similarities, experienced textual critics might legitimately suspect that *The Historie* passage, written in 1566 but referring to events twenty years earlier, contains a 'backward-projection' of the 1560 material, and indeed, we should not dismiss the theory too lightly given the fact that Knox would not be averse to the idea that he was ahead of his time, and generally much cleverer than everybody else. But we can see other ideas, such as his belief in the legitimacy of resistance, developing over a period of years, so there is no reason to suppose that Knox, in this instance, deliberately short-circuited the process. In any case, Dr. John Durkan has shown that the figure of Martin Luther looms large behind even the earliest of Knox's controversies.[3] (And to appreciate just how vituperative Luther could be, one need only consult pamphlets such as the one *Wider das Papstumm zu Rom, vom Teufel gestiftet*). Anyhow, here we have evidence that the 'relatedness' of Knox's various prose-works, spills over from the private letters and *The Historie*, to the theological division and *The Historie*.

But this is not all, in general terms, that we can glean from the present category. Take the preface to Knox's *A Sermon on Isaiah xxvi, 13–21, Preached in St.Giles Church, Edinburgh, 19th August, 1565*, (1565); this contains what is certainly the longest existing statement of how Knox perceived his own vocation, and this makes it extremely interesting for critics who want to discover what motivated him. Knox says:

> Wonder not, Christian Reader, that of al my studye and travayle within the Scriptures of God these twentye years, I have set forth nothing in exponing anye portione of Scripture, except this onely rude and indigest Sermone preached by me in the publicke audience of the Church of Edinbrough, the day and yeare above mencioned. That I did not in writ communicat my judgement upon the Scriptures, I have ever thought and yet thinke my selfe to have most just reason. For considering my selfe rather cald of my God to instruct the ignorant, comfort the sorrowfull, confirme the weake, and rebuke the proud, by tong and livelye voyce in these most corrupt dayes, than to compose bokes for the age to come, seeing that so much is written (and that by men of most singular condition), and yet so little well observed; I decreed to containe my selfe within the bondes of that vocation, whereunto I founde my selfe especially called (Laing VI: 229).

It is Knox himself who brings us to the recognition that unlike other major reformers, he refrained from dedicating his life to scriptural commentaries and doctrinal works (as, say, Calvin did).[4] Against this, however, we must balance Pierre Janton's assertion that, in spite of

3 Durkan, J., 'The Cultural Background to the Scottish Reformation'; 304, n. (165).

4 See Firth, K. R., *The Apocalyptic Tradition*, p. 126.

Knox's disclaimer, 'no British reformer of that period published so much in the vernacular'.[5] Perhaps it is at this point that we can fully appreciate Knox's comments concerning his vocation in his *An Epistle to the Congregation of the Castle of St. Andrews, With a Brief Summary of Balnaves on Justification by Faith* (above, p. 73).

Approaching from a rather different angle, David Murison cites this passage as evidence that Knox: 'never claimed to be a literary man at all'[6] but we need not, in fact, take Knox's comments as literally as Dr. Murison does. After all, by the 19th of August 1565, when Knox wrote the above preface, he had certainly completed Book II of *The Historie*. More probably, the passage expresses a train of Knoxian thought, designed to refute charges such as those Ninian Winzet had brought before him in 1562–63:

> [Authority] […] wes geuin to zow in the sacrament of ordinatioun be auctoritie of preisthed. Quhilk auctoritie geue ye esteme as nochtis, be reason it wes geuin zow (as ze speik) be ane papiste bischope, and thairfor renunceis it, and seikis ane uther ordinatioun of secularis, – it followis consequentlie that ze (quhilk God forbid) sulde renunce your baptism also, geuin to zow be ane papist preist […][7]

In the light of charges like this, Knox had to respond, that like John the Baptist, or even Christ Himself, he was 'especially called'. Winzet replied that an especial calling was always accompanied by miracles (although the Baptist's wasn't); where were Knox's miracles? Knox made a reply of sorts from the pulpit at St. Giles, but thereafter, he let the matter pass, probably not, as C. S. Lewis has said, because he: 'was learning the shabbiest of all *arcanum imperii* – never answer'[8] but because, by that time, Winzet was in exile. Only a very stupid opponent would re-open a controversy which had been terminated so finally by circumstance[9].

So far, then, this general introduction to the theological material has established two main points; in Knox's case, writing theology and

5 Janton, P., 'John Knox and Literature', 426.

6 Murison, D., 'Knox the Writer', 33.

7 Hewison, J. K., (ed.), *Winzet's Works*, vol. I: p. 21.

8 Lewis, C. S., *English Literature in the Sixteenth Century*, p. 202.

9 See Watt, H., *John Knox in Controversy*, p. 47.

writing literature are not mutually exclusive; often quite the reverse is true. Moreover, texts like the Isaiah sermon allow us vivid and unique insights into Knox's self-view, such as we do not get from the admonitory public or even the private epistles.

We have seen Knox at work revising his own thoughts and also adapting them to suit the changing situation. In this chapter we can see Knox revising the work of another contemporary theologian, Henry Balnaves. Balnaves is one of those curious but crucial figures of the Scottish Reformation. He is mentioned frequently in the early part of *The Historie* (see, for example, Laing I: 70, 99, 102, 114–116, 182) and was one of those who tried, and failed, in an attempt to impose the role of Preacher upon Knox. Knox tells how, in St. Andrews Castle, Balnaves (among others) approached and challenged him:

> Thei of the place, but especiallie Maister Henry Balnaves and Johne Rowght, preachear, perceaving the maner of his doctrin, begane earnestlie to travaill with him, that he wold tack the preaching place upoun him. But he utterlie refuissed, alledgeing "That he wold nott rynne whare God had nott called him;" meaning, that he wold do nothing without a lauchful vocatioun (Laing I: 186).

Working on the basis of one of his taunts, we can conclude that Ninian Winzet evidently knew that Knox carried Wishart's double-handed sword;[10] (above, p. 77) but it is less probable that he knew of the subsequent charge to Knox, perhaps devised by David Lindsay, which Knox did find 'lauchful' (this forms an important topic in chapter five;[11] below, pp. 211–213).

But Knox's most important reference to Balnaves (at least in the present context) comes when he tells us of Balnaves's experiences as a fellow-prisoner of Knox. Balnaves was taken to Rouen for a more subtle interrogation than others:

> Maister Henry Balnaves, who was in the Castell of Rowane, was most sharplie assaulted of all; for because he was judged learned, (as he was, and is, in deid,) tharefoir learned men war appointed to trawall with him, with whome he had many conflictes, but God so ever assisted him, that thei departed confounded, and he, by the power of Goddis Spreit, remaned constant in the trewth and

10 See Hewison, J. K., (ed.), *Winzet's Works*, vol. I: pp. 18–20.

11 See Reid, W. S., *Trumpeter of God*, p. 226.

> profession of the same, without any wavering or declynyng to idolatrie. In the preasone he wrait a most profitable Treatise on Justificatioun, and of the workis and conversatioun of a justified man: but how it is suppressed, we know nott (Laing I: 226–227).

In fact, Balnaves's text was not made generally available until after Knox's death, when it was printed by Thomas Vautrollier in 1584. Indeed, the 'epistle dedicatory' to this edition contains a remarkable story of how the lost text was discovered by Richard Bannatyne: 'in the towne of Hormistoune [...] in the handes of a child, as it were serving to the childe to playe with him' (Laing III: 434).

Knox tells us how he received the work when he was in chains in a galley named *Nostre Dame* and how it afforded him: 'great confort and consolation' (Laing III: 8). In fact, Knox decided to summarise the treatise, for the use of his brethren. In what follows we get a rare insight into Knox's thoughts as an editor (although as E. G. Rupp points out: 'he does scant justice to Balnaves's remarkable work').[12]

> I thought expedient it should be digested in chapters; and to the better memory of the Reader, the contents of every chapter proponed briefly unto them, with certaine annotations, to the more instruction of the simple, in the margent. And also that an Epitome of the same work should be shortly collected, wee have likewise digested the same in chapters [...] Which thing I have done, as imbecilitie of ingine and incommoditie of place would permit [...] (Laing III: 8–9).

Prose like this reminds one very much of, say, John Gau's introduction and concluding epistle to the reader and nobles in *The Richt Vay*,[13] in which he outlines what his text is about, what it is for, and how to use it, and of Adam Bell's introduction to *The Roit or Quheill of Tyme*. Knox, moreover, is very much concerned to aid the reader's memory, with marginal notes for greater clarification of difficult points and with a careful technique of selection which preserves salient details in a palatable form. We are now in a position to assess exactly what sort of an editor Knox was, by comparing the original

12 Rupp, E. G., 'The Europe of John Knox', 7.

13 Mitchell, A. F., (ed.), *The Richt Vay*, pp. 7–8, pp. 103–109.

work with his version of it; and this analysis ought not to be disparaged, since its results *do* tell us something.

Balnaves, in his Twentieth Chapter, writes:

> Here is a cleare solution to all the objections of workes, made by the adversaries of faith: for, seing the Apostle saith, "It is impossible to please God without faith;" where then are the works which preceede faith, and move God to give grace and favour, (which ye call *De Congruo*). And then ye worke of your own strength and power, as yee say, the workes which deserve remission of sinnes and everlasting life; yea, not only sufficient to your selfe, but also superaboundant to save others (which yee call *De condigno, et opera supererogationis*) (Laing III: 504).

> The Scriptures are plaine against your false superstitions and sophisticall argumentes: concluding that neither workes preceeding nor following faith have entres in making of a wicked man just, nor yet may save you. It is written, "All which is not of faith is sinne." (Laing III: 504–505).

Balnaves's technique and his argumentative skills are matters to which I shall return. First of all, we shall concern ourselves with Knox's 'sommarie' of this particular section. He writes:

> And that proveth Paull, saying, "Without faith it is impossible to please God:" and also, "All which is not of faith is sin." Whereof it is plaine, that Sophistes alledging that workes preceeding faith deserve the grace of God *de congruo*, say as much as Sin deserveth the grace of God: for all workes preceeding faith, is Sinne (Laing III: 22).

Knox's job, here, of course, is to condense; to select the kernel of the original and to shed the rest, but he has actually done more than this. For example, Balnaves places a strong, initial emphasis on clarity ('Here is a cleare solution'), an emphasis which he reinforces in the second paragraph ('The scriptures are plaine against [...]'). Indeed, the latter instance sets up a contrast or opposition, with the scriptures on one side and 'false superstitions and sophisticall arguments' on the other. Knox cuts the double emphasis and turns it into a single one 'Whereof it is plaine [...]'. He takes Balnaves's two scriptural examples ('It is impossible to please God without faith', Hebrews 11: 6, and 'All which is not faith is sinne', Romans 14: 23, *Coverdale*) which occur quite far apart from each other, and juxtaposes them more closely. This is in line with *synonymia/paraphrasis*, whereby 'thoughts of a similar content' are grouped together for greater emphasis.[14] Significantly (for Knox), he dispenses with Balnaves's oppositions and changes 'sophisticall argumentes' to a mere mention of 'Sophistes'. Balnaves is addressing a putative adversary, who presumably argues from the Catholic point of view; ('ye', 'your', and 'you' invoke the personality of the opponent). Knox edits this feature because the purpose of his revised text is more edificatory than refutatory. His anticipated audience, after all, is Protestant. Balnaves makes good use of scholastic Latin ('*De Congruo*' and '*De Condigno* [...]' etc.) and *gradatio/concatenatio* to build up to the point where he introduces his own argument. Knox retains only vestiges of the Latin, and concludes with a contradiction; sin cannot deserve God's grace. He was to do much the same thing in a later letter to Mrs. Bowes: 'And na mair can God deny his mercie and grace to sic as asketh, than he can ceas to be God' (Laing III: 374, Letter XVI). He has performed his task well.

Not only does Knox revise the work of a fellow theologian, he translates the work of a contemporary, though continental, historian, in *On Predestination*, which we have already touched on (above, pp. 26–27). The historian in question is, of course, John Sleidan, and it is to Knox's version of his work that we now turn. One may, perhaps, be puzzled as to how such material found its way into our theological category, but the translation actually forms part of Knox's refutation of anabaptism, prevalent in the treatise. It outlines what the less radical reformers thought of the anabaptists' apparently outrageous behavior, and hence, discredits them. But the translation is of far greater significance to our understanding of Knox's *The Historie*. (Sleidan's history, in fact, went on to become a popular university text-book. James Melvill for instance recalls how 'Mr. Piter Blackburn, a guid man' taught at St. Andrews 'the Historie, with the twa lights thairof, Chronologie and Chirographie, out of Sleidan, Menarthes and Melanchthon'.[15] Furthermore, Milton mentions Sleidan

14 Sonnino, L. A., *A Handbook*, p. 116.

15 Pitcairn, R., (ed.), *The Autobiography and Diary of Mr. James Melvill*, pp. 48–49.

in *An Apology for Smectymnuus*, and elsewhere). Knox, indeed, had other models, and this we know from Buchanan:

> as to maister knoks his historie is in hys freindis handis, and thai ar in consultation to mitigat sum part of the acerbite of certaine wordis and sum taintis quhair in he has followit to muche sum of your inglis writaris as M. Hal *et suppilatorem eius Graftone*, & c [...][16]

The allusion of course is to Edward Hall's *The Union of the Noble and Illustre Famelies Lancastre and York* (Hall's *Chronicle*) and Richard Grafton's continuation, but we should not overlook the possible influence of more ancient works such as the histories of Tacitus or Sallust. For all this, the influence of Sleidan on Knox has been generally passed over. Here, and in later chapters, we examine his influence. As E. G. Rupp points out, Sleidan's work contains: 'an account of the decline and fall of Thomas Müntzer, the radical reformer of Saxony, who was a leader in the Thuringian sector of the Peasant war' and who 'was executed by the Princes after the Catastrophe of Frankenhausen in the summer of 1525'.[17] (It was this revolt, incidentally, that led Luther to write his ferocious work *Against the Murderous and Thieving Hordes of Peasants*, and for Luther, Müntzer was 'the Satan of Alstedt'.)[18] Sleidan describes one of Müntzer's atrocities in the following terms. The style is particularly terse:

> *Sleidan's Version*
> Missus antea fuerat ad ipsos adolescens quidam nobili genere natus. Hunc Muncerus, contra militiæ morem, contraque ius gentium interfecerat. Eo facto magis exacerbati Principes, comittendi prælii dant signum, & copias instruunt.[19]

Knox's translation of this is almost exactly contemporaneous with a complete version of Sleidan's work, made by a certain John Dawes, and entitled *A Famous Chronicle of our Time called Sleidan's Com-*

16 Hume Brown, P., (ed.), *Vernacular Writings of George Buchanan*, p. 58.
17 Rupp, E. G., 'The Europe of John Knox', 15.
18 See Bainton, R., *Here I Stand: A Biography of Martin Luther*, p. 263. Luther, in turn, was derided as 'Dr. Easy-Chair' and 'Dr. Pussyfoot', p. 262.
19 Sleidan, J., *Commentariorum de Statu Religionis et Republicæ*, p. 67.

mentaries, (1560). A comparison of the two translations is illuminating:

> *Knox's Version*
> But before this, a certen yong man, of noble birth, was sent unto them, whom Muncer (contrary to the lawes of armes, and to the custom of any nation) slew; wherwith the Princes were so provoked, that they blew their trompettes to batell, and set their men in arraye (Laing V: 430).

> *Dawes's Version*
> Ther was sent vnto them before a noble yong man: whom Muncer (against the lawes of Armes) had slayne, wherewith the Princes being more displeased caused the trompettes to sounde to the battle & set their men in order.[20]

The commentaries went through two editions, one in 1555 and one in 1559. The texts are identical, but the later version contains summarising marginal notes. The earlier text does not, at least in the editions that I have seen. Knox had access only to the text of 1555.[21] Dawes, conceivably, could have had access to both. Thus, it is all the more significant, that Knox, independent of the 1559 text, notes in passing that these events are symptomatic of 'the Anabaptistes great mercie' (Laing V: 430). Dawes's marginal note concerns itself only with: 'a messenger slaine against the Lawe of Armes', following the marginal 'Legatus contra gentium cæsus' of the 1559 edition.

The relative merits of the two translations are not to be overlooked, but first, attention should be drawn to the striking similarities between Knox's version of Sleidan and the following passage from Book II of *The Historie*. Knox tells how the house of one Patrick Murray: 'a man fervent in religioun' (Laing I: 345), was destroyed during the siege of St. Johnstone, and he records the Queen Regent's putative response:

> All man eschaped, except the sone of the said Patrik, a boy of ten or tuelf yearis of aige, who being slayne, was had to the Quenis presence. Bot sche understanding whose sone he was, said in mokage, "It is a pitie it chanced on the sone, and nocht on the father; bot seing that so it chanced, me can nocht be

20 Dawes, J., *A Famous Chronicle*, f. lvii.
21 See Firth, K. R., *The Apocalyptic Tradition*, p. 127, n. (44). Knox's *On Predestination* was actually completed by 1558.

against fortune." This was hir happie entress to Sanct Johnestoun, and the great zealle sche tendeth to justice (Laing I: 345).[22]

The powerful irony of the two Knox passages is identical (if we allow the marginal note to the former), and he may well have recalled the Sleidan work when he was writing. Sleidan's sense of injustice is perhaps the most compelling aspect of his passage, and he makes his lines all the more inflammatory by stressing that the victim was young, noble and slain against international custom, for no legitimate military reason. All of these points come out in Knox's translation of Sleidan and some of them in *The Historie* narrative. Dawes's version is less successful, but only Knox consistently presents devastatingly scathing material.

Knox's translation is, without doubt, stylistically superior to Dawes's. It is in the closing sections (my text) that this becomes apparent. Knox's: 'wherewith the Princes were so provoked, that they blew their trompettes to batell' is much better than the truly awkward 'wherewith the Princes being more displeased caused the trompettes to sound to the battel'. Knox gets his information across in a more direct, even relaxed, manner, without the jerky rhythms ('to sounde to the battel') we find in Dawes. One very curious similarity between the two translations, however, emerges (although its significance, if it has any, lies outside this study). So far as I can see, Sleidan does not actually mention trumpets ('tubæ'); his 'commitendi prælii dant signum' denotes the sign for battle. We have known, since chapter two at least, that trumpets were among Knox's favourite things! Indeed, the 'trumpet' becomes a highly appropriate metaphor for the Reformer's religious and political denunciations.

To both Knox and Sleidan (together with the Lutherans), Müntzer's extravagances were symptomatic of the fulfilment of Divine prophecy: 'There shal many come under my name, and saye, I am Christ, & shal deceave many: But when ye shal heare the noyse of warres, be not ye afrayed; for so it must be: but ye end is not yet' (Mark 6: 13, *Coverdale*). To Knox, Müntzer, as much as Cardinal David Beaton, is

22 See also Knox's letter to Mrs. Locke; 23/06/1559, Laing VI: 24, 'When children were slaine, she did but smile, *excusing* the fact by *chance of fortune*' (italics added). Knox is actually saying the *opposite* of this in *The Historie*!

a limb of Antichrist, which God will lop off, according to His ultimate plan. To make interesting reading of all this, a degree of irony is useful, since it allows both the author and reader a chance to appreciate, and be a part of, the secret plan.[23] (It need hardly be said, however, that the Reformation historians always did this with the advantage of hindsight; if Knox is to be accused of 'reading-back' in his *The Historie*, it is here he must answer the charge).

Quite an exquisite irony, then, works it sway into Sleidan's text, and Knox learned from it. Here is Sleidan's description of one of Müntzer's irresponsible companions, who bears the somewhat comical name of 'Phifer' ('Phiferus Munceri socius'):

> *Sleidan*
> Socius erat ei consiliorum omnium quidam insigni præditus audacia, Phiferus, qui somniis nocturnisque spectris plurimum tribuebat: ac interalia tum forte iactabat, per quietam se vidisse quodam in stabulo maximam vim copiamque murium, quos fugasset omneis. Hoc sic accipiebat, a Deo sibi esse mandatum, ut sumptis armis & eductis copiis, nobilitatem omnem exturbaret.[24]

Again, both Knox and Dawes have versions of this narrative:

> *Knox*
> He had a companion of mervelous audacitie who was of all his counsell, whose name was Phifer. This man attributed much to dreames and visions of the night; and amongest other thinges, he chanced to boast that he saw in his slepe, in a certen stable, a mervelous great multitude of mice, and that he did drive them all away. By which dreame he understode that God commanded him to take his armour, and go furth with an armie to destroy all the nobilitie (Laing V: 425).

> *Dawes*
> He had of his counsell one Phifer, a bold and a desperate felow, which was much given to dreames and visions in the nighte who dreamed that he saw in a certeine stable, an innumerable hoste of myse, which he put to flight al: This toke he, as yat God had commaunded him to lead forth his armie against the Nobilitie, & to scatter them […][25]

23 James Melvill understood this as well as Knox or Sleidan; see Reid, D., 'Writing History: Buchanan and the Two James Melvills', 430.

24 Sleidan, J., *Commentariorum de Statu Religionis et Republicæ*, p. 66.

25 Dawes, J., *A Famous Chronicle*, f. lv.

The characterisation in the three versions is acidic and deeply telling. Sleidan achieves his subtle critique of absurd behaviour almost without effort; he steps back and has a cold look at 'Phifer' and the 'fellow' more-or-less condemns himself. Satirists seldom find such easy prey. In a later chapter, we shall see that Knox did not find Cardinal Beaton so accommodating (below, p. 288). In *The Historie*, the closest Knox comes to letting ludicrous action condemn itself is with the following:

> [...] from glowmyng thei come to schouldering; frome schouldering, thei go to buffetis, and from dry blawes, by neffis and neffelling; and then for cheriteis saik, thei crye, *Dispersit dedit pauperibus* [...] (Laing I: 146).

There are other instances, of course, but that material more properly belongs to the later chapters. We can see that Sleidan's method, and Knox's, are the same. But be that as it may, it is worth remembering that Knox did not deny the significance of visions; he was, after all, a product of the sixteenth century. At times he in fact shows himself to be deeply superstitious. It is not hard to find episodes in *The Historie* which are very similar to the Sleidan narrative; for instance, Knox writes of James V's troubles in 1540:

> And yit did not God cease to give to that blynded Prince documentis, that some suddane plague was to fall upoun him, in case hie did not reapent his wicked lief; and that his awin mouth did confesse. For after that Sir James Hammyltoun was beheaded, (justlie or injustlie we disput nott,) this visioun came unto him, as to his familiaris him self did declare: The said Sir James appeared unto him, having in his handis a drawin sworde, by the which fra the King hie stroke baith the armes, saying to him these wourdis, "Tak that, whill thow receave a finall payment for all thy impietie." This visioun, with sorowfull conteanance, hie schew on the morow; and schortlie thairefter deid his two sonnes, baith within the space of 24 houris; yea, some say, within the space of sex houris (Laing I: 67–68).

Obviously it is not Phifer's vision which Knox objects to, since James's is clearly the same sort of thing. Indeed, Knox sees the events of the latter narrative as having a symbolic significance, which works its way into history in a very concrete sense. It is Phifer's *interpret-*

ation of his dream, on the other hand, which is faulty, and more than bordering on the ridiculous.

Both translations rely rather too much on adjectivals ('who was of all his counsall', 'whose name was [...]' [Knox], 'which was much given [...]', 'who dreamed that [...]' [Dawes]). Knox's is rather like the 'Mar Lodge' version of Boece; too literal, while Dawes omits details such as Phifer taking his armour, However, Sleidan says '[...] nobilitatem omnem *exturbaret*'; Knox translates this as to 'destroy/ extirpate' the nobility, (he is thinking of '*exstirpo*'). Dawes's version implies only a rout ('to scatter them [...]'), (from '*exturbaret*'; italics added, all instances), which is less powerful, but closer.

At any rate, we have established the quality of Knox's translation by assessing it alongside another contemporary version. We need no longer quote Dawes's text in juxtaposition with Knox's, but rather, examine our one remaining Sleidan narrative, keeping in mind only what it meant to Knox. When Sleidan turned to the central character, the infamous Müntzer himself, Knox must have studied the text and absorbed all of his literary techniques. According to Sleidan, after Frankenhausen:

> *Sleidan*
> Profugerat in oppidum Muncerus, inque domum non procul a porta sese abdiderat. Huc forte nobilis quidam diuertit. Eius famulus quum in superiorum aedium partem ascendisset, spectandi causa domicilii, reperit quempiam decumbentem in lecto. Rogat qui sit, an ex tumultu profugerit, an sit e seditiosis vnus. Inficiatur ille, seque iampridem ait febricitare. Forte iacebat ad lectum crumena: corripit eam alter, vt aliquid auferret praedae.[26]

> *Knox*
> Muncer fled into the towne, and hid himself in a house not farre from the gate; into the which it happened, that a certen gentilman entered, whose servant going up into the upper parte of the house, of purpose to viewe the dwelling, he found a certaine man lying upon a bedde, of whom he demanded what he was, and whether he were one of the rebelles which fled out of the tumult. That he denied, saying, "That even then he was sicke of an agew." It happened that besides the bedde there laye a purse, which the other snatched up, hoping to gette some pray in it [...] (Laing V: 431).

26 Sleidan, J., *Commentariorum de Statu Religionis et Reipublicae*, p. 68 (1555) or p. 74 (1559).

Instead of money, however, the dishonest servant found letters addressed to Müntzer, and thus the fanatical preacher was discovered. Knox probably considered the thief as much an agent of the Deity as the 'meary Englishman' (Laing I: 261; marginal note), who taunted the fleeing Catholic celebrants after a very famous but unsuccessful St. Giles Day procession in Scotland:

> "Fy upoun yow, hoorsones, why have ye brockin ordour! Doun the streat ye passed in array and with great myrth. Why flie ye, vilanes, now, without ordour? Turne and stryk everie one a strok for the honour of his god. Fy, cowardis, fy, ye shall never be judged worthy of your wages agane!" (Laing I: 261).

(As we saw in chapter three, Knox marvelled that Mrs. Bowes was the Divine agent who brought him back to a Scotland hungry for Protestantism; above, p. 143). Elsewhere in Knox's writings, we find him dealing with the topic of mercenary inclination, like the servant's. For example, when John Leslie, James Melvill and Peter Carmichael are busy hammering at the door of Cardinal Beaton's castle stronghold, with righteous godly zeal (murder) in their hearts, we have prose like this, from *The Historie*:

> In this meanetyme, whill thei force at the doore, the Cardinall hydis a box of gold under coallis that war laide in a secreat cornar. At lenth he asked, "Will ye save my lyef . . . ?" The said Johnne answered, "It may be that we will." "Nay," sayis the Cardinall, "Swear unto me [...]" (Laing I: 176).

The obvious implication here is that Knox's Beaton is so avaricious that he values his box of gold more than his life. This, of course, is bordering on slander, (although we can excuse it because of the good humour), and, as such, it performs a different function from the detail in Sleidan's narrative; a general similarity, however, deserves to be noted.

Returning to the Latin text and Knox's rendering of it, we can see that they both contain a whole tapestry of fine details presented as if they were coincidental but, which, in retrospect, seem to correspond to a (Divinely inspired) pattern. Some features imply chance occurrence ('forte', translated here as 'it happened') or a lack of precision ('quidam', 'a certen gentilman'), but each version retains the intrinsic excitement of a good story by not connecting the man in the bed with the fleeing Müntzer until the narrative naturally unfolds the fact.

We have now seen Knox as an editor and a translator of material which, to him, had deep theological relevance. We have yet to examine Knox's own literary theological methods. One of the earliest and most important works in this respect is his *A Vindication of the Doctrine that the Sacrifice of the Mass is Idolatry*, (1550); a text which belongs to Knox's Newcastle period. The title is self-explanatory and lacks the skilfully deceptive nature of, say, Antoine Marcourt's *Declaration de la Messe, le fruict dicelle, la cause, et le moyen, pour quoy et comment on la doibt maintener*, (1534), which represents an earlier Reformation work on exactly the same theme,[27] although it is not as aggressive as the same author's anonymous *Articles véritables sur les horribles, grands & importables abuz de le Messe papalle*.[28] However, Knox's work was intended neither for 'clandestine circulation among the unsuspecting populace'[29] nor for shock value. Rather, the work was presented in public before the 'Council of the North for public affairs', spear-headed by Dr. Cuthbert Tunstall, who also appears in Sleidan's history: 'as one of the commissioners at the consultations with Franz Burkhardt, Georg von Boyneburg and Francis Myconius [...] which produced the XIII Articles of 1538'. Indeed, Tunstall was sufficiently interested in the doctrine of the Lord's Supper to write a tract entitled *De Veritate corporis et Sanguinis domini nostri Jesu Christii in eucharistia*, published in Paris in 1554.[30]

A Vindication is one of Knox's most skilful works, as Muir's testimony has already hinted (above, p. 141) (and the more obvious logistic devices we have already touched on). For instance, near the introduction, Knox observes:

> And becaus men of great erudition in your audience affirmed the contrarie, most gladlie wold I that heir thai wer present, ether in proper persone, or ellis by thair learnit men, to ponder and wey the causis movyng me thairto; for unles I evidentlie prufe myne intente be Godis halie Scriptures, I will recant it as

27 See Higman, F., *Three French Treatises of John Calvin*, pp. 12–13.

28 See Greengrass, M., *The French Reformation*, pp. 24–25.

29 Higman, F., *Three French Treatises of John Calvin*, p. 12.

30 See Shaw, D., 'Zwinglian Influences on the Scottish Reformation', 124–125.

wickit doctrine, and confes my self maist worthie of grevious punishment (Laing III: 33).

This is *libera vox* or *synchoresis*. In *The Garden of Eloquence*, Henry Peacham provides a very full definition of the situation which calls for its use and the effect it is designed to achieve:

> The orator speaking before those whom he feareth, or ought to reverence, and having some-what to say that may either touch themselves, or those that they favour, preventeth the displeasure and offence that might be taken, as by craving pardon afore hand, and by showing the necessity of free speech in that behalf. [31]

Knox's passage follows the scheme exactly. He nods to 'men of great erudition' in his audience, differentiates between 'proper persone[s]' and 'thair learnit men' and places 'Godis halie Scriptures' between himself and criticism. However, if he is proved to be in the wrong, he will recant and subject himself to punishment as a heretic. Here we see him as a defendant. But Knox also knew that the best means of defence was attack. As counsel for the prosecution, he levels a forceful '*j'accuse*':

> O Preistis! Hath thair not as great iniquitie aboundit in your dayis as ever did from the beginning? Have ye not bene intyseris and leidaris of the pepill to all idolatrie? Yea, hath not the mischeivous exampill of your abominabill lyves provokit thousandis unto iniquitie? [...] Heir ye not that God never will accept prayeris nor sacrifice whillis trew repentance wer found? (Laing III : 60).

The vehemence here anticipates that of *The Appellation* (and specifically the passage we examined above; pp. 108–109), and the method, that of Letter VIII (above, p. 136). But in the latter, Knox was using questions *quid* and *quando*; here he introduces *quæstio camparativa*[32] and *conjuncta*,[33] '*Have* ye not [...]' gives way to '*Heir* ye not [...]', (italics added), while the pejorative items (such as 'iniquitie', 'intyseris', 'mischievous', 'abominabill', 'provokit') come in with power and a consistent force.

31 Sonnino, L. A., *A Handbook*, p. 128.
32 Janton, P., *L'homme et l'oeuvre*, p. 422.
33 ibid., p. 422.

This brings us to one of Knox's favourite tools; *abominatio*. *A Vindication* contains the most memorable instances in all of Knox's writings. According to Melanchthon, this feature is a sub-species of *exclamatio*, used primarily to express revulsion and severe aversion to things base, lowly or disgusting. Jean Calvin was an adept in the use of this device. His influence on Knox is evident:

> And that sall testifie dyvers Massis celebratit for divers causis: sum for peace in tyme of war; sum for raine; sum for fair weather; yea, and (allace, my hart abhorreth sic abominatioun!) sum for sicknes of bestial (Laing III: 65).

> Then suld it not be useit to pray that the tuthe-acke be takin away from us; that oure oxen suld not tak the lowing ill, our horse the spavin or fersie, and so of all maner diseasses for oure cattell (Laing III: 65).

> In the Papisticall Masse, the congregation getteth nothing except the beholding of your jukingis, noddingis, crossingis, turnyng, uplifting, whilk all ar nothing but a diabolicall prophanation of Chrystis Supper. Now juke, cross and nod as ye list, thai ar but your awin inventionis. And finallie, Brethrene, ye gat nothing, but gaseit and beheld whill that one did eat and drink all (Laing III: 67).

In each case, but especially the third, Knox is fiercely critical. The first two draw upon the cycle of seasons, political events, banal human experience and the farmyard. In his article '*D.O.S.T.*: How we make it and what's in it', Pr. A. Jack Aitken tells us that the phrase 'lowing [or lowand] ill' is unique to Knox and the Haddington burgh records[34] and this in itself makes the example stimulating. What Pr. Aitken does not say, and what is worth remembering, is that Knox himself was from a farming family;[35] hence his deep knowledge. But, as I have said, the final passage is the most impressive.

Knox's best literary critics (Prs. Jack and Janton) have had something to say about it. The latter points out: 'Knox sait tirer profit des images radicales qu'il rehausse au moyen de l'accumulation, de la répétition et du polyptote'.[36] (He is presumably referring to *polyptoton*, whereby words are repeated with different inflexions). Although I

34 Aitken, J., '*D.O.S.T.*: How we make it and what's in it', 40.
35 See Reid, W. S., *Trumpeter of God*, p. 16.
36 Janton, P., *L'homme et l'oeuvre*, p. 496.

have shown in my introduction that some of Pr. Jack's evidence is inadmissible (even Laing points out that in the original edition of 1550, the word 'duck', not 'juke', is used),[37] he does draw attention to 'the initial list of nouns'.[38] In fact (and this is the present author's contribution), they are a special kind of noun: verbal-nouns or gerunds ('jukingis', 'noddingis', 'crossingis', 'turnyng', 'uplifting')' which are used for the purposes of derision.

In chapter two we encountered a formidable Knoxian adversary, Quintin Kennedy (above, p. 113), and I promised we would meet him again. Kennedy, it seems, was familiar with Knox's *A Vindication* and his *Ane Compendious Reassonyng* contains the proof. As we know, Knox had stated that Mass was said for 'sicknes of bestyall'. Kennedy's text was ostensibly a debate 'betwixt twa brethir' (Quintin himself (Q) and James (I)). James is given the role of aspiring Protestant (one hesitates to say 'Devil's Advocate', but that's the general idea). It is James who echoes Knox's tract: 'I harde sum of oure preacheouris preche that the papistes will say mess for are kow and als for ane sow'.[39] Quintin calls these statements 'intollerable mokkis and leys' as well he might, while James goes on to level the charges implicit in the last Knox passage:

> We of the new learning ar heichtlie offendit with your cerimoniis, sic as bekking, kneylling, blissing, crocesing, gapeyng, glowring, lyftyn vp of your handis, and knokking on your breist.[40]

The phrase 'We of the new learning', like Ninian Winzet's 'throw curiositie of nouationis'[41] catches, with superb precision, what the faithful Catholics saw as the pomposity of Protestantism. Those who subscribed to it were upstarts, Johnny-come-latelys and too sure of themselves by half. Like Knox, Kennedy obviously had an ear for the absurd, only this time it is Knox who is being caricatured. But

37 See Laing II: 67, n.s (3), (4) and (6).

38 Jack, R. D. S., 'The Prose of John Knox', 249.

39 See Kuippers, C., (ed.), *Quintin Kennedy (1520–1564): Two Eucharistic Tracts*, p. 178.

40 ibid., p. 178.

41 Hewison, J. K., (ed.), *Winzet's Works*, vol. I: p. 38.

obviously, his contemporaries were fully aware of Knox's literary methods as well as his message.[42] It is significant that his primary rhetorical tools, the gerunds ('bekking', 'kneylling', 'blissing', 'crocesing', 'gapeyng', 'glowring', 'lyfting'), survive more-or-less unchanged in Kennedy's text.

A Declaration of the True Nature and Object of Prayer, (1553), one of Knox's most attractive theological works, has just as much to offer as *A Vindication*. For instance, Knox's printer, Hugh Singleton, mentions on the title page that it was composed:

> [...] vpon the death of that moste verteous and moste famous king / Edward the VI. kynge of Englande / Fraunce and Ireland / in which confession / the sayde Jhon doth accuse no lesse his owne offences / then the offence of others / to be the cause of the awaye-taking of that moste godly prince / nowe raininge with Christ whyle we abyde plagues for our unthankfulnesse[43] (Laing III: 89).

Material such as this, coming from the printer himself, suggests that authorial self-deprecation was becoming a selling-point, for Protestant, or at least for Knoxian, prose. Catholicism spoke with authority, from a hierarchy; Protestantism did away with all that. As one French Protestant put it (in a way that reminds us strikingly of Andrew Melvill's address to James VI:[44] 'In church [...] there is no head save Jesus Christ [...] the least person is equal to the greatest; all are equal; the prayers of a layman are as good as those of a priest'.[45] The issues which Knox discussed with Mrs. Bowes (see Letter I, above, p. 138) become more understandable when we take in the above information.

Unlike *A Vindication* and the other theological works in this chapter, *A Declaration of the True Nature and Object of Prayer* is non-polemical. Indeed, it has more in common with a catechism than

42 Hugh MacDiarmid's idea that Knox achieved the whole Scottish Reformation more-or-less single-handedly, by 'amazing fire and magnetism' and without rhetorical skills is not a sound one; see MacDiarmid, H., Ross, A., Maclean, C., (eds.), *John Knox*, p. 82. Dr. Kirk is right when he says that, despite its recent date, this study is one of 'the least penetrating'; see 'The Scottish Reformation and Reign of James VI: A Select Critical Bibliography', 136.

43 Laing's page numbering is irregular here. The above reference is to the *first* p. 89 in vol. III. There are, in fact, two.

44 See Watson, R., *The Literature of Scotland*, p. 71.

45 See Greengrass, M., *The French Reformation*, p. 61.

anything else. It belongs to the species of *apologia*, that which deals with exegetical commentary: *exergasia*.[46] Its structure is simple. It exhibits a series of headings mainly in the form of propositions and queries, and there is a clear movement towards climax in the final passages. A sample of the headings offers: 'WHAT SULD BE PRAYIT FOR' (Laing III: 99); 'IMPEDIMENTS CUMMETH OF THE WEAKNESSE OF THE FLESCHE' (Laing III: 101) 'WHAT IS TO BE GATHERED IN THE NAME OF CHRIST' (Laing III: 103). In short, what we have is a kit designed to ensure salvation in terms of a Protestant understanding of the word. Knox even uses the phrase: 'the rycht way' (Laing III: 95), and of course John Gau's work comes to mind. Indeed, comparison of the two texts is very helpful. Gau for example outlines '*Quho* ve suld pray' and '*Quhat* ve suld pray', (italics added), and he is very much concerned with sincerity and simple practice set over against hypocrisy and elaborate practice:

> [...] to pray in ye spreit yat is said aganis thayme quhilk prays wtuerlie with ye mutht and notht ye hart / to pray in verite yat is said aganis ye prayer quhilk is lik to ane schaudou quhilk aperis wtuerlie in ye air as it var ane oder thinge in verite / sua quhen men mwvis the mutht and the lippis and the tunge wtuertlie without ye hart and mind thair apone / this prayer aperis vtuertlie to be for men.[47]

Knox is rather more tolerant than Gau, although he tackles similar problems:

> [...] we suld expell furth of oure myndis in tyme of our prayer, all vane cogitatiounis [...] I mene not to heir pyping, singing or playing; nor to patter upon beiddis, or bukis whairof thai haif no understanding; [...] Also, in this congregatioun suld be maid commoun prayeris, suche as all men heiring mycht understand; that the hartis of all, subscryving to the voyce of one, mycht, with unfeaned and fervent mynd, say, Amen (Laing III: 102–103).

Gau is making careful use of John 4: 24 'God is a sprete / and they that worshippe hym / must honoure him in sprete and veritie' and

46 See Sonnino, L. A., *A Handbook*, p. 93, p. 97, p. 241.

47 See Mitchell, A. F., (ed.), *The Richt Vay*, p. 83, and *Den Rette Vey till Hiemmerigis Rige* (1533); Brandt, C . J. and Fenger, B. T., (eds.), *Danske Skrifter*, vol. IV: III, pp. 303–304.

combines it with Matthew 5: 7–8: 'But when ye praye / bable not moche / as the gentyls do: for they thincke they shalbe herde / ffor there moche bablynges sake. Be ye not like them therefore' (*Tyndale* 1526). Knox, too, presumably had this latter example in mind, but much of his passage is a response to 1 Corinthians 14: 16: 'But whan thou gevest thankes with the sprete, how shal they that occupieth the rowme of the unlearned, say Amen at thy geyynge of thankes, seynge he knoweth not what thou sayest?' (*Coverdale*).

Both extracts are in a plain style: *claritas* or *perspicuitas*. Gau's is marginally more elaborate, since we find a simile ('quhilk is lik to ane schaudou') in the text, presumably designed to stress the fleeting, intangible nature of false prayer. Knox avoids figurative language but he is still listing gerunds ('pyping', 'singing', 'playing') as he did in *A Vindication*. There may also be a use of *incrementum*; Knox enhances the gerunds by presenting progressively more elaborate ritualistic behavior; 'patter[ing] on beiddis' and use of 'bukis whairof thai haif no understanding'.

Although twenty years separate *The Richt Vay* and *A Declaration*, years which saw the publication of Calvin's celebrated religious text-book *Christianæ Religionis Institutio*, there is little, theologically speaking, to set them apart. Both texts contain similar opinions on religious mediation. Here is Gau again:

> sancte Brigitteis prayer and ye xv o and s Gregoris vii o and alexandri and sixti and ilii and oder papis prayers hes beyne haldine mair precious na our lord Iesus Christis prayer for causz thay haiff giffine sic leinge and pardone to thayme ye quhilk hesz blindit ye pepil [...] / Mony prayis ye psalter of our ladie part with queral bedis for causz thai suld thairfor haiff greit pardone [...][48]

After outlining the function of the Redeemer under the heading of 'WHO MAKETH OTHIR MEDIATOURIS NOR JESUS CHRYST TAKETH HONOUR FRA HIM' (Laing III: 96), Knox asks:

> May any other (Jesus Chryst exceptit) in theis wordis mak intercessioun for synneris / Yf thai may not, than ar thai neither mediatouris nor yit intercessouris? "for albeith (sayith Augustine) Christianis do commend ane

48 Mitchell, A. F., (ed.), *The Richt Vay*, pp. 84–85; Brandt, C. J. and Fenger, B. T., (eds.), *Danske Skrifter*, vol. III: p. 306.

> another unto God in thair prayeris, yit mak thai not intercessioun, neither dar thai usurpe the office of a Mediatour; no not Paule, albeit under the Heid he was a principall member, becaus he commendith him self to the prayeris of faithfull men." (Laing III: 97).

(cf. 1 Timothy 2: 5 and 2 Timothy 2: 2). Gau attacks the Popes Alexander and Julius, the Saints Bridget and Gregory, liars and false teachers, and finally undermines the authority of the Virgin Mary. Knox, on the other hand, builds up to a quotation from Liber II of Augustine's *Contra Epistolam Parmeniani*, and if he has done some editing, it was not in his interests to pervert the original. This is the second time we have found Knox using the Fathers (compare Letter IV, above, p. 126) and there are many more instances. Perhaps at this point it is fitting to say something about the Reformer's attitude to, and use of, Patristic authority. Medieval theologians of course had relied heavily on Augustine and others such as Jerome (Erasmus's favourite), Origen and Chrysostom, usually quoting them in short sentences from *florilegia* or *summa*, as substantiation of a particular point. Thus, it was often almost impossible to check the quotation against the original work, since the only existing manuscripts at that time remained obscure within their libraries. But the printed Amerbach edition of the *Augustini Opera Omnia* (1506) (and Augustine was *the Father* to the Reformers)[49] allowed conscientious theologians to verify that the Patristic writer had been reliably represented. As we saw in chapter one, (above, pp. 43–44), the earliest Scottish Protestants were referring to Augustine and both George Wishart's *Confession of Fayth* [50] and letters contained in Knox's *The Historie* present fairly significant statements of support for the 'ancient Fatheris' (Laing I: 305) on the part of Scottish Protestants.

49 According to B. B. Warfield 'The Reformation, inwardly considered, was just the ultimate triumph of Augustine's doctrine of grace over Augustine's doctrine of the Church'; Warfield, B. B., *Calvin and Augustine* p. 322; see also McGrath, A., *Reformation Thought*, p. 93.

50 Wishart's *Confession* went so far as to state that, provided the Fathers did not exceed the bounds of their vocation: 'not onlye do we receive them as interpretours but also we honour and worship them as Chosen and beloved instruments of God'; see Laing, D., (ed.), *The Miscellany of the Wodrow Society*, p. 12.

Their purpose in citing the writers was obvious; if it could be shown that the Catholic faith was belied by its own ancient champions (as well as by scripture) the Catholics would be left 'high-and-dry'. Quintin Kennedy, for one, recognised the danger, and set about countering it to the best of his ability.[51] Knox's use of Augustine, however, has a rhetorical as well as theological function. It allows him to achieve *dictu commeratio*, or *dictu memorabilis*, whereby: 'the orator reciteth some saying or sentence of another, wholly worthy of remembrance and observation'.[52]

Again Knox's text seems more moderate in tone than Gau's, and Knox only finds a more familiar voice in his final climactic passage (this is vintage Knox, and a full dissertation in the apocalyptic mode which we first identified in *John Knox to the Congregation at Berwick*, and in Letter VIII to Mrs. Bowes; above, p. 75, pp. 135–136):

> The multitude sall not eschape, but sall drink the dregis, and have the cupe brokin upon thair heidis. For judgement begynneth in the house of the Lord, and commounlie the leist offender is first punissit, to provoke the mair wickit to repentance. But, O Lord! infinit in mercie, yf thow salt puniss, mak not consummatioun, but cut away the proude and luxuriant branches whilk beir no frute: and preserve the Commonweillis of sic as gif succour and harbour to thy contempnit messingeris, whilk lang have sufferit exyle in desert. And lat thy Kingdome schortlie cum that sin may be endit, death devorit, thy enemyis confoundit; that we thy pepill, be thy Majestie delyverit may obtene everlasting joy and felicitie, throw Jesus Chryst oure Savioure, to whom be all honour and prais, for ever Amen (Laing III: 105).[53]

Clearly, this belongs more to a sermon than a catechism. It begins with a vehement denunciation ('The multitude [...] repentance') but then it becomes a prayer (an *imploratio*) which shades into liturgy, especially towards the end. The opening image is extraordinary; it borrows from Isaiah 51: 17, but the scriptures say nothing about having

51 For example, see his *Ane Compendius Tractive* in Laing, D., (ed.), *The Miscellany of the Wodrow Society*, especially p. 149.

52 See Sonnino, L. A., *A Handbook*, p. 73.

53 The final sentence here 'And lat [...] Amen' does not occur in the original edition, see S.T.C. 15073. Laing says: 'it has been conjectured that the alterations which appear on collation with the manuscript [M'Crie MS.] were made by the author while it was passing through the press'; Laing III: 88.

the cup broken on the heads of the multitude. We may well have a joke here, although it is not all that obvious at first sight. Likewise, Knox seems to have adapted 1 Peter 4: 17–18: 'For ye tyme is come, that judgement must begynne at vs, what shal the end be of them which beleue not the Gospell of God? And yf the righteous scarcely be saved, where shal ye vngodly synner appeare' (*Coverdale*). The adaptation this time, however, is positive; it envisages possible repentance where the scriptures do not. The remainder of the images: fruit, branches, desert, and afflicted messengers are used with less innovation (compare Daniel 4: 14, Job 18: 16, Isaiah 9: 14, 18: 5, Hosea 9: 16, Luke 3: 9, 13: 9, John 15: 2 and 2 Chronicles 13: 16, to name but some of the likely sources), while the final sentence echoes the third clause of the Lord's Prayer, although there is an extraneous adverb ('shortlie').

Knox's *An Exposition Upon the Sixth Psalm of David, Addressed to Mrs. Bowes*, (1554), also has parallels with the 'Familiar Epistles', as the title implies. Unlike the epistles, however, it seems that *An Exposition* may have been intended for publication, perhaps as a model of how pious Protestants ought to give spiritual comfort. It was probably the last work which Knox wrote before fleeing from England and it just predates *A Godly Letter* and *A Faithful Admonition*. Rhetorical foretastes of both, without the bitterness, surface in *An Exposition*. Thus, in a sense, the text is doubly important. It represents a bridge between the familiar and public letters, having much in common with both. One cannot read the following without thinking of the passages from *A Godly Letter* which we examined above; (pp. 83–84):

> [...] even as the beames of the brycht sone perseth throuch the mistie and thick cloudis and bringeth doun his naturall heit, to confort and quicken suche hearbis and creaturis as, throuch violence of cold, wer almost fallin into deadlie decay; and thus the onlie gudness of God remaneth in all stormes, the sure fundatioun to the afflictit, aganis whilk the Devill is never abill to prevaile (Laing III: 147–148).

In *The Style of John Calvin in his French Polemical Treatises*, Francis Higman states that Calvin's imagery exists only in a rhetorical context.[54] It has no existence outside the texts themselves. Whether or not this is true, the same, however, cannot be said for Knox. There is evidence to suggest that his imagery *is* drawn from experience and observation. He could indeed find 'Sermons in stones' (*As You Like It*, Act 2., Sc. 1., l. 17), but certainly not 'good in everything'! In the above passage he mentions 'hearbis' and 'creaturis' which 'throuch violence of cald, wer almost fallin into deadlie decay'. Writing in *The Historie* of the 'greit weit and frost in Januare 1563', Knox observes:

> [...] upone the 20th day of Januare thair fell weit in grit aboundance, quhilk in the falling freisit so vehementlie, that the eirth was bot ane scheit of ysce. The foules baith grit and small freisit, and mycht nocht flee: monie deyit, and sum wer tackin and laid besyde the fyre, that thair fetheris mycht resolve (Laing II: 417).

One automatically thinks of the powerful lines in Robert Henryson's *The Preiching of the Swallow*: 'bewis bene ar bethit bair off blis / Be wickit windis off the winter wair [...]' and 'The foulis fair, for falt thay fell off feit / on bewis bair it wes na bute to byde'.[55] Knox, however, makes a theological point in both passages; in the first, nature functions as a sign of God's beneficence; in *The Historie* passage it is God's: 'declaratioun that he wes offendit at the iniquitie that wes committit evin within this Realme' (Laing II: 417). In each case, Knox uses *ratiocinatio*; in *An Exposition* he argues from effect to cause, and in *The Historie* from cause to effect.

Interestingly, in *An Exposition*, Knox abandons the familiar Pauline introductory formula:

> The desyre that I have to heir of your continewance with Chryst Jesus, in the day of this his battelll, whilk schortlie sall end to the confusion of his proude enemyis, neither by toung nor by pen can I express, beloved Mother (Laing III: 119).

54 Higman, F., *The Style of John Calvin in his French Polemical Treatises*, p. 147.

55 Fox, D., (ed.), *The Poems of Robert Henryson*, pp. 66–67, ll. 1701–02, 1835–36.

In *Elementorum Rhetorices*, Philip Melanchthon calls the admission 'that our message is beyond the power of words to convey' *adynaton*;[56] Knox covers both oral expression ('by toung') and written communication ('by pen'). Moreover, the word 'desyre' quite deliberately suggests his fervency.

Of more interest is the following passage, in which Knox reveals his nationalistic feelings:

> Somtyme I have thought that impossible it had bene, so to have removed my affection from the Realme of Scotland, that eny Relame or Nation coulde have bene equall deare unto me. But [...] the trubles present [...] in the Realme of England, are double more dolorous unto my hert, then ever were the troubles of Scotland.[57] (Laing I: 133).

His tools are now *laudatio* and *antapodosis*, involving praise and comparison. Rhetorically, if not ideologically, there are striking similarities in *The Complaynt of Scotland* which is roughly contemporaneous with *An Exposition*.

> inglis men ar humil quhen thai ar subieckit be forse and violence, and scottis men ar furious quhen thai ar violently subieckit. inglismen ar cruel quhene thai get victorie, and scottis men ar merciful quhen thai get victorie. and to conclude, it is onpossibil that scottis men and inglis men can remane in concord vndir ane monarche or ane prince, be cause there naturis and conditions ar as indefferent as is the nature of scheip and voluis.[58]

Knox, evidently, did not agree, and he himself is proof against 'The Complayner's' absolute rule that 'it is onpossibil' for Scotsmen and Englishmen to remain in concord (The Complayner, moreover, could not have foreseen the advent of James VI and I). But both writers are using the same sort of juxtaposition to argue their case (The Complayner, of course, is also using the type of parallelism which we have associated with Knox's *A Godly Letter* (above, p. 82).

An Exposition also contains some profound religious advice which is, at times, noticeably superior to that of Knox's shorter letters to

56 See Sonnino, L. A., *A Handbook*, p. 61.

57 This passage is not in either of the printed editions; see Laing III: 132, n. (1).

58 Murray, J. A. H., (ed.), *The Complaynt of Scotland*, pp. 106–107.

Mrs. Bowes. However, in the shorter texts, he was applying himself to immediate religious problems. In this instance, he can find spiritual meaning which is more contemplative, and independent of the specific issues which concerned Mrs. Bowes at any one time. Sustained and elaborate *inopinatum* is the trope he chooses:

> Evident it is that David in theis his prayeris susteanit and felt the verie sense of Godis wraith; and also that he understude cleirlie that it was God onlie that trubillit him, and that had laid that soir scourge upon him. And yit no whair else but at God allone (who appeireth to be angrie with him) seeketh he support or ayde. This is easie to be spokin, and the maist part of men will judge it but a lycht matter to flie to God in thair trubillis. I confes, in deid, that yf our trubillis cum be mannis tyranny, that then the maist sure and maist easie way is to rin to God for defence and abyd. But lat God appeir to be oure enemye, to be angrie with us, and to haif left us, how hard and difficill it is then to call for his grace and for his assistance none knaweth, except suche as have learnit it in experience [...] (Laing III: 135).

Knox himself was very much attached to the figure of King David,[59] and the counsel he gives here certainly shows that he had thought deeply on the meaning, and the situation, behind the Psalms. And he goes on to conclude that this kind of experience is a guarantee of Election: 'neither yit can any man so do, except the elect children of God' (Laing III: 135). Janton identifies these factors as characteristic of Knox's 'agonistic view of life'.[60] Moreover, we saw in chapter three and in the present chapter, that Knox often reworked existing ideas, and this example is no exception; see also Laing I: 468, and VI: 265).

Knox's exegetical work on the Psalms was succeeded by another exposition: *An Exposition Upon Matthew IV, Concerning the Temptation of Christ in the Wilderness*, (1556), a text which was: 'first had in the publique Church, and then afterwards written for the comfort of certaine priuate friends' (Laing IV: 89; facsimile page). Since the *Matthew* work is a sermon, it deserves analysis alongside Knox's only other surviving example of the genre, the *Sermon on Isaiah xxvi*. Of

59 For the significance of King David to Protestants, see Hannay, M. P., *Silent but for the Word: The Role of Women as Patrons, Writers and Translators of Religious Works*, p. 159.

60 Janton, P., 'John Knox and Literature', 428.

the two sermons, the latter certainly has the more compelling introduction. Writing in 1565, Knox observes:

> As the cunninge maryner, beinge maister, having his ship tossed with vehement tempest, and windes contrarious, is compelled oft to traverse, leaste that eyther by too muche resisting to the violence of the waves, his vessel might be overwhelmed; or by too much liberty graunted, to be carried whither the furie of the tempest would, his ship should be driven upon the shore and so make shipwreck. Even so doth our Prophet Isaiah [...] (Laing VI: 234).

The Matthew text, which of course, is ten years earlier, opens in a much less inspired way:

> The caus moving me to intreat this place of Scripture is, that sic as be the inscrutabill providence of God do fall in dyvers tentationis, judge not thame selves be reasone thairof less acceptabill in Godis presence; but contrariwyse, having the way preparit to victorie be Chryst Jesus, sall not feir above measure the craftie assaltis of that subtill serpent, Sathan; but with joy and bold corage, having sic a gyd as heir is payntit furth, such a champioun, and sic weaponis as heir ar to be found, (yf with obedience we will heir, and with unfeaned faith believe,) may assure ourselves of God's present favour, and of finall victorie, by the meanes of Him, who, for oure saifgaird and delyverance, hath enterit in the battell, and triumphed over his adversarie, and all his rageing furie (Laing IV: 95).

There is no need to identify Knox's literary medium with the Isaiah text, but in *An Exposition Upon Matthew* he begins with *præparatio*, which outlines why he has undertaken his current task (the *præparatio* moreover, ties in with Knox's subsequent use of systematic rhetoric. On the very same page he further notes:

> [...] we purpois to observe, in treating this matter: [...] First, *What* this word Tentatioun meaneth, and *how* it is usit *within the Scriptures*. [...] Secundlie, *Wha* is *heir* temptit, and *at what tyme* this tentatioun happinit. [...] Thridlie, *How* and *be what meanis* he was temptit. [...] And last, *Why* he suld suffer theis tentationis, and *what frute* enseweth to us of the same (Laing IV: 95, italics added).

These methods have been characterised as arguments *a persona*, *a tempore*, *a loco*, *a modo* and *a causa*,[61] working within the auspices of *enumeratio*).

With the Isaiah introduction, we meet the: 'sermon as organ of a virile, picturesque speech' and a 'medium for vivid illustration',[62] but most commentators are too surprised by its content; its 'tendance quiétiste',[63] to do justice to its form and structure. W. C. Dickinson exemplifies this: 'Is this the Knox we knew? The Knox to who all temporizing was abomination before the Lord'.[64] While edifying, Dickinson's comments rely too heavily on the use of a text-book image of Knox. That he was a seasoned 'survivor' is well-known. What we should be focusing upon is Knox's illustration, the cunning mariner with his attempts to find the middle course in a storm. (*The Historie* also bears witness to the fact that Knox was fond of naval language: 'Navigatioun' (Laing I: 82), 'assalt by sey' (Laing I: 203), 'rowaris', 'galayis', (Laing I: 204), 'schopped' (Laing I: 206), 'playne seas' (Laing I: 216), 'the sitting doun of the schip called the Cardinall' (Laing I: 220), 'forsaris' (Laing I: 227), 'streicking saill', 'making as thai wald cast anker', 'burded thame' (Laing II: 12), and so forth).[65]

There is nothing quite so vivacious in the second introduction, although there are appealing metaphoric touches; Christ as a 'champioun' (think again of Dunbar's: 'Our campioun Christ confoundit hes his force')[66] who is 'payntit furth' (and this is remarkable, coming from a man who condemned unequivocally all religious icons. But for all the dissimilarities between the two sermons, they are similar in one significant, fundamental and striking way. Take these three passages (the first two from the Isaiah sermon and the last from the Matthew):

> Shal ye then thinke that the dew of God's heavenly grace shall not be as effectuall in you to whome he hath made his promises, as that it is in the herbes

61 Janton, P., *L'homme et l'oeuvre,* p. 423.

62 Owst, G. R., *Literature and Pulpit in Medieval England,* p. 55.

63 See Janton, P., *L'homme et l'oeuvre*, p. 543.

64 Dickinson I: lxiv.

65 See also Janton, P., *L'homme et l'oeuvre*, p. 478, n. (23), and also p. 501, n. (112), for the possible influence of Miles Coverdale on Knox's Isaiah sermon.

66 Bawcutt, P., (ed.), *The Poems of William Dunbar*, p. 69, l. 2.

> and fruites that from yeare to yeare buddeth forth and decayeth? If ye doe so, the Prophet would say your incredibility is inexcusable [...] (Laing VI: 262).

> After this same maner God speaketh to his people; as he shoulde say, The tempest that shall come upon this whole nation shall be so terrible, that nothing shall appeare but extermination to come upon the whole body. But thou, my people, thou I saye, that hearest my worde, belevest the same, and tremblest at the threatenings of my Prophetes, now when the world doth insolently resist, let such, I say, enter within the secrete chamber of my promises [...] (Laing VI: 265).

> For thus, me think our Maister and champioun, Chryst Jesus, doth provoke oure enemy to battel: – "Sathan, thou gloriest of thy power and victorie over mankynd, that thair is nane abill to withstand thy assaltis nor eschape thy dart, but at a tyme or uthir thou givest him a wound! Lo, I am a man lyke to my brethren, having flesche and blude and all properteis of manis nature (sin, whilk is thy vennoume, exceptit;) tempt, try and assalt me: I offer thee heir a place most convenient (the wildernes); thair salbe na mortall creature to comfort me against thy assaltis; thou sall have tyme sufficient, do what thou canst, I sall not flie the place of battell: Yf thow becum victour, thow may still continew; in possessioun of thy kingdome in this wreachit warld. But yf thow can not prevaill aganis me, then must thy pray and unjust spoyle be tackin from thee: Thow maun grant thy self vanquischit and confoundit, and must be compellit to leif off frome all accusatioun of the memberis of my bodie; for to thame doith apperteane the frute of my battell; my victorie is thairs, as I am apoyntit to tak the punishment of thair synnis in my bodie." (Laing IV: 103–104).

For a radical Protestant like Knox such passages exhibit what, at first sight, seems to be an extraordinary licence. After reading them we can appreciate why Thomas Randolph wrote to Cecil, saying of Knox that he appeared: 'as thoughe he wer [...] of God's privie consell' (see Laing VI: 146), but there is nothing arrogant about Knox's utterances. He responded in general terms to such an implication: 'Gif thai understoude how fearfull my conscience is, and ever hes bene, to exceid the bowndis of my vocatioune, they wold nocht so boldlie have accused me' (Laing VI: 592) and more specifically: 'in the publike place I consulte not with flesh and bloud [...] but as the Spirit of my God [...] moveth me, [...] so I speke' (Laing VI: 230). When Milton wrote in *Paradise Regain'd*: 'Thou Spirit who ledst this glorious Eremite / [...] inspire / As thou art wont, my prompted song else mute' (Bk. I, l. 8, ll. 11–12),[67] he believed, like Knox, that he was a vehicle of the Holy Spirit. The whole notion is scriptural; in the gospels it constitutes the very essence of Apostolic preaching, and Presbyterianism stands in this tradition. In practice, however, this did not mean *extempore ad lib* discourses; (*that* was an anabaptist heresy). Rather, material was often highly prepared. However, readers of Sir Walter Scott's *The Heart of Midlothian* will recall that Jeanie Deans was very much surprised to discover that an English clergyman preached *from a script*.

But even allowing for the orthodoxy behind the above passages, they show Knox's Protestantism at its most dynamic, visionary and audacious. Both of the Isaiah extracts are somewhat derivative. The metaphor 'dew of God's heavenly grace' borrows its vehicle from Isaiah 26: 19: 'thy dewe is a dew of herbes' (*Coverdale*) but it owes more to the marginalia which accompanied that 'most remarkable book' the Geneva Bible.[68] The Geneva translators have appended to the same verse: 'As the herbes, dead in winter, florish againe by the raine in the spring time, so they that lie in the dust, shal rise ye to ioye when they fele *the dewe of God's grace*'[69] (italics added). Knox himself goes on to chastise those who would draw any silly conclusions from the verses in question ('If ye doe so, your incredibility is inexcusable'). The second passage from the Isaiah sermon, perhaps reminds us of the lines from *John Knox to the Congregation at Berwick*, (above, p. 76), where he concludes 'as God would say […]'. Pr. Jack is right when he observes that the Deity acts almost 'as an energetic second in the Reformer's corner'[70] (even if the remainder of the extract draws more or less straight-forwardly upon Isaiah 26: 16).

It is the Matthew passage which is really astonishing. Christ, speaking through the mouth of Knox, is presented as infinitely more accommodating than He is in the Gospel (see Matthew 4: 1–11), and enters into a provisional pact with the Devil rather like that between King Hamlet and Old Fortinbras in Act 1, Scene 1 of *Hamlet* (ll. 80–

67 See Campbell, G., (ed.), *John Milton: The Complete Poems*, p. 391.

68 Greenslade, S. L., *The Cambridge History of the Bible: The West from the Reformation to the Present Day*, p. 156.

69 See *The Geneva Bible*, (Crespin's ed.), 1558, p. 311.

70 Jack, R. D. S., (ed.), *Scottish Prose 1550–1700*, p. 20.

95). In a scene worthy of *Paradise Regain'd*, the Saviour removes all possible barriers between himself and Satan; He is 'a man' like 'to [his] brethren', He offers a place of combat which is suitably 'convenient', the adversary shall 'have tyme sufficient' (and here Christ, like Knox, is very intent on *loco* and *tempore*); if He loses the contest, Satan may 'still continew' at his old tricks. However, should Christ emerge the victor, stipulations come into play (and this is where Knox's idea reaches an effective crux). Satan will be 'confoundit', 'vanquischit' and 'must be compellit to leif off [...]'. To be sure, this constitutes a great deal to hang upon 'me think' but, as Knox presents Him, Christ reveals an interesting sense of fair play. Not only this, however, He evidently has an astute legal mind, and reveals a propensity for verb-triplets ('tempt, try and assault me') and existential phrases ('I am apoyntit [...]'). Knox, then, interweaves traditional material with more challenging qualities: imagination and originality.

After the inspired and inspiring preaching in *An Exposition Upon Matthew IV, Concerning Christ's Temptation in the Wilderness*, Knox apparently turned to rather more procedural topics, and he wrote certain *Answers to Some Questions concerning Baptism*, (1556), (see Laing IV: 119–128). Although he was not alone in addressing these issues (for instance, Tyndale composed *A Fruitful and Godly Treatise expressing the Right Institution and Usage of the Sacrament of Baptism*, and in Scotland John Ireland treated it in some detail in the *Meroure of Wyssdome*), the work is one of Knox's least interesting as literature.

A much more significant exercise is his *On Predestination*; Knox's only attempt at systematic theology and a text which we have already considered as a translation. It was apparently written for two reasons. An anonymous anti-predestinarian tract entitled *Against the Careless by Necessity* (possibly composed by Robert Cooke who previously had connections in Edward VI's court)[71] had been circulating in Geneva, and on request, Knox undertook to answer its charges. Secondly, Knox's relationship with Calvin, at that time, needed mending, and he saw his work against anabaptism as a means of achieving this. As Alister McGrath notes, despite an evident mistrust of monarchy in itself: 'Calvin was in the habit of dedicating

71 See Laing V: 16, and Reid, W. S., *Trumpeter of God*, pp. 151–152.

works to European monarchs, in the hope of winning them to the Reformation cause. Among the dedicatees of Calvin's published works were Edward VI and Elizabeth I of England'.[72] However, because of Knox's *The First Blast*, which was published in Geneva without the French Reformer's knowledge, Calvin's own *Commentaries on Isaiah* had been cooly received in England by Elizabeth. When he had established the reasons for this, Calvin upbraided Knox's rashness and (extreme) lack of foresight. (Calvin, indeed, lamented that his difficulties with the Queen had come about solely: 'ob inconsideratum unius hominus fastum'; on account of one arrogant man's lack of consideration).[73] To soothe this indignation, Knox set about writing the 170,000 word theological dissertation, which, as Katharine Firth observes, eventually constituted: 'a substantial defence of Calvin's doctrine of predestination'.[74] (This belief of course also comes from certain parts of the Gospels, it was held by St. Paul, St. Augustine, Duns Scotus, Wycliffe, Hus, Luther, Zwingli and then Calvin; indeed it meant more the Beza than to Calvin.[75] In the *Meroure of Wyssdome*, even Ireland shows that he was thoroughly familiar with the concept, although he writes within a Catholic appreciation of St. Paul and St. Augustine).

On Predestination marks Knox's first published debate (the Genevan printer, Jean Crespin, undertook to publish it, but only after receiving assurances that: 'nothing unorthodox was expressed',[76] and this was indeed the case). It follows a set polemical form; the opponent's work is quoted, then his points are subsequently disputed. All written controversies in the sixteenth century were carried out in this manner (compare, for example John Davidson's *Ane Answer to the Tractiue set furth in the zeir of God, 1558, be Maister Quintine Kennedy, Abbote of Crosraguell, for the establishing of ane Christiane mannis conscience* [...], (1563), or William Fowler's *An Answer to the*

72 McGrath, A., *Reformation Thought*, p. 191, n. (21).

73 Robinson, H., (ed.), *Zurich Letters*, 2nd series, pp. 35–36; see also Greaves, R. L., *Theology and Revolution in the Scottish Reformation*, p. 28.

74 Firth, K. R., *The Apocalyptic Tradition*, pp. 123–124.

75 See McGrath, A., *Reformation Thought*, p. 92, and Quinn, F., (ed.), *Meroure of Wyssdome*, vol. 2: pp. 146–147.

76 Reid, W. S., *Trumpeter of God*, p. 152.

Calumnious Letter and Erroneous Propositions of An Apostat named M. Io. Hammiltoun, (1581).

As we have already established, *On Predestination* has little value as original theology, but at times it contains what is perhaps Knox's most deeply penetrating rhetoric. Here he is challenging the anabaptist belief that all mankind would be saved, and inviting proof of the same:

> For ye must first prove all to be saintes by vocation, all to be blessed with spiritual benediction and to have obeyed, and all to be builded upon the foundation of the Prophetes and Apostles, before that ye be able to prove that all were Elected and Predestinate in Christe Jesus before all tymes (Laing V: 109).

Knox plays the role of *operis exactor*; moreover, the task which he presents is a mountainous one, and he also knows all too well that 'nullo modo fieri potest'; it is quite impossible.

Or again, he responds to another specific charge:

> And farther, how ye be able to prove that Sardanapalus, Croesus, and Tarquinus the proude, can be placed in this rank of your Especially Elected, I can see no good reason; for except that calamatie and God's just vengeance did follow their insolencie, filthie life, and pride, I find in histories no speciall message sent unto them from God. But this ye may understand by some secrete revelation, which ye have received of late in your perfection (Laing V: 118–119).

Ironically, Knox accuses his opponent of assuming exactly the same kind of charismatic qualities which he himself had adopted, but as is often the case, he was unaware of any inconsistencies in his thought. He gives the impression that he has had a quick glance through Cicero, Livy or Herodotus, and the passage embodies *inter se pugnantia*, which is used to reprimand the opponent's insolence.

Although *On Predestination* is a very long text, it is Knox's least representative and it ought not to be juxtaposed with *The Historie*, simply because of its length.[77] Earlier in the present chapter, (above,

77 C. S. Lewis, unfortunately, adopts this approach to Knox's works; see *English Literature in the Sixteenth Century*, pp. 201–202.

pp. 160–168), I have suggested more fruitful ways of making the connection between these two works. Moreover, although Church historian David Calderwood recommends the work to readers as evidence of 'how profound' the Reformer was 'in divinitie',[78] it was not known in Scotland until many years after Knox's death, and in any case, the later writer's assessment is rather too generous.

Only two works remain, then, to be mentioned in the present division; *The Order of the General Fast, and the Form of Excommunication Approved by the General Assembly of the Church of Scotland*, (1566–1569), and *The Order of Excommunication and of Public Repentance*, (1569). The latter may even be excluded from further discussion since it is almost wholly procedural. Both, admittedly, are what Janton calls 'les traités doctrinaux',[79] but the former, of which Knox is only a co-author, contains the more memorable of literary strokes. Knox's influence is surely discernible in the passage which anticipates a response to the proposed implementation of fasting:

> But now we knowe, that suche as neither lufe God, nor trewly feare his judgements (for mo Atheistes we have nor consumate Papistes within this Realme) shall grudge and crye, What new ceremonie is this that now we here of? Wherefore shall we Faste! and who hath power to command us so to do? A feg for their Fasting! we will fill and farse our bellies upone the oulde fassion [...] (Laing VI: 406).

We may think of Henryson's description of Mercury as the poet of the old fashion, but the imagery, especially the 'feg', is Knoxian. At the time of composing *The Order and Doctrine of the General Fast*, Knox may not yet have written his famous account of Cardinal Beaton, so again we get a revealing insight into his thought and how it developed.

This brings us to the end of the theological division and to an appreciation of what a mixed-bag it contains: revisions, translations, sermons, disputations, expositions, vindications and statements concerning ecclesiastical procedure. It may not be possible for twenty-first century readers to appreciate just how important such matters were to

78 Calderwood, D., *The Historie of the Kirk of Scotland*, vol. VII: p. 29; see also Laing V: 17.

79 Janton, P., *L'homme et l'oeuvre*, p. 427.

Knox's contemporaries, but theology and religious doctrine, to many of them, ranked a long way ahead of, say, politics or economic issues. Knox himself dismisses these as 'trifeling questionis' (Laing I: 77), and after we have perused his theological works, we can perhaps understand why. And at any rate, fine literary qualities are just as evident here, as they are in *The Historie* and the remainder of Knox's work.

Chapter Five: Knox's *The Historie of the Reformatioun*, Models and Methods

The following chapters isolate nine topics relevant to the study of Knox's *The Historie*. Chapter five, which incorporates five divisions, deals first of all with the writing of histories and with the sixteenth century models available to Knox. The chapter then goes on to examine textual and manuscript evidence relating to *The Historie*, dates of composition and so forth, before looking in greater detail at Knox's autobiography. Finally, it further analyses Knox's rhetorical techniques insofar as they impinge upon preaching, prophecy and polemics. First of all, however, we shall explore the 'historical genre'. Indeed, Janton is the only Knox critic to have done this satisfactorily in the past, but he treats *The Historie* only as part of his general literary analysis of Knox; in passing, and without the extensive commentary that it undoubtedly deserves.[1] The present study is intended to rectify this situation.

The Historical Genre

We have already seen in chapter one the intellectual climate which Knox inherited, but there we set certain necessary parameters. Our task here is to trace the historiographical genre in Scotland, pre- and post-Knox, in order to assess his overall importance and significance. As Janton observes: 'Quand Knox écrit l'histoire, ce genre populaire a un passé jalonné de grand noms'.[2] We must place John Barbour and Blind Harry in this tradition together with Andrew of Wyntoun, al-

1 See Janton, P., *L'homme et l'oeuvre*, p. 428.

2 ibid., p. 428.

though their medium was verse not prose. More in line with Knox's work but not in the vernacular is John of Fordun's *Chronica Gentis Scotorum*, which dates from the late fourteenth century and terminates its narrative at 1153. Fordun's continuator was Walter Bower who completed the work in 1449.

In the sixteenth century John Major had begun with his *Historia Majoris Britanniæ tam Angliæ quam Scotiæ*, (1520), and of course Boece followed with his *Scotorum Historiæ*, as we have seen. Although we have already looked at the latter, more general commentary is called for here since these two works clearly embody two differing literary strands, both of which are relevant to Knox. C. S. Lewis calls Major's work: 'dry and annalistic in narrative' and fastens onto his account of Merlin's birth in Book II as an example of scholarly plodding,[3] in much the same mode as John Ireland. All this is generally recognised as thoroughly medieval and: 'un genre aride, exact, sans imagination ni flatterie',[4] while Boece, who was a humanist, represents not a declining movement but an ascending one. Indeed, historiographical humanism was to reach its literary peak in George Buchanan's *Rerum Scotticarum Historia*, a work which was only slightly later than, and certainly influenced by, Knox's. In contrast to medieval scholasticism, humanism was the 'new learning'. Those who advocated it bowed the knee to Erasmus in the sixteenth century (stylistically rather than historiographically), and to the classical authors of antiquity such as Cicero and Livy. Indeed, in his *Defence of Martin Luther against the Furibund Decree of the Parisian Theologasts* (*Ein urteil der theologian Zu Paris vber die lehre d. Luthers*) the reforming humanist Philip Melanchthon attacked Major as the supreme spokesman of scholastic tail-chasing.[5]

As we know, Boece's work heavily influenced Adam Bell, and stimulated two fine Scots prose translations which testify to a popular taste for the new histories, and although Knox probably shared something of Buchanan's frank dislike for the fantastic elements so evident

3 Lewis, C. S., *English Literature in the Sixteenth Century*, p. 116.

4 Janton, P., *L'homme et l'oeuvre*, p. 429.

5 See Sanderson, M. H. B, *Cardinal of Scotland*, p. 76.

in Boece, we know that he was not above turning to *Scotorum Historiæ*. Knox was far from being a dazzling humanist like Melanchthon, or even a precocious one, like Calvin, but was not unaware of the movement nor unresponsive to it (above, p. 94) even if his deepest roots, initially, lay in Major's scholasticism. Roughly contemporary with Knox's *The Historie* is the anonymous *Historie of the Estate of Scotland from July MDLVIII to April MDLX*, which is too slight to have anything but historical significance, and *A Diurnal of Remarkable occurents that have passed within the country of Scotland since the death of King James the Fourth till the year 1575*, a useful companion to Knox's work but nothing like as important. After Knox, come the works of a Roman Catholic, John Leslie, who first wrote *The History of Scotland, from the death of King James I, to the year 1561*, then turned it into the Latin *De Origine, Moribus et Rebus Scotorum*, before it found its final form as *The Historie of Scotland, wrytten first in Latin by the most reverend and worthy Johne Leslie, Bishop of Rosse, and translated in Scottish by Father James Dalrymple* in 1595. From the Protestant side, Robert Lindsay of Pitscottie's *Historie and Chronikles of Scotland* cannot boast such a complicated origin, but both writers lack the greatness of Knox. Leslie has a wide knowledge of classical writing and English histories, but proceeds schematically and is somewhat didactic, while Lindsay, although he cannot match Leslie's scholarship and range, is more lively and anecdotal. After these we can see the emergence of diaries and autobiographies such as James Melvill's *The Autobiography and Diary of Mr. James Melvill*, which shares a similar religious orientation to Knox's, but is the work of a man without guile and full of naïve charm (like Nathanael, an Israelite indeed). His namesake, James Melville of Halhill, wrote *Memoirs of his Own Life* and David Moysie produced *Memoirs of the affairs of Scotland from 1577 to 1603*.

It should be easy to see that Knox's position is central and therefore crucial. To be sure, he is not as learned as Buchanan or Leslie, but he brings a genius to his text which is all his own and quite inimitable. His asperity is just as distinctive and only when he combines it with his partisan committedness does he find a parallel in the other histories, most notably in Buchanan, Leslie and Lindsay. As well as sharing some of Boece's subject matter, he has much in common with the others, and the bitty *Historie of the Estate of Scotland* provides some striking parallels, which we shall explore later on (below, pp. 272–273). In terms of style, he probably ranks above all of the sixteenth century historians, or at least those who write in the vernacular, since his prose is comparatively free of Latin antecedents (unlike Boece's translators at their most extreme) and strikingly vivacious to boot. Knox's truest legacy, however, is probably with our first James Melvill, although it need hardly be said that there is an enormous difference in the characters of the two authors.

Manuscripts of Knox's The Historie

There are two sixteenth century manuscripts of *The Historie*: one in Glasgow University Library, one in Edinburgh. The former is later in date and consequently less valuable, to the linguistic critic at least. It consists of 242 leaves, written in a hand which varies in neatness throughout. Book IV of *The Historie* may have been copied out at an earlier date than the rest of the manuscript. *The Buke of Discipline* is omitted. Conjoined to the text is a title sheet referring to a separate work entitled *Contextus Historiæ Evangelicæ Secundum tres Evangelistas Mat. Mar. Et Lucam*, which was once bound together with *The Historie* and which is signed by a certain 'Mr. Jo. Knox' (probably the Reformer's nephew. He has no connection whatever with the composition of *The Historie*). The title sheet is dated '*augusti* 18. 1581'. Until Laing discovered the Edinburgh MS., the Glasgow text: 'was long considered to be the earliest and most authentic copy' (one might say the *textus receptus*): 'and consequently no small degree of importance was attached to it'[6].

The Edinburgh text formerly belonged to Laing and the editor has traced its history in a handwritten note, prefixed to the manuscript. He first alludes to Matthew Crawford's printed edition of the Glasgow version (1732) which contains the following notice:

6 Laing I: xxxiii

> There is also a compleat MS. copy of the first four books of this History belonging now to Mr. Gavin Hamilton, Bookseller in Edinburgh, which formerly belonged to the late Reverend Mr. Matthew Reid, Minister of the Gospel at North Berwick; it is written in a very old hand, the old spelling is kept, and I am informed that it exactly agrees with the Glasgow MS. with which it was collated, during the time this edition was a-printing.

Laing then adds:

> Of its subsequent history I don't know any particulars, till I purchased it at the sale of the late Rev. Dr. Jamieson's library. That it should agree with the Glasgow Manuscript, is what was to be expected, inasmuch as I am satisfied, from comparison, that that MS. must have been transcribed from the present one, before the close of the 16th century – but not earlier than the year 1584.
> This manuscript I consider to be peculiarly valuable and interesting from two circumstances. The first is that it presents the work in its most genuine and authentick form; being undoubtedly the most ancient copy that exists. The second that it has internal evidence of portions of it having been written in the year 1566, with occasional corrections between that date and 1571, and some of these at least appear to be made by *the Reformer* himself.[7]
>
> [Signed] David Laing (italics added)

Although the 'Laing MS.', as it is now called, has been thoroughly examined by Pr. Dickinson in his bibliographical note prefixed to his own modern edition of *The Historie*, it is to be hoped that this study has at least something new to offer. For the present moment, however, we shall explore some of the evidence which Dickinson, and Laing before him, have already established. For example, the corrections to which Laing was referring, have all been traced by Dickinson, and he finds no less than twenty-four instances where Knox himself has apparently made some form of emendation to the text. He adds phrases such as: 'to wit, Jhone Knox' in order to clarify who was speaking in one narrative (see Laing II: 297, f. 312), and at another point he even found it necessary to attach a separate page to the text of *The Historie* to clear up an oversight. He writes in the margin: 'Tak in this that is sewed in this place quhar it is scraped out' (see Laing II: 392, f. 355). The material on the separate sheet now constitutes the

7 MS. La. II. 210, Edinburgh University Library; see also Laing I: xxxi, and Dickinson I: xcvi. Dickinson does not include the whole of Laing's note.

only section of the work which remains in Knox's hand (see Laing II: 392–393). The scribe who worked on the Glasgow MS. of *The Historie* was evidently the first who had to make sense of Knox's directions and to incorporate all the corrections in a fully coherent text.

By-and-large, however, the Glasgow MS. is much less interesting than the other, even though the one fact which consistently emerges from their collation is that the former exhibits an orthographical system which is more Scots in form. If we juxtapose the opening passage to each, (italics added), we can see this clearly:

> *Glasgow MS. (1584?, 1590?)*
> It is not vnknow*in* (Christiane R*e*id*a*r) that the same *cloude* of ignorance that long *hes* darkned many *R*ealmes vnder *yis* accursed kingdome of *yat* Romane antichrist; *had* also owercoverit this *pure* Realme, yat idolatrie *has* bein m*ai*nteined, The blud of innocentis ha*the* be*i*n sched and *c*hrist Jesus his eternall treu*t* hathe beine abhorred, detested and blasphem*it*.[8]

> *Edinburgh MS. (1566)*
> It is not vnknow*en* (Christ*ea*ne R*ea*d*er*), that the same Clud of ignorance that long *hath* dark*en*ed many realms under *this* accursed kingdome of *that* Romane Antichrist, *hath* also owercover*ed* this *poore* Realme; *that* idolatrie hath bein m*a*nteined, the bloode of innocentis hath b*ene* sched, and Christ Jesus his eternall treut*h* hath bein abhorred, detested *and blasphemed*.[9]

The first thing to point out is that neither version is in Knox's handwriting,[10] but even so, we can see clearly in what forms the first readers of *The Historie* must have encountered the text. (We know of the existence of a third sixteenth century manuscript, copied: 'directly from the MS. of 1566'[11] and used by Thomas Vautrollier for the first printed edition of *The Historie* in 1586, but since the transcript is lost, we can only speculate as to its orthography. What we can be certain of, is that Vautrollier's final print is in no way an accurate reflection of the original system). Laing himself deprecates the collation of such texts by pointing out that all we can expect to find are 'slight occa-

8 MS. La. II. 210, Edinburgh University Library, f. (1).
9 MS. Gen. 1123, Glasgow University Library, f. (1).
10 Laing I: xxxiii.
11 Laing I: xxxiii.

sional changes in orthography'. Laing is right, but such disparities are bound to be more significant to a twentieth or twenty-first century literary critic than they were to him. For instance, it is evident that the Glasgow scribe, whoever he was, occasionally lapses into '-it' suffixes, suggesting that he perhaps preferred this form to the English '-ed', but has, as often as not, retained the suffixes of the Edinburgh MS. More consistently, he employs the pronoun-forms 'yis' and 'yat', he uses three distinct spellings of the third person singular present indicative ('hes', 'has', 'hathe') to the Edinburgh MS.'s one ('hath'), and 'ei' or 'ai' diphthongs usually occur when the other scribe has chosen differently. He also seems to have used the English 'cloude' for the more Scots 'clud' but Scots 'pure', and 'blud' for the English 'poore' and 'bloode'. At any rate, we have established something about scribal idiosyncrasies.

A more rewarding discipline by far is criticism of the literary features of the text, and speculation as to its possible sources. All the typical Knoxian literary features are here; symmetry and balance, the use of *isocolon*, and a proleptic metaphor ('cloude of ignorance') which is applied literally with the verbs 'darkened' and 'overcovered'. The latter belongs to a family of similary structured verbs ('vnknowen', 'accursed'), while the passage culminates with parallel verbs in the form of a triplet (the Glasgow scribe in fact slightly lessens the force of this strategy). Knox heightens specificity when he moves from the rather general 'many realmes' to 'this [...] realme', and so on. He continues:

> But that same God that caused light to schyne out of darkness, in the multitud of his mercyes, hath of long tyme opened the eis of some evin within this Realme, to see the vanitie of that which then was universally embrased for trew religioun; and hes gevin unto them strenth to oppone thame selfis unto the same; and now into these last and moist corrupt dayis, hath maid his treuth so to triumphe amonges us, that, in despyte of Sathan, hipochrisye is disclosed and the trew wyrschipping of God is manifested [...] (Laing I: 3).

If we juxtapose these two passages with the introductory epistle contained in the Geneva Bible we can see a clear similarity:

> Besides the manifolde and continual benefites which almightie God bestoweth vpon vs bothe corporal and spiritual, we are especially bound (deare brethren) to give him thankes without ceasing for his great grace and unspeakable mercies, in that it hath pleased him to call vs unto this mervelous light of his gospel, & mercifully to regarde vs after so horrible backesliding and falling away from Christ to Antichrist, from light to darckness, from the liuing God to dumme and dead idoles: & that after so cruel murther of Godes Saintes, as alas, hathe been among vs, we are not altogether cast of, as were the Israelites, and many others, for the like, or not so manifest wickednes, but receyued agayne to grace with moste euident signes and tokens of Gods especial loue and fauour.[12]

Janton asks of Knox: 'A-t-il, à Genève, modelé son langage sur celui des traducteurs, de la Bible de 1557?'[13] and this is surely perceptive. Knox's own introductory passage in *The Historie* resembles the above passage in at least seven different ways (address to reader, murder of saints, idolatry / true worship, Christ / Antichrist, God's great mercy, light / darkness and in the chosen nation idea). In fact there is no doubt that the Geneva text was his original model.

If the collation of manuscripts is less worthwhile than literary criticism and source analysis, detailed study of the 'Laing MS.' itself is much more rewarding, and allows us to draw significant conclusions about the process of composition. This manuscript is the work of eight scribes, discounting Knox's own sporadic additions. Dickinson labels the hands (A)–(H) and follows them to their termination points using the numbered folios. However, he does not trace these points to Laing's printed text, which is, in terms of its orthography, still a better and more accurate edition of *The Historie* than his own. This information, with conclusions, is supplied here in tabular form, as a new contribution to Knox studies.

Hands / Instances	Folios	Laing Text	Scribe (?)
(A) 1	1–114	I:3.1– I:327.33	J. Gray
(B) 1	115–136	I:327.33– I.381.13	(?)
(C) 1	137–158	I.381.13–I:433.8	R. Bannatyne

12 See Crespin, J., (ed.), *The Geneva Bible*, (1558), Introduction.

13 Janton, P., *L'homme et l'oeuvre*, p. 404.

Hands / Instances	Folios	Laing Text	Scribe (?)
(A) 2	159–180	I:433.8–II:7.25	J. Gray
(D) 1	181–204	II:7.25–II:56.14	(?)
(C) 2	205–228	II.56.14–II.103.16	R. Bannatyne
(A) 3	229–249	II.103.16–II.143.8	J. Gray
(E) 1	250–272	II.143.8–II.201.2	(?)
(F) 1	273–294	II.201.2–II.243.31	(?)
(G) 1	295–309	II.342.31–II.391.12	(?)
(A) 4	310–355	II.391.12–II.393.8	J. Gray
(H) 1	356–358	II.393.8–II.399.16	P. Knox
(C) 3	359–387	II.399.16–	R. Bannatyne

Hand (A) has been tentatively identified by Laing as the scribe John Gray.[14] An early draft of the manuscript, ff. (1)–(355), probably existed and was written throughout by (A); Knox himself then revised (A)'s work (since all of the remaining corrections occur in this section). The original text was so heavily annotated that he deemed it necessary for a number of scribes to work on a fair copy. The best part of 'original (A)' remained and went on to constitute much of the manuscript, while the newly revised sections were copied out and re-integrated into the narrative. Indeed, there is internal evidence to suggest that the other scribes were working from an original. For instance, in f. (126), (B) writes of a signature ('the vther subscriptioun we culd nocht read, but the Simile is this [...]'.[15] Only two other hands have been identified; hand (H) seems to have been that of Knox's young nephew, Paul,[16] and (C) that of Richard Bannatyne, his trusty secretary.[17] As we can see from the table, three sections belong to Scribe (C); (ff.

14 See Laing I: xxx, and *The Miscellany of the Wodrow Society*, vol. I: p. 287.

15 See Dickinson I: cix, and Laing I: 354, n. (2).

16 See Finlayson, C. P., 'A Volume Associated with John Knox', 170–172.

17 See Laing I: 411, n. (1), Dickinson I: xcic.

137–158, 205–228 and 359–387). The third of these is written in a hasty, very untidy manner. Laing dates this section to after December, 1571, and notes that it is: 'more like a scroll copy from dictation than an accurate transcript'.[18] Dickinson suggests that: 'these folios may be an example of part of the History in its earliest form'.[19] Thus, they must rank in importance with Knox's 'appended narrative' in f. 355 from a textual point of view. We can conclude from all this that Knox composed *The Historie* either in his own hand, then turned it over to (A) for tidying up, or perhaps he dictated it to Bannatyne (C) and gave Bannatyne's text to (A). After this, six others worked on the script to incorporate Knox's corrections. If Knox did dictate to Bannatyne, the secretary at times would have found himself reworking sections of (A)'s text, which he himself had taken down originally.

Dates of Composition, Contents and Purpose of The Historie

Both Laing and Dickinson trace the dates of Knox's composition using his own references to *The Historie* in official correspondence and internal evidence from the text itself as the basis for their conclusions. This work has been done very thoroughly, but this new study can build very constructively on established conclusions. After all, *when* and *why The Historie* came together, as well as *how*, are fundamental concerns of the literary critic. Moreover, we have placed Knox's text in its proper Scottish context. This section allows us the opportunity to place it more properly in its overall European, as well as Scottish, context. First however, we present a brief summary of the evidence which Knox's finest editors have amassed relating to the composition of his text. Knox's earliest reference to the work is included in a letter to Gregory Railton, dated October, 23, 1559:

> The authoritie of the Frenche King and Quen is yet receaved, and wilbe in wourd till thei deny our most just requeastes, which ye shall, God willing, schortlie hereafter understand, togetther with our hole proceadings from the begynninge of this mater, *which we ar now to sett furth in maner of Historie* (Laing VI: 87, Letter XXXVIII; italics added).

18 Dickinson I: xcic.
19 ibid., cv.

Knox is referring to the raw material which went on to constitute Book II.[20] This section was certainly finished by September, 23, 1560, when Thomas Randolph wrote to William Cecil:

> I have tawked at large with Mr. Knox concerning his Hystorie. As mykle as ys written thereof shall be sent to your Honour, at the comynge of the Lords Embassadours, by Mr. John Woode. He hath written only one Booke. If yow lyke that, he shall continue the same, or adde onie more. He sayethe, that he must have farther help then is to be had in thys countrie, for more assured knowledge of thynges passed than he hathe hymself, or can come bye here: yt is a work not to be neglected and greatly wyshed that yt sholde be well handled (Laing VI: 121, Laing I: xxvi).

Laing himself apparently doubts that the book was actually sent to Cecil, since he found no trace of it among Cecil's papers during a subsequent search,[21] yet the information which Randolph presents is invaluable. Moreover, it attests to Knox's future care as a historian (even though writing history is not just about gathering reliable facts; once one has the facts, the more creative acts of interpretation and presentation must be attempted). Indeed, there is further evidence of Knox's efforts to produce a historically accurate text. In Book III for instance, there is a long passage dealing with those: 'cruell and conjured ennemyes of God' (Laing II: 133), the Duke of Guise and the Cardinal of Lorraine. This passage has apparently been 'corrected be Mr. George' [Buchanan] (see Laing II:134), who was in France at the time of the events narrated. As Dickinson points out, we find Knox: 'inviting the criticism of expert witnesses'.[22] Moreover, in 1571, the Reformer was evidently in correspondence with Alexander Hay, 'Clerk of the Privy council in 1564 and Director of Chancery in 1577',[23] seeking material to facilitate composition, and Hay apparently sent him *Leges Ecclesiasticæ Anglicanæ* or *Reformatio Legum Ecclesiasticarum*, 'which is the worke of Johne Foxe' together with other 'thingis' more fit 'to decoir the Historie' (Laing VI: 610–611).

20 See Laing I: xxvi; Dickinson I: lxxxviii, and Lang, A., 'Knox as Historian', 6.

21 See Laing VI: xxvi

22 Dickinson I: lxxxi.

23 See Laing VI: 608, n. (1).

Book II, however, was composed in the midst of events which were happening all around.

In his perceptive article 'Knox the Historian' in *The Scottish Historical Review*, the author Andrew Lang was first to suggest that this particular book: 'was apparently intended for instant publication'[24] and this is also the view taken by Dickinson.[25] Although it has now become commonplace to cite the opening of the Book as evidence of this assertion, it would be difficult to find a more apposite point at which to introduce it. Here, then, are the lines in question (written originally in Hand (A)):

> Least that Sathan by our long silence shall tak occasioun to blaspheym, and to sklander us THE PROTESTANTIS OF THE REALME OF SCOTLAND, as that our fact tendit rather to seditioun and rebellioun then to reformatioun of maners and abuses in Religioun; we have thocht expedient, so trewlie and brievlie as we can, to committ to writting the causes moving us, (us, we say, ane great parte of the Nobilitie and Baronis of the Realme,) to tak the sweard of just defence against those that most injustly seak our destructioun (Laing I: 297–298).

Pr. Jack calls Book II a: 'polemical and heated justification of the Protestant cause',[26] and the above passage typifies these qualities while relying heavily on the subjunctive mood to augment the patently apologetic tone.

This, more than the introductory passage prefaced to Book I, represents the point at which *The Historie* entered into literary history, since the paragraph introducing Book II as we now have it (see Laing I: 297) is evidently an attempt to link Books I and II together, and is therefore of a much later date than the above passage. The above has all the power which we can associate with the best of Knox's deliberative rhetoric; confidence, volatility and an embattled spirit wholly in its familiar element.

Book III seems to have been composed after II, although as Pr. Dickinson notes, 'internal evidence for the time of writing is scanty'.[27]

24 Lang, A., 'Knox as Historian', 113.

25 Dickinson I: xc.

26 Jack, R. D. S., (ed.), *Scottish Prose 1550–1700*, p. 19.

27 Dickinson I: xc.

Knox later tells us that he intended to conclude *The Historie* after Book III, having narrated the: 'thingis done frome the fyftie-awght year of God, till the arrivall of the Quenis Majestie furth of France' (Laing I: 4), but upon the instigation of 'some faythfull', he resumed a task which he 'never minded further to have travailled in' (Laing I: 4).

The product was of course Book I, which unquestionably represents Knox's finest artistic achievement both from the point of view of style and creative power. David Murison says of its *raison d'être*:

> It was ostensibly meant to tell the story of the Protestant martyrs, Hamilton, Wishart, etc.; and his writing reflects the moods aroused by the events as he remembered them, hope, despair, humour, exasperation, bitterness and rancour, the last exacerbated by his own gloom about the future. Nowhere does Knox reveal his whole character more fully, warts and all, than in the first and last books of the *History*, and, whether one approves or not of Knox, it should be remembered that most of the evidence against as well as for him comes from the candour of his own writing.[28]

It is significant that Dr. Murison links Books I and IV, for they are indeed very similar in temper and mood, although an extraordinarily rich vein of humour is more prevalent in the former. Book I is in fact the longest of the books which Knox contributed to *The Historie*, and it was written in Kyle, Ayrshire, a district which has the Knoxian distinction of being: 'a receptackle of Goddis servandis of old' (Laing I: 105). At any rate, Pr. Dickinson agrees that: 'in Book I the narrative runs freely and in Book I Knox's style is at its best'.[29] In what follows we shall see why.

In the preface to Book I (see Laing I: 5–6), Knox seemed only to envisage three books, but soon after the completion of I, the highly dramatic events which he himself had been involved in, outwith the scope and range of the narrative contained in III, necessitated a fourth book, which is probably Knox's most unrestrained. With reference to Book IV, Pr. Jack cites: 'a heavy reliance on reported speech, as Knox, Queen Mary and Lethington argue out religious problems in a fashion always designed to give victory to the Protestant side'[30] and

28 Murison, D., 'Knox the Writer', 46.

29 Dickinson I: xci.

30 Jack, R. D. S., (ed.), *Scottish Prose 1550–1700*, p. 19.

Dr. David Reid confirms these observations when he classifies Knox's *The Historie* as: 'the outstanding Scottish example of speech based prose'.[31] Book IV was finished by the end of 1566, and its concluding phrase, probably written in Knox's own hand ('In all that tyme the Erle of Murray was so formed to Johne Knox, that nowther be word nor write wes there ony communicatioun betwix thame') (Laing II: 461) represents his final, definite contribution to that astonishing work, *The Historie of the Reformatioun of Religioun within the Realme of Scotland.*

Book V was not written by Knox but probably prepared for the publisher, David Buchanan, by an unknown writer from Knox's remaining scrolls and manuscripts, gathered together latterly by Richard Bannatyne. Dr. Murison says, however, that: 'Book V contains enough to show that Knox had drafted considerable passages'[32] and this can easily be substantiated. For example, early on in this anonymous text, Knox's 'Continuator' writes of the arrival in Scotland of Lord Darnley:

> In the meanwhile there was nothing in the Court but banquetting, balling, and dancing, and other such pleasures as were meet to provoke the disordered appetitie; and all for the entertainment of the Queen's cousin from England, the Lord Darnley, to whom she did shew all the expressions imaginable of love and kindness (Laing II: 473).

Mary's attraction for Darnley came to fruition when:

> The next day following, at six hours in the morning, they were married in the Chappel Royall of Halyrud-House, by the Dean of Restalrig, the Queen being all clothed in mourning: But immediately, as the Queen went to Masse, the King went not with her, but to his pastime [...] In the mean time, the Earl Rothesse, the Laird of Grange, the Tutor of Pitcur, with some gentlemen of Fyfe, were put to the horne, for non-appearance [...] (Laing II: 495–496).

Although the first paragraph here resembles very much a passage in *A Diurnal of Remarkable Occurents*,[33] the sudden and almost sinister

31 See Reid, D., (ed.), *The Party-Coloured Mind*, p. 201, n. (3).

32 Murison, D., 'Knox the Writer', 42.

33 See Laing II: 495, n. (3).

change of mood seems typically Knoxian. Both passages are designed to meditate upon the disparity between appearance and reality, and certainly this does indicate that Knox's world-view lies behind the lines. All the raw material, if not the explosive capacity of expression, is there. Perhaps the best way to express one's overall impression, however, is to say that after reading the first four books of *The Historie*, coming to the fifth book is like coming to a hearth after the fire has been extinguished.[34] As an indication of the inferiority of these passages, one need only juxtapose them alongside an authentic Knoxian passage. Consider how he ridicules the effeminacy of the Frenchman, Châtelard, for example:

> In dansing of the Purpose, (so terme thei that danse, in the which man and woman talkis secreatlie – wyese men wold judge such fassionis more lyke to the bordell than to the comelynes of honest wemen,) in this danse the Quene chosed Chattelet, and Chattelet took the Quene. *Chattelet had the best dress* (Laing II: 368; italics added).

One recalls Gonerill's comment on Lear's hundred knights and his court: 'epicurism and lust / makes it more like a tavern or brothel / than a graced palace' (*King Lear*, Act 1, Sc. 4, ll. 240–242) and this is evidently how Knox conceived of Mary's activity. It has become a commonplace of Knox criticism to point out that his views on dancing were identical to those of the Catholic church prior to, and during, the Reformation. Even Erasmus thought it improper for monarchs (although Baldassare Castiglione, in *Il Cortegiano*, did not).[35] In Scotland the trend is witnessed by *Archbishop Hamilton's Catechism*. Under its definition of 'the saxt command' ('thou sall nocht commit adultery'), the catechism reproves:

> [...] quhasa prouokis othirs to lechorie, be foule speiche, sangis, taillis and pictouris, quha be foule thinking or feling, fylis thameself, quha eschewis nocht the occasionis of lichorie, drounkynnes, ydilness, owir lang sleeping,

34 See also Macgill, F. N. and McGreal, I. P., (eds.), *Masterpieces of Christian Literature in Summary Form*. The editors agree that 'the style of the fifth book lacks the sparkle and pungency of the other four', p. 413.

35 See Bainton, R. H., *Erasmus of Christendom*, p. 149.

> wantone & licht company, *dancing*, singing, with othir siclik prouocationis[36] (italics added).

Knox evokes the attraction between the two participants which he admits was 'honest yneuch' (Laing II: 368), but he creates a polarity between what he sees as proper and improper behaviour and tops things off with an economical but devastatingly telling final sentence. These flashes of literary genius are notably absent from Book V of *The Historie*, very much to its detriment.

We have now examined the composition of the work. This leaves us to consider Knox's fullest statement of intent. The preface to Book I, addressed to the 'gentill Readeris' (Laing I: 4), contains this material and it is here that the general similarity with Sleidan's *Commentariorum de Statu Religionis et Reipublicæ, Carolo V, Cæsare* is at its most pronounced (so much so that Katharine Firth labels Knox 'a poor man's Sleidan',[37] somewhat unfairly, as it happens). Pierre Janton has also noted the resemblance and says additionally of Knox: 'Il a beacoup lu les histoiries [...] il mentionne le nom de Lampridius, Julius Capitolinus, Elius Spartianus; il est imprégné de l'histoire des dogmes et des institutions ecclésiastiques'[38] (and it seems that Knox was even familiar with the works of Urbanus Rhegius, see Laing V: 446, and p. 39, above). Like Sleidan, however, he begins *The Historie* by asking an indulgence of his readers:

> And yit, in the begynnyng, mon we crave of all the gentill Readaris, not to look of us such ane History as shall expresse all thingis that have occurred within this Realme, during the tyme of this terrible conflict that hes bene betuix the sanctes of God and these bloody wolves who clame to thame selves the titill of clargie, and to have authoritie ower the saules of men; for, with Pollicey, mynd we to medill no further then it hath religioun mixed with it. And thairfoir albeit that many thingis wer don be omitted, yit, yf we invent no leyis, we think our selves blameless in that behalf (Laing I: 4–5).

Here is Sleidan's *praefatio* to the commentaries printed by Conrad Badius, together with Edmund Bohun's translation (which is con-

36 See Mitchell, A. F., (ed.), *Archbishop Hamilton's Catechism*, f. liii.

37 Firth, K. R., *The Apocalyptic Tradition*, p.77.

38 Janton, P., *L'homme et l'oeuvre*, p. 429.

siderably later than that of John Dawes, but is included here to give a stylistic example of another interpretation).

> *Sleidan*
> Bellicas autem res, & quicquid est eius modi, non quidem omitto, neque sane potui: sed tamen ex professo non sumpsi tractandas. Nam vt paulo supra dixi, causae religionis hic est potissimum dedicatus labor. Itaque Lectorem, quum ad id genus loca perueniet, admonitum esse volo, ne prolixiorem aliquam narrationem expectet: nec enim instituti mei fuit, & ex aliorum libris qui sibi partem hanc scribendi sumpsirunt, haurire licebit quicquid in eo desiderabitur.[39]

> *Bohun*
> As to Military actions, of what pass'd in the Wars, I have not wholly pass'd them over, nor indeed could I, and yet I have not made them any principal part of my business, because that of Religion was my main design. And therefore when my reader falls upon anything of that Nature, I would have him know before-hand, he is not to expect an exact and large account: That being contrary to my undertaking, and which may easily be found in other Authors who have made those thingis their principal care, tho I have not.[40]

The passages are apologistic, insofar as they are concerned with the expectations of the readers, but one should remember that a history of religious affairs was not a new kind of history (Eusebius of Cæsarea established the traditional genre in the fourth century). However, it *was* new in Scotland, at least in an exclusively non-legendary form. Of course 'Military actions', as Bohun calls them, will impinge. But Knox, for all his protestations, was fond of military matters and, as we know, his whole religious personality was built around a battle strategy. Here, then, we get an indication that we ought not to take his preface too literally. And he did make concessions to aesthetic expectations. We have noted that after Book II was completed Knox: 'never mynded further to have travailled in that kynd of writting' (Laing I: 4). However, 'after consultatioun with some faythfull' he was persuaded to continue. It is not surprising to find that Sleidan visualises a similar pious conference (though with a charm which we do not find in Knox):

39 Sleidan, J., *Commentariorum de Statu Religionis et Reipublicæ*, f. Aiiij.

40 Bohun, E., *The General History of the Reformation*; the author's preface and dedication, p. 2.

Sleidan

Porro superioribus aliquot annis nonnulli magna virtute & doctrina viri, quum istarum rerum mentio nonnunquam fierit, coeperunt mihi esse monitores, vt quicquid in haec tempora, præcipue vero causam religionis, incidisset, literis mandarem: & hortabantur quidem, non quod ipse hoc optime præstare possem aut quod non alii multo magis essent idonei: sed quod illa me viderent exercitatione delectari cum primis, ideoque fore putabant [...][41]

Bohun

Some years since, many men of eminent Learning and Virtue, when these things happen'd to be accidentally mention'd, began to be earnest with me that I should commit to Writing the affairs of our times, especially what related to Religion; And this they did, not out of an opinion that I was better able to do it than another, or because there were not abler men to be found for that purpose; but because they saw me particularly fancy and love these composures.[42]

The phrase: 'when these things happen'd to be accidentally mention'd', is more contrived and transparent than anything in Knox's preface. Unlike Sleidan, Knox does *not* write because he loves composition and he certainly *was* in a position which made him more competent than others. Only the vague but compelling figure of John Willock, whose stature exceeded Knox's in his own day, can come anywhere close to matching Knox's experience and expertise.

The final similarity between Knox and Sleidan which I wish to draw attention to is the most important, since the passages I shall consider deal with the very concept of history-writing in the sixteenth century. This indeed was a subject much studied by the university educated Reformers, and the knowledge derived therefrom was often thought of as part-and-parcel of a decent education (witness Adam Bell, above, p. 55). Jean Bodin, for example, later classified such material in his well-known textbook *Methodus ad facilem historiarum cognitionem*, (1566), (*Method for the Easy Comprehension of History*). Here are Sleidan's views on just what constitutes a proper history, again followed by Bohun's elegant English translation. A comparable passage written by Knox himself is then juxtaposed (and is taken from a very early part of *The Historie* as it now stands):

41 Sleidan, J., *Commentariorum de Statu Religionis et Reipublicæ*, f. Aiii.

42 Bohun, E., *The General History of the Reformation*, p. 2.

Sleidan

Historiam nihil magis decet quam veritas atque candor. Ego certe, nequid in ea parte posset in me desiderari, diligenter incubui. Nec enim ex vano quicquam hausi, vel auditione leui, sed scribendi materiam mihi suppeditarunt acta, quae studiose collegi, de quorum fide nemo dubitare posit.[43]

Bohun

Candour and Truth are the two most becoming Ornaments of an History: and in truth, I have taken the utmost care that neither of them might be wanting here: To that end, I have taken up nothing upon surmise or light report, but I have studiously collected what I have written from the Publick Records & Papers; the Faith of which can justly be call'd in question by no man.[44]

This time Knox cuts right through the elaborate aesthetic as well as historical concerns of Sleidan, but presents lines which are nonetheless the child of the above. He says:

> Of one other [thing] we mon foirwarne the discreat Readaris, which is, that thei be not offended that the sempill treuth be spokin without partialitie; for seing that of men we neyther hunt for reward, nor yitt for vane glorie, we litill pass by the approbatioun of such as seldome judge weill of God and of his workis (Laing I: 5).

Many critics, of course, reject Knox's claim to complete veracity, and rightly so. Ralph S. Walker put it simply and well when he said: 'truth is far from absolute when selected and arranged for purposes of self-justification'[45] and Andrew Lang warns that as a historian Knox: 'needs careful watching'.[46] But innuendos and fanaticism aside, Knox does present a *reasonably* reliable body of facts, and his method of substantiating material with contemporary documents obviously came from his reading of Sleidan.

Katharine R. Firth observes that there were three types of the new religious history: (i) martyrology, which was especially attractive to Erasmian humanists, (ii) Lutheran and 'eastern German Reformation',

43 Sleidan, J., *Commentariorum de Statu Religionis et Reipublicæ*, f. Aiii.

44 Bohun, E., *The General History of the Reformation*, p. 3.

45 Walker, R. S., (ed.), *The Historie of the Reformatioun*, p. 5.

46 Lang, A., *John Knox and the Reformation*, p. xi. See also Kirk, J., 'The Scottish Reformation and Reign of James VI: A Select Critical Bibliography', 122.

which saw the Catholic Church as a corruption of the ancient, and the Reformation as a return to original values, and (iii) the school of Sleidan: 'in which public records and documents were consulted [...] this too was a legacy of humanism, but showed the influence of the more southern variety, which followed after Lorenzo Valla and reached maturity in the Italian city histories'.[47] Knox, like John Foxe, was familiar with all three strands. Unfortunately, Pr. Dickinson does not draw our attention to this fact, and at no point mentions Sleidan.[48] Consequently, Scottish scholars, literary critics especially, have come to regard Knox's *The Historie* not as an expression of European as well as Scottish traditions, but as the amputated limb from a body they have not seen.

Knox's work is of course different in tone and temper from Sleidan's, and we have already noted all of the main similarities. In fact, of the three historiographical strands which Firth isolates, only the first remains to be considered and this we shall do when we come to Knox's treatment of Patrick Hamilton and George Wishart. It is to be hoped, however, that the above material will enable the literary critic to appreciate not only Knox's method of composition, the textual problems to be faced and the basic shape of *The Historie*, but also what his sources were and how he conceived of his task.

Autobiography in The Historie

We know little about the early part of Knox's life, apart from a handful of sketchy details and a good deal of speculation. Certainly, he was at least eight, and perhaps ten, years younger than Laing and M'Crie thought, and this means that he was a relatively young man in his thirties when he entered the Castle of St. Andrews as a tutor. The idea that Knox was over forty when he began his ministry has itself been out of date for fifty years, even though it still finds its way into very recent literary studies. However, the want of information surrounding his first thirty years seems deliberate, since Knox could so

47 Firth, K. R., *The Apocalyptic Tradition*, p. 74.

48 See Dickinson I: lxxxi. Even the most recent literary criticism contains no mention of Sleidan in this respect; see Reid, D., 'Prose after Knox', 189.

easily have supplied it in his *The Historie*. Perhaps the knowledge that he possessed information denied to future generations appealed to him, but the real reason is that these early years were those of his own Catholicism. It is not our purpose here to write biography however.

This present study will consider the autobiography contained in *The Historie* simply as literature. With this in mind we shall begin with the passage which describes the moment when Knox's career first began: the fateful 'call' to preach at St. Andrews Castle. As we know, Knox had at first refused to accept any such charge (above, p. 157):

> Whareupone thei prively amonges thame selfis advising, having with thame in counsall Schir David Lyndesay of the Mont, thei concluded, that thei wold geve a charge to the said Johnne, and that publictlie by the mouth of thare preachear. And so upoun a certane day, a sermone had of the electioun of ministeris, What power the congregatioun (how small that ever it was, passing the number of two or three) had above any man, in whome thei supposed and espyed the giftes of God to be, and how dangerous it was to refuise, and not to hear the voce of such as desyre to be instructed. These and other headis, (we say,) declaired, the said Johne Rowght, preachear, directed his wordis to the said Johne Knox, saying "Brother, ye shall nott be offended, albeit that I speak unto yow that which I have in charge, evin from all those that ar hear present, which is this: In the name of God, and of his Sone Jesus Christ, and in the name of these that presentlie calles yow by my mouth, I charge yow, that ye refuise not this holy vocatioun, but that as ye tender the glorie of God, the encrease of Christ his kingdome, the edificatioun of your bretherne, and the conforte of me, whome ye understand weill yneuch to be oppressed by the multitude of laubouris, that ye tack upoun yow the publict office and charge of preaching, evin as ye looke to avoid Goddis heavye displeasur, and desyre that he shall multiplye his graces with yow". And in the end, he said to those that war present, "Was not this your charge to me? And do ye not approve this vocatioun?" Thei answered, "It was; and we approve it". Whairat the said Johnne abashed, byrst furth in moist abundand tearis, and withdrew him self to his chalmer (Laing I: 186–188).

This passage ought to show that Knox was not the insensitive (and fearless) bully-boy of the Scottish Reformation, but at the other extreme, Charles Warr used it as an example of a: 'yellow streak of enervating cowardice' which 'ran through his complex character'.[49]

49 See Reid, W. S., *Trumpeter of God*, p. 23, and Warr, C. L., *The Presbyterian Tradition*, p. 256.

As Katharine R. Firth more reservedly observes, Knox evidently faced: 'a personal and professional crisis'.[50]

The above, strictly speaking, does not constitute an official ordination, but Knox included it in his *The Historie* presumably for the benefit of sympathetic readers who wished to understand fully the nature of his mission. He evidently regarded Lindsay with respect and as a figure of considerable personal authority. Indeed, it may have been Lindsay who, in light of Balnaves's and Rough's failure to win Knox over to the pulpit, came up with the idea of a public address. We do not know which passages of scripture Rough relied upon to carry out the charge, but enough of his sermon survives, at least vestigially, for us to consider Matthew 18: 20 a safe bet:

> [...] yf two of you shal agree vpon earth (for what thinge soeuer it be yat they wolde desyre) they shal haue it of my father which is in heauen. For where two or thre are gathered together in my name, there am I in the myddest amonge them [...] (*Coverdale*).

St. Paul too may have figured in it: 'wo vnto me, yf I preache not the Gospell. Yf I do it with good wyll, I shal haue my rewarde: but yf I do it agaynst my wyll, yet is the office commytted vnto me' (1 Corinthians 9: 16–17). Rough's methodology of preaching apparently entailed the division of his material into 'headis', a technique adopted by Knox (see for example Laing I: 190) but not used by Wishart of any of the pre-Reformation preachers who appear in *The Historie*.

Laing observes that Rough himself had acquired a considerable reputation as a Preacher[51] and this is borne out in the address to the diffident Knox. After receiving the request from Lindsay, Balnaves and the others, Rough had to preach his sermon, always bearing one thing in mind. When he was done, Knox must not be able, in good conscience, to evade the responsibility thrust upon him. To this end, Rough's words had to be rock solid. They were. Knox burst into tears because he knew they were. Memories of Wishart's death must have loomed large in his mind when he made that particular journey to his

50 Firth, K. R., *The Apocalyptic Tradition*, p. 115.
51 See Laing I: 187, n. (1).

solitary 'chalmer'. Whether Rough used conscious art or not, his speech is far from haphazard. For instance, he persistently invokes a hierarchy of authority: 'God [...] Jesus Christ [...]' and the Congregation. The second time around, he comes at it from a different angle. God is to be glorified, Christ's Kingdom must be increased and the brethren must be edified. Rough finishes up by introducing a personal note which ends with an admonition. Since he is: 'oppressed by the multitude of laubouris', Knox must relieve him, and for two reasons. He is more able to do so than any other, and as a Christian, he simultaneously seeks to eschew 'Goddis heavye displeasur'. Rough of course was able to play his cards so confidently because he was thoroughly immersed in the Protestant Christian ideology and he knew that Knox shared his ethic even if he lacked the practical experience. As we noted earlier, perhaps Lindsay pressed the trigger, and it was especially to him and his close colleagues that Rough turned and, using *quæstio conjuncta* (cf. above, p. 169), said: '"Was not this your charge [...]? And do you not approve [...]?"'. When they answered in the affirmative, Knox must have felt like a drowning man without even a straw to cling to.

There are many other episodes in *The Historie* in which Knox's character is revealed in an autobiographical context. Perhaps the finest of them all occurs in a narrative relating to 1562, when Knox tells how the Earl of Bothwell came to him, repenting 'his formare inordinate lyef' and seeking reconciliation between himself and Arran:

> To the whiche the said Johne ansuered, "My Lord, wold to God that in me war counsall or judgement that mycht conforte and releave you. For albeit that to this hour it hath nott chaunsed me to speik with your Lordship face to face, yit have I borne a good mynd to your house; and have bene sorry at my heart of the trubles that I have heard you to be involved in. For, my Lord, my grandfather, goodsher, and father, have served your Lordshipis predecessoris, and some of thame have died under their standartis; and this is a part of the obligatioun of our Scotische kyndnes: but this is not the cheaf. But as God hes maid me his publict messinger of glaid tydings, so is my will earnest that all men may embrase it, which perfytlie thei can not, so long as that thair remaneth in thame rancour, malice or envy. I am verray sorry that ye have gevin occasioun unto men to be offended with you; but I am more sory that ye have offended the Majestie of God, who by such meanes oft punishes the other sinnes of men. And thairfoir my counsall is, that ye begyn at God, with whom yf ye will enter

in perfyte reconciliatioun, I doubt not but he shall bow the heartis of men to forget all offenses. And as for me, yf ye will continue in godlynes, your Lordship shall command me als boldlie as any that serves your Lordship." (Laing II: 323–324).

From these remarks, Gordon Donaldson finds in Knox: 'the man […] who expressed more clearly than any other, the traditional Scottish bands of kinship and service, which were assuredly mediæval and not modern […]', matched only by: 'a Borderer who said that if his Chief would turn him out at the front door he would come in again at the back'.[52] Laing too values the passage because: 'it furnishes the only information that can be relied upon respecting [Knox's] ancestors'.[53] Certainly this is a fascinating encounter in which Knox is able to indulge his preference for face to face relationships, and he was also able to draw upon his experience as a spiritual counsellor to get straight to the core of the problem. He specifically invokes his role as a preacher of the Gospel, the 'glaid tydingis', to reinforce his own authority, but on the whole the impression is one of moderation, goodwill, loyalty and sound common sense on Knox's part (all qualities which he revealed to Mrs. Bowes in his earlier correspondence). Here we also have the key to his religious assurance, which was so effective because of its very simplicity: trust wholly in and be reconciled to, God, and success will follow.

It is to Knox's credit that he practised what he preached, and this comes out during the run up to his trial for treason. It was Lethington himself who drove Knox to the following assertion, which gives rise to another autobiographical narrative:

> "Gif God stand my friend" said the uther [Knox], "as I am assurit he of his mercie will, so lang as I depend upon his promeise, and prefer his glorie to my life and warldlie proffeit, I litill regaird how men behave thame selffis towardis me; nether yit knaw I quhairin till ony man hes borne with me in times past, unles it be, that of my mouth thay haif heard the word of God, quhilk in times to cum, gif thay refuise, my hairt wilbe persit, and for ane seasone will lament; but the incommoditie wilbe their awne […]"

52 Donaldson, G., 'Knox the Man', 27.

53 Laing II: 323, n. (9).

> The bruit of the accusatioun of Johne Knox being divulged, Mr. Johne Spens of Condie, Advocat, a man of gentill nature, and ane that professit the doctrine of the Evangell, came, as it wer, in secreit to Johne Knox, to inquyre the cause of that grit bruit. To quhom the said Johne wes plane in all thingis, and schew unto him the dowbill of the letter. Quhilk heard and consydderit, he said, "I thank my God, I came to you with ane feirfull and sorrowfull hairt, feiring that ye had done sick ane cryme as lawis mycht haif punischit, quhilk wald haif bene na small trubill to the hairtis of all sik as hes ressavit the worde of life quhilk ye haif preichit; but I depairt gritlie rejosit, alsweill becaus I persaif your awin confort, evin in the myddis of your trubillis, as that I cleirly understand, that ye haif committit no sik cryme as ye are burdenit with. Ye wilbe accusit, (said he,) but God will assist you". And sua he departit [...] (Laing II: 400–401).

The image of Knox glorying in the evangel regardless of his own discomfort is one which emerges consistently throughout his writing. It as, after all, a positively Pauline office. But Knox makes it relevant politically as well as spiritually, and this, Lethington must have realised. Knox's purpose in including the Spence episode is to indicate the mood of mainstream Protestants, but it also suggests the extent of the congruence between his own world-view and theirs. With these two episodes, closely juxtaposed as they are, it is hard to decide who sounds more pious, Knox or Spence (and 'pious' need not be a wholly pejorative adjective here) but again Knox is able to draw upon his position as a Preacher to get one up on his godly comrade. The governing neatness and the interlocking of the two narratives makes the passage more compelling when taken as a whole, because Spence, a latter-day Nicodemus, furnishes Knox (and the reader) with the Preacher's natural counterpart, the Congregation. If Knox's sermons offer 'the word of God', Spence speaks for 'all sik as hes ressavit' it. In each episode certain similarities emerge not only in ideology, but in vocabulary. There is emphasis on the 'hairt' being 'persit' or troubled. The collocation of the two words is not strictly scriptural but it does create pathos of sorts, which is augmented by such items as 'lament', 'sorrowfull' and 'burdenit', which *are* scriptural.

I wish to consider one more autobiographical incident, which has fascinated critics, among them Dr. Murison and Pr. Donaldson. It has something in common, at least superficially, with an episode, which we shall consider later, in which Knox encounters the courtiers after one of his interviews with the Queen. The pattern certainly is the same; an offended Mary Stewart dismisses Knox from her presence; he subsequently encounters one or two stray members of the court and cracks a joke which toys with their expectations (and he was always good at that):

> "Yow will not alwayis" said sche, "be at your book," and so turned hir back. And the said Johne Knox departed with a reaonsable meary countenance; whairat some Papistis offended said, "He is not effrayed". Which heard of him, he answered, "Why should the pleasing face of a gentill woman effray me? I have looked in the faces of many angrie men, and yit have nott bene effrayed *above measure*". And so left he the Quene and the Courte for that tyme (Laing II: 334–335, italics added).

Dr. Murison calls this: 'an occasion for one of Knox's rare pleasant jokes', but Donaldson penetrates further when he considers its significance in relation to Knox's: 'attitude to physical danger'.[54] He finds the phrase 'above measure' of crucial importance because it suggests that Knox was often fearful, but had the capacity to overcome the emotion. Acting in his capacity as a historian, Pr. Donaldson has moved into the domain of the literary critic. Such a critic can of course cite supporting authorities to colour Donaldson's observation. For instance, in *Discoveries*, Ben Jonson observes: 'Language most shows a man: Speak that I may see thee. It springs out of the most retired and inmost parts of us, and is the image of the parent of it, the mind. No glass renders a man's form, or likeness, so true as his speech'.[55] No observation could be more crucial to this study.

Preaching, Prophecy and Polemics

The Reformation as a world-movement undoubtedly had a lasting effect on the sermon as a literary genre and as a force within society. Only as society became increasingly secularised did this force lessen, for better or for worse. However, it would be both naïve and unfair to think that the Reformers invented preaching. This is certainly not the case, but where their real contribution lies is in their undoubted exalt-

54 Murison, D., 'Knox the Writer', 49 and Donaldson, G., 'Knox the Man', 19, 23.
55 Herford, C. H. and Simpson, P., (eds.), *Ben Jonson*, vol. VIII: p. 625.

ation of the genre. Like the Word of John's gospel, it was made flesh and came alive in a very relevant way.

This did not, of course, come about overnight. In his major work on Knox, and in a later, equally fine, but more exclusively literary study, *L'eloquence et la rhetorique dans les Sermons de Hugh Latimer*, Pr. Janton has traced how the sermon in the sixteenth century took shape through the continual publication of practical handbooks such as Andreas Gerardus Hyperius's *De Formandis Concionibus Sacris* and *De Tradendis Disciplinis* of Juan Luis Vives, and Knox was in the right place at the right time to inherit the best of the new learning, and apply it to his preaching. The textbooks gradually found their way into English translations such as Thomas Wilson's *The Arte of Rhetorique*, (London, 1553), Richard Rainolde's *A Booke Called the Foundation of Rhetorike*, (London, 1563), and Hyperius's own *The Practice of Preaching*, (1577), during and after the Reformation, and augmented the rhetorical training which the university educated Reformers already had. Just as Knox's conception of history and how to write it involved detailed knowledge of complex strands of thought and experience, so too his knowledge of how to preach came from a milieu of highly intellectual material. Only when one properly appreciates this can one approach Knox's sermons. I propose to examine five samples in order to give a fair indication as to the range of Knox's preaching. They are: (i) his first sermon preached at the Castle of St. Andrews in 1547 (Laing I: 189–192), (ii) at Stirling in 1559: 'in the greatest of our trubles' (Laing I: 465–473), (iii) at Cowper (Laing II: 8): 'when the Reformers were in full retreat',[56] (iv) in 'Sanct Geilis Kirk' before 'the haill Nobilitie' in 1560 (Laing II: 84–87) and finally (v) before the dissolution of Parliament in 1563 when Knox preached against the Queen's proposed marriage (see Laing II: 386). Janton has developed useful categories, under which sermons (i) and (v) are classified as *controverse*, (ii) and (iii) as *exhortation*, and (iv) as belonging to *sermons de circonstance*.[57] In one way or another, all of the above differ from Knox's published works on Isaiah and Matthew, which are commentaries. With the sole exception of (iv), the sermons in *The*

56 Donaldson, G., 'Knox the Man', 24.

57 Janton, P., *L'homme et l'oeuvre*, p. 410.

Historie are in summary form, although upon occasion Knox does appear to be quoting directly from an original text, or from his own memory. Enough survives, however, for us to appreciate why Knox was so successful and why the Reformers on the front line turned eagerly to him for encouragement and support, and also why he caused controversy after the return of Mary. He does not claim authorship of sermon (iv), but as Laing says, it: 'was undoubtedly conducted by Knox himself'.[58]

The St. Andrews text marks the beginning of Knox's career (and we have already explored the episode in which he received his call in the earlier autobiographical section). For a first effort it was remarkably confident, although as W. Stanford Reid observes: 'that Knox was very nervous […] goes without saying'.[59] His courage seems to have mounted with the occasion, and after he had finished: 'Some said, "otheris sned the branches of the Papistrie, but he stryckis at the roote, to destroy the hole"' (Laing I: 192).[60] His text, significantly enough, was from the prophet Daniel 7: 24 (later, he was to preach effectively on Haggai, see Laing II: 88), but he was still teaching on Daniel twenty-four years after his first sermon, when James Melvill saw him on that famous occasion in 1571.[61] In this instance, he combined *Old Testament* prophecy with Revelation 13: 5, to produce the following radical rejection of papal authority:

> […] he willed men to considder yf these notes, "Thare shall ane arise unlyk to the other, having a mouth speaking great thinges and blasphemous" could be applyed to any other, but to the Pape and his kingdome; for "yf these" (said he,) be not great wordis and blasphemous, 'the Successor of Petir', 'the Vicare of Christ,' 'the Head of the Kirk,' 'most holy,' 'most blessed,' […] yea, 'that has power of all, and none power of him;' Nay 'not to say that he dois wrong' [...] "Yf these," (said he) "and many other, able to be shawin in his own Canone Law, be not great and blasphemous woordis, and such as never mortall man spak befoir, lett the world judge." (Laing I: 191).

58 Laing II: 84, n. (1).

59 See Reid, W. S., *Trumpeter of God*, p. 48.

60 See *O.E.D*, IX, 314, (1).

61 See Pitcairn, R., (ed.), *The Autobiography and Diary of Mr. James Melvill*, p. 26.

The relationship between this sermon and Sir David Lindsay's *Ane Dialogue betuix Experience and ane Courteour*, has been noted from time to time, although different conclusions have been drawn. In 'Sir David Lindsay, Reformer', an article in *The Innes Review* of 1950, Brother Kenneth states the one recognised fact, that: 'the general resemblance is too close to be accidental'.[62] Lindsay, of course, *was* present in the Castle at the time of Knox's sermon). In a highly readable work, *John Knox in Controversy*, Hugh Watt posits two things: that Knox ultimately inspired Lindsay to write part of his poem, and that the particular juxtaposition of Daniel and Revelation produced a reading of history which was unique to Knox at that time.[63] Both statements have been challenged.

Brother Kenneth suggests that: 'it is more likely that the scholar and humanist presiding at the council suggested the line of thought to the diffident young preacher'.[64] As to Watt's second point, Katharine Firth argues that while:

> [...] one cannot be quite certain that Knox did not arrive at the thesis independently [...] possibly [he] had a copy of [George] Joye's *The Exposicion of Daniel the prophete gathered out of Philip Melanchthon, Johan Ecolampadius, Chonrade Pellicane, and out of John Draconite & C.*, (Geneva 1545), or else access to some of the German authors. Another source could have been Frith's translation of Luther's *De Antichristo*.[65]

This would mean that texts such as Melanchthon's *In Danielam Prophetam Commentarius* or the ideas of Oecolampadius's more general *Commentariorum in Prophetam* ultimately lie behind the sermon. Nor should we rule out *Chronicon Carionis Expositum et auctum multus et re teribus et recentibus histories*, (1532), by John Carion, in a Latin or German version, although it is still too early for the English translation by Walter Lynne and John Funcke (London, 1550). Indeed, by his own admission, Knox was relying on an: 'originall whare my

62 Brother Kenneth, 'David Lindsay, Reformer', 80.

63 Watt, H., *John Knox in Controversy*, p. 13.

64 Brother Kenneth, 'David Lindsay, Reformer', 80, n. (6).

65 See Firth, K. R., *The Apocalyptic Tradition*, pp. 116–117.

testimonyes ar written' and he only offers to prove: 'that the wrettaris ment as I have spokin' (Laing I: 192).

In places, the sermon itself draws heavily from the *Ius Canonicum* of orthodox Catholicism (and it is in this that the resemblance with Lindsay's poem is at its most pronounced). Knox is presumably alluding to such common papal titles as *Romanus Pontifex Sanctissimus*, *Sanctissimus Dominis Noster* and *Servus Servorum Dei*, and after listing some of these in translation, he introduces a 'yea', then a 'nay' section which recalls Matthew 5: 37 (or 2 Corinthians 1: 17–20): 'your communicacion shalbe, yee, yee; nay, nay. For whatsoever is more then that, commeth of euel' (*Coverdale*). This is presumably to ensure that the congregation (and, later, the readers of *The Historie*) fully appreciated that he was rejecting every aspect of the papacy. He evidently succeeded in creating that impression. (This brings us incidentally to a recognition of the fact that, ultimately, Knox had two audiences, which each wanted different things). As he says in *The Historie*, his audience at St. Andrews specifically wanted 'the probatioun' of that which, previously, he had affirmed (that the Catholic Church was hopelessly corrupt): '"for yf it be trew, we have bene miserable deceaved"'. (Laing I: 189). The original readers of Knox's memoirs may have been more interested in his autobiography than in the veracity of such issues, which by that time had been decided by most Scots anyway, for better or for worse. Not a few of Knox's works, as we now have them, deal with this dual audience. For instance, his *An Exposition Upon the Sixth Psalm of David, Addressed to Mrs. Bowes*, which we considered in chapter four (above, pp. 177–180), is one such text.

Aside from catering to a range of listeners and readers, Knox writes at a level where grammatical structure and rhetorical design smoothly interface. For example, his *apodosis*, ('lett the world judge'), is crucially important. It is used in the imperative rather than the optative mood, but at the same time fulfils all the requirements of *permissio*. In using this figure, the orator leaves to his audience the final pronunciation of judgement on a matter which has been more-or-less decided by him. But at least it invokes the participation of the listeners if it is properly used. Knox's understanding of rhetorical practice was at this stage probably influenced by what he calls the 'humane authoris' (Laing I: 186). This would mean Cicero and the pseudo-Ciceronian textbook *Rhetorica ad Herrenium*. Quintillian's *Institutio Oratoria* also contains a definition of the above device. The *apodosis*, moreover, has more than one *protasis*, or antecedent conditional clause. The phrase '"yf these"', accompanied by a parenthetical 'said he', for the benefit of *The Historie* readers, occurs twice and helps to tease one's sense of expectation. The above sermon was delivered before the Reformation gathered any strength in Scotland, so Knox had no guarantee of support. That he summoned eloquent resources in order to persuade is not surprising.

The Cowper Sermon as it exists in *The Historie*, is only barely salvageable, and certainly it is more fragmentary than the earlier work. Indeed, it is better to get it out of the way quickly and move on to the Stirling text of 1559. It appears to be a variation of a theme which Knox first considered in *A Faithful Admonition to the Professors of God's Truth in England* (above, pp. 85–90), and there are parallels in the *Familiar Epistles*. It is based on a combination of texts (Matthew 14 and John 6). Again Knox employs the same mode of presentation; the combination of narrative and quotation:

> His exhortatioun was, "That we should not faint, but that we sould still row aganis these contrarius blastis, till that Jesus Christ sould come; for (said he,) I am assuredlie persuaded that God sall delyver us frome the extreme trowbill, as that I am assured that this is the Evangell of Jesus Christ whiche I preche unto [you] this day. 'The fourth watche is nocht yet come;' abyde a lytill: the boit salbe saved, and Peter, whiche has left the boit, sall not droune. I am assured, albeit I cannot assure you, be reason of this present rage; God grant that ye may acknawledge his hand, after that your eyes hes seine his deliverance." (Laing II: 8).

Like his sermon at St. Andrews in June 1559 (see Laing I: 349) which only survives in narrative form, what impresses about this is its relevance and applicability to the situation which it addresses head on. In a famous, remark Knox's value to the Reformers had been assessed: 'the voice of one man is able in one hour to put more life in us than five hundred trumpets continually blustering in our ears'.[66]

66 See *Calendar of the State Papers Relating to Scotland and Mary, Queen of Scots*, (eds.), Bain, J., et al, vol. I: no. 1017.

Knox places great emphasis on his own personal vision. The item 'assured' in one form or another occurs four times and is accompanied by 'delyver' and 'delyverance'. He is not altogether convinced that he can communicate his faith to the congregation: 'be reason of this present rage', (that is, political turmoil, not personal anger) but he asks its members to accept his judgement until relief, in the symbolic shape of the 'fourth watche' ultimately arrives. The allusion is presumably to Matthew 14: 25, (and the same reference occurs at least twice in *A Faithful Admonition*, cf. Laing III: 273 and 288, the first implicitly). Here, the notion of the 'fourth watch', which by the Roman reckoning, denotes the last quarter of the day (we might say the 'eleventh hour'), is especially important. Aside from its literal meaning it has a metaphorical function signifying the very depths of despair. Knox calls the overall technique here *specialis applicatio* (Laing I: 469, marginal note) and his use of it reached a literary peak at Stirling in 1559, and it is to this superb text that we now turn.

David Murison calls the Stirling text: 'Knox's greatest sermon as padre in chief to the army'[67] but it is worth noting that Knox preached only because: 'Johne Willock was departed to England, as befoir he had appointed' (Laing I: 465). When we add to this the fact that our Quintin Kennedy, whom we have met in previous chapters (above, pp. 112–113, p. 171), called Willock the 'Chosin primat' of Protestantism in Scotland,[68] Knox begins to occupy his proper place in our perception. (Even if we treat Kennedy's information with caution it is difficult to see why he would make such a point if it weren't a true reflection, since he would only be exalting one enemy at the expense of another. In the 1980s, political activist Arthur Scargill would not have said that Norman Tebbit was the Leader of the British Conservative party to slight Margaret Thatcher!)

The sermon itself was initially based on Psalms 80, and as E. G. Rupp suggests (admittedly, with reference to Knox's Isaiah 26 text), Knox adheres to: 'the expository method [...] of following through a passage, breaking the text in pieces, feeding the flock with the bread

67 Murison, D., 'Knox the Writer', 44.

68 See Laing, D., (ed.), *The Miscellany of the Wodrow Society*, p. 267.

of life'.[69] Knox concentrates at first on verses four to eight, then tells how he had been studying Psalm 80 during his recent stay in Edinburgh, and in doing so: 'he was assured of trubles suddanlie to come' (Laing I: 466). After some references to such figures as Saul, Nebuchadnezzar and Balthasar, Knox quotes directly, and subsequently gives us access to prose like this:

> Oure faces ar this day confounded, our ennemyes triumphe, oure heartis have quaiked for fear, and yitt thei remane oppressed with sorrow and schame. But what shall we think to be the verray cause that God hath thus dejected us? Yf I shall say, our synnes and formar unthankfulness to God, I speik the treuth. But yitt I spack more generalie then necessitie required: for when the synnes of men ar rebucked in general, seldome it is that man discendeth within him self, accusing and dampnying in him self that whiche most displeaseth God (Laing I: 469).

The power and intensity of the language here matches that of the passage dealing with Mary Stewart's arrival in Scotland which we shall look at in a subsequent chapter (below, pp. 316–318). The mood is identical and so too is some of the language. But nowhere does Knox come closer to the above passage than in his Preface to Book IV which was written some seven years after the crisis described above. Indeed, it was on the heels of another crisis, after the murder of Rizzio, that it was written:

> "[…] But frome whence (allace) cumeth this miserable disperioun of Goddis people within this Realme, this day, Anno 1566, in Maij? And what is the cause that now the just is compelled to keap silence? Good men ar banished, murtheraris, and such as ar knowin unworthie of the commoun societie, (yf just lawis war put in deu executioun) bear the hoill regiment and swynge within this Realme? We answere, Becaus that suddandlie the most part of us declyned from the puritie of Goddis word […]" (Laing II: 265).

Strictly speaking this is not part of a sermon, for when Knox wrote he had no audience and the popular support which he undoubtedly enjoyed when he preached in 1559 had been almost wholly dissipated. Even so, the general similarities in content and form are undeniable. In the first, and for the benefit of his congregation, Knox attempts to make

69 Rupp, E. G., 'The Europe of John Knox', 9.

sense of an ostensibly inexplicable situation, with some considerable success, and he moves on to ponder the dubious efficacy of preaching based on general rather than particular examples. Obviously, in the second passage, Knox has gone beyond the desire to encourage. He had burst into a desolate attic where his hopes for, and dreams of, a theocracy were crushed. Things are topsy-turvy, as indeed they were in 1559, but then there was in Knox's mind a solution which people were willing to explore. By 'Anno 1566, in Maij' he was not confident that they would be so again.

Two stylistic features emerge in these texts which Knox also used in his outstanding sermon of 1563 (as we shall see). In the Stirling text he uses both of them; rhetorical questions and a sense of shared experience. His frequent use of the genitive plural ('our(e)') creates a feeling of solidarity, while the series of past-participles ('confounded', 'quaiked' and 'oppressed') outlines precisely what this experience has entailed. These three verbs are of especial interest. The first comes from an imprecatory register which is nevertheless a scriptural one, the second is more visually suggestive (and may owe something to Daniel 10: 7: 'a greate quaking fell vpon them, soe that thay fled to hyde themselues') (*Great Bible*) and the third perhaps carries just a hint of injustice, or apparent injustice (which in Protestant thought is not the same thing at all). Knox's rhetorical answer: '"Yf I shall say [...] I speik the treuth"', is designed to invoke humility, and the noun-couplet 'sorrow and schame' in the previous sentence adds not a little poignancy. Knox also dwells on the fact that the Protestants are wholly 'dejected'. One may argue that his reminders were more likely to depress the Congregation than to encourage it, but this notion would be fundamentally alien to Knox's way of thinking, and probably to his listeners' as well. Self-criticism, (the more the better) was, in Knox's view, the only way to convince God of one's penitence. Thereafter, the Deity is more likely to respond favourably to requests and prayers, and will unfold His divine plan in a more readily comprehensible way. Once the Brethren got that straight, they were by no means home and dry, but they were on the way to ultimate victory. Knox concluded by vehemently exhorting: 'all man to amendment of lyffe, to prayaris, and to the warkis of charitie'. He tells us that subsequently: 'the myndis of men began wounderously to be erected' (Laing I: 473). Knox had evidently passed the acid test which all orators must undertake if they are to succeed in moving men to action. Here, indeed, was an Anthony to: 'ruffle up [their] spirits' (*Julius Caesar*, Act. 3, Sc. 2, l. 229).

In the second passage, Knox laments 'this miserable dispersioun' as he lamented the 'dejection' of the Protestants in 1559, but the language is less geared to persuasion. He does not attempt to identify with any particular group, but he does answer his own three-fold series of questions in a similar way to the previous passage. When we come to our final sermon, Knox's appearance before the Lords in 1563, we shall see how he harnessed some of his best and shrewdest rhetoric, but for the moment we shall have to consider some rather different material.

When we turn to the sermon at St. Giles in 1560, we see Knox neither in despair nor seeking to enliven the Reformers. The Reformation had been established, and Knox turned to devout thanks-giving and prayer; thus we find a very different kind of exhortation. In what follows, however, I want to suggest that the form of Knox's service was one which he had established some time earlier. The document known as: *The practies of the Lorde's Supper yewsed in Barvike-upon-Twyed by John Knoxe, precher to that congregation in the Church there*, (1550), is useful in this attempt (again this text belongs to the 'Morrice Collection' published by Peter Lorimer). We can juxtapose material like the following, and some striking similarities begin clearly to emerge:

> *St. Giles Sermon (1560)*
> "[...] O Eternall and Everlasting God, Father of oure Lord Jesus Chryst, quha hes nocht onlie commandit us to pray, and promeisit to heir us, but alsua willis us to magnifie thy mercies, and to glorifie thy name quhen thou schawis thy self pitiefull and favoribill unto us, especiallie quhen thou deliveris us frome disperatt daingearis [...] Out of thir miseries, O Lord, could nather our witt, policey, nor strength delyver us; yea did schaw unto us how vayne was the help of man, quhair thy blessing gevis not victorie. In thir our anguischeis, O Lord, we suitit unto thee, we cryit for thy help, and we reclameit thy name, as thy trubillit flock, persecutit for thy treuth sake. Mercifullie hes thow hard us, O Lord, mercifullie, we say, becaus that neither in us, neither yitt in our confederatis was thair any caus quhy thou souldest have gevin unto us sa joyfull

and suddane a deliverance: for neither of us bayth ceassit to do wickitlie, evin in the myddis of oure gretest trubillis [...]" (Laing II: 84–85).

Berwick Text (1550)
Allmyghtie and everlastynge Lord, unyversall but yet most mecifull Father, we have offended and daylye do offend the ees of thy majestie in all the actions of our lyffe. Just cause hast Thou, O Lord, to thrist us into hell for our manyfold offencis, the remembrance wherof is grevous to our conscience, so paynfull and dollorous that easse nor relaxation in ourselves can we fynd none. Whome to shall we call? Whom shall we seke? Who maye release owr sorrow and restore gladness but Thou alone, O mercyfule Lorde? [...] We are encoraged to aske mercie of Thee, for when we were Thine enemyies, dead by synne, and colde do nothyng but blaspheme Thee in thy face, Thou wast movyd to have mercie; Thou loved and colde not hait us; and so Thou loved us that Thou gave thy onlye-begotten Sonne Jesus Chryst for our redemption; and by Him has Thou mayd unto us one promyse that whensoever two or three gathered in his name asks any thing of thee, the same they shall obtain by Him.[70]

The Berwick text pre-dates the St. Giles Sermon by ten, perhaps even eleven, years,[71] and we can see in it how Knox first constructed his prayers, and that he did not alter the basic framework very much in the later sermon, although he has obviously worked in some contemporary references. A notable similarity is the reference to God's command for prayer and guarantee of acceptance when man is at his least acceptable, 'quha hes nocht onlie commandit us to pray, and promeisit to heir us', (1560), / 'We are encouraged to aske mercie of Thee [...] when we were Thine enymies', (1550). Then there is the reference to man's anguishes which takes the form of urgent questions in the earlier text: 'Whom to shall we calle? Whom shall we seke? Who maye [...]?', although Knox may be referring to particular events in the 1560 version (which he does not develop). In the St. Giles text there is some emphasis placed on martyrdom ('persecutit for thy treuth'), none in the Berwick thanks-giving. Of course, we can account for this difference by remembering that Knox's congregation at Berwick had another world-view and had inherited different experiences from those of the Scottish Reformers in 1560. There is equal stress on God's 'mercy' and mercifulnes in both passages, with a high concentration

70 Lorimer, P., *John Knox and the Church of England*, p. 291.
71 ibid., p. 292.

of reverential pronouns used vocatively and genitively (thirteen instances in each case). Only in the sermon of 1560 does Knox use an ordinary pronoun to refer directly to God ('quha'). It is noticeable that the St. Giles sermon builds in intensity and is more immediately compelling than the Berwick text, since it uses a 'nocht onlie […] but […] especiallie' form, while the sentences in the 1550 text are generally shorter and more frequent (six sentences in the Berwick, to four in the St. Giles). To be sure, there are many further similarities and contrasts, but we have established that the ground-work of the 1560 passage already existed in Knox's mind long before. When he preached in 1563, his topic, the Queen's marriage, was much more inflammatory.

Knox was evidently worried that Mary's marriage to another Catholic Monarch would be enough to stimulate a counter-Reformation, but we should also note that he was modelling himself on John the Baptist, who rebuked Herod over his proposed marriage to Herodias in the gospels (compare for example Luke 3: 19: 'But Herode the Tetrarcha, whan he was rebuked of him because of Herodias his brother's wife […]' (*Coverdale*)). Most of the text of this sermon survives, although there has been some editing for final inclusion in *The Historie*; how much we cannot really be sure. But Knox of course quotes the best parts directly and thus saves the reader some effort. There are some justly famous and truly memorable moments, of which the most impressive is this:

> "[…] In your most extreame dangearis I have bein with you: Sanct Johnestoun, Cowper Mure, and the Craiggis of Edinburgh, ar yitt recent in my heart; yea, that dark and dolorouse nyght whairin all ye, my Lordis, with schame and feare left this toune, is yitt in my mynd; and God forbid that ever I forgett it. What was (I say) my exhortatioun unto you, and what is fallen in vane of all that ever God promised unto you by my mouth, ye your selfis yitt lyve to testifie. Thair is nott one of you against whom was death and destructioun threatened, perished in that danger: And how many of your ennemyes hes God plagued befoir your eyis! Shall *this* be the thankfulness that ye shall render unto your God […]?" (Laing II: 384–385, italics added).

This is supremely accomplished rhetoric from a wily, shrewd politician *par excellence* (even if *The First Blast* had been politically disastrous). Knox reinforces former ties, exploits loyalties, invokes commitment and hints at punishment to come, all by turns. For a sermon it is strikingly autobiographical rather than theological, and it is a far cry from the wordy, doctrinal excesses of the Matthew sermon or *An Epistle to the Congregation of the Castle of St. Andrews*.

When this text was delivered, Knox no doubt saw his reforms slipping into oblivion and much hard, bitter effort being wasted by an insidious process precipitated by the presence of the Queen. But its most remarkable literary feature is one which we have met before (in Knox's letter from Dieppe to Scotland during one of the most frustrating episodes in his life: above, pp. 97–99). It is the ability to load just one word, a demonstrative pronoun, 'this', with the whole import of a passage. '"Shall *this*"' says Knox, with what must have been more than a trace of incredulity, '"be the thankfulness ye shall render [...]?"' (italics added). Remembering always that a sermon is designed for oral delivery, we can only speculate as to how much vocal emphasis Knox put on the item, but we can be fairly sure that it was considerable (and it may be significant that the famous tribute to Knox in the *Calendar of State Papers* refers not to his words, but to his *voice*). Indeed, if we read the lines aloud once or twice, the summarising pronoun can be used with such power that it becomes easy to imagine how deeply the Lords must have been stung by Knox. His *cri de coeur* involves the same kind of lumbering rhetorical question which we examined earlier, but this time the answer remains implicit. In fact, if the Lords did not come away with the impression that they were betraying the trust placed in them by God, through Knox, it could only be because the Reformer's rhetoric had failed.

But all this was by way of preamble. By comparison Knox delivers his *coup de grâce* quite casually:

> "And now, my Lordis, to putt end to all, I hear of the Quenis marriage: Duckis, brethren to Emperouris, and Kingis: stryve all for the best game; but this, my Lordis, will I say, (note the day, and beare witnesse efter,) whensoever the Nobilitie of Scotland professing the Lord Jesus, consentis that ane infidell (and all Papistes are infidellis) shalbe head to your Soverane, ye do so far as in ye lyeth to banishe Christ Jesus from this Realme; ye bring Goddis vengeance upoun the countrey, a plague upoun your self, and perchaunse ye do no small confort to your Soverane." (Laing II: 385–386).

Knox seems to have foreseen that both 'Papistis and Protestantis' would be offended, but that hardly needed supernatural, prophetic powers. As he says: 'even his familiaris disdained him for that speaking' (Laing II: 386), but Knox, perhaps more than any other, had no faith in a so-called *simultaneum*, or a society in which two religions co-existed. Moreover, there is much evidence to suggest that he knew exactly what he was doing. W. Stanford Reid is not wrong when he says that, long before, Knox had learned: 'to count the cost before he made a move'.[72] Having already been summoned to the Queen's presence thrice, the likelihood of fourth encounter must have been on his mind. Already he seems to be preparing. Knox the notary surfaces ('note the day, and beare witnesse efter'), and he makes sure of the time and his witnesses before he gives his final inflammatory judgement.

As in the Stirling sermon of 1559, Knox's logic comes across as rather alien to modern minds, but once the reader begins to comprehend how, and according to what principles, he thought, it is extremely simple. It goes something like this. Join a 'papist' to a 'papist Queen', then an infidel will be the supreme ruler (even if Mary was already an infidel), *ergo*, Christ will be banished from Scotland. This could only lead to Divine punishment. Knox then played his final card; perhaps Mary herself would ultimately be the worse for it. Of course, that was the way things actually worked out in the event, but as Pr. Dickinson observes: 'Mary's own actions and character' rather than the efforts of Knox were: 'to deprive the Roman Church of any victorious recovery'.[73]

The analysis of these five sermons, then, hopefully brings us to an appreciation of the literary merits inherent in Knox's preaching and to an understanding of his success. When Pr. R. Watson argues that: 'it is impossible to warm to Knox's harsh, authoritarian nature', he does the Reformer something of an injustice, perhaps because his notions about Knox do not seem to have been fully 'de-mythologised'.

72 Reid, W. S., *Trumpeter of God*, p. 103.
73 Dickinson I: lxi.

But Pr. Watson is certainly right to say that Scotland was fertile ground for Knox's preaching[74].

There are many other traces of the sermon in *The Historie*, especially in the Wishart narrative. In fact, Knox recorded several of Wishart's sermons, and he invariably commented on them. Certainly they provide useful material for comparison with Knox's own charismatic preaching, and that they influenced him greatly, there is no doubt. And since Wishart's only other literary production was the Zwinglian *Confession of Fayth* now contained in *The Miscellany of the Wodrow Society* and printed posthumously in 1548, we should be grateful to Knox for preserving these literary reminders.

During what Jenny Wormald has called Wishart's: 'peripatetic ministry to Ayrshire, Fife, Lothian and Perth in 1544',[75] he preached on Romans (Laing I: 125), Psalms 107 (Laing I: 130) and 'The Parable of the Sowar' from Matthew 13 (Laing I: 134). (It will be recalled that 'The Parable of the Unforgiving Servant' was John Gau's most lengthy exercise in scriptural quotation (above, pp. 38–43) and similarly in John Johnsone's *An Confortable Exhortation of Oure Mooste Holy Christen Faith*, we find 'The Rich man and Lazarus' (Luke 16) and the 'Parable of the Rich Fool' (Luke 12) (both lifted *verbatim* from Tyndale's 1526 *New Testament*). Knox too may have been attached to this literary form, since his account of the murder of Beaton is based at least partly on the same parable: '"Eitt and be glade my saule, for thow hast great riches laid up in store for many dayis"' (cf. Luke 12: 19, Laing I: 173).

Now all this is not to say that the use of parables was a peculiary Protestant phenomenon; there are examples of 'The Good Samaritan' and the 'Rich Gluttone' in *Archbishop Hamilton's Catechism* of 1551,[76] but with the Reformation's renewed emphasis on preaching, it is not all that surprising that homiletic genres made something of a come-

74 Watson, R., *The Literature of Scotland*, p. 96.

75 Wormald, J., *Court, Kirk and Community*, p. 106. According to Duncan Shaw, Wishart was following not just the obvious example of Christ, but also of Zwingli's disciple Conrad Schmidt; see 'Zwinglian Influences on the Scottish Reformation', 123.

76 Mitchell, A. F., (ed.), *Archbishop Hamilton's Catechism*, f. xli.

back in vernacular religious prose. And there were difficulties too. As early as 1528, William Tyndale warned against a 'good-works' orientated interpretation of *The Parable of the Wicked Mammon* in Luke 19 and re-asserted the Lutheran/Pauline gospel of justification by faith alone.

Unlike Knox, however, Wishart preached from a: 'bill conteanyng the purpose' (Laing I: 137) but he often extemporised, as in this sermon, preached in Haddington when his support was waning. Knox tells how Wishart, as it were, 'walked that room and issued thence / In Galilean turbulence'[77] (to borrow a strikingly apt phrase from a poem by W.B. Yeats). Wishart remonstrated thus, using *perclusio/cataplexis*:

> "O Lord, how long shall it be, that thy holy woorde shalbe despysed, and men shall not regard thare awin salvatioun. I have heard of thee, Hadingtoun, that in thee wold have bein at ane vane Clerk play two or three thowsand people; and now to hear the messinger of the Eternall God, of all thy toune nor parische can not be nombred a hundreth personis. Sore and feirfull shall the plagues be that shall ensew this thy contempt: with fyre and swerd thow shalt be plagued; yea, thow Haddingtoun, in speciall, strangearis shall possesse thee, and yow, the present inhabitantes shall eyther in bondage serve your enneymes, or ellis ye shalbe chassed fra your awin habitationis; and that becaus ye have not knawin, nor will nott know the tyme of Goddis mercifull visitatioun." (Laing I: 138).

Knox tells us that: 'In such vehemency and threatnying continewed that servand of God neyr ane hour and ane half' (Laing I: 138). If Knox is not exaggerating, it is clear that he edited and shortened Wishart's speech for *The Historie*, but it still holds our attention by virtue of its ominous strength. In her biography *Mary, Queen of Scots*, Antonia Fraser calls Wishart: 'a leading Protestant preacher of outstanding gentle character, in an age not over-endowed with the pure in heart'[78] and there is certainly some evidence to confirm this (as we shall see in a later chapter dealing with Knox's dramatic narratives). W. Stanford Reid understates things a little when he says that: 'Wishart could, from what we know of his sermons, be quite violent and fiery, and the fact that he went around with a body guard carrying a double-

77 Jeffares, A. N., (ed.), *Poems of W. B. Yeats: A New Selection*, p. 251. This quotation is from 'Two Songs from a Play', II.

78 Fraser, A., *Mary, Queen of Scots*, p. 45.

handed sword hardly bespeaks of a man wholly devoted to peace'.[79] Furthermore, since he was known to favour the Swiss theology of Huldreich Zwingli, he could hardly have been unaware of that Reformer's violent death on the battlefield of Kappel, where he fell with sword in hand, nearly fifteen years before Wishart's return to Scotland. Even Luther, who in any case is known to have personally disliked Zwingli, had condemned his actions.

These things aside, however, the above passage represents a special kind of preaching. It is, for the most part, prophecy. (And Knox tells us that Wishart's predictions were fulfilled in 1550, when Haddington was devastated by both French and English forces, and by: 'a peast so contagious, that with great difficultie could thei have thare dead buryed' (Laing I: 236). Wishart's technique, however, is more important than the veracity of his prophecy. It should be obvious that Wishart makes use of recurrent scriptural formulae and that they create the whole flavour of the passage. The imagery is presumably from the books of Jeremiah and Isaiah. For instance Jeremiah 17: 4 reads: 'I wil subdue you vnder the hevy bondage of youre enemies', while Isaiah 1: 17 and 66: 15 respectively read: 'Youre londe lieth waist, youre cities are brent up, youre enemies deuoure youre lande and ye must be fayne to stande and luke vpon it: and it is desolate' and: 'ye Lorde shall judge all flesh with the fyre and with his swerde, and there shalbe a greate nombre slayne of the Lorde' (*Coverdale*). It is perhaps significant that Wishart suggests two possibilities. After all, the more alternatives the prophet offers, the more chance he has of getting it right.

Of course, in addition to this, there is the speaker's own sensitivity, which manifests itself as righteous Christ-like indignation, and the scriptural patterns revolve around a core made up of contradistinctions between a rich past and a depleted present, between Clerk Play and Gospel, and by extension, between vanity and religious truth. Interrogative phrases such as: 'how long shall it be [...]' invoke duration rather in the fashion of Psalms, Isaiah or the gospels. Christ, for instance, often queries: 'how longe shall I be with you? How longe shall I suffre you' (Matthew 17: 17, *Tyndale* 1526). Wishart's address

79 Reid, W. S., *Trumpeter of God*, p. 28.

to Haddington itself neatly falls into that category of preaching which E. G. Rupp calls geographical expostulation – 'O Manchester, repent. Turn to God O Bolton!',[80] although he does not mention its probable sources. It recalls Christ's stern rebuke to the unbelieving towns of Capernaum, Chorazin and Bethsaida (see, for example, Matthew 11: 23, Luke 10: 15), and His lamentation over Jerusalem, specifically in Luke 19: 44; 'because thou hast not known ye tyme, wherein thou hast been visited' (*Coverdale*).

Wishart uses the phrase 'O, Lord', with its interjection positioned before the substantive in the vocative relation to convey his sudden, devotional vehemence and he relies heavily on pronouns to spike his admonition. 'Thee', 'thow', 'thy', occur seven times in total, and when we compare this with similar passages in Knox we can conclude that Wishart was less prone to this kind of language than his successor. Wishart in fact drives his point home relentlessly. The prepositional phrase 'in speciall', which performs adverbially, intensifies the threat to Haddington, and Knox must have thought of the prophet never being accepted in his home country (see Matthew 13: 57, Mark 6: 4, John 4: 44). Such intensification occurs in other ways too. Wishart twice uses the negative particle 'nor' ('toune nor parische' [...]; 'have not knawin, nor will nott knaw') but in these instances the intensification takes the shape of expansion not particularisation. Pr. Janton is right when he says that, in Knox's writings, 'La prédiction précise, la véritable *ominatio*, comme celle de Wishart sur Haddington ou Dundee, apparaît rarement',[81] but like Wishart, Knox was soon to experience similar despair as his preaching apparently fell upon deaf ears. Even so, rejection is itself often a necessary component of the prophetic experience, as it is outlined in the Bible. It may seem bizarre to twenty-first century readers that such activity could lead to violent death, but indeed it did.

Just as Knox assumed the role of preacher after Wishart's death (albeit unwillingly), he took up the fallen prophetic mantle like Elisha after the departure of Elijah (see 2 Kings 2: 13, 14). Indeed, no sooner had he embarked on his reforming career, when he was apparently

80 Rupp, E. G., 'The Europe of John Knox', 13.
81 Janton, P., *L'homme et l'oeuvre*, p. 469.

practising prophecy and the sermon as interrelated strands of the one vocation. This first produced the typically thrasonical style which we so readily associate with him. 'The sentence of Johne Knox to the Castell' (of St. Andrews) is a good example. When the Castle was being bombarded by French galleys:

> […] he ever said, "That thare corrupt lyef could nott eschape punishment of God;" and that was his continuall advertisement, fra the tyme that he was called to preache. When thei triumphed of thare victorie, (the first twenty dayis thei had many prosperous chances,) he lamented, and ever said, "Thei saw not what he saw." When thei bragged of the force and thickness of thare walles, he said, "Thei should be butt egge schellis". When thei vanted, 'England will reskew us' he said, "Ye shall not see thame; but ye shalbe delivered in your ennemyis handis, and shalbe caryed to ane strange countrey." (Laing I: 204–205).

In much the same vein, Knox tells of an incident in the galleys during his subsequent imprisonment.

> And lyeing betwix Dundeye and Sanctandrois the second tyme that the galayis returned to Scotland, the said Johne being so extreamlye seak, that few hoped his lyeff, the said Maister James willed him to look to the land, and asked yf he knew it? Who answered, "Yes, I knaw it weall; for I see the stepill of that place, whare God first in publict opened my mouth to his glorie, and I am fullie persuaded, how weak that ever I now appear, that I shall nott departe this lyif, till that my toung shall glorifie his godlie name in the same place." (Laing I: 228).

Pr. Dickinson has pointed out that: 'this prophecy may be *ex post facto*' and in any case: 'was not committed to writing until about 1566'.[82] Gordon Donaldson expands on these facts when he says: 'we all know the kind of man who likes to say: "And I just said to him […]" or "And I just told him"'.[83] Anyone with a critical mind, then, would obviously approach Knox's prophecy, like Wishart's, with a good deal of skepticism. But what makes up Knox's prophecy in terms of its literary structure, and how does it differ from Wishart's?

In both Knox passages the prophecy itself relies on an apparent disparity between expectation and reality. Wishart, as we have seen,

82 Dickinson I: lxxi.
83 Donaldson, G., 'Knox the Man', 32.

made much of distinctions too, but of a different sort: between obligation, (on the part of man to attend to his own salvation) and reality (that many would rather watch a vain play). Knox's approach allows him to undercut complacency and false beliefs in the first example and to confound those who had written him off as a dead man in the second. In terms of literary merit, the first passage is by far the better. Knox attacks the pronouncements of the castilians like a boy with a pin puncturing balloons. Each one is inflated, and subsequently meets the same sorry fate as its predecessor. It is certainly significant that his fulminations and vaticinations are given in direct speech, while the remarks of the others survive for the most part only in reported speech (and think again of Ireland's clerk, whom we met previously; above pp. 36–37). This gives Knox's words an immediacy with which he does not grace the speech of others. But these are Knox's memoirs after all, not anyone else's. Moreover, the others 'brag' and 'vant'. His use of these verbs is explicitly pejorative, especially the latter, which is an aphetic form of 'avaunt'. Vainglory (one of the Scottish preacher's favourite topics) is clearly suggested, as in this contemporary usage: 'they laude their verses, they boast, they vaunt [...]'.[84] Knox, then, sketches in the dispositional qualities of his companions without individualising detail but with the knowledge of an enduring substructure of consistently predictable behaviour. This is the Preacher's knowledge of his flock, which relies on him to keep its members on the right path.

Another sort of characterisation comes into play with Knox's choice of imagery. Admittedly, egg-shells are a common sixteenth century symbol of fragility and worthlessness ('I gat not so muche [...] as [...] an poore egshell',[85]) but the juxtaposition of this with brick walls, is powerfully and cynically reductive. He is not as vivid as Wishart, but the notion of a 'strange countrey' is common to both preachers. Knox's sources are probably Acts 7: 6: 'But thus sayde God unto hym: thy sede salbe a stranger in a strange lande and they shal make bonde men of them', Judges 2: 10: 'he solde them into the hands of their enemies'; and Luke 21: 24: 'They shall fall thorow the edge of

84 *O.E.D.*, X., II, 67.
85 ibid., X, II, 67.

the swerde and be led captyve amonge all nations' (*Coverdale*). Indeed, the prediction that one's enemies will triumph is common to the prophecy of both Knox and Wishart, and in each case, the prophet apparently suggests that this is because of unthankfulness which thoroughly deserves punishment. Banishment to foreign shores, invasion of foreign powers or enslavement seem to be topics which appeal to the preachers, perhaps because of the politico-religious climate which they found themselves in. The suppression of Protestantism was, after all, imminent. Not only are the images poetic, their vision is realistic.

The second Knox passage is rather different. What was initially and ostensibly a gesture of encouraging kindness to the Reformer, at the lowest point in his career, is turned into something else entirely; a proclamation of his own secret relationship with the Deity. In fact, what we have here is the second phase of Protestant prophecy. The first warns of punishments to come, the second suggests that the troubles which are subsequently endured are in fact an assurance of ultimate triumph. Wishart was dead before a second phase arrived for him, but such a fate was not for Knox. '"Nay, returne to your barnes, and God blisse you"' Wishart had told him, '"One is sufficient for one sacrifice."' (Laing I: 139).

Also in the second passage, Knox places much emphasis on 'that place' where he first began preaching (St. Andrews) so evidently he entertained a special affection for the town as a potent symbol of the single, most important turning-point in his life. And Knox does not just hope to return to St. Andrews, he is in fact 'fullie *persuaded*' (italics added). In its deep structure the verb implies dialogue. The transitive 'departe this lyif' is a rhetorical (and typically Knoxian) synonym for 'die', and Knox concludes by outlining the character of a future sermon.

We have already explored Knox's overt preaching techniques and established that prophecy is an integral and stimulating part. And in spite of the fact that *The Historie* contains only a handful of such sermons (not all of which we have explored), the art of the sermon never really lies far from the surface of Knox's prose. What follows is an attempt to justify such an assertion. The *moralitas* is among the most homiletic of literary devices, and Knox has given us one very famous example of it. After his account of Cardinal David Beaton's murder, he says (and cf., for example, 1 Corinthians 1: 9, Philippians 3: 19, and 1 Thessalonians 5: 3):

> But we wold, that the Reader should observe Goddis just judgementis, and how that he can deprehend the worldly wyse in thare awin wisdome, mak thare table to be a snare to trape thare awin feit, and thair awin presupposed strenth to be thare awin destructioun. These ar the workis of our God, whareby he wold admonish the tyrantis of this earth, that in the end he will be revenged of thare crueltye, what strenth so ever thei mack in the contrare. But such is the blyndnes of man, (as David speakis,) "That the posteritie does ever follow the footsteppes of thair wicked fatheris, and principallye in thair impietie;" (Laing I: 180).

Even if it strikes us as *Deus ex Machina*, this would not sound out of place at the end of, say, one of Henryson's fables, the only difference being that Henryson's characters are (at least ostensibly) fictitious. Quotations from scriptural exemplars of wisdom such as Solomon and David often form part of the morality, and this is clearly the case here. Take the following lines, which are from Henryson's *moralitas* to *The Taill of the Upounlandis Mous and the Burgess Mous* (and we notice how little room the poet leaves for alternatives):

> And Solomon sayis, gif that thow will reid,
> 'Vnder the heuin I can not better se
> Than ay be blyith and leif in honestie'.[86]

It is not really clear what scriptural passage Henryson is actually referring to (there are parallels in, for example, Ecclesiastes 3: 12, 5: 18, 8: 15 or Proverbs 16: 8, 27: 1); he may even have had a poem by Lydgate in mind[87], but the Solomonic authority carries much weight. Even more relevant to our current argument is a passage from Sir David Lindsay's short poem *The Tragedie of the Cardinall* which, judging by internal evidence, Knox almost certainly knew. Lindsay has the Cardinal's ghost pronounce the following lines from beyond the grave, with great solemnity and sorrow:

86 See Fox, D., (ed.), *The Poems of Robert Henryson*, p. 19.

87 See Wood, H. H., (ed.), *The Poems and Fables of Robert Henryson*, pp. 228–229.

> Now fynd I trew the saw quhilk Dauid said:
> Without God of ane hous be maister of wark
> He wyrkis in vaine, thocht it be neuer so stark.[88]

Lindsay is thinking of Psalms 127: 1: 'Excepte the LORDE byylde the house, their labour is but lost that byylde it' (*Coverdale*), and he even adds a qualificatory adverbial 'thocht it be neuer so stark' to reinforce the argument. Surely these lines provided Knox with a model for his own narrative, although, as ever, he has incorporated it into a larger scheme which itself functions around a multiplicity of related models. And not only does he integrate Lindsay's idea, he actually expands on it. Knox makes highly effective use of two Davidic Psalms, quoting one with acknowledgement of his source, one without. This feature allows one reference to function within the sub-text, the other, on the surface, and in clear view of the reader. The first, Psalms 69: 22, 'Lette their table bee made a snare to take themselves with alle, and lette the thynges that should have bene for their wealth be vnto them an occasion of fallynge' (*Great Bible*), deals with a theme which evidently struck Knox as a good parallel to his Beaton narrative, so he borrowed from it. The psalmist, however, is importuning God, Knox on the other hand, is being wise in retrospect. The second quotation is presumably from Psalms 109, but David in fact says no such thing. He implores the Deity: 'Lette his posteritie be destroid, & in ye generacion following let their name be put out. Let the iniquitie of his father be had in remembrance with the Lord' (*Geneva Bible*). Knox, then, has turned the lines into a *sententia* (although the quotation marks are Laing's and do not occur in either the Glasgow or Edinburgh MSS.[89] None of the contemporary scriptural translations (*Coverdale*, *Matthew*, *Great*, *Genevan*,) mention 'follow[ing] in the footsteppes [...]' as a metaphor for guidance, so we can be safe in assuming that Knox is adapting things just a little. How did Knox himself view this kind of preaching?

During one of his celebrated interviews with Mary, he gave the following definition of his vocation (which actually enhances upon the Isaiah 26 sermon):

88 See Hamer, D., (ed.), *The Works of Sir David Lindsay*, p. 137.

89 See MS. La. II. 210, Edinburgh University Library, f. 46.

> "[...] I am send to preache the Evangell of Jesus Christ, to such as please to hear it; and it hath two partes, Repentance and Fayth. And now, Madam, in preaching repentance, of necessitie it is that the synnes of men be so noted, that thai may know whairin thei offend [...]" (Laing II: 387–388).

Unfortunately, Knox was prevented from giving his views on the preaching of faith (but see Laing II: 103–104) by an anguished cry: '*What have ye to do* [...] *with my marriage?*' (and that's another story!; italics added). Even so, from this we can conclude that the repentance part of the Knoxian gospel covers the above *moralitas*. Beaton of course was beyond redemption (as Knox thought anyhow), but he provides a kind of negative exemplar to induce repentance in others.

Of course, Knox was not always able to maintain consistency of theme in his preaching of repentance. Indeed, at one time earlier in his career he was apparently forced by circumstance to preach exactly the opposite:

> Why did God suffer the men that had professit his name, be ressaving the sign of circumcisioun, sa unmercifullie to be intreatit? I myght answer, God sufferis his awn, in all ageis, be the ungodlie to be cruellie tormentit. (Laing III: 396–397, Letter XXV).

On the one hand, the charge of using ready-made interpretations can be levelled, but must be balanced by the fact that Christ rebuked those who could not read the signs of the times (see Matthew 16: 3, Luke 12: 56).

Returning to the Beaton passage, however, Dickinson suggests that there is a 'vast stress' on the word 'but' in the *moralitas*.[90] It comes hard on the heels of Knox's most infamous sentence: 'These thingis we wreat mearelie' (Laing I: 180), which ought to be interpreted in the Henrysonian sense as, 'we have chosen to treat a serious theme with levity for the purpose of entertainment as well as moral edification', not just as 'these things we write gleefully'. (Yet Knox was obviously not sorry that Beaton was murdered, and it would be foolish, even crass, to excuse him overmuch). On the other hand it is utterly essential that modern critics do not apply value judgements here;

90 See Dickinson I: lxii.

'men are as the time is. To be tender-minded does not become a sword' (*King Lear* Act 5, Sc. 1, ll. 32–33).

In fact there is less stress on the conjunctive than Dickinson would have us believe, and his approach perhaps perpetuates too rigid a distinction between narrative and moral. Modal verbs are a more reliable guide to interpretation. 'Wold' for instance, implies desire (to inculcate), and 'should' duly implies duty (on the reader's part, to be inculcated). It is noticeable that the emphasis on responsibility moves rather neatly from preacher to Congregation (or, more accurately, to reader), before the introduction of the final arbiter, who is of course God. 'Just judgementis' leaves no doubt about moral rectitude, although it is a borrowing from the Genevan marginalia where it is appended to Psalms 109 (or from Foxe, who also uses it). Knox subsequently introduces the adverb 'how' to pick up the verb of perception 'observe' and the stress is on manner and one's response to it rather than on message. That comes presently. 'Whareby' carries the reader one step closer to the kernel of the morality, while phrases such as 'in the end' and 'what strenth so ever thei mack' reinforce the message by creating an aura of inevitability. One can hardly deny that this is a solid, confident and competent piece of preaching, even a *tour de force* from a man uniquely qualified to write on such a topic.

In *The Historie*, Knox the polemicist is just as fascinating as Knox the preacher. Admittedly, nearly all the early texts which we discussed in previous chapters were to a great extent polemical; some have even been oral or written debates. Indeed, it is debate which particularly interests us here, and there are several instances of it which cannot be overlooked. The first takes place between Knox and one Friar Arbuckle in 1547 (Laing I: 195–200). This encounter is essential because it represents a record of Knox's earliest debate (waiving the twenty year gap between event and actual writing-up). Thus, it provides a fascinating counter-point to Knox's first sermon.[91] Next comes the series of interviews between Knox and Mary, and Knox's trial scene, since they represent the climax of the whole story and because, as Dr. Murison says, they belong to: 'the immortal scenes in

91 See Laing's notes, f. III. 4.

Scottish history'.[92] Finally, there is the epic confrontation between Knox and Maitland of Lethington, itself another memorable scene and a keener intellectual battle than anything represented in Knox's arguments with the Queen.

So then to the Arbuckle incident. John Hamilton, Abbot of Paisley, had initiated an inquisition into the heresies being preached at St. Andrews, and it was a luckless pair of clergymen who had the misfortune to find themselves opposed to Knox in debate. One was 'Supprior Dean Johnne Wynrame' and the other, a certain 'Arbuckill Gray-Freir' (Laing I: 193) (identified by John Durkan as 'F. Alexander Arbuckle, O.F.N., scholar of Latin, Greek and Hebrew',[93] and according to Knox himself, 'a learned man' (Laing I: 199). Evidently, the Sub-prior came unprepared for the rigorous contest which Knox demanded and he soon resigned the floor to Arbuckle, who fared little better. Knox's speeches in *The Historie* are much longer than those of his opponents; perhaps this is a distortion or perhaps it argues for the fact that he had done his homework. Whatever his faults, one must admit that Knox did not enter into anything less than wholeheartedly.

The controversy began with Winram defending the significance of the symbolic elements in church ceremonies. Knox denied their scriptural warrant and provoked this response: '"Will ye bynd us so strait, that we may do nothing without the expresse word of God? What! and I ask a drynck? think ye that I synne? and yitt I have nott Goddis word for me"' (Laing I: 196). This was his first, and last, mistake. Knox quickly accused him of *improprietas*: '"I wold we should not jest in so grave a mater [...]"'. Thereafter, he had the upper hand, and the Sub-prior was in retreat'. '"Forgeve me"', he says, '"I spak it but in mowes, and I was dry"'. Arbuckle was marginally more potent:

> "Sayis not Sanct Paule, 'That another fundatioun then Jesus Christ may no man lay'. But upone this fundatioun some buyld, gold, silver, and pretious stones; some hay, stuble and wood. The gold, sylver and precious stones, ar the Ceremonyes of the Church, which do abyd the fyre, and consumes nott away.

92 Murison, D., 'Knox the Writer', 50.

93 See Durkan, J., 'Book Review: Dickinson's *Knox*', 160.

This place of Scripture is most plaine." (sayis the foolish Feind.) (Laing I: 197–198).

Hugh Watt finds: 'signs that Knox was completely nonplussed for the moment'[94] but Knox probably considered this a better argument than the Sub-prior's for two reasons. It is scriptural and it places emphasis on unequivocal interpretation. Arbuckle's text was 1 Corinthians 3: 11–15, which he rendered faithfully, but Knox wasted no time before addressing the very issue of right understanding. The following rejoinder is unquestionably a masterpiece of lucid and intelligent deliberative rhetoric:

"I prayse my god, throwght Jesus Christ, for I fynd his promeis suyre, trew, and stable. Christ Jesus biddis us 'Nott fear, when we shalbe called befoir men, to geve confessioun of his trewth;' for he promisses, 'that it shalbe gevin unto us in that hour, what we shall speak [...] Now to your argument: The Ceremonyes of the Kirk, (say ye,) ar gold, silver and pretious stonis, because thei ar able to abyde the fyre, but I wold learne of yow, what fyre is it which your Ceremonies does abyd? And in the meantyme, till that ye be advised to answer, I will schaw my mynd, and make ane argument against youris, upoun the same text. And first, I say, that I have heard this text adduced for pruf of Purgatorie, but for defence of Ceremonies, I never heard [...] But omitting whetther ye understand the mynd of the Apostill or not, I maik my argument, and say, That which may abyd the fyre, may abyd the word of God. But your Ceremonies may not abyd the word of God: *Ergo*, Thei may not abyd the fyre, and yf they may not abyd the fyre, then ar they not gold, silver nor precious stones. Now, yf ye find any ambiguite in this terme, Fyre, which I interpret to be the woord, fynd ye me ane other fyre, by the which thingis buylded upon Christ Jesus should be tryed then God and his woord, which both in the Scriptures ar called fyre, and I shall correct my argument." (Laing I: 198).

This is a rebuttal designed to vanquish all opposition (which it seems to have done). Knox achieves it first of all by lauding Christ, presumably to convince the audience of his piety (which was real enough). Like his introduction to *An Epistle to the Congregation of the Castle of St. Andrews*, composed the following year, it is praise with a practical application. There is some thanksgiving too of course and Knox displays his knowledge of the gospels by quoting Matthew 10: 19 (or

94 Watt, H., *John Knox in Controversy*, p. 19.

Luke 12: 12): 'But when they delyyer you vp, take no thought how or what ye shall speake, for it shall be geuen you euen in that same houre, what ye shall saye' (*Coverdale*). Knox's use of this scriptural passage explicitly casts him in the mould of a Christian apologist before unfaithful magistrates, despite Sub-prior Winram's protestation: '"I came nott hear as a judge, but only familiarlie to talk"' (Laing I: 195). Knox, however, did not let him off so easily. (We saw, above, p. 132, an example of how Knox was a proto-Bunyanite; here is another. This scene reminds us, perhaps, of Bunyan before Judges Keelin and Cobb in his *A Relation of the Imprisonment of Mr. John Bunyan*).[95]

Also in this instance, we have particularly competent and striking examples of Knox's use of syllogisms, which are well worth bringing to the reader's attention. Janton identifies: '"That which may [...] *Ergo* [...] fyre"' as a syllogism in *baroco*; that is to say, a syllogism in which the major premise is a universal affirmative, the minor, a particular negative. This, in itself is impressive, but on top of it, Knox immediately introduces another, a syllogism in *ferio*: '"I prove, that abydis not the tryall of Goddis word, which Goddis word condempnes: But Goddis word condempnes your Ceremonies: Therefor thei do not abyd the tryall thairof"' (Laing I: 199). This time, the major premise is a universal negative, followed by a minor and a conclusion which are particular affirmative and negative respectively.[96] Not to be outdone by our distinguished French predecessor in 'Knox studies', however, the present writer has at least something to offer. Knox also introduces two instances of *reditus ad propositum*; neat returns to the main theme after digressions (and they are introduced rather more subtly that my editing allows them to appear). The first comes with: '"Now to your argument"', and the second with '"But omitting"', and between these, Knox sums up his opponent's arguments quite fairly. There is no simplification such as we find in his work on Balnaves's *Treatise on Justification*, (above, pp. 157–160), but Balnaves's ideas were ideologically similar to Knox's own views and he didn't need to spell them out. Here, he does. As in his

95 See Sharrock, H., (ed.), *Grace Abounding to the Chief of Sinners*, p. 85 ff.

96 See Janton, P., *L'homme et l'oeuvre*, p. 443.

brief clash with Dean John Annand (see Laing I: 189), he demands complete accuracy and precision, which he does not get from Arbuckle. For his own definition of 'fyre', around which his whole argument revolves, he could have turned to a wide range of scriptural sources. Jeremiah 20: 9 will suffice (but cf. Jeremiah 23: 39): 'ye word of the Lord was a verray burning fire in my heart' (*Coverdale*). This not only suited his argument, it constituted a memorable manipulation of scriptural semiotics.

Watt notices Knox's remark that he had heard the Pauline text adduced as proof of purgatory, 'probably in his training as a priest',[97] although Watt does not develop this point. *Archbishop Hamilton's Catechism*, however, can shed some light on the matter, since it contains just such an argument from the same passage: 'And the work of ilk man, quhat it is ye fyre sall trie or prief [...] Quha sa will consider diligently this auctoritie of S. Paule, he sall esely find purgatory to be efter yis lyfe'.[98] This is compelling evidence that Knox had his finger on the pulse of Catholicism. Furthermore, in his *Memorial to the Privy Council* we find unmistakable echoes of the St. Andrews debate, remoulded and re-presented, but still strongly reminiscent:

> So shall your Honors' careful dilygence provide that Christs Religion in this realm – all praise and honor be unto God, now tending to perfection and maturitie, – so surely be founded upon Chryste and upon his expresse word, that not only it may abyde the stormy warrs of mens judgement, but also the warfare, the trial of Gods sacrat word we mean, which when it cometh, as it must needs consume and burn away the stuble haye and wood, without respect of persons; so must it try and declare to be fine the gold, silver, and precious stones, how contemned [soever] that other builder appered that builded such fine stuff upon the sure foundement.[99]

When Knox wrote these lines he must surely have remembered Friar Arbuckle's argument, even if, as he said at St. Andrews, he had been a long time familiar with 1 Corinthians 3: 11–15 and its uses. (When we come to analyse the Cardinal Beaton narrative in Knox's *The Historie* we shall see how an idea that was first formulated in his letter-writing

97 Watt. H., *John Knox in Controversy*, p. 19.

98 Mitchell, A. F., (ed.), *Archbishop Hamilton's Catechism*, f. cciii.

99 Lorimer, P., *John Knox and the Church of England*, p. 274.

found its way into narrative (below, pp. 288–290). With the Arbuckle incident, we have, if not exactly the reverse of that situation, at least a different process of transmission. It is this. An idea which took shape during an academic debate early in Knox's career afterwards found its way into a letter, then into narrative, but it is in that very narrative that we learn of the original debate!).

In the passage immediately above, there are of course new features. There is a rich metaphor which is not scriptural ('stormy warrs of mens judgement'). 'Warfare' is a common enough scriptural concept (cf. 1 Timothy 1:18 'war a good warfare') but no passage seems to match Knox's context. However, he evidently returned to the aforementioned Pauline epistle and introduced verse 10: 'Accordynge to the grace of God which is geuen vnto me, as a wyse bylder haue I layed the foundacion, but another byyldethe thereon' (*Coverdale*). This gives him another chance to identify with Paul, but also to suggest that he, Knox, is more wretched.

Returning to the original debate, then, we can see that Knox was not about to let the lessons he had learned go to waste, even if Arbuckle and Winram were no match for his dialectical expertise. Scriptural passages, for Knox, evidently accumulated significance and were to be developed and sharpened for future arguments. But this is not all we can learn from the memorable Arbuckle incident. Thanks to Knox's *The Historie* we know how the controversy ended, although the narrative is inevitably coloured by his bias. Arbuckle, he tells us, was forced into a *lapsus linguæ* of monumental proportions when he concluded that the: '"Apostles had not received the Holy Ghost, when thei did wryte thare Epistles, but *after*, thei receaved him, and then thei did ordeyn the Ceremonies" (few wold have thought, that so learned a man wold have gevin so foolische ane answer; and yit it is evin as trew as he bayre a gray cowl)' (Laing I: 199, italics added). Apparently, Knox was completely taken aback and gave a 'starte', for he knew as well as the Sub-prior, that if such were the case: '"then fayre weall the ground of our fayth"' (Laing I: 200) and he meant the Christian, not just the Protestant, faith. What's more, there is much colourful figurative language from Knox, although some of it at least belongs to the historical narrative rather than to the debate. In his own opinion the '*optima collatio*' (or best comparison) came when he said:

'as the theaf abydis the tryall of the inqueist, and thareby is condempned to be hanged, evin so may your ceremonies abyd the tryall of Goddis word', but perhaps even this is excelled when Knox tells us that the Friar: 'wanderis about in the myst' before 'he falles in a fowll myre' (Laing I: 199). As we saw in his *A Vindication of the Doctrine that the Sacrifice of the Mass is Idolatry*, the imagery is from the farmyard (above, p. 170).

Knox's four interviews with Mary some fifteen years later (see Laing II: 277–286, 331–335, 371–376, 387–398), and his trial before her in 1563 on charges of treason (Laing II: 398–412) provide even more compelling reading and again most of the prose is of a dialectical and polemical nature. The issues discussed, moreover, are of greater political import than before, since, by the time Knox met the Queen, he had developed fully his revolutionary belief in lawful resistance to 'ungodly' sovereigns. (And not only is this the topic of his first clash with Mary, it forms the core of his long argument with Lethington, who was, as David Murison points out: 'the chief theorist of absolute monarchy in Scotland'[100] and, as Knox himself thought: 'ane far better dialectician' (Laing II: 406) than the Queen.

W. J. Anderson has suggested that the interviews with Mary were conducted in French[101] but this is unlikely. Of these, the first and fourth are the most memorable, the latter particularly, because of the keenness of its conflict, which was becoming deeply personal, but the former more consistently produced high quality rhetoric throughout. When asked: '"Think ye, […] that subjectis having power may resist their princes?"', Knox produced the following bold *similitudo*, perhaps suggested by '"Plato, the philosopher," who "wrote his Bookis of the Commounwealth, in the which he dampneth many thingis that then war manteaned in the world […]"' (Laing II: 279).

> "[…] the father may be stricken with a phrensye, in the which he wolde slay his awin childrene. Now, Madame, yf the children aryse, joyne thame selfis togetther, apprehend the father, tack the sweard or other weaponis frome him, and finallie bind his handis, and keape him in preasone, till that his phrenesy be over past; think ye, Madam, that the children do any wrang? Or, think ye,

100 Murison, D., 'Knox the Writer', 50.

101 See Anderson, W. J., 'John Knox at Dieppe', 104–105.

> Madame, that God wilbe offended with thame that have stayed thair father to committ wickedness? It is even so (said he,) Madam, with Princes that wold murther the children of God that are subject unto thame. Thair blynd zeall is no thing but a verray mad phrenesie; and thairfoir, to tack the sweard frome thame, to bynd thair handis, and to cast thame selfis in preasone, till that thei be brought to a more sober mynd, is no disobedience against princes, but just obedience, because that it aggreith with the will of God." (Laing II: 282).

As one commentator says: 'there was no court flattery in such sentiments'[102] and indeed what this lacks in subtlety it makes up for in sheer audacity. Knox probably prepared it according to the principle that the most effective similitudes ought to be simpler than the matter which they seek to illustrate. Another literary criterion is vividness, and if Knox does not really achieve this, there is an intensity of commitment which sculpts the imagery into heavy blocks and ultimately improves clarity. Moreover, there is an almost episodic nature to the remedial steps which Knox then outlines ('joyne', 'apprehend', 'tack', 'bind', 'keape').

To make her point, Mary had contrasted the Biblical decree that subjects ought to obey their Princes (Romans 13: 1, 'Let every soule submytte him selfe to the auctorite of the hyer powers [...] The powers that be, are ordeyned of God' (*Coverdale*), with the actions of the Reformers under Mary of Lorraine. Knox answers by coming up with a similar contrast, this time presumably between the Fifth Commandment ('Honour thy Father and Mother', see Exodus 20: 12, *KJV*) and a hypothetical situation where its rule is temporarily suspended. His language is overtly didactic. Infinitives again occur in the latter part of the analogy ('to tack', 'to bynd') and 'keape' has become 'to cast', which was probably even more inflammatory.

Significantly, there is an attempt to turn the analogy into prophecy, since we find in the margin: 'when this was written, thar wes no appearance of Marie's empreasonment'. This comment allows scholars to date the transcription of the manuscript to: 'between 16 June 1567 and 2 May 1568',[103] but the marginal note itself provides us with an

102 Macgill, F. N. and MacGreal, I. P., (eds.), *Masterpieces of Christian Literature in Summary Form*, p. 413.

103 See Laing II: 282, n. (1), Dickinson II: 17, n. (1).

example of Knox (or a scribe) yoking together heterogeneous things by violence. As we have seen, Knox's prophecy and his polemic do not have all that much in common, and there is nothing whatsoever about this passage to suggest that he originally thought of it as a prediction.

Evidently Mary was astonished by Knox's comparison, even if, as Dr. Duncan Shaw points out, 'she undoubtedly had already a picture in her mind of the person of Knox'.[104] She: 'stood as it war amased, more then the quarter of ane hour' (Laing II: 282). To Mary: 'if such actions shall have passage free, / Bondslaves and pagans shall our statesmen be' (*Othello*, Act 1, Sc. 2, ll. 100–101). 'The Quenis conclusioun' (Laing II: 283), however, exhibits a reductive simplicity which was often the mainstay of Knox's own controversial technique:

> "[...] Weall then I perceave that my subjectis shall obey you, and not me, and shall do what thei list, and nott what I command: and so man I be subject to thame, and not thei to me." (Laing II: 282–283).

And she achieved this sort of effect quite consistently. For example, she assessed the fundamental issue of the whole Reformation thus:

> "Ye interprete the Scripturis [...] in one maner, and thei [members of the Catholic Church] interprete in ane other; Whome shall I beleve? And who shalbe judge?" (Laing II: 284, parenthesis added).

With reference to this passage, J. H. Millar awards Mary: 'complete dialectical victory',[105] but there is surely more to such victory than simply an expression of the nature of the problem, astute as it is. And one cannot overlook the fact that Knox actually answers the Queen's questions directly and unequivocally. Like Friar Arbuckle, Mary found him '"oure sair"' (Laing I: 285), but she remains admirably defiant; '"yf thai war here that I have heard, thai wold answer you"'. Knox had a reply for that too, but we have already explored this particular debate long enough.

104 Shaw, D., 'John Knox and Mary, Queen of Scots', 53.
105 Millar J. H., *Literary History of Scotland*, p. 136.

If we pass over their second encounter, to the third and fourth, which are of higher quality, we can juxtapose prose of a very different character. At Lochleven, Mary was deferential, later she was bitterly offended. In the first instance, deferential or not, Mary go from Knox the very opposite of what she desired. Was it lawful for the Protestants of the West Country to take up for themselves the sword of justice which properly belonged to her? '"The Sweard of Justice" quod he "Madam, is Goddis"'. Furthermore:

> "The examples ar evident: for Samuell feared not to slay Agag, the fat and delicate King of Amalech, whom king Saule had saved. Neather spaired Helias Jesabellis fals propheittis and Baalis preastis, albeit that king Achab was present. Phyneas was no magistrat, and yit feared he not to stryck Cosby and Zimbrye in the verray act of fylthie fornicatioun." (Laing II: 372).

Before his Queen one final time prior to his trial, Knox was asked '"what ar ye within this Commounwealth?"':

> "A subject born within the same," said he, "Madam. And albeit I neather be Erle, Lord, nor Barroun within it, yitt hes God maid me, (how abject that ever I be in your eyes,) a profitable member within the same: Yea, Madam, to me it apperteanes no lesse to foirwarne of suche thingis as may hurte it, yf I foirsee thame, then it does to any of the Nobilitie [...]" (Laing II: 388).

This of course is Knox's finest moment; his '*Hier stehe ich / ich kan nicht anders*', and it transforms what was, to all intents and purposes, a personal attack, into an overtly political statement which is, simultaneously, a personal defence.

The first passage uses *peristasis*, a device with which the author enlarges upon an issue by providing copious parallels. Here Knox manages to pack four Biblical references (1 Samuel 15: 9, 33, 1 Kings 18: 40, Numbers 25: 14, 15) into a comparatively short passage. Each deals with overcoming fear or hesitation and relies on frequent use of proper nouns ('Samuell', 'Agag', 'Amalech', 'Helias', 'Jesabell(is)', 'Baal(is)', 'Achab', 'Phyneas', 'Cosby', 'Zimbrye'). Indeed, this is the technique used by Knox in the very sermon which so offended the Queen. One recalls references to place-names such as 'Cowpar Mure' and the 'Craiggis of Edinburgh' (above, p. 227).

The second and more famous of the passages uses *necessitas*: 'the representation of the necessity of a thing',[106] and titles ('subject', 'Erle', 'Lord', 'Barroun', 'member') if not proper nouns, play the dominant role there. Moreover, Mary had attacked the propriety of Knox's sermon, and he responds by using the verb 'appertean' which refers explicitly to fitness and rectitude.[107] Again there is an attempt to turn the passage into prophecy ('lett the papistis judge this day 1567') (Laing II: 388).

In Knox's trial scene, from the latter part of Book IV, there is no such use of marginal comment, but these scenes are doubly interesting because Knox is contending with two opponents, Mary and Lethington, at the one time. And one should not overlook the fact that he is on trial for his life. Again Knox plays to two audiences, the jury and the readers of *The Historie*. When he addresses the latter, he often includes asides which are obviously designed to give the impression that he is before a kangaroo court. He makes Mary look vindictive, vengeful and unbecoming: 'Hir pomp lackit one principall point, to wit, womanlie gravitie; for when sche saw John Knox standing at the uther end of the tabill bair-heided, sche first smyleit, and efter gaif ane gawf lauchter' (Laing II: 404).[108] The smiling Lethington too seems more slippery than ever. He and the Queen are often pictured together, whispering secretly, 'what it wes, the tabill hard nocht' (Laing II: 409).

For all that, Knox's polemic is even more inspired than ever (no mean achievement by anyone's standards, let alone Knox's). Compelling indeed is this foretaste of things to come, when he engages in pre-trial sparring with Lethington.

> "Lat us heir" said thai, "your defensses; for we wald be glaid that ye mycht be fand innocent."
>
> "Nay," said the uther, "for I am informit, and that be diverse, and evin be you, my Lord Secreatarie, that I am allreaddie condampnit, and my cause prejudged: Thairfoir I mycht be reputed ane fooll, gif I wald mak you previe to my defensses." (Laing II: 402).

106 See Sonnino, L. A., *A Handbook*, p. 130.

107 See *D.O.S.T.*, I: 95, 2, (2).

108 I am not suggesting that Knox's presentation was a fiction. Mary, of course, had little reason to like him and no reason to be sorry he was where he was. But the whole thing seems to take on the form of an *Ecce Homo*, with Knox as the innocent man on trial.

Knox tells us that: 'At thoise wordis thai semeit baith offendit' (Laing II: 402). Although he is courteous, it is obvious that the naïveté with which he addressed Mary of Lorraine in his first letter to her, (above, pp. 90–91), is gone completely. This comes out again and again during the trial. Knox consistently refuses to take the bait which his antagonists offer him, presumably with his downfall and humiliation in their minds.

Knox had written a letter (see Laing II: 395) which subsequently fell: 'by the meanis of false brethren' into the 'handis of the Quene' (Laing II: 397) and this text was construed as treasonable. In the two extracts following, Knox's method in turning aside the charges is similar:

> Quhill that no man gaif ansuer, Lethingtoun addressit him to John Knox, and said "Maister Knox, ar ye nocht sorie from your hairt, and do ye nocht repent that sick ane letter hes past your pen, and from you is cumin to the knawlege of utheris."
> John Knox ansuerit, "My Lord Secretour, befoir I repent I maun be taucht of my offence." [...] (Laing II: 405).

> "Ye shall not eschaip so," said the Quene; "Is it nocht treasoun, my Lordis, to accuse ane Prince of creweltie? I think thair be Actis of parliament aganis sick whisperaris." That wes grantit of monie.
> "But whairintill," said Johne Knox, "can I be accusit?" (Laing II: 407).

When all seem to agree that Knox is in an impossible situation, with 'eneuch ado' (Laing II: 407) to be getting on with, his rejection of the accusations is not partial or even consensus-seeking, but utterly fundamental. This was undoubtedly a bold course of action, but the only way to secure complete victory. Significantly, the Secretary addresses Knox in religious language, while the Queen's charge is political. For these reasons Knox probably responded more readily to Lethington, and indeed, he picked up the verb 'repent' and carried the vocabulary one stage further in his subsequent response to the Queen: '"Is it lauchfull for me, Madam, to ansuer for myself? Or shall I be dampned befoir I be hard?"' (Laing II: 407). Mary on the other hand had belittled Knox, implicitly suggesting that he was a seditious 'whisperar' (Laing II: 407), certainly not a term designed to be flattering.

Knox went on to deny that the charge of 'creweltie' had been laid against the Queen, and he finally carried the day. After describing the scene in which he had been dismissed 'for [the] nicht' (Laing I: 410), Knox provides some humour, as he did during and after his debate with Friar Arbuckle back in the early days at St. Leonards. He tells us that Lethington and Master Maxwell were: 'the two stoupeis' of the Queen's chair, and no doubt recalling his own comments on William Arth, he suggested that the corrupt jury which he had faced, were governed by: 'this same God reuling thair tounge that sometymeis reulit the toung of Balaam, when gladlie he wald haif cursit Godis pepill' (Laing II: 411). It is evidently with some satisfaction that Knox concludes: 'That nycht wes nether dansing nor fyddilling in the Courte' (Laing II: 412).

His debate with Lethington at the General Assembly in 1564 (see Laing II: 425–469) was much less conclusive. David Murison calls it 'tedious' and says that: 'like most arguments it got nowhere'.[109] Dr. David Reid, on the other hand, emphasises that 'Knox's debate with Lethington, recorded of course as a triumph for himself in his *[The] Historie* is a good example […] [of] the controversies between Church and state' and Dr. Reid goes on to assess this kind of polemic in general:

> […] at least it sets out to make a disinterested appeal to the mind and is the product of great mental agility and stamina. Of course asperity comes in and malice, invective and imprecation. But on the whole what is striking is the discipline and trust in rationality the Scottish Presbyterians show in their disputing in this earlier period.[110]

Knox in fact plays down his own love for dialectics, in favour of his desire to make the 'truth' known (although one is compelled to ask, with Pilate, 'What is truth?'; see John 19: 38, *KJV*). For instance, when Lethington tires of the debate and George Hay is appointed to take his place, Knox tells the latter: '"I wald be sorie that I and ye suld be reputed to ressoun as two scolleris of Pythagoras, to schaw the

109 Murison, D., 'Knox the Writer', 50.

110 Reid, D. S., *The Party-Coloured Mind*, p. 9.

quicknes of our ingyne, as it wer to ressoune on boith the pairties"' (Laing II: 434).

The reasoning itself is, however, far from tedious, and Lethington is no Friar Arbuckle or John Annand. He reveals his wide knowledge not only of scripture, but a whole range of recognised authorities, from Luther, Melanchthon and Bucer, to Musculus and Calvin. It is his cynicism and his refusal to be forced into a position which has not been adequately proven, which make him such a good dialectician. For instance, he says: '"Prove that and win the play"' (Laing II: 438), '"The cases ar nothing lyke"' (Laing II: 439), '"I doubt whidder [...] thay did weill or nocht"' (Laing II: 449) and '"Weill, [...] I think nocht the ground sa sure as I durst builde my conscience thairupon"' (Laing II: 449). In this he reveals a world-view which is perhaps more akin to that of the twentieth or twenty-first century than the sixteenth.

Knox of course counters more than adequately. Here is one such example (cf. 2 Kings 9: 10, 36 and 1 Kings 22: 38):

> "That Helias said, 'Doggis sall lyck the blude of Achab'" said Johne Knox, "'and eat the flesche of Jesabell', the Scriptouris assuris me; but that it wes whisperit in thair awin eir, or in ane cornar, I reid nocht." (Laing II: 432–433).

This is an example of *irrisio*, or a bitter taunt full of irony, and Knox gets his own back on the Queen, who had called him a 'whisperar'.

And this brings us to the conclusion of chapter five. We have seen how and when the text of *The Historie* came into being, vital concerns of Knox studies. Even more importantly, we have now examined Knox's oratorical tools, as he developed them over a period of almost twenty years. We have seen that they fall into three sections: the three 'P's of preaching, prophecy and polemics. In which area he is the most skilled is difficult to determine, since each appeals in a different way. Knox's preaching, at least as it occurs in *The Historie*, is less spiritually-orientated than in his two published sermons, but his goal is no longer the consolation of the individual or of a small flock. We can say with certainty that *he aimed always to provoke, to stir men into thought or action*. When we turn to the prophecy, we must look at it with two things in mind. It tells us, first of all, about Knox's own psychology and self-view, and we must recognise that it supplemented his preaching by lending it charismatic qualities. His polemics appeal almost *solely to the intellect*, even if Knox does use scripture as a guide to reason. The finest qualities of the debates, and they are *very fine*, are lucidity and intellectual precision, although, as Dr. Reid observes, rancour and distrust are also in evidence. We can see at all times, however, that Knox exerted very considerable literary skill, at every turn, and in everything he said.

Chapter Six: Narrative and Descriptive Art in *The Historie*

This chapter comprises a further four sub-divisions of Knox's *The Historie*: merry tales, dramatic narratives, forensic rhetoric and descriptive writing. All of these features have generally been over-looked in former studies of Knox and, again, an attempt is made to redress this situation. And with this simple recognition, we can get straight down to business.

Merry Tales and Humorous Narratives

One of Knox's intentions in writing a history was, as he says, to: 'enterlase merynes with earnest materis' (Laing I: 145). Like Henryson, he knew that: '[...] clerkis sayis, it is richt profitabill / Amangis ernist to ming ane merie sport'[1] (and a *specific* similarity with Henryson is something which one can frequently notice in Knox, as we shall see). Of course, the type of humour we find in the Reformer's writings, especially in his 'merry' moods, has a long tradition behind it, in Scotland and beyond. Chaucer's *fabliaux* come to mind and the apocryphal *Merie Tales* which gathered around the name of Skelton. Anticlericalism often goes hand-in-hand with such narratives, and Knox's work fits in well with the combination of two literary strains which were coming together prior to, and indeed during, the Reformation. Even so, the satire became less a laugh at oneself, less of a fond indulgence, when the possibility of *real* reform and a new Church began to present itself. In Scotland, David Lindsay epitomised the changing mood in

1 See Fox, D., (ed.), *The Poems of Robert Henryson*, p. 3, ll. 19–20.

poetry and drama, and in France, Francois Rabelais did so in prose. Knox, however, was the first to do so in Scots prose.

Although the following narratives overlap with other genres such as preaching, they are of such a fine literary quality that they deserve consideration in themselves and in a special category. This is why I have chosen to isolate them from the more mainstream type of preaching in *The Historie* which we have just considered in the preceding chapter. The narratives themselves are masterpieces of their kind, and each one constitutes a complete artistic unit in itself, as intrinsically and aesthetically satisfying as, say, MacDiarmid's 'The Watergaw', but perhaps more attractive because of its medieval origins. The first stories are contained in William Arth's sermons (of which there are four, as retold by Knox) and in the Sandie Furrour, Richard Carmichael and Alexander Setoun narratives, which were shaped by Knox himself.

William Arth was a Friar who had evidently become dissatisfied with the moral conduct of the clergy and who took to preaching critical sermons in the early 1530s. At St. Andrews in the presence of John Major, George Lockart and Patrick Hepburn (who was the butt of one of Arth's later stories), the Friar preached, and:

> The theame of his sermone was "Veritie is the strongest of all thingis." His discourse of Curssing was "That yf it war rychtlie used, it was the moist fearfull thing upoun the face of the earth; for it was the verray separatioun of man frome God: but that it should nott be used rashlie, and for everie light cause, but onlie against open and incorrigible synnaris. But now (said he,) the avarice of preastis, and the ignorance of thair office has caused it altogitther to be vilipended; for the preast, (said he,) whose dewitie and office is to pray for the people, standis up on Sounday, and cryes, 'Ane hes tynt a spurtill. Thair is ane flaill stollin from thame beyound the burne. The goodwyiff of the other syd of the gait hes tynt a horne spune. Goddis maleson and myne I geve to thame that knowis of this geyre, and restoris in not.'" – (Laing I: 38).[2]

Ostensibly Knox merely recounts the sermon of another preacher here, but his were the acts of selection and presentation. These are more

2 Cf. a similar definition in 'The Twa-penny Faith'; see Mitchell, A. F., (ed.), *Archbishop Hamilton's Catechism*, penultimate page, unnumbered: 'Cursing cuttis, and deuydis the Curset fra the haly congregatioun off the Kirk of God'.

important than they at first seem, since Arth's narrative embodies a sermon (or mock sermon) within a sermon. In its new context of Knox's *The Historie*, the telescoping continues. It subsequently becomes *a sermon within a sermon within yet another sermon* (*The Historie* itself), and part of a longer narrative-series than Arth himself employed. Running parallel to these generic extensions is a striking use of dialogue, *and dialogue within dialogue*. This narrative consists of roughly one hundred and fifty words, and nearly a third of them fall into this category. It may be no accident that the use of the Scots language correspondingly becomes thicker and more richly textured as the presentation of speech becomes more sophisticated. (The use of Scots is a point to which I shall return, but for the moment, structure, rather than content, is our topic).

It is impossible to tell whether Knox touched up the narrative himself, since Arth's sermons do not survive independently, but it is unlikely that the later Reformer tampered with things. He knew the value of a good narrative and he has obviously chosen his material well. Knox of course is not the most self-effacing of reporters, but here he seems to have satisfied himself with the slightest of narratorial interpositions. With his timely and well-placed '(said he)'s, Knox pokes in his nose, and thus employs one of the expert story-teller's most functional tools. The tale itself moves from serious observation about a matter of ecclesiastical procedure through to blatant comedy, and this is undoubtedly deliberate (although Arth and not Knox is the real artist here). The phrase 'but now' marks the turning point, and the introduction of low burlesque, or travesty, is unmistakable. Arth's vocabulary is impressive, and like Knox's own, wide-ranging. He does not pull any punches by using 'incorrigible' or 'vilipended', 'avarice' and 'ignorance'. This brings us to Arth's use of Scots, and to an important point about W. Dickinson's edition of Knox's *The Historie*. My reasons for choosing the Arth narratives to make this point will become apparent. In his foreword, Dickinson says:

> Laing's transcript (corrected here and there from the manuscript) has formed the basis of the text, but the spelling has been modernized throughout [...] the modernization of the spelling *should call for no apology* [...] This should be said, however, – and the exception is an important one – *those vernacular*

words which still remain vernacular whatever their spelling may be, have been everywhere retained (italics added).[3]

If one looks at Dickinson's presentation of the above narrative, it will be evident to those who like their medieval texts undiluted, that the modern version is less attractive than the original.[4] Whether this calls for an apology or not remains a matter of personal taste. But much can be gathered from Pr. Dickinson's assertion that he has everywhere retained vernacular words. Take one example from the above. The word 'gait', as used by Arth does not mean 'gate' (so, Dickinson), as in: 'an opening in a wall for the purpose of entrance and exit', so such a rendering, or indeed, translation, is uncalled for. Only if Knox had recorded 'yett' or 'yate' would this have been justified. 'Gait' is in fact an old Scots word meaning 'street', dating from 1220. *D.O.S.T.* says that the item is: 'to be found in the names of streets in various towns, as *Horsmangate*, *Segate*, *Briggate*'.[5] Murray's *New English Dictionary* (*O.E.D.*) adds that this: 'spelling first appears in the 15th century but was almost confined to Scots and northern writers until the beginning of the 17th Century'.[6] Thus, in light of this information, the phrase: 'on the other syd of the gait' conjures up rather a different mental picture than Dickinson's text suggests.

Arth makes good use of prepositional phrases, the above being an example, which is complemented by: 'beyound the burne'. This is a kind of metaphor like: 'the other syd of the gait', suggesting things beyond immediate reach or outwith one's immediate circle, although it does have its literal uses too. *The Antiquities of the Shires of Aberdeen and Banff* of 1493 has an entrance: 'the croftis on the yond syd of the burn [...] to perteyn to the said wicar'.[7] In the final stages of the tale, the vocabulary nearly all comes from a domestic context ('spurtill', 'flaill', 'horne spune', 'geyre') and is used to make priestly concerns look extremely banal, while the Scots 'goodwyiff' is the most easily visualised of all typical stock-characters. Arth returns to his theme of

3 Dickinson I: xi–xii.

4 For the irony of this, see Dickinson I: 15–16.

5 *D.O.S.T.*, II: 627.

6 *O.E.D.*, IV: 73.

7 *D.O.S.T.*, I: 389.

incongruity, however, when he has the priest combine 'Goddis maleson' with the summarising noun 'geyre'. (Dickinson's 'gear' is somewhat misleading), and on the whole, we are left with the impression of vivacity couching a serious and important theme. The following narrative is more entertaining, and increases the comic intensity two-fold.

> [...] he [Arth] ferther told a meary tale; how, after a sermoun that he had maid at Dunfermling, he came to a house whair gossipis was dryncking thair Soundayis penny, and he, being dry, asked drynk. "Yis, Father, (said ane of the gossopes) ye shall haif drynk; bot ye mon first resolve ane doubt which is rissen amongis us, to witt, What servand will serve a man beast on least expenssis". "The good Angel, (said I,) who is manis keaper, who maikis great service without expenssis." "Tush, (said the gossope,) we meane no so heigh materis: we meane, What honest man will do greatest service for least expensses?" And as I was musing, (said the Frear,) what that should meane, he said "I see, Father, that the greatest clerkis ar nott the wysest men. Know ye nott how the Bischoppis and thair officiallis servis us husband men? Will thei not give to us a lettir of Curssing for a plack, to laste a year, to curse all that looke ower our dyke and that keapis our corne better nor the sleaping boy, that will have three schillings of fye, a sark, and payre of schone in the year. And thairfoir, yf thair curssing dow any thing, we held the Bishoppis beast chaip servandis, in that behalf, that ar within the realme." (Laing I: 38–39).

With this tale it is more difficult to assess Knox's contributions, and we cannot differentiate between literary voices as sharply as we did in the previous example. Probably, the first three lines (my text) (from 'He [...] drynck') belong to Knox, who is using Arth's information if not his exact words. The patterning of 'how, after a sermoun [...] he came' is caught up again in 'he, being dry, asked drynck', and this has a peculiarly Knoxian ring about it. Furthermore, the parenthetical phrase ('"said I"') obviously belongs to Arth, although ('said the Frear') must be Knox's, while the double '(said ane of the gossopes)' could belong to either of the narrators. Of course, the 'gossops' are never named, and even if they were, the names would probably mean nothing to us, but in all probability, a real encounter lies behind the lines (and we only get at it second or third-hand), so a claim of multiple-authorship would have to be sustained.

Especially impressive here are the subtly worked, tongue-in-cheek intellectual confrontations and the deft characterisation. Arth's initial response: '"the good Angel"', has a sort of ready-made seriousness about it which is not quite convincing, almost as if he were anticipating an ulterior motive behind the voiced question. The 'gossop's' quick impatience is realised through his dismissal of such '"heigh [presumably theological] materis"', before he finally ridicules the 'Bishoppis'. When he says: '"the greatest clerkis ar nott the wysest men"', there may of course be an echo of Chaucer or Henryson or simply an independent use of a popular oral proverb (see *Tilley* C.409, first recorded 1481, Caxton).

One critic who has written perceptively on this passage is Thomas Carlyle, though his historical observations are somewhat idiosyncratic. He writes: 'Knox never heard this discourse himself; far away, He, from Arth and St. Andrews. But he has contrived to make out of it and the circumstances surrounding, a little picture of old Scotch life, bright and real looking, as if by Teniers or Ostade'.[8] According to Laing's rather out-dated table of the chronological events in Knox's life, he was at this time in 'priest's orders, [...] with one of the religious establishments in the neighbourhood of Haddington',[9] but W. Stanford Reid is probably right when he suggests that: 'from Knox's detailed account of Arth's speech it would seem that he too had been present at the time'.[10] Whatever the case, the most remarkable (and indeed reliable) thing about Carlyle's observation is that it equates Knox's text with the visual arts and focuses on a deep 'Scottishness'. If there is any connection between Knox and Teniers/Ostade, it is in their use of satire and coarse peasant types as subject matter, but the second point (Scottishness) is more our concern here.

In the Scots of Knox's day, the word 'gossops', for instance, could not possibly have had the meaning which we attach to it today (Dickinson simply uses 'gossip').[11] Even as late as the 1530s it was used to denote a 'god-parent' as in this instance from the *Book of the Thanes of Cawdor*: 'Quhen eyr the caus iniuris to eyther of us the saidis parteis [are to] fulfill the band of gossaprie [...] as gossapis suld do' (1533). Not that this was Knox's meaning, however. A second

8 Carlyle, T., *Latter-Day Pamphlets: John Knox*, p. 112.

9 Laing I: xiv.

10 Reid, W. S., *Trumpeter of God*, p. 17.

11 See Dickinson I: 16.

meaning, derived from the first, had entered circulation by Arth's time, signifying: 'a familiar acquaintance, friend, chum' as in 'She is to her Gossypes gone to make merry'.[12] Its use is not at all pejorative. The use of 'gossop', then, goes along well with 'Soundayis penny'. The latter is an allusion to the traditional drinking of one's 'penny (worth)' of ale on the Sabbath; as much in quantity as a penny affords.[13] Again, as in the preceding Arth narrative, the richest Scots items come towards the end. 'Plack' for instance, denotes, as Dickinson says, 'a small copper coin, originally worth four Scots pennies, but the word was soon used, as here, to indicate a merely nominal sum'.[14] The commonest use of the item, however, can probably be traced back to proverbs (*Tilley* P.379, first recorded 1520, Dunbar) and typical expressions ('not worth a plack', 'plack and boddle', 'neuer left ane plak').[15] Thus, it ties in both with '"the greatest clerkis"' and 'Soundayis penny'). 'Sark' and 'schone' refer to items of clothing, of course, and as we saw in Ireland's sermons, (above, pp. 34–35), this kind of vocabulary did have positive homiletic uses.

On the whole, G. R. Owst would have classified this material: 'anecdote based on personal reminiscence, whether at first or second hand', as opposed to: 'another variety of the *exemplum* [...] which is really a development of the animated figure, and might be termed hypothetical narration'.[16] Indeed Knox seems to have been wholly receptive to creative homiletics. For example, he writes of the years 1538–1539:

> Ane Black freir, called Frear Kyllour, sett furth the Historye of Christis Passioun in forme of a play, quhilk he boith preached and practised opinlie in Striveling, the King him salf being present, upoun a Good Friday in the mornying: In the which, all thingis war so levelye expressed, that the verray sempill people understood and confessed, that as the Preastis and obstinat Pharisyes persuaded the people to refuise Christ Jesus, and caused Pilat to condampne him; so did the Bischoppes, and men called Religious, blynd the

12 See *O.E.D.*, IV: 311.

13 *O.E.D.*, VIII: 651

14 Dickinson I: 16.

15 *O.E.D.*, VII: 931.

16 Owst, G. R., *Literature and Pulpit in Medieval England*, p. 169, p. 177.

people, and perswaid Princes and Judgeis to persecute sick as professis Christ Jesus his blessed Evangell (Laing I: 62).

Knox's responsiveness here quite distinctly sets him apart from the earlier Wycliffites, who condemned such performances, and he seems to be alluding to a type of late Miracle play, possibly evincing Lutheran sympathies. David Calderwood's *The Historie of the Kirk of Scotland* also refers to Kyllour, but Calderwood is evidently recalling Knox's words rather than displaying any independent knowledge. Laing says of Kyllour: 'unfortunately his play, which probably was represented in 1535 or 1536 has not been preserved. Neither has any information respecting Friar Kyllour himself been discovered'.[17] Certainly a printed version or a manuscript would have been of great interest to Reformation scholars.

Just as Arth originally considered 'curssing', he turned to 'miracles' soon after:

> As concernying miracles, he declaired, what diligence the ancientis took to try trew miracles from false. "But now, (said he,) the greadynes of preastis not onlie receave false miracles, bot also thei cherise and feis knaiffis for that purpoise, that thair chapellis may be better renouned, and thair offerand may be augmented. And thairupon ar many chapelles founded, as that our Lady war mychttiar, and that sche took more pleasour in one plaice then in ane uther; as of laite dayis our Lady of Karsgreng hes hopped fra ane grene hillock to ane uther. But honest men of Sanctandrose, (said he,) yf ye luif your wyffis and your doughtaris, hald thame at hame, or ellis send thame in honest companye; for yf ye knew what miracles war kithed thaire, ye wold neyther thank God nor our Lady." And thus he mearelie tanted thare trystis of hurdome and adulterye used at such devotioun (Laing I: 39).

This particular tale is more carefully constructed than the previous two, and can be more readily divided into recognisable sections. Admittedly, some of the patterning we detected in the first narrative re-emerges (such as the use of '"But now"' to turn the tables) but even so, the structure is distinctive. For example, for the first time Knox introduces and concludes, with an 'As concernyng' and an 'And thus' respectively.

17 See Calderwood, D., *The Historie of the Kirk of Scotland*, vol. I: p. 125, and Laing I: 62, n. (1).

This hints at the fact that Knox is steadily asserting his own narratorial presence (a presence which will soon take control and pass judgement on Arth, as we shall see). Between introduction and conclusion, there seems to be a further two phases, first of mounting affectation and high comedy, then of a more sombre warning.

In the first section, the language is initially pejorative. 'Feis' is surely used in its bad sense ('Heire the Inglis knycht feys a tratour')[18] and 'knaiffis' is blatantly condemnatory. 'Offerand', which is a substantive, is tonally neutral, denoting Church emoluments, but when Arth follows things through, we get an image of the Virgin Mary (presumably), hopping from: '"ane grene hillock to ane other"'. The verb is particularly useful in comedy, as William Dunbar, for example, knew ('He hoppit lyk a pillie wantoun').[19] Arth has no concomitant simile, but still, we laugh. In the next section, filial loyalty is invoked to frustrate the supposedly libidinous 'miracles' of the clergy, with 'kithed' suggesting a gradual realisation of what is going on; (compare: 'it kythit be his cognisance ane knight that he wes').[20] In Knox's final summing up, he uses contractual terminology ('trystis') and implies corruption all round.

Arth's final tale, the Patrick Hepburn narrative, is perhaps the finest of the four (and Knox knew about the climatic structure of the tales, there is no doubt). This is the only tale to have a particular individual as the butt of its humour, although as Arth narrated it, he left the name out (and Knox delightedly supplied the deficit):

> "There was (said he) a Prelatt, or a least a Prelattis peir, a trew servand of the King of luiff, who, upoun a nycht after suppar, asked at his gentillmen, be the fayth that thei awght to the king of luiff, that thei should trewlie declare how many syndrie wemen everie ane of thame had haid, and how many of thaime war menis wyffis. Ane answered, He had lyne with fyve, and two of thame war maryed. The other answered, I have haid sevin, and three of thame are maryed. It came at last to my Lord him self, who macking it veray nyce for a lytill space, gave in the end ane plane confessioun, and said, 'I am the yongest man, and yitt have I haid the round desone; and sevin of thame are menis wyffis'. Now, (said the Frear,) this god and king of luif, to whome our Prelaittis maikis

18 *D.O.S.T.*, II: 427.

19 *D.O.S.T.*, III: 150.

20 *D.O.S.T.*, III: 487.

> homage, is the maister devill of hell, frome whome such werkis and fruitis do procead." This Prelatt was knowin by his proper tockenes to have bene Priour Patrik Hepburne, now Bischop of Murray, who to this day hes continewed in the professioun that he anes maid to his god and king of luif (Laing I: 40–41).

Arth probably refrained from naming names in this instance because Hepburn himself was in the audience, but even so, the 'Prelattis peir' could hardly have escaped the reference. More than this, however, the tale is impressive for its shrewd observation, which is matched by a skilful, teasing presentation. For instance, the phrase: 'macking it veray nyce for a lytill space' is crucial to the humour and the progression of the narrative. Indeed Knox uses the phrase elsewhere: 'The Bischope, and his band of the exempted sorte, maid it nyse to entrye befoir the Erle of Argyle who sat in judgement' (Laing II: 379) probably to suggest vanity or even effeminacy: (cf. 'Mak nyce and gar the larbair lowne beleue ye be a mayd').[21] Arth also uses some gentle irony. For instance the use of 'gentillman' must be implicitly ironic. Like Robert Henryson, Arth knew that 'it is contrar the lawis of nature A gentill man to be degenerate'.[22]

The whole tale in fact parodies the sacrament of confession ('ane confessioun' is of course not idly chosen) and Arth finishes off by defining the 'king of luiff'. The object of ecclesiastical devotion should be Jesus Christ, but Arth makes it clear that these clerics worship the 'maister devill of hell'. Indeed, with '"Now"', Arth introduces a little *moralitas*. Janton accurately observes that: 'Les anecdotes dont Frère Arth [...] témoignent de la vitalité de l'*exemplum* à la veille de la Réforme'.[23] Knox himself brings things right up to date (presumably to around 1566) and tells us where Hepburn is and what he is (still) doing. And one cannot have expected Knox to have had any sympathy for Hepburn, who, as W. Stanford Reid observes, was: 'well-known as an opponent of the Reformation and a persecutor of the brethren'.[24] Knox's assessment of Friar Arth itself is a little harder to swallow, considering that he evidently entertained the young Knox

21 *D.O.S.T.*, V: 541.
22 *D.O.S.T.*, II: 637.
23 Janton, P., *L'homme et l'oeuvre*, p. 449.
24 Reid, W. S., *Trumpeter of God*, p. 174.

(who would have been barely twenty when he heard the Friar), as much as anyone else:

> It was supposed, notwithstanding this kynd of preaching, that this Frear remaned papist in his heart; for the rest of the Frearis, fearing to losse the benedictioun of the Bischoppes, to witt, thair malt and thair maill, and thair other appoincted pensioun, cawsed the said Frear to flye to England, whair, for defence of the Paip and Paipistrie, hie was cast in preasone at King Hary his commandiment. But so it pleasith God to open up the mouth of Balaames awin asse, to cry out againest the vitious lyves of the clergie of that aige (Laing I: 41).

Here, Knox has taken over completely, lest he should be eclipsed by the remarkable Friar, and he is using his favourite device: the appeal to scripture. ('And the Lorde opened the mouth of the asse, and she sayde vnto Balaam: What haue I done unto thee, that thou hast smitten me now three times?' Numbers 22: 28, *Great Bible*). He even includes a few anticlerical touches himself, although their flavour is totally different from that of Arth's efforts. He suggests that the Friars' easy lives ('malt', 'maill' and 'pensioun') take precedence over their duty to preach, and this is a theme to which he will return.

The Arth tales apparently allowed Knox a chance to limber-up, and in their context of *The Historie*, they constitute a kind of literary praxis. After their inclusion Knox himself presents what must be his first, wholly original attempt at telling 'a merry bourd': the Sandie Furrour narrative. He manages it superbly. Knox has saved the best until last, as he cheerfully admits: 'hear followis the moist meary of all' (Laing I: 42). This is the longest of the tales, and as such, we shall divide it into four sections of roughly equal length. (The tale itself is of such quality that any editing is undesirable).

> Sandie Furrour, who had bene empreasoned sevin yearis in the Toure of Londone, Sir John Dingwaill, according to the cheritie of Churche men, enterteneid his wyiff, and waisted the poore manes substance. For the which caus, at his returnying, he spaik more liberallie of preastis then thei could bear, and so was he declaired to be accused of heresye, and called to his ansuer to Sanctandrose. He lapp up mearely upoun the scaffold, and, casting a gawmound, said, "Whair ar the rest of the playaris?". Maistir Andro Olephant, offended thairwyth, said, "It shalbe no play to yow, Sir, befoir that ye depart." And so began to read his accusatioun [...] (Laing I: 42).

Unlike Friar Arth's anecdotes, this is full-blooded narrative rather than sermon-narrative, although it certainly contains an obvious moral point about the corruption of 'preastis'. Knox, however, does continue the Friar's theme of sexual dalliance, and this time 'John Dingwaill' is the unfortunate (but not innocent) victim. The aggrieved Sandie Furrour, at any rate, is not under any illusions about him.[25] Interwoven with the theme of illicit behaviour are metaphors apparently drawn from theatrical sources: ('*enterteneid* his wyiff', 'He *lap up* […]', 'casting a *gawmound*', '"whair ar the rest of the *playaris*?"', and '"it shall be no *play* to yow, Sir, [...]"') (italics added). In fact, compared to Furrour's incorrigibly irreverent remarks, 'Andro Olephant's' attempt to restore order with a threat only makes him sound more ridiculous. When Furrour's hearing properly begins, the jokes come thick and fast:

> The first article whareof was, That he dispyssed the Messe. His answer was, "I hear mo Messis in awght dayis, then thre Bishopis thair sitting sayis in a year." Accused secoundarly, Of contemptioun of the sacramentis. "The preastis (said he,) war the maist commoun contempnaris of sacramentis, and especially of matrimonye," and that he witnessed by any of the preastis thare present, and named the menis wyffis with whome thei had medled, and especiallie Sir Johne Dignwaill, who had sevin yearis togitther abused his awin wyff, and consumed his substance; and said, "Becaus I complayne of such injuries, I am hear summoned, and accused, as one that is worthy to be brunt. For Goddis saik (said he,) wil ye taick wyeffis of your awin, that I and utheris, whose wyiffis ye have abused, may be revenged upoun yow." (Laing I: 43).

Had this part of the tale been narrated orally, the phrases: 'That he had dispyssed the Messe' and: 'especiallie Sir Johne Dignwaill' could have been delivered with a mock seriousness (like Arth's '"the good Angel"') and an exaggerated emphasis, respectively. Furrour's reply to the first charge, moreover, relies upon equivocation: '"I hear mo Messis in awght dayis then thre Bishopis […] sayis in a year."'. (Evidently he is not such a fool as the clergymen think). Knox, it seems, is implying that the Bishops say no Masses at all, and that they are deficient in administering their own Catholic practices (and one feels that the irony of that, if it were true, must have particularly amused Knox). But the fact that Furrour equivocates (and equivocates successfully) is the

25 See Laing I: 42, n. (2).

more important point, because it prepares the reader for the evasive rhetoric of Friar Alexander Seton, who is the major character in a subsequent narrative.

When the second charge ('comtemptioun of the sacramentis') is levelled, the story moves into its first major phase. The humour draws its dynamic from the fact that the accusers are more crooked than the accused (a theme with which Knox, again like Henryson, could work wonders). And one should remember that Knox is not wholly in sympathy with Mr. Furrour either, since he too is evidently a Balaam's ass (of a cruder kind than William Arth). Even so, Furrour has a compelling sense of being mocked by outrageous fortune: '"Becaus I complayne of such injuries, I am hear summoned and accused"'. When he demands of the priests that they marry, so that he might cheerfully fornicate with their wives and thus revenge his own injuries, another shift in direction is evident. Furrour evokes the following response:

> Then Bischope Gawin Dumbar, named the Old Bischop of Abirdein, thinking to justifye him self befoir the people, said, "Carll, thow shalt not know my wyff." The said Alexander ansuered, "My Lord, ye ar too old; bot with the grace of God, I shall drynck with your dochtter or I departe". And thareat was smylling of the best, and lowd laughtter of some; for the Bishop had a dowghter maryed with Andro Balfour in that same toune. Then the Bishoppis bad "Away with the Carll." But he ansured, "Nay; I will not departe this houre; for I have more to speak against the vices of preastis, then I cane expresse this haill day." (Laing I: 43–44).

Knox explores the motivation behind Dunbar's pompous action. Dunbar thought: 'to justifye himself befoir the people', while the subsequent phrase 'the said Alexander' perhaps implies that Knox knew, or at least, was familiar with Furrour. There is surely a degree of intimacy. The Archbishop's reply: '"Carll, thow shall not know my wyff"' demands a riposte, and Furrour's response is hilarious. Knox himself evidently provides the information about Dunbar's daughter, who was: 'maryed with Andro Balfour in that same toune'. 'For the [...]', a key justificatory link, shows his concern to keep his readers fully informed, since it seems that Furrour's comments hit the mark only by accident. That there was 'smylling of the best' and 'lowd laughter of some' are attractive details, the first suggesting a sort of grudging but good natured response, the other rather less restrained and perhaps with a touch of mockery about it (aimed at the Archbishop). They are laughing *with*, not *at*, Furrour, and we can follow suit. Furthermore, having been dismissed by an understandably offended Dunbar, Furrour can now gainsay with an obvious relish (like the Henrysonian husbandman, he is no king!): '"Nay, I will not departe this houre"'. After all, he has enough explosives to last the '"haill day"', as he says himself. The tale's climax is as follows:

> And so, after diverse purposes, thei commanded him to burne his bill. And he demanding the caus, thei said, "Because ye have spoken these articles whairof ye ar accused." His ansuer was, "The mekill devill bear thame away, that first and last said thame." And so he tuck the bill, and chowing it, hee after spatt it in Mr. Andro Oliphantis face, saying, "Now burne it or drune it, whitther ye will: ye heir na mair of me. Butt I man have somewhat of everie ane of yow to begyn my pack againe, which a preast, and my wyif, a preistis hoore, hes spentt;". And so everie prelate and riche preast, glaid to be qwyte of his evill, gave him somwhat; and so departed hie, for he understood nothing of religioun (Laing I: 44–45).

In this part of the narrative, one senses that the priests are becoming desperate. Furrour is now 'demanding' of *them*. Dialogue such as '"The mekill devill bear thame away"', together with Dunbar's '"Carl [...]"' rather recalls that of the Soutar and his wife in David Lindsay's *Ane Satyre of the Thrie Estaitis*. The detail of Furrour chewing his bill and spitting it in Olephant's face is perhaps something too earthy, even if, in terms of vulgarity, it falls a long way short of Lindsay's 'arse-kissing' divorcees. That the priests end up buying Furrour off, 'glaid to qwyte of his evill', is Knox's final missile; that Furrour 'understood nothing of religioun', is almost superfluous.

The Richard Carmichael narrative is much shorter and thus satisfies the reader without relying on a careful build up of humorous material. It seems no coincidence that it comes between the longest anecdotes (Sandie Furrour and the Seton sermons), though of course, Knox may be following the chronological order of events:

> But so fearfull it was then to speak any thing against preastis, that the least word spokin against thame, yea, albeit it was spokin in a manes sleip, was

> judged heresye; and that was practised upoun Richart Carmichaell, yet leving in Fyfe, who being young, and ane singar in the Chapell Royal of Striveling, happened to say, "The devill tak away the Preastis, for thei ar a gready pack". Hie, thairfoir, accused be Sir George Clappertoun, Deane of the said Chapell, was compelled tharefore to burne his bill (Laing I: 44–45).

Carmichael has perhaps been reading Isaiah 56: 11: 'they are shameless dogges, that be neuer satisfied' (*Great Bible*). This is a theme which emerges in Seton's sermons, so Knox is obviously preparing the reader for more detailed material. Here, however, he concentrates on what he sees as the inquisitorial excesses of the clergy. The first four lines (my text) sketch in a situation which the remainder of the passage substantiates. Thus we have an attempt at *confirmatio*. The style is of course competent, although like the author of *The Complaynt of Scotland* (above, p. 60), Knox is drifting towards participial excess in conjunction with his habitual use of absolutes ('yet leving in Fyfe', '[...] who being young', and 'He [...] accused by Sir George [...]'). (It is occasionally suggested that Knox's prose is un-Latinate, but such statements should not be made without qualification. For instance, he does use ablatives quite frequently: '*Which understood*, he *ran* to the posterne [...]' (Laing I: 175), '*Which perceaved*, the Cardinall or his chalmer child, (it is uncertane,) *opened* the doore [...]' (Laing I: 177; italics added)). In the final sentence (above), the repetition of 'tharefore' may be thought of as clumsy, unless perhaps there is some mimicry of Clapperton. Knox might have expected his original audience to share knowledge to which modern readers cannot now have access.

After the Carmichael episode comes Knox's treatment of Seton: 'a Blak Frear, of good learning and estimatioun' (Laing I: 45). As Dr. John Durkan says in '"Scottish Evangelicals" in the Patronage of Thomas Cromwell', Seton preached at St. Andrews '[...] a memorable course of Lenten sermons, softening the stark Lutheran emphases with distinctions borrowed directly or indirectly from Melanchthon',[26] but, like Arth, this Friar was extremely critical of clerical abuses. For instance, he condemned idle bishops as dumb dogs, and the report of

26 Durkan, J., '"Scottish Evangelicals" in the Patronage of Thomas Cromwell', 141.

one such sermon came to the ears of a bishop who subsequently summoned the Friar. Seton denied that he had said any such thing, and, with the audacity of an experienced equivocator, concluded:

> "In verray deid, My Lord, I said that Paul sayis 'It behoveth a Bishop to be ane teichear.' Isai sayith, 'That thei that feid nott the flock ar dum doggis.' And Zacharie sayeth, 'Thei ar idol pastouris.' I of my awin head affirmed nothing, butt declared what the Spreitt of God had befoir pronunced; at whome my Lord, yf ye be nott offended, justly ye cane nott be offended at me. And so yit agane, my Lord, I say, that thei are manifest leyaris that reported unto yow, that I said, That ye and otheris that preach nott ar no Bischoppis but belly Gods." (Laing I: 47).

Like Carmicheal, Seton appeals to Isaiah 56: 11, but also to 1 Timothy 13: 2: 'a Bizhoppe must be blamelesse [...] apt to teach' and Zechariah 11: 17: 'O Idols shepherde, that leauethe the flocke' before he concludes with a veiled reference to Philippians 3: 9: 'whose God is the bely' (*Coverdale*). Seton's successful attempt to avoid being held responsible for his attacks revolves around his abnegation of self in favour of the '"Spreitt of God"', but as well as being a shrewd evasion it was also a legitimate use of a main strand of all Reformation thought. We can also enjoy a joke at the Bishop's expense, but in the end it is Seton's dexterous intellectual manipulation which impresses us.

We now turn to the richest vein of humour in *The Historie*; Knox's use of farce. Three narratives concern us, all of which have become justly famous. They are, of course, the tussle for precedence of entry into Glasgow Cathedral Church between the followers of Cardinal Beaton and Archbishop Dunbar in 1546, the incident in the French galleys when an anonymous Scotsman was confronted with an image of the Virgin Mary, and finally, the St. Giles day ceremony with the Queen Regent in 1558. The first comes in the midst of George Wishart's dramatic narrative and changes the mood quite drastically, but again, Knox is not at liberty to re-arrange the order of events to please himself and the artistic sensibilities of his readers. (All historians, however partisan, have responsibilities which cannot be ignored). In the subsequent lines, Knox's *glorious* sense of humour manifests itself to the fullest extent:

> The Cardinall was knowin proude; and Dumbare, Archbischope of Glasgw, was known a glorious foole; and yitt, becaus sometymes he was called the Kingis Maister, he was Chancelour of Scotland. The Cardinall comis evin thus [sic] same year, in the end of harvest befoir, to Glasgw; […] But whill they remane togither, the one in the toune, the other in the Castell, questioun ryses for bearing of thare croces. The Cardinall alledgeid, by reasson of his Cardinall-schip, and that he was *Legatus Natus*, and Primat within Scotland, in the kingdom of Antichrist, that he should have the pre-eminence, and that his croce should not onlye go befoir, but that also it should onlye be borne, wharesoever he was. Good Gukstoun Glaikstour, the foirsaid Archibishop, lacked no reassonis, as he thowght, for mantenance of his glorie: He was ane Archibishop in his awin diosey, and in his awin Cathedrall seat and Church, and tharefor awght to give place to no man: The power of the Cardinall was but begged from Rome, and apperteined but to his awin persone, and nott to his bischoprik […] (Laing I: 145–146).

Writing in the traditions of 'folly literature', Knox observes that this indeed is: 'a questioun worthy of such two prelattis' (Laing I: 146, marginal note). Pr. Dickinson enjoys: 'the half-humorous, half-serious description' of 'the doubts and difficulties of the case'[27] and it is the extraordinary blend of opposites which flavours the prose. The way in which Knox moves from the above pseudo-intellectual high comedy to physical horse-play, belly laughs and blatant farce is irresistibly compelling:

> Many of thame lacked beardis, and that we the more pitie; and tharefore could not bukkill other by the byrse, as bold men wold haif doune. Butt fy on the jackmen that did nott thare dewitie; for had the one parte of thame reacontred the other, then all had gone rycht. But the sanctuarye, we suppose, saved the lyves of many. How mearelye that ever this be writtin, it was bitter bowrding to the Cardinall and his courte. It was more then irregularitie; yea, it mycht weall have bene judged lease majestie to the sone of perdition, the Papes awin persone; and yitt the other in his foly, as proud as a packoke, wold lett the Cardinall know that he was a Bischop when the other was butt Betoun, befoir he gat Abirbrothok. This inemitie was judged mortall, and without all hope of reconsiliatioun (Laing I: 147).

The passive voice and mock remonstrance ('Butt fy on […]'), together with the account of what the 'jackmen' could not do ('bukkill other by

27 See Dickinson I: lxxv.

the byrse'), changes this from a violent encounter ('bitter bowrding') to a more jolly occasion which can be thoroughly enjoyed by the reader. As we can see, the technique here is far more controlled than that of, say, the Sandie Furrour narrative, and even more farcical. Knox uses a more sophisticated vocabulary alongside a rich, homely one. 'The sone of perdition' echoes John 17: 12 (or 2 Thessalonians 12: 3) while the medieval Latin of '*Legatus Natus*' competes with the alliterative aptronym 'Good Gukstoun Glaikstour' (Mr. Trifling Folly), and '*lease majestie*' with 'Abirbrothok' (Arbroath). Alliterative name-calling was indeed a frequent device in Reformation polemics. Sir Thomas More, for example, writing on the Catholic side in England, called Tyndale the Apostle of the Apostates. Knox even introduces a neat pun with: 'the other was butt Betoun'.

The same sense of spectacle and absurd fun re-emerges towards the end of Book I, and again there is an introductory passage which sets things up for the ensuing silliness. The following passage overlaps with sections of an anonymous work entitled *A Historie of the Estate of Scotland, from the year 1559 to the year 1566*, and this allows us to juxtapose prose which focuses on the same material (the technique employed, for example, when we looked at the work of Gau and Nisbet; above, pp. 38–39). The work as we now have it is a late seventeenth century transcript of a much older manuscript, but Laing suggests that it is: 'somewhat doubtful whether the first writer was a person living at the time, and describing events as an eye-witness'.[28] Even so, the text corroborates Knox's *The Historie*, as we can see:

> *The Historie of the Reformatioun*
> Yit wold nott the Preastis and Freiris cease to have that great solempnitie and manifest abominatioun which thei accustomablie had upoun Sanct Geillis day, to witt, thei wold have that idole borne; and tharefor was all preparatioun necessar deuly maid. A marmouset idole was borrowed from the Gray Freiris, (a silver peise of James Carmichael was laid in pledge:) It was fast fixed with irne nailles upon a barrow, called thare fertour. Thare assembled Preastis, Frearis, Channonis, and rottin Papistes, with tabornes and trumpettis, banneris and bage-pypes, and who was thare to led the ring, but the Quein Regent hir self, with all hir schaivelingis, for honour of that feast. West about goes it, and

28 See Laing, D., (ed.), *The Miscellany of the Wodrow Society*, vol. I: p. 51.

cumis doun the Hie Streat, and doun to the Canno Croce. The Quein Regent dyned that day in Sandie Carpetyne's housse [...] (Laing I:259).

A Historie of the Estate of Scotland
Always the said first of September, called St. Giles day, loath to want any jott of the devill's service, [they] borrowed of the Gray Freirs a litill Idoll of St. Giles and putt on a golden coate upon the same, and presented it in that guise according to the wicked custome, to be carried through the toune. It wes soone taken up by the blind ignorant, and carried in procession through the most parte of the Toune, till at length it wes pulled downe and broken by some brethren of the towne, who, moved with zeall, could not suffer such manifest idolatrie, (the Queene Regent being neere by,) nothwithstanding no man received any harme; albeit the number of people wes exceeding great; bot the Papists, priests, ffriers, and Bishops, were altogether dashed and confused and thair array broken: Alwayes the Queene discembled the matter for the tyme [...][29]

Pr. Jack Aitken had Knox very much in mind when he observed that a Middle Scots author who:

> [...] thematically fronts motion adverbials, uses successions of minimal simple sentences, prefers present participle subordinate clauses to finite verb clauses, employs the *who was there but* idiom [and] uses historic present tense [...] may be assumed to be aiming at the effect of a racy, personal narration of folk-tale or popular anecdote.[30]

It is obvious from the above juxtaposition that the unknown author is less intent on creating, or less *able* to create, such an effect. However, he does provide us with material which Knox leaves out, that the 'Idoll' has a 'golden coate' for instance. The parenthetical: 'the Queene Regent being neere by' cannot match Knox's use of idiom, although both authors use lists to convey the 'busy-ness' of the scene. From the quality of Knox's story, it should be evident that we are entering a comical phase that perhaps has no equal anywhere else in *The Historie*. As the narrative progresses our expectations are not disappointed. Knox unfolds the episode in a further two distinct phases. The first culminates in a marvellous *mot d'esprit*:

29 ibid., pp. 54–55.
30 See Aitken, J., 'Oral Narrative Style in Middle Scots', 109.

[…] some of those that war of the interprise drew ney to the idole, as willing to helpe to beare him, and getting the fertour upoun thare schulderis, begane to schudder, thinking that thairby the idole should have fallin. But that was provided and prevented by the irne nailles, as we have said; and so, begane one to cry, "Doun with the idole; doun with it," and so without delay it was pulled doun. Some brag made the Preastis patrons at the first; but when thei saw the febilness of thare god, (for one took him by the heillis, and dadding his head to the calsay, left Dagon without head or handis, and said, "Fye upon thee, thow young Sanct Geill, thy father wold haiff taryed four such […]" (Laing I: 260).

Finally we have description like the following; 'le pêle-mêle comique'[31] in which: 'the words themselves become the panting, gasping tussle of men in hand-to-hand affray':[32]

[…] this considdered, (we say,) the Preistis and Freiris fled faster than thei did at Pynckey Clewcht. Thare mycht have bein sein so suddane a fray as seildome hes bein sein amonges the sorte of men within this realme, for doun goes the croses, of goes the surpleise, round cappes cornar with the crounes. The Gray Freiris gapped, the Black Frearis blew, the Preastis panted, and fled, and happy was he that first gat the house; for such ane suddan fray came never amonges the generatioun of Antichrist within this realme befoir […] (Laing I: 260).

Because of their obvious similarities, the previous three Knox passages deserve consideration together, although each offers something unique. The first illustrates just how keenly Knox felt for an occasion. In modern times he might have been especially skilled in the description of a cup final crowd or a coronation. One can almost hear the tuning of musical instruments and see the surging marchers with the Regent out in front. The second draws upon the narrative contained in 1 Samuel 5: 4 as a backdrop to the current story: 'beholde, Dagon laye vpon the grounde beefore the arke of the Lorde, and hys head, and hys two handes cut of vpon the threshold […]' (*Great Bible*), but more than this, it contains a conclusion which, in terms of wry humour, deserves to rank alongside Henryson's delightful: 'Me think na man may speik ane word in play, / Bot now on dayis in ernist it is tane',[33] and alongside the immortal scenes in Scottish literature,

31 Janton, P., *L'homme et l'oeuvre*, p. 485.

32 Dickinson I: lxxv.

33 See Fox, D., (ed.), *The Poems of Robert Henryson*, p. 33, ll. 770–771.

such as *Tam O'Shanter*'s: 'Weel done, Cutty-Sark!'.[34] It has always been a Scots propensity to measure son off against father, always to the detriment of the former (the 'kent his faither' syndrome). The ignominious flight of the Friars in the final extract is realised with explosive energy, and Knox turns from *Old Testament* to Scottish history in his allusion to 'Pynckey Clewcht'. David Murison places this kind of prose in: 'the good old *Christ's Kirk* and *Peblis to the Play* tradition in Scottish literature',[35] and it is our final selection which comes closest to the genre. To get some idea of what Dr. Murison means, and to test his theory, we can juxtapose Knox's lines with a passage like this from *Christis Kirk on the Grene*, which represents Scottish medieval poetry at its most attractive:

> With forkis and flalis thay leit grit flappis
>   and flang togither with friggis
> with bougaris of barnis yai brist blew cappis
>   Quhill thay of bernis maid briggis
> The rerde rais rudlie with the rappis
>   Quhen rungis was layd on riggis
> The wyffis come furth with cryis and clappis
>   lo quhair my lyking liggis Quod scho
> at chrystis kirk.[36]

Surely there is much, but not absolute, continuity between Knox's writing and the earlier alliterative verse, although in this instance at least, the (anonymous) poet makes use of matrimonial loyalties to remind us of the fact that there are victims of, and spectators to, the chaos. But the whole tradition has a crazy beauty, full of imaginative qualities, pyrotechnic displays, and is fired by the sheer silliness of its subject matter. Knox, in fact, is probably the finest exponent of the genre *in prose,* although in verse (such as Robert Fergusson's) the line continues with as much quality. But Knox also introduces what Ralph Walker calls: 'a prevalent asperity of his own'.[37] In a phrase such as 'the generatioun of Antichrist' this is clearly evident, while Knox's

34 See Barke, J., (ed.), *Poems and Songs of Robert Burns*, p. 207.

35 Murison, D., 'Knox the Writer', 47.

36 See Craigie, W. A., (ed.), *The Maitland Folio MS.*, p. 152, ll. 131–140.

37 Walker, R. S., (ed.), *The Historie of the Reformatioun*, p. 6.

overall sarcasm does not really have any earlier counterpart in the tradition.

Now that we have seen what each passage contributes in terms of individuality, it seems apt to turn to their stylistic features. In the first, Knox uses the rhetorician's *dissimulatio*, saying 'one thing' and meaning 'in heart another',[38] when he observes that the priests' great solemity is a manifest abomination. He consistently employs Scots diction; 'marmouset', 'fertour' and 'shaivelingis' being the most elaborate items, and he augments their use by suggesting a strong sense of familiarity. 'James Carmichaell' and 'Sandie Carpetyne' were evidently people he knew, or knew of. In the second, he relies heavily on alliteration and combines it with verb and noun couplets or triplets ('provided and prevented', 'head or handis', '"Fye [...] father [....] four" [...]'). 'Dadding' is onomatopoeic and helps add to the splendidly vivid picture of the scene. Knox varies his technique of anaphora ('as we have said') and introduces a journalistic economy ('and so without delay it was pulled doun'). In the final passage, Knox begins with hypothetical comment ('Thare mycht [...]'), but quickly smooths it into the actual narrative.

With just a change of preposition ('*doun* goes' becomes '*of* goes', italics added), Knox manages to convey each inevitable stage of the brawl. And not only do the priests and Friars battle it out, the items of their clothing seem to do so too ('round cappes cornar with the crounes'). Knox's final touch comes with his use of *similiter desinens* as defined by Quintillian and Johannes Susenbrotus: 'When clauses conclude alike, the same syllables being placed at the end of each'.[39] ('The Gray Freiris gapped, the Black Frearis blew, the Preistis panted'). Each clause has no object and ends with a similar past-tense verb which alliterates with the preceding adjective or noun (as in the third phrase).

This brings us to our final jocular narrative, one which is certainly less lively than the above, but again it has something significant to offer. The event it describes took place in the galleys in 1548, and the narrative is contained in Book I of *The Historie*:

38 Sonnino, L. A., *A Handbook*, p. 77.

39 ibid., p. 170.

> Sone after the arrival at Nances, thare great *Salve* was song, and a glorious painted Lady was brought in to be kissed, and amongis otheris, was presented to one of the Scotishmen then cheyned. He gentillye said, "Trubill me nott; such an idole is accurssed; and tharefoir I will not tuich it." The Patron and the Arguesyn with two officeris, having the cheaf charge of all such materis, said, "Thou salt handill it;" and so thei violentlie thrust it to his face, and putt it betuix his handis: who seing the extremitie, tooke the idole, and advisitlie looking about, he caist it in the rivare, and said, "Lett our Lady now saif hir self: sche is lycht aneuch, lett her learne to swyme." After that was no Scotisch man urged with that idolatrie [...]
>
> These ar thingis that appear to be of no great importance; and yit yf we do rychtlie considder, thei expresse the same obedience that God requyred of his people Israell, when that thei should be caryed to Babylon; for he gave charge unto thame [...] that thei should say, "The Goddis that have nott maid the heavin and the earth shall perish frome the heavin and out of the earth." (Laing I: 227–228).

There are two distinct parts to this passage, and one might say that the old separation between tale and *moralitas* applies (and this is something which is also apparent in the Cardinal Beaton narrative, above, pp. 237–238). If we look at each constituent part of the passage, it is obvious that the story itself is more aesthetically pleasing. It is apparently modelled on Judges 6: 31: 'But Joas sayde vnto all them that stode by him: Wyl ye stryve for Baal? He yat stryveth for him shal dye this mornyng. Yf he be God, let him avenge himself, because his altare is broken downe' (*Coverdale*).[40]

Laing observes that 'this "merry fact" evidently happened to Knox himself'[41] but there is really no evidence for this at all. Indeed, on the contrary, we know that Knox was seldom slow to claim credit for himself, by name. His failure to do so in this instance may be significant. W. S. Reid observes that: 'this has all the earmarks of a typical Knoxian action'[42] but one should not go any further. These things aside, however, the phrase 'advisitlie looking about' is a superb *mot juste* and to find anything comparable, one has to return to the 'macking it veray nyce [...]' of Patrick Hepburn's narrative (above,

40 See Janton, P., *L'homme et l'oeuvre*, p. 463, n. (166).

41 Laing I: 227, n. (3).

42 Reid, W.S., *Trumpeter of God*, p. 57.

p. 264). Then there is the understatement of: 'After that was no Scotische man urged with that idolatrorie'.

The homiletic part evidently follows a pattern. Knox becomes self-conscious and reminds us that although the preceding narrative may be very funny, it expresses something profound about God and His relationship with the Chosen People. (Knox seems consistently to have envisaged a reader who was rather more stern than he was himself, and was forever making excuses for such humorous diversions). The Biblical allusion this time is to Jeremiah 10: 11: 'As for their Goddes, it may well be sayde of them: they are goddes, that made nether heauen nor earth, therefore shal they perish from the earth, and from all thingis vnder heauen' (*Coverdale*). Again it seems that Knox is citing from memory, since the quotation does not match precisely any of the scriptural translations which were circulating at the time. Generally speaking, however, it is accurate enough to enhance his point.

Dramatic Narratives

Having considered Knox's undoubted ability as a teller of the 'merry tale' we must examine another facet of his work which draws at least partially on similar talents. Certainly, the narratives which this section considers are often, though not always, humorous, but their primary characteristic is their dramatic power. Indeed, it is perhaps in his dramatic narration that Knox's true literary greatness rests.

I propose to begin with Knox's treatment of Scotland's protomartyr of the Reformation, Patrick Hamilton. The inception point of this narrative lies in Knox's description of the high-ranking clergyman James Beaton (uncle of the better known David):

> [...] who was moir cairfull for the world then he was to preach Christ, [...] for it was weill knowin that at onis he was Archbishop of Sanctandrosse, Abbot of Dumfermeling, Abirbroth, Kylwynnyng, and Chancellare of Scotland (Laing I: 13).

Such a disparity between the ideal and the actual is the very stuff of Knox's Juvenalian satire (as it was in Wishart's prophecy). Hamilton on the other hand was only: 'providit to *reassonable* honouris and leving, (he was intitulat Abbot of Ferne);' (italics added), and Knox's special stresses cannot be overlooked. Again unlike Beaton, Hamilton hated: 'the world and the vanitie thairof [...]' (Laing I: 14–15).

When Knox actually gets down to business, to a description of Hamilton's death scene, he sets the mould for a memorable fusion of tenderness and fierce declamation, and this allows him to prepare for his later treatment of Wishart's martyrdom. He tells us that: 'At the plaice of executioun', Hamilton 'gave to his servand':

> [...] who had bene chalmer-child to him of a long tyme, his gown, his coit, bonet and such lycht garmets, saying, "These will nott proffeit in the fyre, thei will proffeit thee: Aftir this of me thow cane receave no commoditie, except the example of my death, which, I pray thee, bear in mynd; for albeit it be bitter to the flesche, and feirfull befoir men, yet is it the entress unto eternall lyif, quhilk non shall possesse that denyis Christ Jesus befoir this wicked generatioun." (Laing I: 17).

Jostling for attention with this, is Knox's description of what happened during Hamilton's torment:

> [...] he was greved by certane wicked men, amongis whome Campbell the Black Freir (of whome we spak befoir) was principall, who continuallie cryed "Convert, heretick: call upoun our Lady: say *Salve Regina*" etc. To whome he answered, "Departe, and truble me not, ye messingeris of Sathan." Bott whill that the foirsaid Freir still roared one thing in great vehemencye, he said unto him, "Wicked man, thou knawis the contrair, and the contrair to me thou has confessed. I appeall thee befoir the tribunall seatt of Jesus Christ!" (Laing I: 18).

In the first passage, Knox shows his ability to captivate the reader's attention with circumstantial details designed simultaneously to exalt Hamilton and to evoke sympathy. This technique, as we shall see, is central to his treatment of Wishart. The second is characterised by the pious bantering between Hamilton and Campbell, with each invoking, in contrasting religious language, absolute authority. For Campbell this is the Virgin Mary, for Hamilton it is: '"the tribunall seatt of Jesus Christ!"'. Knox gives Hamilton the final word, as we would expect, but the martyr is hardly in a position to relish a dialectical victory even if Knox recalls the precise facts. Knox himself was not present at the St. Andrews martyrdom (see Laing I: 500, Appendix III).

What he is about here, is trying to create a Scots *Book of Martyrs*, which has its English equivalent in Foxe, its French in Crespin's *Actes des Martyrs deduits en sept livres depuis le temps de Wyclif & Huss. jusques a present*, (Geneva 1565), and its Catholic European counterpart in the *Legenda Aurea* of Jacobus de Voragine. The last had in fact worked its way into Scottish literature *via* the popular saints tales which had penetrated the vernacular, and when the Reformation began, there was a need for similar documentation of heroic deeds. The Reformers, however, could not take refuge in what they saw as religiosity and superstition, and the subsequent impression both of realism and veracity permeates their work in this area. What impresses us about Knox's treatment of Hamilton (which is his first foray into martyrology) is the way in which it makes the issues clear from the start by working them out through dramatic dialogue.

When Knox turned to his next major martyr, George Wishart, he was able to bring us into contact with more detailed narratives and more historically reliable material, since he was an acquaintance of this Reformer and an eyewitness to his ministry if not his death. In this instance, it is wholly unlikely that Knox adapted the events in order to make himself look more important than he actually was. His material on Wishart concerns itself not just with preaching. There is some serious dramatic narrative which demands attention because of its superb quality. For instance, there are two episodes which deal with attempts on Wishart's life. First, one 'disperat preast [...] Schir Johne Wightone' (Laing I: 130), tried to assassinate him but was thwarted, then a more subtle plan was apparently hatched with which to lure him to Edinburgh. This, as Knox tells us, also fell through. Here is the earlier narrative:

> And upoun a day, the sermoun ended, and the people departing, no man suspecting danger, and tharefore nott heading the said Maister George, the Preast that was corrupted stood waiting at the foot of the steppis, his goune lowse, and his whinger drawin into his hand under his gown, the said Maister George, as that he was moste scharpe of eie and judgement, marked him, and as he came neyr, he said, "My freind, what wald ye do?" And tharewith he clapped his hand upoun the Preastis hand, wharein the whingar was, which he

tooke from him. The Preast abassed, fell down at his feitt, and openly confessed the veritie as it was. The noyse rising, and cuming to the earis of the seik, thei cryed, "Deliver the tratour to us, or ellis we will tack him by forse;" and so thei birst in at the yett. But Maister George took him in his armes, and said, "Whosoevir trubles him shall truble me; for he has hurte me in nothing, bot he hes done great conforte boyth to yow and me, to witt, he hes lattin us understand what we may feare in tymes to come. We will watch better." And so he appeased boith the one parte and the other, and saved the lyif of him that soght his (Laing I: 130–131).

The second of two related incidents is much more skilfully narrated, and one says this bearing in mind the very high standard of the first. Knox tells us that Wishart:

[...] passed to Montrose, to salute the Kirk thare; whare he remaned occupyed sometymes in preaching, but most parte in secreat meditatioun, in the which he was so earnest, that nycht and day he wold continew in it. Whill he was so occupyed with his God, the Cardinall drew a secreat drawght for his slawchter. He caused to writt unto him a letter, as it had bein frome his most familiare freind, the Larde of Kynneyre, "Desyring him with all possible diligence to come unto him, for he was strickin with a suddane seakness." In this meantyme, had the tratour provided thre score men, with jackis and spearis, to lye in wate within a myll and a half of the toune of Montrose, for his dispatche. The letter cuming to his hand, he maid haste at the first, (for the boy had brought a horse,) and so with some honest men, he passes furth of the toune. But suddandlye he stayed, and musing a space, returned back; whereat their wondering, he said, "I will not go: I am forbiddin of God: I am assured thare is treassone. Lett some of yow, (sayis he,) go to yonder place, and tell me what ye fynd." Diligence made, thei fand the treassone, as it was [...] (Laing I: 131–132).

In both passages, Wishart is portrayed as a potential healer, or at least one who attends the sick. Laing suggests that Wishart visited Dundee in August 1545, and for this time there is an entry in *A Diurnal of Remarkable Occurents*: 'the pest was wonder greit in all burrowis townis of this realme, quhair mony pepill deit with great skant and want of victuallis'.[43] In the second, there are faint echoes of the Lazarus story in John's gospel: 'Mary [...] sent unto him saying: Lorde, beholde / he whom thou lovest is sicke' (John 11: 3, *Tyndale*

43 See Laing I: 129, and Thomson, T., (ed.), *A Diurnal of Remarkable Occurents*, p. 39.

1526). Of course, the only treason in the gospels is that of Judas Iscariot. In Knox's Wishart narrative, that particular role is reserved not for renegade priests or even Cardinal Beaton, but for the Earl of Bothwell: 'But as gold and wemen have corrupted all worldlye and fleschlye men from the begynning, so did thei him' (Laing I: 143).

In spite of all that they have in common, there is a major difference between the two episodes. The first may be said to inculcate a moral, in two senses. Wishart learns: 'what we may feare in tymes to come' while his followers (and the readers of Knox's *The Historie*) learn: 'for and yff ye shall forgeve other men thare treaspases / youre father in heven shal also forgeve you', (Matthew 6: 17, *Tyndale* 1526) or something along those lines. In the second, Knox wants to give the impression that Wishart has supernatural powers of observation. For Wishart, the: 'time is not yett full come' (John 7: 6, *Tyndale* 1526). The language used in these passages is as fascinating as ever. Knox's choice of 'whinger', for instance, is significant. It denotes a short stabbing-sword well suited to the purpose for which Wighton intended to use it. Rolland's *Book of Seven Sages* has a good parallel: 'incontinent his quhinyear furth he drew'.[44] Knox uses it elsewhere, and one suspects that his sense of justice as well as his veracity as a reporter have something to do with it: after Wishart's death 'Johne Leslye', one of the assassins of Beaton, 'spared not to say "That same *whingar*, (schawin furth his dager,) and that same hand, should be preastis to the Cardinall" (Laing I: 172; italics added).

Knox consistently calls Wishart 'Maister George' and this too has a special meaning. The *D.O.S.T.* entries for 'Maister' are extensive. The relevant sense, of course, is when: 'Prefixed to the Christian name […] alone, chiefly of one who is a master of Arts. Masters in this use were often clergymen or schoolmasters and so the occurences are very numerous indeed'.[45] In 'George Wishart: His Early Life', John Durkan says that Wishart's: 'first appearance in Scottish records [was] at Montrose in 1534, when he was already a Master of Arts' and he may have been a graduate not of Aberdeen but 'of the University of

44 *O.E.D.*, X, II: 51.
45 *D.O.S.T.*, IV: 27–32.

Louvain'.[46] Laing's notes on the distinction between 'Schir' and 'Maister' are still a good reference point (Laing I: 555–8). There are one or two other interesting Scotticisms. For instance, Knox tells us that the 'seik', to whom Wishart had presumably been ministering, were so angered by the news of the attempt on his life that they 'birst in at the yett'. In the *Glasgow MS.* of *The Historie*, 'birst' has been replaced by 'thay thrist in', but in both cases the sense of outrage is vividly realised. Interestingly, in Wishart's subsequent speech he uses the Scots past-participle of 'lat': 'he hes lattin us understand [...]'. Wishart probably did use such a phrase, since the above form is quite common, so Knox, to his credit, is successfully bringing us very close to vivid and actual historical events.

I implied earlier that the second narrative was a greater artistic success than the first. This is so because it opens with a pair of vignettes. Wishart is pictured at prayer; a man wholly devoted to God and the well-being of his fellow men. Beaton, on the other hand, is plotting *how he might kill him* (and we may be reminded of Psalms 30: 'they haue gathered a councel together agaynst me, and are purposed to take awaye my life' (*Coverdale*)). The juxtaposition constitutes *synkrisis* and the implications of this very subtle pairing-off gradually emerge the more one reads the passage. Again, incidental details such as the fact that 'the boy had brought a horse' keep the story flowing, and the climax comes when Wishart: 'suddanlye [...] stayed'. For Knox, this is the moment when God imparts to Wishart his miraculous knowledge.

Knox's assured control of his medium is something which also comes out in the early part of the first narrative. As we saw with the merry tales, he is an intrusive narrator, but his point of view falls short of omniscience, and if we apply the standard literary distinction between 'showing' and 'telling', it is obvious that he does the latter, but there is still much elaborate scene-setting, and this is accompanied by careful explanatory material. But the most striking feature is Knox's use of terse, climactic dialogue ('"My freind, what wald ye do?"'). Indeed, it should be noted that Wishart's dialogue itself seems

46 Durkan, J., 'George Wishart: His Early Life', 98.

more assured than that of his wild prophesying at Haddington, which we considered earlier (above, pp. 231–232).

Even so, Wishart does reproduce these tones with great fidelity during a notable incident when he was preaching at 'Enresk' (Inveresk), near Edinburgh. Two gray Friars entered the Church and, according to Knox, Wishart welcomed them; '"It may be that thei be come to learne"' (Laing I: 135). The Friars, however, evidently did not appreciate Wishart's offer of edification, and they disrupted his sermon. He subsequently addressed them:

> 'O sergeantis of Sathan, and deceavaris of the soules of men, will ye nether hear Goddis trewth, nor suffer otheris to hear it? Departe and tack this for your portioun – God shall schortlie confound and disclose your hipochrisie [...]". This sentence he pronounced with great vehemencye, in the myddist of the sermoun; and turneyng to the people, he said "Yone wicked men have provocked the Spreat of God to angar." And so he returned to his mater, and proceaded to the end (Laing I: 136).

Here Wishart acts as Christ rebuking the Pharisees, in Matthew 23:13, 33: 'Wo be vnto you scribes and pharisees dissemblers / for ye sheet up the kyngdom of heven before men: ye youre selves goo not in / nether suffre ye them that come to enter in [...] ye serpents and generation of vipers / how shall ye escape the damacion of hell?' (*Tyndale*, 1526, cf. also Matthew 24: 51). (We have already seen Knox using similar imagery; above p. 154). Wishart's most memorable phrase, however, is the alliterative 'sergeantis of Sathan'. We can detect something of his Zwinglianism coming through, and can use this passage as evidence that Knox's militant language came to him from Wishart (above, pp. 73–74).

The most blatant Biblical parallels in the Wishart narrative occur earlier on in *The Historie*. When the preacher was residing at 'Inner Gowrye', some two miles from Dundee, with 'Williame Spadin, and Johne Watsoun, both men of good credyte,' (Laing I: 132), he was observed by them to pass 'furth into a yard:'

> When he had gone up and doune into ane alay a ressonable space, with many sobbes and deape grones, he platt upoun his knees, and setting thareon, his grones increassed; and frome his knees he fell upoun his face; and then the personis fornamed heard weaping and, as it war ane indigest sound, as it war of

prayeris, in the which he continewed neyre ane hour, and after begane to be qwiet; and so arrose and came in to his bed. They that awated prevented him, as thei had bein ignorant, till that he came in; and than begane thei to demand whare he had bein? Butt that nycht he wold ansuer nothing. Upoun the morrow, thei urged him agane; and whill that he dissimuled, thei said, "Maister George, be plaine with us; for we heard your grones; yea, we heard your bitter murning, and saw yow boyth upoun your kneis and upoun your face." With dejected visage, he said, "I had rather ye had bein in your beddis, and it had bein more profitable to yow, for I was skarse weall occupied." When thei instantlie urged him to lett thame know some confort; he said, "I will tell yow, that I am assured that my travall is neir ane end; and tharefor call to God with me, that now I schrink not when the battell waxis maist hoote." And whill that thei weaped, and said, "That was small conforte unto thame;" he ansured, "God shall send yow conforte after me [...]" (Laing I: 132–133).

This seems to be a fusion of the Gethsemane story and the Last Supper (and these motifs are also present in the section of the 'Wishart narrative' attributed to John Foxe, see Laing I: 149–171, especially 168–169), while 'Spadin' and Watson act as (rather make-shift) apostles. And, indeed, as Knox himself implies, they must have been the sole source of the story ('as informatioun was gevin to us [...]', Laing I: 132). One can read in the gospels: 'he [Christ] was in agony / and prayed somewhat longer. And his sweate was lyke droppes of bloud / tricklynge doune to the grounde' (Luke 22: 44), and 'the spirite ys willynge / but the fleshe is weeke' (Matthew 26: 41, *Tyndale*, 1526). The frequent references to 'conforte' recall the office of the Comforter in John's gospel (see John 14: 16–18). As we have already speculated, Knox himself seems to be St. Peter in the narrative (although he does not deny Wishart, as Peter denied Christ).

As to the language of the above; 'personis fornamed' is straight from a contract, and an adjective, such as 'indigest', is striking also. Normally it is pejorative, as in this instance from Douglas's *Aeneid*: 'Into counsalys geuyng he was hald a man nocht indigest, bot wys and cald'.[47] It actually means 'undigested' in figurative and literal applications, and in the former usually refers to sounds, as it does here. A noun like 'travall' moves us back to religious experience and probably echoes Isaiah 53: 11: 'he shall see of the travail of his soul' (*Great*

47 *D.O.S.T.*, III: 242.

Bible), but the sense that climactic passages of the *New Testament* are being re-enacted before us is over-powering. Even so, *The Historie* is none the worse for that.

Not only do we find very blatant Biblical parallels during those narratives in which Wishart himself appears. They also permeate the plot-structure of *The Historie*. For example, Knox says of Archbishop Gavin Dunbar and Cardinal Beaton, who were engaged in bringing Wishart to the stake, but were not themselves on the friendliest of terms:

> In that day was wrought no less a wonder than was at the accusatioun and death of Jesus Christ, when that Pilate and Herode, who befoir war ennemyes, war maid Freindis, by consenting of thame boith to Christis condempnatioun, differis nothing, except that Pilate and Herode war brethrene under thare father the Devill, in the Estaite called Temporall, and these two, of whome we ar to speak, war brethren (sonnes of the same father the Devill) in the Estaite Ecclesiasticall (Laing I: 145).

This puts the final touches to the Christ-parallels (cf. Luke 23: 12) and places Knox firmly within a Lutheran tradition. Luther's contemporaries had viewed the German Reformer's hearing at Worms along exactly the same lines, linking Albert of Mainz with Caiaphas, Car-dinal Lang with Annas, Frederick the Wise with Peter, and Charles V with Pilate. Knox is obviously entering the final scenes of his Passion Play. The tone is typically satirical, and Knox exhibits aesthetic precision when he first outlines the similarities between the figures, then the differences. Even if the 'Estaite[s]' differ, all are: 'sonnes of the same father'.

The culmination of the Wishart story comes of course with his martyrdom, which is also narrated in *The Historie*, but here we encounter problems over authorship. Knox himself says that the manner of Wishart's: 'Accusation, Process, and Ansueris [...] we have receaved […] frome the Book of Martyres, which, woord by woord, we have hear inserted' and the reasons he gives for this are: that Foxe's book is both too expensive for ordinary readers and something of a collector's item (Laing I: 148). Laing is non-commital, and his suggestions are tentative, but as always he gives us the reliable facts with the assurance of a responsible scholar. Foxe enlarged and revised his own work for an edition of 1570 and added material relating to Scottish martyrs. He says that his information about Wishart is taken '*Ex Scripto Testimonio Scotorum*'. Laing adds that:

> In many places of these additions, the details are more minute than the corresponding passages in Knox's *History*, yet there is such a coincidence in the information, that Foxe may be indebted for some of them to the Scottish Reformer. The account of Wishart, [Knox's], however, is copied from a printed book [Foxe's].[48]

Since there is such uncertainty, it seems advisable to pass on to the more authentic material which follows. This of course is the Beaton narrative in which Knox: 'attains his highest eminence as a writer'.[49]

Knox tells of the Cardinal's castle stronghold, and we should read the following with 1 Corinthians 3:19 (or Job 5:13) in mind: 'For it is written 'He compaseth the wyse in their craftynesse'' (*Coverdale*):

> And thare he remaned without all fear of death, promissing unto him self no less pleasur, nor did the riche man, of whome mentioun is maid by our Maister in the Evangell; for he did nott onlie rejois and say, "Eitt and be glade, my saule, for thow hast great riches laid up in store for many dayis" but also he said "Tush, a feg for the fead, and a buttoun for the braggyne of all the heretikis and thair assistance in Scotland. Is nott my Lord Governour myne? Witness his eldest sone thare pledge at my table? Have I not the Quene at my awin devotioun? (He ment of the mother to Mary that now myschevouslie regnes.) Is not France my freind, and I freind to France? What danger should I fear?" [...] But yit he had devised to have cutt of such as he thought mycht cummer him; for he had appointed the haill gentill men of Fyff to have mett him at Falkland, the Mononday after that he was slane upoun the Setterday (Laing I: 173).

48 See Laing I: 148, n. (2), and M'Crie, T., *Life of John Knox*, p. 400. Foxe's account was taken from a rare printed tract entitled *The Tragical death of David Beaton, Bishoppe of Sainct Andrews in Scotland: Whereunto, is ioyned the martyrdom of maister George Wyscharte gentleman, for whose sake the aforesayed bishoppe was not longe after slayne. Wherein thou maist learne what a burnynge charitie they shewed not onely towardes him, but vnto al suche as come to their handes for the blessed Gospels sake* from 'Roberte Burrant to the reader'. If Knox was actually the author of Foxe's material, Burrant was an intermediary.

49 Millar, J. H., *Literary History of Scotland*, p. 143.

This remarkable passage, which presents the Cardinal trying his best to 'out-Herod Herod', involves a more sophisticated use of the Scots language, of rhetoric and the Bible than anywhere else in Knox's writings. As I said earlier in the section dedicated to preaching, the narrative is based on one of Luke's parables. (Just as Shakespeare could create comedy using Falstaff and the parable of Dives and Lazarus, Knox could do something similar). Yet he had another model for Beaton. The Cardinal sounds much like the unrepentant children of Judah in Jeremiah 5: 11–31, who are subsequently punished by God. This long section, incidentally, makes use of the 'fig' image. In Miles Coverdale's version, verse 11 reads: 'Tush, there shall no miszfortune come upon us'. In the 'Knox-Papers', collected by Peter Lorimer in the 1870s, the letter *John Knox to the Congregation of Berwick* contains what must be a literary embryo of the above passage, and enables us to reconstruct something of its genesis (see also Laing V: 483 and Isaiah 22: 13). Originally, it seems, Knox combined Jeremiah 5: 11–13, Isaiah 5: 19 and 1 Thessalonians 5: 3 to produce the following very significant lines:

> In thiis [sic] most feirfull prayer of the propheit wer his eyes oppined that he assuredlye saw all these plagues which short after apprehended this obstinat natioun, albeit in the meane season with contempt thay cried, "Tushe, their words be but wynde. Latt the counsall of the Holy One of Israel cum to pass. We shall have peace and wealthe in our dayes, for we are the pepill yat call upon the Lorde. His law and holie temple are with us." By these meanes did this sinfull natioun persuade themselves to rest, peace and tranquillite, when suddane destructioun approched at hand.[50]

(Cf. also Job 6: 26). Given what we know about Knox's writing, this letter is self-authenticating, and Lorimer is right when he says that its '*genuineness* [...] does not admit of doubt. It bears the strong impress, throughout, of his well-known style, both of thought and language'[51] (italics added). We can see that when Knox came to incorporate the idea behind the above into his Beaton-narrative (an idea, which, as we now know, he first formulated some years earlier), he

50 Lorimer, P., *John Knox and the Church of England*, pp. 256–257.
51 ibid., p. 265.

dropped, or replaced the references to Isaiah. One (5: 19) implied self-righteousness; he no doubt felt that the Cardinal did not even make the pretence of piety, and the other (22: 13) could be superseded. But the Jeremiah text *has* survived the transition from earlier letter (1552) to later narrative (1566), although the only specific trace is the tell-tale interjection 'Tush(e)' (cf. Laing III: 204 etc.). This word no longer occurs in the Bible as we now know it, having been finally edited out by the compilers of the *King James Version* of 1611. Thus, Knox's audience would recognise it immediately where we cannot, unless we have special access to older Bibles. There are also non-scriptural traditions and no comparable difficulties prevent us tracing them, but before doing this, it may be helpful to compare Knox's version of things with that of the only pre-existing, highly literary treatment of the same material; David Lindsay's. In *The Tragedie of the Late Cardinal Beaton*, the Cardinal says:

> Our Gouernor, to mak hym to me sure
> With sweit and subtell wordis I did him syle,
> Tyll I his Sone and Air gat in my cure.
> To that effect, I fand that crafty wyle,
> That he no maner of waye mycht me begyle
> Than leuch I, quhen his liegis did allege
> Quhow I his sone had gottin in to plege.

Shortly afterwards, he says that through God's 'hie power Diuine':

> [...] I was [...]
> Richt dulefulliye doung down amange the asse,
> Quhilk culd not be throch mortal mannis ingyne:
> Bot, as Dauid did slay the gret Gollyasse,
> Or Holopharne be Judeth keillit wasse,
> In myd amang his tryumphant Armye,
> So was I slane in to my cheiff Cietie.[52]

The first similarity to note between Knox's and Lindsay's respective presentations is that they both use leitmotifs. There is Knox's 'Tush' which in English and Scottish literature, more often than not, sug-

52 See Hamer, D., (ed.), *The Works of Sir David Lindsay*, vol. I: pp.136–137, ll. 204–210, 239–245.

gests arrogance and silliness. For instance, one can read in Bunyan's *The Pilgrim's Progress*: '"Tush" said Obstinate, "away with your book"'. In Shakespeare's *Othello*, the vain and stupid Roderigo opens the play by saying: 'Tush, never tell me, […] that you, Iago […]' (Act 1, Sc. 1, l. 1). Robert Louis Stevenson could mock, that: 'every tusher tushes me so free that I may be tushed if the whole thing be worth a tush', and so on.[53] On Lindsay's part there is the Cardinal's 'than *leuch* I […]' (italics added). This phrase often implies imminent disaster and is probably derived from the gospels: 'Wo vnto you that laugh here, for ye shal wepe and wayle' (Luke 6: 25, *Coverdale*). In *The Preiching of the Swallow*, Henryson's silly lark says: 'Schir Swallow […] and *leuch*' (italics added), and is later pictured 'lauchand',[54] only to end up, with the other birds, in the fowler's net. Of course, Lindsay's Cardinal lacks the magnificent insolence of Knox's and the Reformer manages to pack all of Lindsay's information about Beaton's dealings with Arran and the Governor's son into two questions: '"Is nott my Lord Governour myne? Witness his eldest sone thare pledge at my table […]?"'. It is hard to decide which author presents Beaton as more Machiavellian, however. Lindsay's 'sweit and subtell wordis' and 'crafty wyle' have no equivalent in Knox, but Knox's '[…] yit he had devised […]' coming, as it does after a vivid picture of the Cardinal's complete disregard for danger, suggests a manipulative and comprehensive subtlety which would be hard to match.

The most rewarding comparison between the two authors, comes, however, when we analyse their use of the Bible. Lindsay places Beaton's temporary resting place as 'amange the asse' whereas Knox indulges in some cosmic irony by putting him in: 'a nuk in the boddome of the sea-toore, […] whare many of Goddis childrene had been empreasoned befoir' (Laing I: 179). In this instance only Lindsay's information is Biblical. Douglas Hamer lists four examples[55] but only one (Job 30: 19) seems to have been definitely in Lindsay's mind: 'I am euen as it were claye & am become like aszshes & dust' (*Coverdale*). In place of Knox's Jeremiah quotation, Lindsay has an

53 See *O.E.D.*, X, 1, 510.

54 See Fox, D., (ed.), *The Poems of Robert Henryson*, pp. 68–69, l.1741, 1762.

55 See Hamer, D., (ed.), *The Works of Sir David Lindsay*, vol. IV: p. 167.

allusion to David and Goliath (1 Samuel 17: 51). This is a *narrative*, with Beaton as Goliath, while Knox's material is part of a *prophecy*. Lindsay's reference to the apocryphal book of Judith (13:10) (*Coverdale*) is much in the same spirit as Knox's report, but the Reformer seldom mentions the apocrypha, although he would have recognised the allusion since, as we have seen, the story is in *Coverdale's Bible*). And of course, Holopharne's 'cheiff Cietie' (Bethulia) has its parallel in Knox's Babylon.

Lindsay, however, cannot match Knox's use of alliteration and of Scots traditions. In Scotland 'fegs' and 'buttouns' are the standard types for worthlessness. For instance, the *Satirical Poems of the Reformation* mention: 'Ane feirfull tratour [...] to crucifie Christ that comptis not a feg',[56] and Wyntoun says: 'I set nowcht thareby a buttowne'.[57] As his published correspondence shows, the Cardinal had a vigorous and lively command of Scots[58] but he is no more likely to have said this than Napoleon is: 'Not tonight, Josephine', and Knox's intention is obviously to stimulate hubris. In her *Cardinal of Scotland*, M. H. B. Sanderson has written well on this point: 'Knox was preaching a sermon with the Cardinal as object lesson, to accentuate his self-reliance made his fall all the more salutary'[59]. Knox, of course, is writing, like Lindsay, in the best fall-of-princes tradition, and our new knowledge of the literary history behind his observations, makes his motivation a lot clearer. But however compelling he is, Knox's Beaton has no real existence. He is not like Shakespeare's Cardinal Wolsey in *Henry VIII*. Moreover, Knox gives him a series of rhetorical questions and the most memorable involves a chiasmus: '"Is not France [A] my freind [B], and I freind [B] to France [A]?"' (parenthesis added). The impression of patness overpowers any credibility we may give to Knox. But credibility and great writing are not interdependent. He subsequently digresses but not much further into the text he achieves similar heights. He tells how the

56 *D.O.S.T.*, II: 436.

57 *D.O.S.T.*, I: 402.

58 See Lang, A., 'The Letters of Cardinal Beaton', 150–158.

59 Sanderson, M. H. B., *Cardinal of Scotland*, p. 224.

conspirators gain access to the Castle, by taking advantage of an opportune moment:

> But airlie upoun the Setterday, in the mornying, the 29. of Maij, war thei in syndree cumpanyes in the Abbay kirk-yard, not far distant from the Castell. First, the yettis being oppin, and the draw-brig lettin doun, for receaving of lyme and stanes, and othir thingis necessar for buylding, (for Babylon was almost finished,) – first, we say, assayed Williame Kirkcaldy of Grange youngar, and with him sex personis, and gottin enteress, held purpose with the portare, "Yf My Lord was walking?" who ansuered, "No," (And so it was in dead; for he had bene busy at his comptis with Maistres Marioun Ogilbye that nycht, who was espyed to departe frome him by the previe posterne that morning; and tharefor qwyetness, after the reullis of phisick, and a morne sleap was requisite for my Lord.) (Laing I: 174–175).

Here Knox moves from routine details to explanatory narrative, and an allusion to Jeremiah 51: 53: 'though Babilon clymmed up into heaven and kepte her power on hie, yet shal I sende her destroyers [...]' (*Coverdale*). A short letter (now contained in the *Papers of the Reign of Henry VIII*) from one 'James Lyndesay' to an unknown recipient, dated the 29th of May 1546, seems independently to confirm much that Knox says. The following extracts are from the original manuscript of this letter.[60] It opens:

> [...] this Satterday betuix v howris and vj in ye mornyng ye cardinale is slane in ye castell of Sanctandros be Normond Leslie in this maner // at ye cumin in of ye masonis & wirk men in ye place to yair wirk, Normond Leslie, and thre wyth hym enterit & eftir hym James melwin & thre men wyth hym // fenyit yair selfis to haue spokin wyth ye Cardinale // & eftir yame, come ye young Lard of Grange and viij men wyth hym, all in geyr.[61]

Although this account is twenty years earlier than Knox's it cannot compare in value. There is no innuendo of course but it lacks the vigour of *The Historie*. Where Knox really scores against the earlier letter is in his use of metaphor. 'Comptis', which presumably alludes to illicit sexual activity, adds to the humour by implying whoredom.

60 See Brewer, J. S. and Gairdner, J., (eds.), *Letters and Papers of the Reign of Henry VIII*, 21, I, no. 948, p. 464.

61 This text was transcribed by R. J. Lyall, PRO, SP, 491/9.

And from a humorous use of language, Knox switches to an equally tendentious, but more subtle one:

> The portar, fearing, wold have drawin the brig; but the said Johnne, being entered thairon, stayed, and lap in. And whill the porter maid him for defence, his head was brokin, the keyis tackin frome him, and he castin in the fowsea; and so the place was seased. The schowt arises: the workemen, to the nomber of mo then a hundreth, ran of the wallis, and war without hurte put furth at the wicked yett (Laing I: 175).

Pr. Janton notes that: 'la brièveté des phrases, le nombre des verbes et l'alternance des temps augmentent la tension dramatique',[62] but has no comment on the passive phrase, 'his head was brokin'. The phrase seems to be a disguised attempt to eschew responsibility. The letter contains no such attempt: the portar refused admittance: '*quhill ane of yame straik hym wyth ane knyff*', (italics added), although the two texts concur in their secondary details. The letter reads '[they] kest hym in ye fowse', and its author goes on: 'incontinent ya shote furtht all ye wirkmen and closit ye yet, syne sowght ye chalmeris, & schote furth all ye howsald men, as yai gat yame, naikit//'. Knox, however, emphasises that the workmen were put out unharmed (even if they were in collusion with the assassins), and this remark is probably designed to counterpoint the treatment of the unfortunate porter. But the crucial difference between the versions is abundantly clear. The letter says that the porter was murdered, Knox says that he somehow got himself killed.

The assassination scene itself is, of course, far more vividly realised in Knox's *The Historie* than in the letter. Here it is. Cardinal Beaton has confronted his ruthless assailants:

> The said Johne Leslye, (according to his formar vowes,) strook him first anes or twyse, and so did the said Petir. But James Melven, (a man of nature most gentill and most modest,) perceaving thame boyth in cholere, withdrew thame, and said, "This worke and judgement of God, (althought it be secreit,) aught to be done with greattar gravitie;" and presenting unto him the point of the sweard, said, "Repent thee of thy formar wicked lyef, but especiallie of the shedding of the blood of that notable instrument of God, Maister George Wisharte, which

62 Janton, P., *L'homme et l'oeuvre*, p. 485.

albeit the flame of fyre consumed befoir men; yitt cryes it, a vengeance upoun thee, and we from God ar sent to revenge it: For heir, befoir my God, I protest, that nether the hetterent of thy persone, the luif of thy riches, nor the fear of any truble thow could have done to me in particulare, moved, nor movis me to stryk thee; but only becaus thow hast bein, and remanes ane obstinat ennemye against Christ Jesus and his holy Evangell." And so he stroke him twyse or thrise trowght with a stog sweard; and so he fell, never word heard out of his mouth, but "I am a preast, I am a preast: fy, fy: all is gone." (Laing I: 177).

One can understand why Melvill's apocalyptic, Messianic language appealed to Knox. After all, he was fond of making similar statements himself. Words like 'judgement', 'gravitie', 'Repent', 'wicked' and 'obstinat' were his own everyday tools. But Knox was probably more interested in Beaton's final comments: '"I am a preast: fy, fy: all is gone"'. The modern reader has to take Knox's (and Foxe's) word that this is actually what the Cardinal said. That Beaton used his priesthood as a last line of defence is surely credible. But Knox almost certainly saw the remarks as a fulfilment of the prophecy contained in Jeremiah 51: 54: 'A piteous crie shall be herde from Babilon' (*Coverdale*).

This brings us to the only passage from Knox's works which is quoted extensively by literary critics. (One recalls Rutland's Ovidian curse on Clifford in *Henry VI Part III* (Act 1, Sc. 3, 1. 48): 'Di faciant laudis summa sit ista tuæ!'):

Whill they war thus occupyed with the Cardinall, the fray rises in the toune. The Provest assembles the communitie, and cumis to the fowseis syd, crying, "What have ye done with my Lord Cardinall? Whare is my Lord Cardinall? Have ye slayne my Lord Cardinall? Lett us see my Lord Cardinal?" Thei that war within answered gentilye, "Best it war unto yow to returne to your awin houssis; for the man ye call the Cardinall has received his reward, and in his awin persone will truble the warld no more." But then, more enraigedlye, thei cry, "We shall never departe till that we see him." And so he was brought to the East blockhouse head, and schawen dead ower the wall to the faythless multitude, which wold not beleye befoir it saw: How miserably lay David Betoun, cairfull Cardinall. And so thei departed without *Requiem æternam*, and *Requiescant in pace*, song for his saule. (Laing I: 178–179).

James Lyndesay's account does not differ in any major detail, although it is notable that it contains derisory references to Beaton as a false god:

> Ye commoun bell of ye tovn rang, ye provust and tovn gaderit in ye nowmer of thre or fower hundreth men, & come to ye castell, quhill Normand Leslie & his companye come to ye wall heid, and sperit quhat ya desirit to se, ane deid man // Incontinent ya brocht ye Cardinale deid to ye wall heid, in ane payr of schetis & hang him ower the wall be ye tane arme & ye tane fute / & bad ye pepill se yer thar god.

Towards the end of his letter he includes an observation (of which Knox, no doubt, would have approved): 'I find few displesit of his deid'.

Knox, however, is much better in capturing the hysteria of the crowd and its loyalty to '"My Lord Cardinall"', and he does so by invoking empathy, but certainly not sympathy (or only unintentionally, and this is an important distinction). And after the insistent questioning of the Provost comes the sombre reply: '"Best it war to return to your awin houssis [...]"'. The 'faithless multitude', moreover, will not believe without seeing, and this phrase recalls John 20: 25–29. Knox's Latin phrases (one of which J. H. Millar renders somewhat casually),[63] are, of course, taken from the Mass for the Souls of the Dead (the *Officium Defunctorum*) in the Catholic tradition, and we have already established that this kind of borrowing (for the purpose of mockery) was quite common among Knox and his contemporaries.

We have seen then, that the whole Beaton episode is a literary *tour de force* superior to the Wishart story in its humour and dramatic strength. But perhaps the most sophisticated literary manoeuvres come not with Knox's great broadsides, but in quieter moments such as this:

63 See Millar, J. H., *Literary History of Scotland*, p. 145. Millar has '[...] without *Requiem alternam*'. This rendering also occurs in Billy Kay's *The Mither Tongue*, see p. 66. The latter part of the phrase is given in Laing as '[...] *Requiescant in pace*' and in Dickinson as '*Requiescat in pace*'. The MS. 1566 / MS. La. II. 210, f. 60, agrees with Laing, but Dickinson's presentation represents the generally accepted form of the phrase; see *O.E.D.*, VIII: 499.

> The death of this foirsaid tyrant was dolorous to the preastis, dolorous to the Governour, most dolorous to the Quene Dowager; for in him perished faythfulnes to France, and the conforte to all gentilwemen, and especiallie to wantoun wedowis: His death most be revenged (Laing I: 180).

From a stylistic point of view this short passage probably constitutes Knox's finest use of building forensic rhetoric, adjectival parallelism and mimesis anywhere in the canon. At the third step, 'dolorous' becomes 'most dolorous' almost imperceptibly and there is an ascendancy of rank from 'preastis' to 'Governour' to 'Quene'. Janton observes that: 'Emphatique, la répétition devient *epizeuxis*,'[64] while a touch of alliteration surfaces with 'wantoun wedowis' and Knox winds things up by using free indirect speech. This comes close to stream-of-consciousness narrative or interior monologue (terms not invented before modern criticism), but is one of those techniques which allows progression to stay within the control of the reporter of the action: in this case, Knox himself.

In the latter part of *The Historie*, the dramatic narratives which most resemble the assassination of Beaton, almost invariably involve Mary of Guise, the Queen Regent. This is because, in Knox's eyes, both were 'tyrants'. The same sort of hubris which dominates the Beaton incidents comes out in: 'the delightful tale of what happened when the Reformers were in full retreat in Fife at the beginning of 1560'[65] (compare the following with Psalms 42: 'myne enemies cast me in the tethe, daylie sayenge vnto me; where is now thy God?' (*Coverdale*).

> The Quene Regent, proude of this victorie, burst forth in hir blasphemous rayling, and said, "Whair is now Johne Knox his God? My God is now stronger than his, yea even in Fyff." (Laing II: 8).

We might juxtapose beside this, the narrative of the Queen Regent at Edinburgh Castle:

> The Queen Regent satt all the tyme of the assault (quhilk wes baith terribill and lang) upon the foir-wall of the Castell of Edinburgh; and quhen sche perceivit

64 Janton, P., *L'homme et l'oeuvre*, p. 494.
65 Donaldson, G., 'Knox the Man', 24.

> the overthraw of us, and that the ensenyeis of the Frenche war agane displayit upoun the wallis, sche gaif ane gawfe of lauchter, and said, "Now will I go to the Messe, and prayse God for that quhilk my eyes have sene!" And sa wes Freir Black reddy for that purpose, quhom sche hir self a little of befoir had deprehendit with his harlott in the chapel. But huredome and idolatrye aggre weill togidder [...] (Laing II: 67–68).

The similarity between the first of these and Psalms (but see also Deuteronomy 32: 37, Joel 22: 17, Jeremiah 2: 6, 8 and two other texts: Psalms 79: 10, 115: 2) does perhaps arouse suspicion. However, the fact that both of these stories are probably untrue, or at best, salacious or highly exaggerated, should not detract from their value to the literary critic. Even so, Gordon Donaldson's remarks are worth bearing in mind: 'in all her quite voluminous correspondence Mary of Guise shows no sign of being aware of Knox's existence at all'.[66] But the fact that the Regent did not behave in a swaggering, arrogant manner, taunt Knox by name and thus call down upon herself Divine Correction, would spoil the story, or rather, render it non-existent, and if she were not a thorough-bred idolater who very naturally sanctioned whoredom (among priests) the second episode would likewise have no substance. Knox's propaganda is sophisticated, witty and carefully orchestrated, but it is still propaganda. That 'gawfe of lauchter' is a tell-tale sign. It was there during Knox's trial for treason before another Mary, (see above, p. 251), and it was intended to reflect just as unfavourably upon its author as it does here.

A dramatic narrative also involving the Regent which is altogether more credible though perhaps less entertaining occurs somewhat earlier in *The Historie*, (in Book I, just before the episode of St. Giles).The Protestants of the West Country are in confrontation with the Queen:

> The Gentilmen begane to complane upoun thare strange internement, considdering that hir Grace had found into thame so faithfull obedience in all thingis lauchful. Whill that the Quein begane to craft, a zelous and a bold man, James Chalmeris of Gaitgyrth, said, "Madame, we know that this is the malice and devise of thei Jefwellis, and of that Bastard, (meanyng the Bischope of Sanctandrois,) that standis by yow: We avow to God we shall maik ane day of it. Thei oppresse us and our tennantis for feading of thare idill bellyes: thei

66 ibid., 24.

> truble our preacheris, and wold murther them and us: Shall we suffer this any longare? Na, Madame: It shall not be." *And tharewith everie man putt on his steill bonet* (Laing I: 257–258; italics added).

Here, Knox describes a scene in which emotions have reached flashpoint and violence seems imminent. His ability to capture the crisis-feeling of the moment is incomparable. The final sentence in fact is remarkable not only for its sinister concision but for its complete simplicity. The adverb 'tharewith' is especially useful since it focuses specifically upon that point of time at which there is nothing more to be said and action must inevitably be taken. 'Chalmer's' final words on the matter ('"It shall not be"') are dominated by the beat of monosyllables and this too augments the tension, but his address to the Regent is bristling with powerful accusations. The priests are worthless fellows, or '"Jefwellis"', and the Bishop receives a harsher appellation '"that Bastard"'. The phrase: '"We avow to God we shall maik ane day of it"' typifies a familiar Scots hard-headedness in cold, lucid, confessional language, which is impossible to ignore if one is on the receiving end of it. This particular incident ended peacefully, and in compromise, but others did not.

In Book II, for instance, the flashpoint comes and an explosion follows:

> It chanced, that the nixt day, whiche was the ellevint of Maij, after that the Preachearis wer exyled, that after the sermoun whiche was vehement against idolatrie, that a preast in contempt wold go to the Messe; and to declair his malapert presumptioun, he wold opin up ane glorious tabernacle which stoode upoun the Hie Altare. Thare stoode besyde, certane godly men, and amonges otheris a young boy, who cryed with a lowd voce, "This is intollerable, that when God by his Worde hath planelie damned Idolatrie, we shall stand and see it used in dispyte." The preast heirat offended, gave the chyld a great blow; who in anger took up a stone, and casting at the preast, did hytt the tabernacle and brack doune ane ymage; and immediatlie the hole multitude that war about cast stones [...] (Laing I: 320–322).

One wonders if the 'young boy' is a King David or a football hooligan, and Knox himself probably shared the reader's dilemma, but the boy, like Mrs. Bowes, William Arth, Alexander Seton or even Beaton's murderers, has a place in God's operations, however small and apparently insignificant.

Again the key stylistic feature is Knox's use of adverbs ('heirat' and 'immediatlie'). The first assesses the situation and updates it, while the second triggers off the wild-fire action. One can well understand the priest taking offence and delivering his 'great blow' but the boy's comment makes the contrast between scriptural admonition and contemporary religious practice which was so fundamentally an issue of the Reformation. The boy's own anger, however, seems to have little to do with any point of religious doctrine and more to do with getting his own back, but this too was possibly symptomatic of the Reformation as a whole.

Nowhere in *The Historie* does Knox achieve a richer narrative than in the incident which he describes as the: 'speaking of ane ancient matrone when Scone was birning' (Laing I: 361, marginal note), an event which took place during the same year as the previous episode. Beginning with an obvious pun, Knox tells how:

> The multitude easilie inflambed, gave the alarme, and so was that Abbay and Palace appointit to saccage; in doing whairof thay took no lang deliberatioun, but committed the whole to the merciment of fyre; whairat no small nomber of us war offended, that patientlie we culd nocht speak till any that war of Dundie or Sanct Johnestoun. A poore aged matrone, seing the flambe of fyre pas up sa mychtilie, and perceaving that many war thairat offended, in plane and sober maner of speaking, said, "Now I see and understand that Goddis judgementis ar just, and that no man is able to save whare he will punische. Since my rememberance, this place hath bein nothing else but a den of hooremongaris. It is incredible to beleve how many wyffes hath being adulterat, and virginis deflored, by the filthie beastis whiche hath bein fostered in this den; bot especiallie by that wicked man who is called the Bischope. Yf all men knew alsmuche as I, thay wald praise God; and no man wald be offended." This woman duelt into the toune, neye unto the Abbay; at whose wordis war many pacified; affirming with hir that it was Goddis just judgement. And assuredlie, yf the laubouris or travell of any man culd have saved that place, it had nocht bein at that tyme destroyed; for men of greattest estimatioun lawboured with all diligence for the savetie of it (Laing I: 361–362).

David Murison detects: 'the ring of realism in the story as we stand in the crowd with Knox […] and overhear with him […]'.[67] Dr. Murison however does not wholly do justice to the passage. There are some formulaic expressions, to be sure, but they detract little. The 'lang' of 'lang deliberatioun' is not unusual but one might have expected 'mature' or 'wyse'. The woman's denunciation of 'hooremongaris', however, epitomises one strand of Reformation thought with complete precision. Three decades earlier, John Gau had written against: 'thay […] that […] committis fornicatione with hwris or ony licht personis'[68] and in the wake of the Reformation in Scotland, Ninian Winzet advocated: 'renuncing […] of plesouris of the body […] fra unlesum huirdom'.[69] 'Hooremongaris' is a less common form but it does occur quite frequently. In *The Register of the Minister, Elders and Deacons of the Christian Congregation of St. Andrews* there is a reference which is almost exactly contemporaneous with the Scone incident: 'Schyr Alexander Gaw and Catren Nesche' are called 'huyrmongaris and adulteraris'.[70]

Knox's own words, however, provide the most characteristic example of a Scots idiom. The phrase: 'this woman duelt into the toune, neye unto the Abbay' is identical in spirit and syntactical construction to: 'Ane knicht dwelt neir hand by'[71] in David Lindsay's *Squire Meldrum* or: 'the eldest duelt in ane borous toun […] the vther […] vponland weill neir' from Henryson's *The Taill of the Uponlandis Mous and the Burges Mous*.[72] Knox of course has a special reason for using such a phrase. It assures us that this woman is uniquely qualified to pass judgement on the priests and especially on 'that wicked man', the Bishop himself. The juxtaposition of 'lauboris or travell' and of the former with 'diligence' again catches an idiom. One need only compare John Ireland's: 'puttand all labour and deligence to his […] seruice'[73] or Gilbert Haye's: 'with the corporale laboure and travaille

67 Murison, D., 'Knox the Writer', 43.
68 *D.O.S.T.*, II: 59.
69 *D.O.S.T.*, II: 183.
70 *D.O.S.T.*, II: 184.
71 *D.O.S.T.*, II: 247.
72 See Fox, D., (ed.), *The Poems of Robert Henryson*, pp. 9–10, ll. 164–165.
73 *D.O.S.T.*, II: 123.

of his members'.[74] Strictly speaking, nearly all of these terms refer to physical exertion, which is not Knox's meaning, be he often exaggerated and this is perhaps an example.

For sheer dramatic intensity, the closest Knox comes to the splendour of this narrative is with his descriptions of the battle of Solway Moss, which of course took place some time before the Reformation itself (although Knox's account of the battle was in fact written after the above passages). As we shall see, he makes use of the techniques he developed in his earlier writing. He tells us:

> The forrow goes furth, fyre ryses, herschip mycht have bein sein on everie syd. The unprovedeid people war all together amased; for brycht day appearing, thei saw ane army of ten thowsand men; thare cornes and housis upoun every syd send flambes of fyre unto the heaven […] The soldeouris caist frome thaim thaire pickis, culveringis, and utheris weaponis fensable; the horsemen left thair spearis; and so, without judgement, all man fled. The sea was filling, and so the watter maid greate stope; but the fear was such as happy was hie that mycht gett a tackar. Such as passed the watter and eschaped that danger, nott weill acquented with the ground, fell into the Sollen Moss. The entrie thairof was pleasing yneuch, but as thei proceaded, all that took that way, eyther lost thare horse, or ellis thame selfis and horse boith. To be schort, a greatter feir and disconfiture, without cause, hes seldome bein sein (Laing I: 85, 87).

There are parallels in romance narrative, but Knox's almost cinematographic visual perception puts him about four centuries ahead of his time. David Murison improves considerably on C. S. Lewis's criticism when he says that: 'Knox is very good at battles [...] the scurrying to and fro [...] the confusion and the panic',[75] but to appreciate just how good, one can compare this compelling passage with, say, the studied elegance and coldness of Buchanan in *Rerum Scotticarum Historia*. Pr. Dickinson has observed of Knox's *The Historie*, that: 'we are present in the times of which we read'.[76] The reason for this sense of 'being there' can be traced of course to style. Again, Knox deliberately uses historic present tenses (a technique which was not used consistently in the vernacular by any other contemporary Scottish

74 *D.O.S.T.*, III: 491.

75 Murison, D., 'Knox the Writer', 44.

76 See Buchanan, G., *The History of Scotland*, p. 322 and Dickinson I: 11.

prose historian), to give us the vivid impression that the action is happening here and now, and the 'seldome hes bein sein' formula, or 'for such […] came never', which we first encountered in our analysis of the merry tales, (above, p. 274), also recurs. Knox thus highlights one's sense of occasion. Shortly after this, he employs rather more satirical methods.

For instance, in the section which leads up to Solway Moss in *The Historie* and in passages which come immediately after the Scone incident with the matron, he employs devices which remind one very much of dialogue in, say, Erasmus's *Encomium Moræ*, (or *The Praise of Folly*).

> All man, (foollis we meane,) bragged of victorie; and in verray deid the begynnyng gave us a fayr schaw […] Stout Oliver was without strack tackin, fleing full manfully; and so was his glorie (stinking and foolishe proudnes we should call it,) suddandly turned to confusioun and schame (Laing I: 88).

Elsewhere, for example, he writes: '[…] befoir whose cuming the rascheall multitude put handis in the thevis, I should say, frearis, places, and utterlie destroyed them' (Laing I: 362).[77] (With the latter example we perhaps have evidence to indicate that originally, Knox was dictating). His technique here is a simple one. He makes a statement in which he apparently forgets himself, and then immediately redefines his previous comment completely. There are many more examples of this throughout *The Historie* and, even if they do not always occur in the scenes of riotous intensity such as the above, they add nonetheless to the rich array of humorous methods which Knox employed.

We saw earlier that Knox's unreservedly humorous tales had much in common with preaching, and the same is undoubtedly true of his dramatic narratives. One passage in which this comes out and which shares the same control of language and Scots forms that emerged earlier, is the following:

77 See also Laing I: 169 for similar phrases. Some are remarkably close to Knox's practice and yet are not attributed to him; see Dickinson, II: 234 and Lang, A., *John Knox and the Reformation*, pp. 20–21.

As the Frenche spoilyied the countrye in thair retourning, one capitaine or soldiour, we cannot tell, bot he had a reid cloik and a gilt morrion, entered upoun a poore woman, that dwelt in the Whytsyd, and began to spoyle. The poore woman offered unto him suche breid as sche had reddy prepared. But he, in no wayis thairwith content, wald have the meill and a lytill salt beif whiche the poore woman had to susteine hir awin lyfe, and the lyves of hir poore chylderein; neather could tearis, nor pitifull wourdis, mittigat the merciles man, but he wald have quhatsoever he mycht carie. The poore woman perceving him so bent, and he stoupped doun in hir tub, for the taking foorth of suche stufe as was within it, first cowped up his heillis, so that his heid went doun; and thairefter, outher by hirself, or if ony uther companie came to help hir, but thair he endit his unhappie lyfe; God so punissing his crewell hairt, quho could nocht spair a misserable woman in that extremitie, "Let all suche soldiouris receve suche rewaird, O Lord, seeing that thou art the revenger of the oppressed." (Laing II: 14–15).

The lesson here is an old one and recognisably part of a Scottish tradition. Henryson had chastised 'mychtie men' who: 'will not thoill in pece ane pureman be' and warned: 'For till oppres, thow sall haif als grit pane / As thow the pure with thy awin hand had slane'.[78] So it is with Knox's French soldier. And there is some detailed observation coupled with old Scots humour. Knox notices that the Frenchman has a 'gilt morrion' (or 'morrow' as the *Edinburgh MS.* would have it).[79] This presumably refers to a variety of helmet. The 'reid cloik', moreover, is probably intended to suggest the soldier's physical splendour, which contrasts markedly with the woman's poverty.

The phrase: 'But he in no wayis thairwith content, wald have the meill [...]' sketches in, with precision, a good deal of information, and helps get the action underway. The alliterative 'mittigat the merciless man' uses a common collocation and heightens the tension by taking things one step further towards confrontation. As to Knox's lexical choice, one can read similar expressions in the *Bannatyne MS* ('and mak hir hairt with mercy mytigat').[80] Then comes the most splendid expression of all. The woman: 'cowped up his heillis, so that his heid went doun [...]'. The same phrase occurs at least once in Cranstoun's

78 See Fox, D., (ed.), *The Poems of Robert Henryson*, pp. 101–102, l. 2731, 2768–2769.

79 See Laing II: 15, n. (1).

80 *D.O.S.T.*, IV: 328.

Satirical Poems of the Time of the Reformation,[81] so we can be fairly sure that this was a typical Scots form. Despite the ideological sympathies between the two texts in which it occurs, we cannot, of course, say that the phrase was used exclusively in Reforming circles.

Pierre Janton has suggested that Knox's concept of preaching (which, as we have seen, permeates his *The Historie* no less than his other texts) was similar to Hugh Latimer's. Two fundamental tenets gird the latter's sermons (and Knox's too). The first is to teach sound doctrine (*exhorti per sanam doctrinam*) and the second is to contradict spurners (*contradicentes convicere*).[82] The second office, which concerns us here, ties in with Ezekiel 33: 9: 'yf thou warne the wicked off his waye, to turne from it, where as he yet wil not be turned from it: than shal he dye because of his synne, but thow has delyuered thy soule' (*Coverdale*).[83] The remainder of the narratives which this section considers, concern themselves with this office.

The following incident occurred after one of Knox's final appearances before Queen Mary, when he was 'commanded' by her 'to pass furth of the cabinet', and: 'to abyd farther of hir pleasur in the chalmer' (Laing II: 389). When describing how the 'Lord Ochiltrie' came to keep him company, Knox introduces a remarkable narrative, but one which, like the previous passages, is deeply Scottish and has its origins in traditions well established before Knox's time.

> [...] thairfoir began he to forge talking of the ladyes who war thair sitting in all thair gorgiouse apparell; whiche espyed, he mearelie said, "O fayre ladies, how pleasing war this lyeff of youris, yf it should ever abyd and then in the end that we myght passe to heaven with all this gay gear. But fye upoun that knave Death, that will come whitther we will or not! And when he hes laid on his areist, the foull wormes wilbe busye with this flesche, be it never so fayre and so tender, and the seally sowll, I fear, shalbe so feable, that can neather cary with it gold, garnassing, targatting, pearle nor pretious stones". And by suche meanes procured he the cumpany of women; and so past the tyme till that the Laird of Dun willed him to departe to his house quhill new advertisement (Laing II: 389).

81 *D.O.S.T.*, III: 90.

82 Janton, P., 'John Knox and Literature', 427.

83 See also Rupp, E. G., 'The Europe of John Knox', 9.

T. F. Henderson and M. P. McDiarmid are among few Scottish critics to notice how 'various allusions' show that Knox's literary art owed something to his acquaintanceship with the works of the old 'makaris'[84] and in his second work on Knox, *Concept et Sentiment dans L'Eglise chez John Knox*, Pr. Janton observes, rather more specifically, 'Quand Knox moralise sur l'éphémère beauté des dames de la cour, il continue la tradition des pessimistes du Xve siècle. Quelques exemples suffiront'.[85] He then cites Henryson and Dunbar, but the above passage contains vestigal traces of a number of literary genres. Of course, the 'all is vanitie' theme of Ecclesiasties is the earliest, but recognisably medieval ideas such as the *danse macabre*, *memento mori*, the 'three living and three dead' motif (although Knox is very much alive), the reasonings between Age and Youth, and *Everyman*, are all present. Although earlier Protestants like Gau had condemned: 'thay that payntis thair body with precious clais or silver or gold precious stenis or gold ringis',[86] the traditions all belong originally to a unified Catholic Christendom. They stress in general terms the fallibility of wealth, decoration and beauty over against the fact that all: 'Mon thole the deid and de',[87] and that the body will inevitably decay through natural processes. (The sixteenth century, on the whole, was not a good time to be squeamish).

The humour on the other hand is distinctively that of the Reformer. W. C. Dickinson suggests that we may have a hard time believing that: 'by suche meanes procured he the cumpany of women'[88] but the whole scene is a broad belly laugh at Knox's own excesses and, apparently, one he could not resist. We cannot label an old Scots poet like Henryson unusually attractive and simultaneously represent Knox as puritanical (in the pejorative rather than the historical sense),

84 See McDiarmid, M., *Robert Henryson*, p. 120, and Hendersen, T. F., *Scottish Vernacular Literature: A Succinct History*, p. 327; see also Laing I: 116, n. (1).

85 Janton, P., *Concept et Sentiment dans L'Eglise chez John Knox*, pp. 22–23.

86 Mitchell, A. F., (ed.), *The Richt Vay*, p. 16; see also Brandt, C. J. and Fenger, B. T., (eds.), *Danske Skrifter*, vol. II: p. 227.

87 See Fox, D., (ed.), *The Poems of Robert Henryson*, p. 182, l. 10.

88 See Dickinson I: lxxvii.

when, between them, there is clearly a relation of pedigree and a shared subject matter.[89]

The subsequent selections are both from Book IV of *The Historie* and, although they have much in common with the above, a clear shift of emphasis is discernible. Knox is moving away from the type of universalism so patently evident in his preaching on temporality, and towards a very specific kind of denunciation. He is still concerned with royalty and with royal courts, but individuals bear the brunt of his attack both directly and indirectly. E. G. Rupp points out how this kind of thing was prevalent among the leading Reformers,[90] who were sure that the gospel must take precedence over all else. The first Knox passage denounces the French King:

> At the entrie of King Harie of France, in the towne of Orleance, the matrones, virgenis, and menis wyffis, war commanded to present thame selfis in the Kingis palice at nycht, to daunse: and thei obeyed; for commounlie the French natioune is not hard to be entreated to vanitie. After fidling and flyngyng, and when the Cardinall of Lorane had espyed his pray, he said to the King, "*Sire, la primiere est vostre, et faut que je suis le second!*" That is to say, "Sire, the first choise is youris, and I man be the secound!" And so the King gat the preeminence, that he had his first electioun. Bot because Cardinallis ar companeounis to Kingis, the Cardinall of Lorane has the nixt: And thairafter the torches war putt out, and everie man commanded to provid for him self the best he myght. What cry was thair of husbandis for thair wyeffis; of wyiffis, for thair husbandis; of auncient matronis, for thair dochteris; and of virgenis for thair freindis; or for some honest man to defend thair pudicitie, Orleance will remember mo kingis dayis then one (Laing II: 318–319).

Knox is using *exprobatio*, defined by Franciscus Robortellus as: 'something [...] neatly criticised and derided by exposing to attack things in it that are disgusting',[91] (and Knox wasn't alone in attacking the Guises; Francois Hotman's *Le Tygre: Satire sur les gestes memorables des Guisards*, (1560), is another notable example of the trend). Knox has a sly dig at the Catholic hierarchy, and the general impression[92] is of the tight interlocking of narrative events. There is a

89 Rupp, E. G., 'The Europe of John Knox', 6.
90 ibid., 13.
91 Sonnino, L. A., *A Handbook*, p. 94.
92 See Greengrass, M., *The French Reformation*, p. 74.

kind of hierarchy among the victims too, since Knox mentions first husbands and wives, mothers and daughters, then virgins and their friends. Moreover, to make sure the reader understands how uncharitable the Cardinal of Lorraine is, Knox provides an instant translation of his remarks. In short, the whole thing is an attack on immoral behaviour and this must surely be where the role of the preacher comes in. It is his job to reprehend the wicked man to turn from his path (and one should re-consult Knox's comments on the gospel of repentance, to appreciate fully what he is about here; above, p. 239). But he has another reason for including such a narrative. If he simply wanted to warn against sinful behaviour he could easily have drawn upon many scriptural examples. But he did not. He deliberately chose contemporary events and the Court of France as his subject matter, and their link with Mary, Queen of Scots, is inescapable.

Knox of course often preached openly against her behaviour. How much of this was personal and how much vocational is a matter for speculation, but we have already recognised that the Scottish tradition lies behind at least some of his sermonising. The Châtelard story (which we have already touched on; above, p. 205) must then be classified with the above, since it is designed along the same lines, with the same purpose. As Dr. Murison says, Knox: 'uses it as a stick against Mary'.[93] Châtelard, as the familiar story goes, was apprehended in the Queen's bedchamber, and for this he was, ultimately, and by due order of law, executed. Knox's version runs thus:

> Poor Chattelett was brocht back from Kinghorne to Sanctandrois, examinat, putt to ane assise, and so beheaded, the twenty-twa day of Februar, the year of God jmvc threscoir twa. He begged licence to wryte to Fraunce the cause of his death, which, said he, in his toung, was "*Pour estre trouvé en lieu trop suspect*;" that is, "Becaus I was found in a place too much suspect." At the place of execution, when he saw that thair was no remeady but death, he maid a godly confessioun, and granted, that his declyning from the treuth of God, and following of vanitie and impietie, was justlie recompensed upoun him. But in the end he concluded, looking unto the heavenis, with these words, "O cruelle Dame," that is, "Cruell Maistress." What that complaint imported, luvaris may devine. And so receaved Chattelett the reward of his dansing; for he lacked his

93 Murison, D., 'Knox the Writer', 48.

head, that his toung should nott utter the secreattis of our Quene. "Deliver us, O Lord, from the raige of such inordinat reullaris." (Laing II: 369).

A dispassionate matter-of-factness blends with at least some compassion for 'poor Chattelett'. Like the small birds: 'who wist weill to die' in Henryson,[94] Châtelard saw that: 'thair was no remeady but death', but at least he is not compelled to 'die as beastis without confessioun'.[95] Knox's artistry emerges best, however, in that devastating and apparently throw-away line: 'What that complaint imported, luvaris may devine'. Furthermore, he carefully juxtaposes two clauses which imply the unfitness of the punishment to the crime. Lacking one's head is of course fatal, but the reason given for the execution is deliberately presented as petty and trivial. Knox concludes with a fine example of *amplificatio* '"Deliver us, O Lord [...]"', which, as Pr. Janton says, 'marshals all rhetorical techniques of development'.[96]

The same techniques are at work in that compelling narrative which comes after Knox's trial when the Nobility unanimously acquitted him, much to Mary's displeasure:

> The Lordis voteit uniformelie thai coulde find no offence. The Quene wes past to hir cabinet. The flatteris of the Courte, and Ledingtoune pryncipally, raged. The Quene wes brocht agane, and placeit in hir chyre, and thai commandit to vote oure agane: quhilk thing heichlie offendit the haill Nobylattie, and began to speik in opin audience, "What! sall the Laird of Lethingtoune haif power to controle us; or sall the presence of ane woman caus us to offend God, and to dampne ane innocent aganis oure conscience for plesour of onie creatour?" And so the haill Nobylattie absolved Johne Knox againe, and praisit God for his modestie, and for his plane and sensible ansueris [...]
>
> This persavit, the Quene began to upbraid Mr. Henrie Synclair, then Bischope of Ross, and said, heiring his vote to agree with the rest, "Trubill nocht the barne: I pray you trubill him nocht; for he is newlie walknit out of his sleip. Why soulde nocht the aulde fule follow the futestapis of thame that haif passit befoir him." (Laing II: 411).

What Knox chooses to present as remarkable is the fact that he was acquitted not once, but twice, and that Mary was hell-bent on having

94 See Fox, D., (ed.), *The Poems of Robert Henryson*, p. 73, l. 1875.

95 ibid., p. 167, l. 21.

96 Janton, P., 'John Knox and Literature', 428.

him: 'in hir will be vote of hir Nobylattie' (Laing II: 412). This satisfaction at the frustrated expectations of the Queen's party charges the whole passage with dynamism, and this comes out best in: 'the tant of the Quene to Mr. Henrie Synclair' (Laing II: 411, marginal note). If Mary did in fact utter these words she reveals a talent for scathing mockery and a withering distaste for what she saw as weak, inconsistent behaviour. Certainly we know enough about her astuteness and personal attributes to admit that there must be some truth in Knox's presentation. This granted, her vigorous use of Scots brings the sting of saltiness to her remarks in a way which is wholly memorable. Her sudden contrast between the '"newlie walknit barne"' and '"the aulde fule"' following stupidly in the footsteps of others, is extremely effective. It is not surprising that Sinclair was driven to answer 'cauldlie'. Knox's own characteristic strain of mockery emerges in the phrase: 'for Madame wes disappoyntit of hir purpois' (Laing II: 412), which makes Mary look both pompous and peevish. This was one prophet's head which was *not* going to be delivered on a platter to a dancing girl (cf. Matthew 18: 8, Mark 6: 25).

We have now looked at over a dozen of Knox's dramatic narratives and one cannot help but be impressed by their range and variety as literature. We have moved from the descriptive richness and realism of the Perth incident, to the humour and the Scottish moralising of the episode with the woman and the French soldier. We saw the extraordinary Christ parallels in Wishart's narrative, and the licence, the dramatic power and also the mendacity of the passages describing the behaviour of Cardinal Beaton and the Queen Regent. Then there were the tense, highly wrought confrontation scenes between the opposing forces of Reformation and *status quo*. We have also looked at the earlier descriptions of the rout at Solway Moss, the French Court and finally the French influence on the Scottish court. From these scenes and episodes, one derives a sense of Knox's remarkable resourcefulness as a writer and as an advocate prepared to go to great lengths to amass evidence for his partisan cause. Ironically, and rather pathetically, he seems only to have succeeded in condemning himself in the eyes of history by so doing, but his efforts were not wholly in vain. Their legacy is fine literature.

The Barbed Pen: Knox's Use of Forensic Rhetoric

Forensic rhetoric is an important aspect of Knox's work, and it would be difficult to overlook. Again the literary value of his efforts in this field is high, and there is much variety both in expression and content. The blurring of genres again creates a problem, however, since Knox's talents and experience all come together, making classification difficult. The present section examines a number of fairly long passages of forensic rhetoric, which reveal a strikingly impressive technique, but does not amass a collection of Knox's more terse, trenchant strokes. The first passage chosen contains his assessment of James V, who died in 1542 (when Knox was in his late twenties). What follows may be in fact a genuine recollection of the opinions which Knox heard expressed at the time, and thus it pre-dates the period of his own earliest appearance in *The Historie* by a few years. We can almost perceive Knox the young priest, with ears and eyes wide open, assessing the *pros* and *cons*:

> All man lamented that the realme was left without a male to succeid: yit some rejosed that such ane ennemy to Goddis treuth was tackin away. Hie was called of some, a good poore manis King, of otheris hie was termed a murtherare of the nobilitie, and one that had decreed thair hole destruction. Some prased him for the repressing of thyft and oppressioun; otheris disprased him for the defoulling of menis wyffis and virgines. And thus men spak evin as affectionis led thame. And yitt none spack all together besydis the treuth; for a parte of all these foresaidis was so manifest, that as the verteuis could nott be denyed, so could nott the vices by any craft be clocked (Laing I: 92–93).

The impression here is one of balance, even moderation and objectivity. 'Yitt' and 'some' are recurrent items, while 'prase' on one hand is matched by 'disprase' on the other. And when Knox says that 'all man lamented', he plays, perhaps unconsciously, a card in his own favour, since it gives us an insight into the general opinion on female rulers at that time. More striking are his remarks on what might be called freedom of speech. Indeed, it is in these comments that Knox the proto-democrat begins to emerge, to find a better platform during his interviews with the Queen. It may be significant that it was the death of her father that gave him his first opportunity to form his belief in the right to speak as he chose, but one should probably be wary of reading too much into historical coincidence.

Knox also uses material relating to James's character to assess others, notably Cardinal Beaton. For instance, after outlining the events which were ultimately to lead to the Battle of Solway Moss, Knox observes:

> Oure King perceaving that the warr wald ryse, asked the Prelattis and Kirkmen, what supporte thei wald maik to the susteanyng of the same; for rather wald he yitt satisfie the desyre of his Uncle, then he wald hasard warr, whare hie saw not his force able to resist. Thei promissed montanes of gold, (as Sathan thaire father did to Christ Jesus yf he wald worshippe him;) for rather thei wold have gone to hell, or he should have mett wyth King Hary: for then, thought thei, Fayr weill our Kingdome; and fayr weill, thought the Cardinall, his credite and glorie in France (Laing I: 77).

This attack revolves around Matthew 4: 8–9:

> [...] the devyll toke hym vp and led hym to an excedynge hye mountayne, and shewed hym all the kyngdomes of the worlde, and all the glorie of them, and sayde vnto hym: all these wil I geue the, yf thou wilt fal downe and worship me (*Coverdale*).

The association of James V with a false Christ admirably epitomises what Knox sees as the King's failure to fulfil the duties of his high office. (Slightly later, when James says: '"Pack you, Jefwellis"' it is: 'a ansure worthie of ane prince'; see Laing I: 82; marginal note). The impression here, however, is of wasted potential rather than of worthlessness, and this ties in well with the moderation of the first passage we considered. More striking than any of this is Knox's use of pithy cartoon-like thought-bubbles to outline the opinions of the clergy and Beaton. The cinema or television screen again comes to mind.

Even more impressive is Knox's treatment of James's death-scene, and the following passage is aimed not just at the Cardinal, but also at Mary of Lorraine. Knox calls it the '*Regis exitus*'.

> In the meantyme, in this [the King's] great extremitie, cumes the Cardinall, (ane apt comfortare for a desparat man.) He cryes in his ear, "Tak ordour, Schir, with your realme: who shall rewill during the minoritie of your Dowghter? Ye have knawin my service: what will ye have done? Shall thare nott be four Regentes

> chosyn? and shall nott I be the principall of thame?" Whatsoever the King answered, documentis war tackin that so should be [...] This finissed, the Cardinall posted to the Quene, laitly befoir delivered [*ReginæNativitas*; Laing I: 91, marginal note], as said is. At the first sight of the Cardinall, sche said, "Welcome my Lord: Is nott the King dead?" What moved her so to conjecture, diverse men ar of diverse judgementis (Laing I: 91–92; parenthesis added).

Laing says that: 'This story of Cardinal Beaton having forged [...] a Will, constituting Beaton Regent during the minority of Mary, has been discredited, [...] but it undoubtedly obtained credence at the time'.[97] Certainly David Lindsay was familiar with it, since, in *The Tragedie of the Late Cardinal Beaton*, he has the ghost say: 'Ane paper blank his grace I gart subscryue / In to the quhilk I wrait all that I plesit'.[98] Knox's insinuations about Mary of Lorraine are hilariously funny, but again a great degree of reservation is necessary.

Pr. Dickinson says that Pitscottie's version of the above scene is more pleasing because of that famous phrase: 'it came with a lass, it will pass with a lass'.[99] (Knox has: '"it came from a woman; and it will end in a woman"' (Laing I: 91), and considering the fact that Knox had such a good ear for the Scots phrase, we must admit that this is a rather curious instance of anglicising). Even so, the Reformer presents an accomplished version nonetheless. He uses *sermocinatio* and ends in *intimitatio*. Desiderius Erasmus defines the former as: 'the attribution to an individual of language in harmony with his age, birth, country, life, spirit and behaviour. *This figure is found in histories*, but is more common in the poets' (italics added). Knox's use, however, is closer to the definition given by Julius Caesar Scaliger in his *Epitome Troporum ac Schematum et Grammaticorum et Rhetorum*: 'When a particular direct speech is attributed to a character [...] [as] a means of portraying his character'.[100] Knox uses this device on both characters, making each look callous and thoroughly self-centred. Knox's Beaton (not the real Beaton) is more vividly characterised since his questions suggest great urgency and fervour. The latter device comes in with

97 See Laing I: 91, n. (2).
98 See Hamer, D., (ed.), *The Works of Sir David Lindsay*, p.134, ll.121–122.
99 Dickinson I: 39, n. (5).
100 Sonnino, L. A., *A Handbook*, p. 168.

Knox's parting shot. 'What moved her so to conjecture, diverse men ar of diverse judgementis'. In his *Direccions for Speech and Style* John Hoskins later defined the scheme as: 'a way of amplifying that leaves the collection of greatness to our understanding [...] and makes our meaning more palpable by a touch than by direct handling'.[101]

Pr. Dickinson points out that: 'in neither Mary Stewart nor her mother, Mary of Guise, could Knox find one redeeming virtue'[102] and the following passage probably represents him at his most outspoken. His subject is of course the woman he loved to hate (Mary, Queen of Scots):

> [...] so was sche sold to go to France [...] for a plague to this realme and for hir finall destructioun. And thairfoir, albeit that now a fyre cumes out frome hir, that consumes many, lett no man wonder, she is Goddis hand, in his displeasur punishing our formare ingratitude. Let men patientlie abyd, and turne unto thar God, and then shall he eyther destroy that hoore in hir hoordome, or ellis he shall putt it in the harttis of a multitude, to tak the same vengeance upoun hir, that hes bein tane of Jesabell and Athalia, yea, and of otheris, of whome prophane historyis mak mentioun; for geattar abominatioun was never in the nature of any woman, then is in hir, whareof we have but sein only the buddis; but we will after taist of the rype fruitt of hir impietie, yf God cutt not hir dayis schorte (Laing I: 218).

David Murison rightly calls these: 'strong intemperate words' and indeed they are powerful enough to place Knox alongside, say, Shakespeare's great cursers; King Lear, Queen Margaret or Timon of Athens. Dr. Murison, however, includes a proviso. They were, he says, written: 'when Mary was in the midst of her amour with the man who had murdered her husband about six weeks before, and was riding headlong for disaster. Like it or not, our prophet was proved sadly right again'.[103] Laing himself says that Knox's language: 'is impossible to vindicate'[104] but the present writer feels no inclination to do so. Dr. Murison has said enough, even if one can only agree *cum grano salis*. What is surprising, and what both Laing and Dr. Murison have passed

101 ibid., p. 120.
102 Dickinson I: lxxiii.
103 Murison, D., 'Knox the Writer', 46.
104 Laing, I: 218, n. (4).

over, is the fact that, in terms both of sentiment and vocabulary, Knox is manifestly the debtor of the book of Revelation 18: 3–8 (with one major difference: *Knox is milder*). Here are the verses, from *Coverdale's Bible*:

> [...] for all nacions haue dronken in the wine of the wrath of her whoredome [...] come away from her my people, that ye be not partakers of her synnes, lest ye receaue of her plages. For her synnes are gone up to heauen, and the Lorde hath remembred her wyckedness. Rewarde her euen as she rewarded you, and geue her double accordinge to her workes. And poure in dubble to her in the same cuppe, which sche fylled unto you. And as moche as she gloryfied her selfe and lyved wantonly, so moch poure ye in for her punysment, and sorowe, for she sayeth in her herte: I syt beinge a quene, and am no wyddowe, and shall se no sorrowe. Therefore shal her plages come at one daye, death and sorrow, and honger, and shalbe brent with fyre [...]

Knox must have been struck by the apparent relevance of this prophecy to the situation with Mary and Bothwell, even if there was a good deal of wishful thinking in the parallel. This time the source of the parallel is especially significant because it again places Knox's prophecy in the apocalyptic tradition. His other references, to Jezebel and Athalia, are presumably based on 2 Kings 9: 33 and 11: 20 respectively, but these figures, together with other Biblical villains such as Ahab and Delilah, were types, commonly used in Scotland and elsewhere during the Reformation. And for all this fiery intemperance, one should not overlook the fact that Knox is offering advice. Buchanan's assessment of Mary in *Rerum Scoticarum Historia* was more subtle, more scholarly, more moderate and less Biblical, but his intentions are evidently very similar to Knox's.[105]

Descriptive Writing

I wish now to consider two passages from Knox's *The Historie* which we might aptly classify as 'descriptive' writing. Yet this is not all they have in common, and I have chosen to juxtapose them for two other reasons. They reveal, very strikingly, a sixteenth century world-view which posits a relationship between natural phenomena ('Des prodiges

105 See Gatherer, W. A., (ed.), *The Tyrannous Reign of Mary Stuart*, pp. 53–54.

célestes'),[106] and world events. And Knox's *The Historie* is not alone in displaying this view, as I propose to show by comparing his text with the earlier history of Hector Boece. The first example describes the arrival of a comet known as the: '"fierie boosome"', (Laing I: 254), which was seen over Scotland in 1558; the second deals with the arrival of Mary Stewart, a few years later. Hopefully their similarities will emerge in due course. The first reads:

> In the wynter that the said Johne aboad in Scotland appeired a comet, the course whairof was from the south and southwest, to the north and north-east. It was seine the monethis of November, December, and Januare. It was called "The fyrie boosome." Sone after dyed Christierne, King of Denmark: And warr raise betuix Scotland and England [...]
>
> In the end of that nixt harvest, was sein upoun the Bordouris of England and Scotland a straunge fyre, which discended from heavin, and brunt diverse cornes in boyth realms, but most in England. Thare was presented to the Quein Regent by Robert Ormestoun, a calf having two headdis, whareat sche scripped, and said, "It was but a commoun thing." *The warr begane in the end of the harvest* [...] (Laing I: 254–255; italics added).

It is not difficult to find may similar passages in Boece. Here is one such, accompanied by Bellenden's translation:

> *Boece's Scotorum Historiae*
> Duo eodem anno Cometae apparuisse dicuntur, vterque ingenti mole, humano aspectui horrendus: orientem solem in autumno vnus præcedebat, occidentem in vere alter sequebatur. Conspectae sunt & frequentius sub noctem ignitae acies ardentibus hastis coelo concurrere, alteraque profligata subito euanescere. Lituus (ita incuruum sacri magistratus ecclesiastici baculum appellant nonnulli) in pontificis manu dum sacra ageret Cameloduni repente igne correptus, ita pertinaciter arsit, vt nulla prorsus arte extingui potuerit.[107]
>
> *Bellenden's Chronicles of Scotland*
> The samyn yere apperit twa cometis, richt horribil to the sicht of man. The tane apperit befoir the sone rising in weir, and the tothir eftir the son ganging to in hervist. Offt tymes wes sene in the nicht ane fyry ordinance of armit men rusching to gidder with speris in the air, and quhen the tane of thame was wincust the tothir sone evanist. Quhen the Bischop of Camelon wes doand

106 Janton, P., *L'homme et l'oeuvre*, p. 441.
107 Boece, H., *Scotorum Historiæ*, Liber X, f. 200.

> dyvyne seruice in his pontificall, his staff tuke neyd fyre, and mycht be slokynnit be na craft quhill it was resoluit to nocht.[108]

Obviously, if one undertook to write a history, it was necessary to compare such phenomena with an event. The comet episodes all move from heavenly to earthly portents, thus preparing the reader for the type of interpretation outlined above. Knox, more effectively than Bellenden, suggests the inevitability of war by his extreme concision in moving from each portent to what he sees as its indirect consequence. Bellenden's language is, however, as tightly controlled in other ways. He makes us of a 'tane [...] tothir' construction, presumably suggested by 'vnvs' and 'alter'. Bellenden's 'son rising' and 'son ganging' (from 'orientam' and 'occidentem') create symmetry which in Knox's passage is likewise to be found with reference to the poles ('south', 'southwest', 'north', 'north-east') and all of the passages share a common vocabulary. For example, the following items play an important part in invoking mood: 'appeired / apparuisse / apperit', 'was seine / aspectui / to the sicht', 'end of that harvest / in autumno / ganging to in heruist', 'straunge / horrendus / horribil', and finally 'fyrie / ignitæ / fierie'. Obviously sixteenth century historians had stock phrases with which to describe such events, and as to interpretation, even Shakespeare's generation inherited something along similar lines. In *King Lear*, Gloucester puts things in a nutshell when he says: 'These late eclipses in the sun and moon portend no good to us' (*King Lear*, Act 1, Sc. 2, ll. 103–104). All three passages finish off with an example of supernormal occurrences closer to hand; but Knox uses his to make the Queen regent sound arrogant whereas the others involve no comparable intention.

This brings us to our second sample of Knox's descriptive writing. He tells us:

> The nyntene day of August, the year of God jmvc three scoir ane yearis, betwix sevin and aught houris befoir noon, arryved MARIE QUENE OF SCOTLAND, then widow, with two galayis furth of France [...] The verray Face of heavin, the time of hir arryvall, did manifestlie speak what confort was brought unto this cuntrey with hir, to wit, sorrow, dolour, darkness, and all impietie; for in

108 Batho, C. and Husbands, H., (eds.), *The Chronicles of Scotland*, vol. II: p. 50.

the memorie of man, that day of the year, was never seyn a more dolorous face of the heavin, then was at hir arryvall, which two days after did so continue; for besides the surfett weat, and corruptioun of the air, the myst was so thick and so dark, that skairse mycht any man espy ane other the lenth of two pair of buttis. The Sun was not seyn to schyne two dayis befoir nor two dayis after. That foirwarning gave God unto us; but allace, the most part war blynd (Laing II: 267–269).

This is unmistakably Knoxian. Pr. Ronald Jack has particularly admired its literary qualities, especially: 'the slow building up of atmosphere'.[109] But Knox has built imaginatively on a real meteorological occurrence. One of Mary's French companions who came with her to Scotland, the chronicler, Pierre de Bourdeilles Brantôme, complained that on arrival, he encountered 'grand brouillard', and there is no reason to doubt him.

The most rhetorically impressive features occur in the second and middle sentence (my text). It is packed full (but not overloaded) with detail, and Knox's complete control of language ensures that the reader's attention does not falter. Disjunctive subordination is used mainly to sketch in time, while Knox interweaves justificatory phrases with adjectivals. However, his definitive: 'to wit, sorrow, dolour, darkness and all impietie' constitutes prose composition of the highest order. Knox obviously regards bad weather as a sign of God's profound displeasure and this is not all that far from the world-view implicit in the earlier passage.

Moreover, Knox's registers are strikingly idiomatic. For example, 'verray', 'manifestlie' and 'impietie' are obviously drawn from the Biblical register. The first is used as an intensive to denote the exceptional prominence of an otherwise ordinary thing, as in: 'the verie heuens declare his righteousness' (*Coverdale*, Psalms 96: 6). The language is consistently metaphoric, with a switch from noun to verb ('Face' to 'speak'). One might legitimately label these effects personification or pathetic fallacy. Knox also mentions 'two pair of *buttis*' (italics added). The substantive here (rendered by W. C. Dickinson as 'boots')[110] is presumably drawn not from the vocabulary of clothing but from that

109 Jack, R. D. S., (ed.), *Scottish Prose 1550–1700*, p. 20.
110 See Dickinson II: 7.

of contemporary sport. *D.O.S.T.* defines the item as 'a mark for practice in achery', as in: 'he wan the pryse abune them all [...] baith at the buttis and the futeball' from Lindsay's *Squire Meldum.*[111] The intense power of the prose is heightened in other ways. The adverb 'skairse' qualifies the degree of the speaker's belief, thus adding just a trace of doubt and helping to create an almost surreal impression. A phrase like 'corruptioun of the air' suggests a Macbeth-like scene, and evidently for Knox, Mary's arrival ushers in a world where: 'Fair is foul, and foul is fair' (*Macbeth*, Act 1., Sc. 1, l. 10). Symmetry, such as we found in the 'comet' descriptions, exists here in the phrases 'two dayis befoir' and 'two dayis after'. It may be fanciful to suppose that this passage was first written at much greater length and selectively condensed to give it such an electrical charge, but we do know that in the *Edinburgh MS.* of 1566, it occurs in one of the heavily revised sections.

This, then, brings us to the end of the material from Knox's *The Historie*. Like his private epistles, *The Historie* has been somewhat neglected by critics who have relied rather too heavily on a one-quotation stereotype. It is to be hoped that this chapter has rediscovered many fine areas in the major work, and interpreted Knox in a more original way than hitherto. We have seen that he was a brilliant teller of merry tales, and that his work in this area provides us with some of his most unexpected and entertaining narratives. If any aspect of his writings gives the lie to the popular notion that Knox was the archetypal dour Scot, it must be these tales.

To be sure, in this respect, he will never be in the same league as Chaucer, or even, if we limit our sphere of investigation to a Scottish context, of Robert Henryson, but nonetheless, his sense of humour is extremely compelling and pervasive. It is, moreover, truly Scottish in its mood and temper. Without Knox, some of the most memorable personalities of the early part of the Reformation in Scotland (such as William Arth, Patrick Hepburn, Sandie Furrour and Alexander Seton) would have descended into an undeserved obscurity, instead of gracing

111 *D.O.S.T.*, I: 397–398.

the pages of an eloquent literary work, with charm, charisma, and at times, downright incorrigibility.

Similarly, we can see that Knox's unashamedly dramatic narratives are subtle, skilful, highly purposive and brilliantly effective. Their explosive power allows them to rank alongside the finest examples of this type of literature, in any literary canon, anywhere in the world. As a descriptive writer, Knox was just as accomplished, even if in many ways he is a product of his own times and their world-view. This is especially evident in the vocabulary which he apparently felt constrained to use (together with Boece, Bellenden and the other writers of Scottish historiographical works). The 'flavour' of the sixteenth century is particularly pungent within this dimension of *The Historie*. But we do not disparage Shakespeare for being a child of the age, nor should we do so with Knox.

But, certainly we can acknowledge that those critics who admire Knox's style, from J. H. Millar to Ronald Jack and even Roderick Watson, have very weighty and considerable reasons for doing so. It is not for nothing that *The Historie* is universally recognised as the first truly great work of Scots prose (and it should not be forgotten that it has many worthy competitors for this distinction, as the discussion in chapter one has already shown. *The Complaynt of Scotland* and Bellenden's *The Chronicles of Scotland* are works of no mean achievement, to say nothing of other major translations from the early part of Knox's period).

And if influence is a guide to the enduring value of a text, we cannot forget that the histories which were written after Knox's, would not have displayed the same merit, technique or efficacy as they do, had the Reformer never put pen to paper. We have also seen that Knox's literary legacy is not limited solely to prose. Poets who wrote as much as centuries later than Knox, still reveal vestigal traces of his presence in their work, (even if other writings, such as those in the tradition of popular alliterative verse, have been the intermediaries). But at this point, we need finally to extend our claims for the permanent value of Knox's greatest work. The present author, indeed, feels himself more than justified in making the following weighty assertion: not only is John Knox's *The Historie of the Reformatioun* the finest literary prose work of the times to which it belongs so inseparably, it is one of the very greatest works of prose in the *whole of Scottish literature – quod erat demonstrandum!*

Conclusion

This study has served to emphasise that Knox was, and is, a crucially important literary voice; he stands at the end of the medieval period as one who has absorbed its teaching and methods as well as its traditions, but who also came under the influence of humanism, and of onward-marching Reformation doctrine. He is regarded by historians as a supremely influential figure, although recently it has been recognised that he was not the sole architect of the Scottish Reformation, and although a man of firm conviction, was not always a fearless champion of his beliefs. He was never 'in power' and it is improper to speak of him 'permitting' things as if he held political office.[1]

1 See Massie, A., *101 Great Scots*, 'John Knox', (pp. 42–45), p. 43. For the most part, a remarkably fair account of Knox in which Massie explodes myths with obvious relish. He says, however, that it is popularly believed that Knox was a patriot and a nationalist, and then attacks *these* notions as false. But there is at least some evidence for them. The whole issue of anglicisation dominates Massie's arguments here. He is right only if we *automatically* associate patriotism with language, as Winzet had done. This would be to ignore characteristic Knoxian pronunciations such as: 'But one thing, in the end, I may nocht pretermit, that is, to give him a lye in his throat, that either dar, or will say, that ever I socht support against my native cuntrie. What I have bene to my cuntrie, albeit this unthankful age will not knowe, yet the aiges to come wilbe compelled to beir witnes to the treuth' (Laing VI: 595–596, cf. John 18: 37), which *do* have nationalistic overtones (whether the speaker is a scoundrel or not). Moreover, Massie corrects the error about Knox's birthdate (ca. 1513 not 1505), but forgets to take this into account when he says that Knox was fifty-nine when he married Margaret Stewart, a girl of sixteen (see p. 42). Considering the fact that Knox had three daughters by his second wife, this is hardly possible, since, according to Massie's own dates, Knox only lived to fifty-nine. This sort of curious arithmetical oversight is not uncommon. For instance, even Pr. Jack is guilty of it. In *Scottish Prose 1550–1700*, like Massie, he corrects the date of birth, but clings to the notion that Knox's: 'voice was silent for the first forty years of his life' (see p. 44). Long-sustained notions, it seems, defy evidence, and die hard. Among Alan Massie's more questionable assertions is the unqualified statement that John Major was a: '*humanist* historian' (p. 44). For a

Literary critics have perhaps been too much influenced by an inaccurate historical image, and historians do not always recognise the relevance of rhetorical technique as an agent of change in belief and therefore in history. However, Pierre Janton has argued very cogently that Knox: 'could not have become the historic figure he is without great literary talent'[2] and this is a fact all too seldom recognised. Knox, of course, did not conceive of his literary talent as a means of achieving a historical reputation, even if he was occasionally egotistical. After his own conversion to Protestantism, he was *first*, *last*, and *always*, a preacher, fishing for the souls of men in the time-honoured fashion. As an intensely practical man, he knew that eloquence and rhetoric were essential tools for a preacher, but only if carefully used. Properly appreciated, his words should fall away and become irrelevant once the religious point is taken. To admire words at the expense of doctrine is to misunderstand the preaching altogether (and this is true with all religious teaching, the language of the Bible being the supreme example). In line with these notions, is Knox's own denial of rhetoric as a vehicle of sophistry, hypocrisy, or both. For the literary critic to stop with such a recognition, however, would be to miss a great deal. The deceptive plainness of Knox's writings paradoxically adds another layer of complexity to his literary work. As I have illustrated in this study, the sixteenth century was a period of rhetorical fecundity and of intense commitment. The combination of these two strands produced sparks of fire, in Knox's works no less than in, say, Martin Luther's.

This study has also shown that language is not simply a means to an end, however important that end. Language itself is often defined and shaped by religion (or any strong belief, for that matter) and also reveals independently the psychological patterns of those who use it. This is true in Knox's case. The correlation is especially pronounced in his private letters (chapter three) and in *The Historie* (chapters five

more informed account, see Durkan, J., 'John Major: After 400 Years', 137 and also MacQueen, J. and W., 'Latin Prose Literature', 236, for reliable information on how Major, in fact, brought *scholastic* techniques to bear on historical traditions.

2 Janton, P., 'John Knox and Literature', 423.

and six), and, surprisingly, rhetorical convention seems neither to undermine his impression of sincerity, nor to diminish our image of Knox's mind. We cannot always say the same about his public epistles and the theological writings, probably because these were intended for publication and Knox was more keenly aware of his audience. Even so, texts such as *The First Blast*, *The Apellation* and *A Godly Letter* do provide compelling evidence that all of Knox's skills, together with the vehement side of his character, at least, are interacting in an electrifying sense.

The Historie of the Reformatioun, however, is Knox's greatest literary achievement and all of his other works, for all their intrinsic interest, look pale beside it. In this work, he has to subordinate his fundamental concerns, so evident elsewhere, to the flow of narrative, but this does not prevent him manifesting his own character and thoughts, consciously or unconsciously. We can divide *The Historie* into sections which reveal the contrasting literary strands operating within it, and having isolated these, establish the revelatory and functional qualities of language within each. It is not possible to read *The Historie* without appreciating the multi-faceted character of its author or without making some kind of decision about sixteenth century Protestantism, and perhaps even about modern Protestantism.

This study, then, has argued for a more realistic and informed recognition of Knox's literary legacy, but it is still true that his voice will probably never reach a great number of readers, simply because his public image puts them off. More problematically, he will always, and immediately, alienate those, who, with good reason, do not stand in a Protestant tradition, however loosely we use the terms. (This is why *The Historie* is a tragically flawed masterpiece). Catholic readers face difficulties which are not easily surmounted. Indeed, even those who share Knox's Protestantism (again with the necessary provisos) must exercise special caution in their analysis of his work. Finally, as W. S. Reid has observed,[3] there will perhaps always be a small number who approve unreservedly of Knox, more because of his world-view and perceived ecclesiastical achievements than literary ones, but it is worth remembering that excessive enthusiasm is often as great a threat

3 See Reid, W., *Trumpeter of God*, p. 285.

to objectivity as is hostility. Knox is forever controversial, but we ought to stop just reacting to him, and start thinking about him; a difficult task, to be sure, but not an impossible one. It is a sobering thought, and amazingly ironic, but perhaps the literary Knox can only be appreciated, for the right reasons, in a secular society. When all is said and done, one knows instinctively that he would readily have sacrificed his undoubted literary talents to prevent this.

Appendix 1: Glossary of Rhetorical Terms Used in this Book[1]

Abominatio – An exclamation of personal hatred against some person or thing.

Acclamatio – A concise statement or exclamation at the close of a section summing it up.

Accusatio – When the speaker accuses someone to his face of a crime previously unknown.

Admonitio – A warning, urging the audience to avoid dangers revealed by the speaker.

Adynaton – To admit that the subject is beyond the power of words to describe.

Antapodosis – A comparison of two things placed clearly side by side.

Ante occupatio – To anticipate the possible objections to one's argument and to answer them in advance.

Ambiguitas – When a word can be understood in two or more senses.

Benevolentia – An attempt to obtain mercy by an appeal for compassion from a stronger opponent.

Boni ominis captatio – To interpret an uncertain outcome as the better possibility; to call an uncertain thing a good one.

Chiasmus – The first thing in a phrase joined to the fourth, the second to the third.

Commoratio – Continual reference to and repetition of one central point.

Comparatio – Analogy. A confrontation between two different things with respect to their similarilty.

Concessio – To concede voluntarily the whole matter to the opponent particularly if the concession will do him some damage.

1 Definitions are taken from Sonnino, L. A., *A Handbook.* All other rhetorical terms are taken from the canon of mainstream literary criticism.

Conclusio – A concluding section, briefly summing up what has been said before.

Congeries – An accumulation of words or phrases which attains a climax by piling up words.

Consummatio – When a number of different arguments tend to one end.

Definitio – The shortest correct exposition of the nature of anything.

Dictu commoratio – The recitation of a memorable saying or sentence from some other author.

Digressio – A discussion departing from the main theme but still pertinent and useful.

Disjunctio – Parallel sentences each with its own nearly synonymous verb.

Enumeratio – When a subject is discussed according to its causes, effects and circumstances.

Exclamatio – A simulated exclamation to display emotion.

Exclusio – To dismiss a point in the opponent's favour.

Execratio – To curse and abuse a person for things that cannot be proved.

Exemplum – A form of rhetorical proof by analogy using the deeds of particular men, historical or fabulous.

Familiaritas – The transposition of the discussion into terms of intimacy and familiarity.

Gratiarum actio – Thanks for benefits received and an admission of inability to repay.

Incrementum – A series of phrases, each stronger than the last. To make the matter seem more important, it begins with the least important.

Inter se pugnantia – To reprove someone of inconstancy or hypocrisy.

Inopinatum – The paradox. The speaker expresses astonishment that such a thing can exist.

Interrogatio – To ask a question which needs no answer.

Inversio – An exchange of syllables which corrupts the whole form of the word.

Irrisio – To taunt savagely under the guise of gentle speech.

Libera vox – To pretend to speak freely, thus getting the audience to believe what is said.

Litotes – Understatement.
Necessitas – To confess to some action but maintain that it was necessary.
Negatio – A refusal to speak which nevertheless tells everything.
Ominatio – To foretell the effects likely to follow some evil cause.
Optatio – The wish.
Partitio – When the whole of a speech is divided at the beginning.
Perclusio – A threat.
Peristasis – To enlarge by expanding the circumstances of the subject.
Permissio – To refer the rest of the case to the judgement of a listener.
Praeparatio – To state fully why something will be said or done.
Propositio – A short statement of the subject of the discourse which follows.
Quaestium – A question used for emotional emphasis.
Ratiocinatio – A process of reasoning from cause to effect.
Reditus ad propositum – The return to a main theme after a digression.
Rejectio – To reject some accusation as unworthy of the accuser.
Repetitio – Repetition of the same sound at the beginning of succeeding units.
Sententia – A succinct and striking general statement.
Sermocinatio – Direct speech attributed to a person or thing.
Similiter desinens – Clauses which end with similar sounding syllables.
Simplicitas – A direct and simple style.
Urbanitas – The sophisticated joke.

Appendix 2: Principal Events in the Life of John Knox (ca. 1513–1572)

1513. Battle of Flodden; probable year of John Knox's birth. He was later to study under John Major, probably at St. Andrews, but he left without a degree.

1517. Martin Luther's protest against indulgences in Wittenberg.

1520. Excommunication of Luther.

1527. Patrick Hamilton of Fern preaches on Justification by Faith in Scotland.

1528. Hamilton is condemned by Archbishop Beaton and burned at the stake for heresy in St. Andrews. Sir David Lindsay's satirical poems on clerical abuses published. William Tyndale's *New Testament*, and *The Gude and Godly Ballads* circulate in Scotland.

1534. Peace with England; Henry VIII breaks definitively from the Pope; further burnings for heresy in Scotland.

1535. Friar Alexander Seton denounces the Papacy.

1536. Publication of Jean Calvin's *Institutes of the Christian Religion* (Basle).

1538. Marriage between James V of Scotland and Mary of Lorraine.

1539. Proposed meeting of James V, and Henry VIII, at York, fails to take place. James comes under the influence of Cardinal David Beaton.

1540. Act against iconoclasm and private gatherings.

1541. Act to promote Church reformation.

1542. Defeat of the Scots at Solway Moss. Birth of Princess Mary, death of James V when his daughter is five days old.

1543. Earl of Arran becomes Regent; Act authorising the reading of Scripture in the vernacular. Mary Stewart crowned Queen. Alliance with England collapses; old alliance with France renewed.

1544. Declaration of war by Henry VIII.

1545. John Knox, aged 32, attaches himself to George Wishart, a popular Zwinglian preacher.
1546. Wishart arrested by Cardinal Beaton, and burned for heresy. Murder of Beaton at St. Andrews.
1547. John Knox is publicly called upon to accept the role of preacher. St. Andrews Castle falls. Knox becomes a prisoner in the French galleys. Death of Henry VIII. Battle of Pinkie.
1548. Queen Mary sent to France.
1549. A Provincial council held at Edinburgh; John Knox appointed preacher at Berwick
1550. Treaty of Bologne, involving Scotland, England and France.
1551. Knox becomes Chaplain to Edward VI; helps revise the Articles and Liturgy of the English Church.
1552. Knox declines the Bishopric of Rochester; a Catholic Catechism is sanctioned by Archbishop Hamilton.
1553. Death of Edward VI; Mary Tudor becomes Queen in England. Marian persecution of uncompromising Protestants causes many to flee to the Continent, Knox included.
1554. Mary of Guise becomes Regent; Knox becomes a minister to the English Congregation at Frankfurt. After a controversy, he moves on to Geneva.
1555. Knox briefly visits Scotland from Geneva.
1556. Knox returns to Geneva, but is burned in effigy in Edinburgh.
1557. St. Giles Day Riot in Edinburgh. Scots nobles form the 'Lords of the Congregation' to defend the Protestant Faith.
1558. Queen Mary marries the Dauphin. Death of Mary Tudor. Elizabeth I accedes to the English throne. Scottish Protestants petition the Queen Regent for religious reform.
1559. Publication of 'The Beggars Summons', claiming a restitution of wrongs from the friars. The Queen Regent forbids public preaching without the leave of bishops. Prominent Scottish preachers disregard her order. Knox returns to Scotland. Riots and burnings at Perth and Scone. Civil war between the Queen and the Protestants, the former supported by France, and the latter by England.
1560. Year of the Scottish Reformation. Treaty of Berwick between Elizabeth I and Scots Protestants. Siege of Leith; Death of

Queen Regent; 'Treaty of Edinburgh' between Scotland, England and France. First Reformation Parliament meets; Confession of Faith ratified, first General Assembly of the Church in Scotland.

1561. A Convention of the Scots nobility held in Edinburgh. Mary Queen of Scots returns to Scotland; her celebration of the Mass interrupted; Knox's first meeting with the Queen.

1562. Earl of Huntly's rebellion suppressed; Knox's second interview with Mary. A public disputation on the Mass held by Knox and the Abbot of Crossraguel.

1563. Knox's third interview with the Queen at Lochleven. The Archbishop of Glasgow is prosecuted for attempting to restore the Mass. Knox preaches against Mary's proposed marriage to Don Carlos of Spain. Fourth and most turbulent interview with the Queen. Knox tried for treason, but acquitted.

1564. Calvin dies at Geneva. David Rizzio becomes a favourite of the Queen's in the Scottish Court.

1565. The Queen marries Henry, Lord Darnley.

1566. Knox occupied in writing a large part of his *The Historie of the Reformatioun*.

1567. Murder of Lord Darnley. Marriage of Mary, to the Earl of Bothwell; Queen's forced abdication; coronation of her son, James VI; Earl of Moray becomes Regent; Reformed Church declared the only Church in Scotland.

1568. Mary flees to England, and is imprisoned.

1570. The Regent, Moray, is assassinated.

1572. Knox preaches his last sermon. Death of Knox.

Bibliography

Aitken, A. J., '*D. O. S. T.*: How we make it and what's in it', *Proceedings of the Third International Conference on Scottish Language and Literature, Medieval and Renaissance*, Lyall, R. J. and Riddy, F. J., (eds.), (Stirling and Glasgow, 1981), 33–52.

Aitken, A. J., 'Oral Narrative Style in Middle Scots', *Actes du 2e Colloque de Langue et de Littérature Ecossaises* (*Moyen Age et Renaissance*), Blanchot, J. J. and Graf, C., (eds.), (Strasbourg, 1978), 98–112.

Aitken, A. J., 'The Pioneers of Anglicised Speech in Scotland; a second look', *Scottish Language*, 16, 1997, 1–36.

Aitken, W. R., (ed.), *Poems of William Soutar: A New Selection*, (Edinburgh, 1988).

Anderson, W. J., 'John Knox at Dieppe', *The Innes Review* 13, (1962), 104.

Bain, J., (ed.), *Calendar of the State Papers Relating to Scotland and Mary, Queen of Scots*, (Edinburgh, 1898–1969).

Bainton, R., *Erasmus of Christendom*, (New York, 1969).

Bainton, R., *Here I Stand: A Biography of Martin Luther*, (New York, 1959).

Bald, M., 'The Pioneers of Anglicised Speech in Scotland', *Scottish Historical Review*, 24, 1927, 179–193.

Barclay, W. R., *The Role of Sir David Lindsay, in the Scottish Reformation*, (Wisconsin, 1956).

Barke, J., (ed.), *Poems and Songs of Robert Burns*, (London, 1983).

Batho, C. and Husbands, H. W., (eds.), *The Chronicles of Scotland*, (Edinburgh and London, 1911).

Bawcutt, P., (ed.), *The Poems of William Dunbar*, (Glasgow, 1998).

Bell, A., *The Roit or Quheill of Tyme*, Nat. Lib. MS. 1746.

Biblia Sacra: *Vulgate Editionis Sixti V Pontifica Maxima jussu Recognita et Clementis VIII*, (London, 1977).

Blanchot, J. J. and Graf, C., (eds.), *Actes du 2e Colloque de Langue et de Littérature Ecossaises* (*Moyen Age et Renaisssance*), (Strasbourg, 1978).

Blayney, M. S. and G. H., 'Alain Chartier and *The Complaynt of Scotland*', *The Review of English Studies*, 9, 1958, 8–17.

Boece, H., *Scotorum Historiæ a primæ gentis origine rerum et Gentium illustratione non Vulgari*, (Paris, 1575).

Bohun, E., *The General History of the Reformation of the Church From the Errors and Corruptions of the Church of Rome*, (London, 1689).
Bower, W., *Johnannis de Fordun Scotichronicon, cum supplementis et continuatione Walteri Boweri, insulæ Sanct Columbæ abbatis. E. Codicibus MSS. Editum, cum notis et variantibus lectionibus, Cura Walteri Goodall, Subjecta est dissertatio de nuptis Roberti senescalli Scotiæ atque Elizabethæ Moræ*, (Edinburgh, 1759).
Brandt, C. J. and Fenger, B. T., (eds.), *Danske Skrifter*, (Copenhagen, 1850–1856).
Brewer, J. S. and Gairdner, J., (eds.), *Letters and Papers of the Reign of Henry VIII*, (London, 1862–1910).
Brown, P. H., 'Reformation and Renascence in Scotland' in *The Cambridge History of English Literature*, Ward, A. W. and Walker, A. R., (eds.), (Cambridge, 1938).
Brown, P. H., *John Knox: A Biography*, 2 vols., (London, 1895).
Brown, P. H., (ed.), *Vernacular Writings of George Buchanan*, (Edinburgh and London, 1892).
Buchanan, G., *The History of Scotland*, Aikman, J., (tr.), (Glasgow, 1827).
Buchanan, G., *Rerum Scotticarum Historia*, (Edinburgh, 1582).
Burns, J. H., 'Knox and Bullinger', *Scottish Historical Review*, 1955, 90–91.
Burns, J. H, 'The Meroure of Wyssdome', *The Innes Review*, vol. 6, No. 2, Autumn, 1955, 77–98.
Burns, J. H., 'The Political Background of the Reformation', *Essays on the Scottish Reformation*, McRoberts, D., (ed.), (Glasgow, 1962), 1–36.
Calderwood, D., *The Historie of the Kirk of Scotland*, (Edinburgh, 1842).
Cameron, J. K., 'Aspects of the Lutheran Contribution to the Scottish Reformation', *Records of the Scottish Church History Society*, 22, (1984–86) 1–12.
Cameron, J. K., 'John Johnsone's *An Confortable Exhortation of Oure Mooste Holy Christen Faith and her Frutes*: An Early Example of Scots Lutheran Piety', *Studies in Church History*, Subsidia 2, 1979, 129–144.
Campbell, G., (ed.), *John Milton: The Complete Poems*, (London, 1980).
Carlyle, T., *Lectures on the History of Literature*, (London, 1892).
Carlyle, T., *Latter-Day Pamphlets: John Knox*, (London, 1885).
Chambers, R. W. and Seton, W. W., 'Bellenden's Translation of the History of Hector Boece', *Scottish Historical Review*, 17, No. 65, Oct. 1919, 5–16.
Cody, E. G. and Murison, W., (eds.), *The Historie of Scotland, wrytten first in Latin by the most reverend and worthy Jhone Leslie, Bishop of Rosse,*

and translated into Scottish by Father James Dalrymple, 1596, (Edinburgh and London, 1895).
Collinson, P., 'The Role of Women in the English Reformation illustrated by the Life and Friendships of Anne Locke', *Studies in Church History*, 2, (1965), 258–272.
Coverdale, M., *The Holy Scriptures* [...] *with the Apocripha faithfully translated from the Hebrue and Greake*, (London, 1535).
Cowan, H., *John Knox, Hero of the Scottish Reformation*, (New York and London, 1905).
Cowan, I. B., *The Scottish Reformation: Church and Society in Sixteenth Century Scotland*, (London, 1982).
Craigie, W. A., (ed.), *The Maitland Folio MS. Contining Poems by Sir Richard Maitland, Dunbar, Henryson, Douglas and others*, (Edinburgh and London, 1919).
Craigie, W. A., Aitken, A. J. and Stevenson, J., (eds.), *A Dictionary of the Older Scottish Tongue*, (Chicago and London, 1937–2002).
Crespin, J., (ed.), *The Bible* [...] *translated according to the Ebrue and Greke*, (Geneva, 1568–70).
Dawes, J., *A Famous Chronicle of our Time called Sleidanes Commentaries, concerning the State of Religion and Commonwealth, during the Reign of the Emperour Charles the Fifth*, (London, 1560).
Dawson, J. E. A., 'The Two John Knoxes: England, Scotland and the 1558 Tracts', *Journal of Ecclesiastical History*, 42, 4, 1991, 555–576.
Dennistoun, J., (ed.), *Memoirs of the Affairs of Scotland* [...] *from 1577 to 1603*, (Edinburgh, 1830).
Dickinson, W. C., (ed.), *John Knox's History of the Reformation in Scotland*, (Edinburgh, 1949).
Donaldson, G., 'Knox the Man', *John Knox: A Quatercentenary Re-appraisal*, Shaw, D., (ed.), (Edinburgh, 1975), 19–33.
Donaldson, G., *The Scottish Reformation*, (Cambridge, 1960).
Droz, E., (ed.), *Le Quadrilogue Invectif*, (Paris, 1950).
Duncan, A. A. M., 'Hector Boece and the Medieval Tradition', *Scots Antiquaries and Historians*, Duncan, A. A. M., Rae, T. I. and Marinell, A., Bruce H., Lenman, P., (eds.), (Dundee, 1972), 1–11.
Durkan, J., 'Book Review: Dickinson's *Knox*', *Innes Review*, I, 1950, 158–161.
Durkan, J., 'The Cultural Background in Sixteenth Century Scotland', *Essays on the Scottish Reformation*, McRoberts, D., (ed.), (Glasgow, 1962).
Durkan, J., 'George Wishart: His Early Life', *Scottish Historical Review*, No. 113, 1953, 32, 98.

Durkan, J., 'John Major: After 400 Years', *The Innes Review*, I, 1950, 131–139.

Durkan, J., '"Scottish Evangelicals" in the Patronage of Thomas Cromwell', *Records of the Scottish Church History Society*, 21, 1981–83, 125–157.

Durkan, J., 'Heresy in Scotland: the second phase, 1546–58'; *Records of the Scottish Church History Society*, 24, 1990–92, 320–365.

Erasmus Rotterodamus, D., *Erasmi Epistulæ*, (Oxford, 1910).

Erasmus Rotterodamus, D., *Novum Testamentum Omne* etc., (Basel, 1516).

Felch, S. M., 'The Rhetoric of Biblical Authority: John Knox and the Question of Women', *Sixteenth Century Journal*, 26, 4, 1995, 805–822.

Finlayson, C. P., 'A Volume Associated with John Knox', *Scottish Historical Review*, 38, 1959, 170–172.

Firth, K., *The Apocalyptic Tradition in Reformation Britain 1530–1645*, (Oxford, 1979).

Fleming, D. Hay, *The Reformation in Scotland*, (London, 1910).

Forshall, J. and Madden, F., (eds.), *The New Testament*, (Oxford, 1879).

Fox, D., (ed.), *The Poems of Robert Henryson*, (Oxford, 1981).

Frankforter, A. D., 'Elizabeth Bowes and John Knox: A Woman and Reformation Theology', *Church History*, 56, 1987, 333–347.

Frankforter, A. D., 'The Chronology of the Knox-Bowes Letters', *Manuscripta*, March, 1987, 31, no. I, 28–41.

Fraser, A. *Mary, Queen of Scots*, (London, 1969).

Gatherer, W. A., (ed.), *The Tyrannous Reign of Mary Stewart: George Buchanan's Account*, (Edinburgh, 1958).

Grant, D., (ed.), *Dryden: Poems and Prose*, (London, 1985).

Greaves, R. *Theology and Revolution in the Scottish Reformation: Studies in the Thought of John Knox*, (Michigan, 1979).

Greengrass, M., *The French Reformation*, (Oxford, 1981).

Greenslade, S. L., (ed.), *The Cambridge History of the Bible: The West from the Reformation to the Present Day*, (Cambridge, 1963).

Grieve, M. and Aitken, W. R., (eds.), *The Complete Poems of Hugh MacDiarmid*, (Harmondsworth, 1978).

Hamer, D., (ed.), *The Works of Sir David Lindsay of the Mount*, (Edinburgh and London, 1937).

Hannay, M. P., (ed.), *Silent but for the Word: Tudor Women as Patrons, Translators and Writers of Religious Works*, (Ohio, 1985).

Hazlett, I., 'A Working Bibliography of the Writings of John Knox', *Calviniana*, 10, 185–194.

Healey, R. M., 'Waiting for Deborah: John Knox and Four Ruling Queens', *Sixteenth Century Journal*, 25, 2, 1994, 371–386.

Healey, R. M., 'John Knox's "History": A "Compleat" Sermon on Christian Duty', in *Church History*, 61, 1992, 319–333.

Hendersen, T. F., *Scottish Vernacular Literature; A Succinct History*, (Edinburgh, 1988).

Hewison, J. K., (ed.), *Winzet's Works*, (Edinburgh and London, 1888).

Herford, C. H. and Simpson, P., (eds.), *Ben Johnson*, (Oxford, 1950).

Higman, F., *The Style of John Calvin in his French Polemical Treatises*, (Oxford, 1967).

Jack, R. D. S., (ed.), *History of Scottish Literature*, vol. I. (Aberdeen, 1988).

Jack, R. D. S., 'The Prose of John Knox: A Re-Assessment', *Prose Studies*, 4, 1981, 239–51.

Jack, R. D. S., *Scottish Prose 1550–1700*, (London, 1971).

Janton, P., 'John Knox, rérformateur écossais', *Dictionnaire de Spiritualité*, 1738–39.

Janton, P., 'John Knox. Réponse à une letter d'un jésuite nommé Tyrie, 1572', *La Revue Réformée*, 1977/1.

Janton, P., 'L'art et la technique du syllogisme chez John Knox', *Théologie pratique et Société. Mélanges à la mémoire de Michel Péronnet*, Montpellier, 2003, t. II, 69–80.

Janton, P., 'Prayer in Prose as Literature and the British Reformers of the XVIth Century', *Cahiers Elisabéthains*, Montpellier, 2004.

Janton, P., *Concept et Sentiment dans L'Eglise chez John Knox*, (Paris, 1972).

Janton, P., *John Knox (ca. 1513–72): L'homme et l'oeuvre*, (Paris 1967).

Janton, P., 'John Knox and Literature', *Actes du 2e Colloque de Lange et de Littérature Ecossaises, Moyen Age et Renaissance*, Blanchot, J. J. and Graf, C., (eds.), (Strasbourg,1978), 422–429.

Janton, P., 'Un projet éducatif pour l'Ecosse: le Livre de Discipline (1560)', *L'éducation au XVIè siècle*, (Le-Puy-en-Velay, 1994), 127–138.

Janton, P., *L'Eloquence et la Rhetorique dans les Sermons de Hugh Latimer*, (Paris, 1968).

Janton, P., 'Prophétie et "prophesying" chez John Knox et dans La tradition puritaine'; *Les Signes de Dieu aux XV17 et XVIIè*, (Clermont Fd., 1993), 37–44

Janton, P., 'La désobeissance chrétienne et le pouvoir selon John Knox'; *Tout pouvoir vient de Dieu*, (Montpellier, 1993), 164–179.

Janton, P., 'John Knox et L'Histoire'; *L'Histoire au temps de la Renaissance*, (Paris, 1996), 161–175

Jeffares, A. N., (ed.), *Poems of W. B. Yeats: A New Selection*, (London and Basingstoke, 1984).

Johnsone, J., *An Confortable Exhortation of Oure Mooste Holy Christen Faith and her Frutes*, (S.T.C. 2, 14668).

Kay, B., *Scots: The Mither Tongue*, (Edinburgh, 1987).

Kenneth, Bro., 'David Lindsay, Reformer', *The Innes Review*, I, 1950, 79–91.

Kenneth, Bro., 'The Popular Literature of the Scottish Reformation', *Essays on the Scottish Reformation*, McRoberts, D., (ed.), (Glasgow, 1962), 169–184.

Kinsley, J., (ed.), *Poems and Songs of Robert Burns*, (Oxford,1968).

Kirk, J., 'The Influence of Calvinism on the Scottish Reformation', *Records of the Scottish Church History Society*, 18, (1972–74), 157–179.

Kirk, J., 'The Scottish Reformation and Reign of James VI: A Select Critical Bibliography', *Records of the Scottish Church History Society*, 23, Part 1, 113–155.

Knox, J., *A Confession & delcaratio of praiers added thereunto / by John Knox / minister of Christes most sacred Evangel / upon the death of that moste verteous and famous King / Edward the VI kynge of Englande / France and Ireland / in whiche confession / the sayde Jhon doth accuse no les his owne offences / then the offences of others / to be the cause of the awaye takinge of that moste godly prince / nowe raininge with Christ whyle we abyde plagues for our unthankfulnesse.* (London, 1553), (S.T.C. 15073, Reel 254).

Knox, J., *A Comfortable Epistell, sente to the afflicted Church of Chryst, exhorting the faythefull to beare his cross wyth pacience, lokyng every houre for hys commynge agayne to the great comfort and consolacion of hys chosen*, (Wesel (?), 1554) (S.T.C. 15072, Reel 555).

Knox, J., *An Answer to a letter of a Iesvit, named Tyrie by Iohne Knox*, (St. Andrews, 1572), (S.T.C. 15062, Reel 473).

Knox, J., *The Coppie of a Letter / sent to the Ladye Mary dowagire Regent of Scotland, by John Knox in the yeare 1556. Here is also a notable sermon, made by the sayde John Knoxe, wherein is euydentlye proued that the masse is and alwayes hath been abhominable before God and Idolatrye*, (S.T.C. 15066, Reel 442).

Knox, J., *John Knox's History of the Reformation in the Realm of Scotland*, Laing MS., MS. 1566 or La. II. 210, Edinburgh University Library.

Knox, J., *The Historie of the Reformatioun of Religioun within the Realm of Scotland*, MS. Gen. 1123, Glasgow University Library.

Knox, J., *The Epistles of Mr. Knox, worthy to be read because of the Wholesome Christiane doctrine to be found thairin*, M'Crie MS. La. III. 345.

Knox, J., *An Exposition upon the syxt Psalme of David, wherein is declared hys crosse, complayntes and prayers*... Harleian MS. No. 416. ff. 40–45 No. 34. British Museum.
Kuippers, C. H., (ed.), *Quintin Kennedy (1520–1564): Two Eucharistic Tracts*, (Nijmegen, 1964).
Kyle, R., 'John Knox and the Purification of Religion: The Intellectual Aspects of his Crusade against Idolatry', *Archiv für Reformation-geschichte*, 77, 1986, 265–280.
Kyle, R., 'John Knox', *Dictionary of Scottish Church History & Theology*, Wright, D. F., Lachman, D. C. and Meek, D.E., (eds.), (Edinburgh, 1993), 465–466.
Laing, D., (ed.), *The Miscellany of the Wodrow Society*, (Edinburgh, 1842).
Laing, D., (ed.), *The Works of John Knox*, 6 vols., (Edinburgh, 1846–64).
Lang, A., *John Knox and the Reformation*, (London, 1905).
Lang, A. 'Knox as Historian', *Scottish Historical Review*, 2, 1905, 113–30.
Lang, A., 'The Letters of Cardinal Beaton', *Scottish Historical Review*, 6, 1909, 150–158.
Law, T. S., (ed.), *The New Testament in Scots*, (Edinburgh and London, 1903, 1904).
Lee, M., 'John Knox and his History', *Scottish Historical Review*, 45, 1966, 79–88.
Lesley, J., *De Origine, moribus, et rebus gestis Scotorum libri decem* [...] *Accessit nova et accurata regionem et insularum Scotiæ, cum vera eiusdem tabula topographia. descriptio*, (Romæ, 1578).
Lewis, C. S., *English Literature in the Sixteenth Century* (*Excluding Drama*), (Oxford, 1954).
Lindsay, M., *History of Scottish Literature*, (London, 1977).
Lorimer, P., *John Knox and the Church of England*, (London, 1875).
Luther, M., *Dr. Martin Luther's Werke: Die Deutsche Bibel*, (Weimar, 1929).
Lyall, R. J., 'Complaint, Satire and Invective in Middle Scots Literature', *Church, Politics and Society*, MacDougall, N., (ed.), (Edinburgh, 1983), 44–64.
Lyall, R. J., 'Vernacular Prose before the Reformation', *History of Scottish Literature*, (ed.), Jack, R. D. S., (Aberdeen, 1988), 163–182.
Lyall, R. J., (ed.), *Ane Resonyng of ane Scottis and Inglis Merchand Betuix Rowand and Lionis*, (Aberdeen, 1985).
Lyall, R. J., and Riddy, F., (eds.), *Proceedings of the Third International Conference on Scottish Language and Literature, Medieval and Renaissance*, (Stirling and Glasgow, 1981).
MacDiarmid, H., Maclean, C. and Ross, A., *John Knox*, (Edinburgh, 1976).

McDiarmid, M., *Robert Henryson*, (Edinburgh, 1981).
McDonald, C., (ed.), *Meroure of Wyssdome*, vol. 3, (Aberdeen, 1990).
Macgill, F. N. and McGreal, I. P., (eds.), *Masterpieces of Christian Literature in Summary Form*, (New York, 1963).
MacKay, A., (ed.) *Historie and Chronicles of Scotland*, (Edinburgh and London, 1899–1911).
MacKenzie, A. M., *A Historical Survey of Scottish Literature to 1714*, (London, 1933).
MacNab, T. M. A., 'Bohemia and the Scottish Lollards', *Records of the Scottish Church History Society*, 5, 1935, 10–22.
MacPherson, C., (ed.), *Johannes de Irelandia's Meroure of Wyssdome*, vol. 1, (Edinburgh and London, 1926).
MacQueen, J. and W., 'Latin Prose Literature', *History of Scottish Literature*, vol. I, Jack, R. D. S., (ed.), (Aberdeen, 1988), 227–243.
Major, J., *Historia Majoris Britanniæ tam Angliæ quam Scotiæ*, (Paris, 1521).
Massie, A., *101 Great Scots*, (Edinburgh, 1987).
McGrath, A., *The Intellectual Origins of the European Reformation*, (Oxford, 1987).
McGrath, A., *Reformation Thought*, (Oxford, 1988).
McClure, J. D., *Scotland and the Lowland Tongue: Studies in the Language and Literature of Lowland Scotland.* (*In honour of David D. Murison*). (Aberdeen, 1983).
McClure, J. D. and Spiller, M. R. G., (eds.), *Bryght Lanternis: Essays on the Language and Literature of Medieval and Renaissance Scotland*, (Aberdeen, 1987).
M'Crie, T., *Life of John Knox* (5th Edition), (Edinburgh, 1831).
Merriamn, M. H., 'Scottish collaborators with England during the Rough Wooing', *Scottish Historical Review*, 47, 1968, 10–34.
Muerman-Solin, A., *Variation and Change in Early Scottish Prose*, (Helsinki, 1993).
Millar, J. H., *Literary History of Scotland*, (London, 1905).
Mitchell, A. F., (ed.), *The Richt Vay to the Kingdome of Heuine*, (Edinburgh and London, 1888).
Mitchell, A. F., (ed.), *Archbishop Hamilton's Catechism*, (Edinburgh, 1882).
Mitchell, A. F., (ed.), *A Compendious Book of Godlie and Spiritual Songs Commonly known as 'the Gude and Godlie Ballatis'*, (Edinburgh and London, 1897).
Moffat, J., *The Bible in Scottish Literature*, (London, 1924).
Muir, E., *John Knox: Portrait of a Calvinist*, (London, 1929).

Müller, G., 'Protestant Theology in Scotland and Germany in the Early Days of the Reformation', *Records of the Scottish Church History Society*, 22, 1984–86, 103–117.
Murison, D., 'Knox the Writer', *John Knox: A Quatercentenary Re-appraisal*, Shaw, D., (ed.), (Edinburgh, 1975), 33–50.
Murison, W., *Sir David Lyndsay, Poet and Satirist of the Old Church in Scotland*, (Cambridge, 1938).
Murray, J. A. H., (ed.), *The Complaynt of Scotland*, (London, 1872).
Murray, J. A. H., *A New English Dictionary on Historical Principles* (*O.E.D.*), (London, 1888–1933).
Nichols, F., (ed.), *Epistles of Erasmus*, (London, 1904).
Offor, G., (ed.), *The New Testament of our Lord and Saviour Jesus Christ (1526)*, (London, 1836).
Owens, W. R., (ed. and intr.), *Grace Abounding to the Chief of Sinners*, (Harmondsworth, 1987).
Owst, G. R., *Literature and Pulpit in Medieval England*, (Cambridge, 1933).
Pedersen, C., *Det Ny Testament*, (Antwerp, 1529, Copenhagen, 1950).
Percy, E., *John Knox*, (London, 1937).
Pine-Coffin, R. S., (ed.), *Confessions*, (Harmondsworth, 1961).
Pitcairn, R., (ed.), *The Autobiography and Diary of Mr. James Melvill* (Edinburgh, 1847).
Pollard, A. W. and Redgrave, G. R., (eds.), *A Short-Title Catalogue of Books Printed in England, Scotland and Ireland, And of English Books Printed Abroad 1475–1640*, (London, 1946–)
Quinn, F., (ed.), *Meroure of Wyssdome*, vol. 2, (Edinburgh, 1965).
Reardon, B., *Religious Thought in the Reformation*, (New York and London, 1981).
Reid, D., *The Party-Coloured Mind*, (Edinburgh, 1982).
Reid, D., 'Prose after Knox', *The History of Scottish Literature*, vol. I, Jack, R. D. S., (ed.), (Aberdeen, 1988), 183–199.
Reid, D., 'Writing History: Buchanan and the Two James Melvills', *Proceedings of the Third International Conference on Scottish Language and Literature*, Lyall, R. J. and Riddy, F. J., (eds.), (Stirling and Glasgow, 1981), 422–438.
Reid, W. S., 'John Knox's Theology of Political Government', *Sixteenth Century Journal*, 19, 4, 1988, 529–540.
Reid, W. S., *Trumpeter of God*, (Michigan, 1974).
Ridley, J., *John Knox*, (Oxford, 1968).
Robinson, H., (ed.), *Zurich Letters*, 2nd Series, (Cambridge, 1842–45).

Robinson, M., 'Language Choice in the Reformation: The Scots Confession of 1560', *Scotland and the Lowland Tongue: Studies in the Language and Literature of Lowland Scotland*, M'Clure, J. D., (ed.), (Aberdeen, 1983), 59–78.
Ross, J. M., *Scottish History and Literature to the Period of the Reformation*, (Glasgow, 1884).
Rupp, E. G., 'The Europe of John Knox', *John Knox: A Quatercentenary Re-appraisal*, Shaw, D., (ed.), (Edinburgh, 1975), 5–19.
Sanderson, M. H. B., *Cardinal of Scotland: David Beaton 1494–1546*, (Edinburgh, 1986).
Scribner, R.W., *The German Reformation*, (London, 1986).
Shaw, D., (ed.), *John Knox: A Quatercentenary Re-appraisal*, (Edinburgh, 1975).
Shaw, D., 'John Knox and Mary, Queen of Scots', *John Knox: A Quatercentenary Re-appraisal*, Shaw, D., (ed.), (Edinburgh, 1975), 50–69.
Shaw, D., *Reformation and Revolution*, (Edinburgh, 1967).
Shaw, D., 'Zwinglian Influences on the Scottish Reformation', *Records of the Scottish Church History Society*, 22, Part 2, 119–139.
Sharrock, R., (ed.), *The Pilgrim's Progress*, (Harmondsworth, 1986).
Shire, H. M., *Song, Dance and Poetry of the Court of Scotland under James VI*, (London, 1969).
Skene, W. F., (ed.), *Chronica Gentis Scotorum*, (Edinburgh, 1871).
Sleidan, J., *Commentariorum de Statu Religionis et Reipublicæ, Carolo, Quinto, Cæsare*, (Paris, 1559).
Smellie, A., *The Reformation in its Literature*, (Edinburgh, 1925).
Smith, G. G., *Scottish Literature: Character and Influence*, (London, 1919).
Smith, J. M., *The French Background of Middle Scots Literature*, (Edinburgh and London), 1934.
Sonnino, L. A., *A Handbook to Sixteenth Century Rhetoric*, (Oxford, 1968).
Sprotte, O., *Zum Sprachengebrauch bei John Knox*, (Berlin, 1906).
Stewart, A., (ed.), *The Complaynt of Scotland*, (Edinburgh, 1979).
Stevenson, R. L., 'John Knox and his Relations to Women', *Familiar Studies of Men and Books*, (London, 1917), 328–397.
Thomson, T., *Proceedings of the Society of Antiquaries in Scotland*, (Edinburgh, 1867).
Thomson, T., (ed.), *A Diurnal of Remarkable Occurents that have passed within the country of Scotland since the death of King James the Fourth till the year 1575*, (Edinburgh, 1833).
Von Weid, H., *Enchiridion Doctrinæ Christianæ, Canoes Concilii Provincialis Coloniensis, Anno Celebrati MDXXXVI,* (Paris, 1547).

Walker, H., (ed.), *Doctrinal Treatises and Introductions to Different Portions of the Holy Scriptures*, (Cambridge, 1849).
Walker, H., *Three Centuries of Scottish Literature*, (Glasgow, 1892).
Walker, R. S., (ed.), *The Historie of the Reformatioun*, (Edinburgh, 1940).
Warfield, B. B., *Calvin and Augustine*, (Philadelphia, 1956).
Warr, C. L., *The Presbyterian Tradition*, (London, 1933).
Watson, G., 'The Franciscan Friary of Jedburgh with Some Account of Adam Bell, its Historian', *Proceedings of Berwickshire Naturalists Club*, vol. xx, 1906–08, 82–88.
Watson, G., (ed.), *The Mar Lodge Translation of the History of Scotland*, (Edinburgh and London, 1946).
Watson, R., *The Literature of Scotland*, (London, 1984).
Watt, H., 'Henry Balnaves and the Scottish Reformation', *Records of the Scottish Church History Society*, 5, 1935, 23–39.
Watt, H., *John Knox in Controversy*, (London, 1950).
Whitley, E., *Plain Mr. Knox*, (London, 1960).
Wood, H. H., (ed.), *The Poems and Fables of Robert Henryson*, (Edinburgh, 1933).
Wormold, J., *Court, Kirk and Community*, (London, 1981).
Wright, D., 'John Knox and the Early Church Fathers', *John Knox and the British Reformations*, Mason, R., (ed.), (Aldershot, 1998), 99–117.
Wright, D., 'The Commoun Buke of the Kirke: The Bible in the Scottish Reformation', *The Bible in Scottish Life and Literature*, Wright, D., (ed.), (Edinburgh, 1988), 155–178

Index